SCANDINAVIAN AIRLINES SYSTEM

aircraft fleet development

1946 - 2016

Aviation Historical Review

SCANDINAVIAN AIRLINES SYSTEM

aircraft fleet development

1946 - 2016

Authors

Birger Holmer
Ulf Abrahamsson
Bengt-Olov Nas

Aviation Historical Review

Swedish Aviation Historical Society (SFF) was estabilshed in 1961. Its objective is to support aviation historical events, research, restauration and taking care of historical aviation material including aircraft and dokumentation.

SFF has around 5,700 members, who recieve six editions annually of the *Svensk Flyghistorisk Tidskrift, (Swedish Aviation Historical Magazin) and a yearbook, Aviation Historical Revie.*

Address: Swedish Aviation Historical Society
P.O. Box 102 67,
S-100 55 Stockholm, Sweden
www.flyghistoria.org

The original version of this book is the SFF 2014 Aviation Historical Review, published in the Swedish language.

The Swedish Aviation Litterature Society awarded the book "The 2015 Swedish Aviation book of the year."

Copyright   Authors and Photographers

This book is a translated version of the SFF 2014 Aviation Historical Review.

The translation is done by Bengt Olov Nas as an independent project with the objective to share the historical events behind the development of SAS aircraft fleet also outside Scandinavia.

All rights reserved. No part of this book may be reproduced or transmitted in any form or by any means electronic or mecanical or other means now known or hereafter invented, including phoyocopying and recording, or in any information storage or retrieval system without permission from the Publisher in writing. All inquires should be directed to the Publisher.

Revision 1, dated 23 Feb 2016.
Layout and production NACE AB, Bengt-Olov Nas,

ISBN 978-91-637-9961-7

Top Photo Christoffer Hammarborg
Bottom Photo Hans Norman, www.scanliners.com

Foreword and acknowledgements

SAS was established on 1 August 1946 as a consortium that was founded by the Danish DLL, Norwegian DNL and Swedish intercontinental air services AB (SILA). The consortium agreement covered only the intercontinental traffic on North and South American routes, where the three companies would cooperate under the unifying name Scandinavian Airlines System. On 14 May 1948 SILA's activities and commitment to SAS were passed to ABA and SILA became the holding company for the emerging private ownership of ABA. ABA entered a new agreement with DDL and DNL regarding coordinated traffic within Europe beginning on 1 July 1948.

The airplanes have been selected and developed to meet the fleet as needed over time. The authors of this book have, during the period from 1946 to the present SAS formation (2007), personally been involved and had responsibility for the evaluation and recommendations of equipment selections. The SAS management and Board of Directors have approved the formal decisions on investment and procurement contracts. The book describes the background and the aircraft selection process as well as why some types were chosen over others. A lot of other people who were involved and influenced decisions are mentioned in the story, but not all. The project organization, with the task to evaluate and recommend appropriate aircraft types and associated components to SAS, and to act as the main contact with the aviation industry, also influenced and contributed to the development of aviation, which is made clear in the book.

The aviation industry language has an aviation technical jargon. The reader can probably perceive certain formulations to that effect. We have tried to clarify this as much as possible in the body of the text and have also attached a list of explanations for the abbreviations. We hope that the meaning of the stories can be understood.

Ulf Edlund and Sven Stridsberg have been of great help with the editing of the content and layout. Bengt Jirvell has proofread the Swedish manuscript. Bengt Olov Nas has translated the text to English and Bob Woodling and Helga Griesbeck has edited and proofread the text.

Kristin Nas has assisted with knowledge and help in handling of the Indesign layout program. Several pictures have been downloaded from the SFF's picture archive. Hans and Ulf Norman have assisted with photos from www.Scanliners.se. Pictures have also been obtained from the manufacturers Airbus, Boeing, Bombardier, CFMI, IAE, Pratt & Whitney, and Rolls-Royce. Hans Kampf has processed illustrations. Some other people have also contributed as evidenced by the captions and in addition we have added a few personal pictures. A number of pilots who have been active in SAS have contributed with personal stories about how certain types were to fly and as a workplace environment. Personal experience observations of the types from cabin crews are also presented

Stockholm and Jonstorp November 2014

Birger Holmer   Ulf Abrahamsson   Bengt Olov Nas

Translated to English November 2015, Bengt Olov Nas

Table of content

Foreword and acknowledgements ... 5
SAS and parent companies' aircraft purchases 1943-1980
Birger Holmer and Ulf Abrahamsson ... 10
   SILA, Swedish Intercontinental air transport AB ... 10
   Douglas DC-4 ... 10
   Boeing B-17 Flying Fortress, ABA's Felix ... 13
   Employment by ABA ... 14
   Boeing 377 Stratocruiser ... 15

Parent companies' fleets ... 18
   ABA ... 18
   DDL ... 18
   DNL ... 19
   SAS development years 1946-1950 ... 21

The propeller era ... 23
   Douglas DC-6 ... 23
   Saab 90 Scandia ... 25
   Douglas DC-6B ... 27
   SAS polar flights ... 29
   Douglas DC-7 series ... 30
   Convair series: CV-240, CV-340 and CV-440 Metropolitan ... 35
   Turboprop Aircraft ... 36

The jet age ... 39
   de Havilland Comet ... 39
   The choice between the Boeing 707 and Douglas DC-8 ... 40
   SAS-Swissair-cooperation ... 54
   Caravelle ... 55
   CV-990 Coronado ... 60
   DC-8 development ... 64
   Short and medium range jet aircraft ... 68
   Douglas DC-9 ... 70
   Boeing 737 ... 73
   The establishment of the McDonnell Douglas Corporation ... 78

Supersonic aircraft ... 81
   Concorde ... 81
   U.S. SST project ... 82

Wide-body aircraft ... 84
   Boeing 747, often called jumbo jet ... 84
   Douglas DC-10 ... 91
   Airbus A300 ... 96
   SAS and Airbus ... 97

New CEO ... 99
Reflections by Birger Holmer ... 100
   Cooperation between international airlines. ... 100
   Criteria and priorities during the evaluation and specification work. ... 101
   Safety ... 101

Regularity and aircraft availability	102
Passenger Comfort and service	102
Aircraft evaluation	102
Technical and flight operational activities	105

New times   Ulf Abrahamsson   106
The Jan Carlzon era	106
SAS Airline of the Year 1983!	106
The economy	107
The aircraft fleet 1980/81	108
The new strategies and new demands on the fleet.	108
Airbus A300	109
McDonnell Douglas DC-9	109
DC-8	109
Boeing 747	112
McDonnell Douglas DC-10	113

New aircraft to the fleet   115
Passenger Pleasing Plane, P3	115
Boeing 7J7	116
MD-87 and DC-9-80 turns MD-80	120
Hovercraft, aerostat or boat	120
McDonnell Douglas MD-11	121
Airbus A340	122
Boeing 767	123
The choice of a new aircraft for long-haul routes.	125
Phase out of the DC-9	128

New strategies   129
SAS evolves as a company	129
Charter Company Scanair aquires their own aircraft	130
SAS Commuter	131
Hard times	132
MD-90 and MD-95	133
SAS acquires Linjeflyg	134
Cooperation with other companies	136
British Midland, BMI	136
EQA - European Quality Alliance	136
EQA becomes Alcazar	137
The phase-out of F28 and DC-9	138
Selection of the "Small" aircraft	140

New CEO of SAS, Jan Stenberg   140
SAS buys Boeing 737-600	144
SAS project organization	149

Reflections by Ulf Abrahamsson   149
SAS Project organization	149
SAS development areas	150
Technology development 1946 - 1995	152
Price development	154
SAS decisions in retrospect	155

The period 1996 to 2016   Bengt-Olov Nas 156
   1996 long term fleet development plan 156

767 replacement 158

"Big" a recurring need 161
   Big becomes Medium 162

Engine selection 163
   Airbus A330-300 163
   Airbus A321 164

Bigger Commuter fleet 165

Saab 2000 at SAS 168

Aircraft projects and evaluation 170
   Star Alliance cooperation 170
   New Regional Jet 171
   Star Alliance long-haul study 173
   The next generation narrow-body 173
   Superjet International 174
   Cooperation within the SAS Group 174

The Q400 operations end in 2007 175

The MD-80 replacement 176

New long-haul fleet 178

Aviation and the environment 179
   The regulatory framework for environmental protection, ICAO Annex 16 179
   Aircraft noise Definitions 179
   SAS fleet and the environment 180

Aircraft come back 185

Reflections by Bengt Olov Nas 186

Aircraft Financing 187
   Financial lease 187
   Operating lease 187
   Sale-leaseback 187
   SAS fleet 187

"This is your captain speaking" 188

"Welcome to the SAS," it's your cabin crew's salute to welcome you aboard. 196

Chief operating officers 1946-2016 202

Two old SAS-ladies: Daisy and Tante Ju 205

Aircraft data 206

Authors 210

Abbrevation   explanation 212

SAS and parent companies' aircraft purchases 1943-1980

Birger Holmer with processing by Ulf Abrahamsson

SAS is based on the three national airlines in Scandinavia, the Swedish ABA, Aktiebolaget Aerotransport AB; the Danish Luftfartsselskap a/s DDL, and The Norwegian Airline DNL sel membership. SAS was formed in its final form in 1951.
Picture SAS.

SAS has a background in the three national airlines in Scandinavia, ABA, DDL and DNL. ABA was formed in 1924, DDL in 1918 and is one of the world's oldest airlines, and DNL was formed in 1938. The companies were primarily engaged in domestic flights. Another name that can be found in several places in the book is SILA, Swedish Intercontinental air transport joint stock company that was formed in February 1943. SILA was established to carry out the planned traffic across the North Atlantic after the end of the war.

SILA, Swedish Intercontinental Air transport AB

The establishment of SILA had been preceded by lengthy discussions that had already started before the outbreak of World War II. In addition to ABA there was also participation by interested parties for Danish and Norwegian air transport, and by concerned government authorities and representatives from business life. The outbreak of the war and the subsequent occupation of Denmark and Norway made it difficult to complete these negotiations but continued mainly through Swedish efforts.

It was noted then that from many aspects it would be advantageous to form a private company for civil air transport instead of making it operate through the predominantly State-owned ABA. It was agreed that ABA would manage the technical activities for the traffic that SILA expected to begin after the end of the war. Howeverthe US authorities demanded, in order to permit the airline operation, that there was an established and well respected technical organization tied to the company.

Karl-Henrik Larsson was appointed to be the head of the project department in SILA's management. He and SILA's CEO, Per Norlin then spent the better part of 1943 in America to prepare for the future traffic over the North Atlantic Ocean, to acquire necessary permits and to obtain suitable flight equipment. After extensive investigation they concluded that the Douglas DC-4 aircraft would be the best option. On 25 November 1943 a contract with Douglas Aircraft Company of Santa Monica, California was signed for the delivery of 10 DC-4 aircraft as soon as possible after the end of the war.

Douglas DC-4

Even before the DC-3 made its first flight on 17 December 1935, Douglas had started to plan for its successor which should have the the capacity twice the size of the DC-3 and had a range of 3,500 km. In February 1936 the studies had progressed so far that five US Airlines showed an interest. In March of that year American Airlines, Eastern Airlines, Pan American, TWA and United Airlines provided $100,000 each to Douglas to build a prototype of a four-engine aircraft, the DC-4E, where E stood for Experimental. The engine chosen was the Pratt & Whitney (PWA) R-2180, a 14-cylinder radial engine with a take-off power of 1,450 HP, an engine that would later show up on Saab's Scandia aircraft.

The DC-4 was the first aircraft of this size with a nosewheel instead of a tail wheel. Performance requirements meant that a takeoff could be completed even if one outboard engine failed and stability during cruise would be satisfactory for continued flight even if two engines on the same side failed. This required a relatively large vertical fin rudder. Douglas chose therefore to introduce a tail section with a triple fin with three rudders in order to limit the height to meet the ceiling height and doors for the airline's hangars as the aircraft were equipped with a nosewheel.

Some other innovations were introduced as power-assisted rudder, air conditioning and two piston engine powered auxiliaries for the supply of the electrical system and other systems when the engines were not running. The electrical system was modernized through the transition to AC power. It was intended to introduce a pressurized cabin for the series production.

Douglas impressed the airlines with the proposal, but TWA and PanAm canceled their participation in the project because they considered it too complex and too costly. They focused instead on the smaller and simpler Boeing 307 Stratoliner.

Douglas completed the design, however, and the plane was ready in May 1938, flying for the first time on June 7 of the same year. Due to technical problems, the airworthiness certificate was delayed until May 1939. It was delivered to United which conducted numerous flight tests on its route network. The flights went well but operating economy was not considered satisfactory even though passenger capacity had been increased from 42 to 52.

The project was canceled and the aircraft was sold to a Japanese company that flew it for a short time. It was reported to have crashed, but in reality it had been dismantled to be used as a model for a Japanese four-engine bomber with great range.

The project resulted in a loss for Douglas of nearly $ 1.5 million. As the DC-4E project closed down, American Airlines, Eastern and United agreed with Douglas that they needed an aircraft with the same capabilities as the DC-4E, but lighter, and simpler, and that it should be called the DC-4.

The airlines were offered two engine options, Wright R-1820 or Pratt & Whitney R-2000. The American engine designation R stands for radial and the numbers of cylinder volume expressed in cubic inches. The three companies all selected the PWA R-2000, which was established as the standard for the DC-4. They also agreed to delete the triple-pronged tail and replace it with a single fin with rudder and a traditional elevator. More important was to simplify the design, making it lighter and thus improve operating costs rather than to take into account the costs of new hangars. The military authorities also supported this when they later came into the picture.

Douglas's main rival at the time was Lockheed with its Constellation that had a triple tail section. The rumor suggested they were misled by the DC-4E prototype, but that has not been confirmed.

Eventually, Douglas received 61 orders for the DC-4 but was forced by the U.S. authorities to cancel them to focus their efforts on the manufacture of military versions of the DC-3 as well as fighter bombers. Despite this, however, Douglas carried on to a very limited extent work on the DC-4. It however turned out well, because after the Japanese attack on Pearl Harbor the plans changed radically. The project was taken over by the USAAF, and the military version was designated C-54. No DC-4/C-54 prototype was manufactured, but the C-54 went straight into series production. The first aircraft was completed in February 1942 and made its first flight from Clover Field in Santa Monica on February 14.

The C-54 was produced in many versions. Most of them had a large cargo door on the left side and a strengthened floor to enable transportation all kinds of cargo and equipment, but some were also equipped for passenger transports. Both President Roosevelt and PM Churchill each had their own specially equipped C-54. A total of 1,315 units of DC-4s and C-54s were produced.

During the war, Douglas carried quietly on with improving the DC-4 so that the appropriate versions could be offered to the airlines after the war. SILA was the first airline to sign a contract for delivery after the end of the war because Douglas was forced to cancel a contract with American customers.

In his letter of December 4, 1943 Donald Douglas, wrote, among other things, "*this is the first contract the Douglas Company has entered into which*

Douglas DC-4E was designed with three tailfins to minimize the aircraft height
Photo Boeing.

extends into the post-war period, and as such is another milestone in air transport history."

The contract was signed on 25 November 1943 or delivery of 10 DC-4s at a total value of $ 4 million In the final phase of the war and shortly after the end of the war, several contracts were signed for delivery as soon as possible. Many carriers opted to buy secondhand C-54s, which eventually became available at the surplus market. Alterations for civilian use were made at Douglas or other aircraft manufacturers or in-house. Surplus plane rates were in the range of $ 50,000-100,000 compared with SAS price of about $ 400,000 for new aircraft.

When purchasing from an aircraft manufacturer, a basic specification is available, which is then complemented by the airline's own requirements. In most cases these concern interior arrangements such as selection of seats, interior materials, and their color schemes. The galley layout is also often quite airline-specific. Similarly, the arrangement in the cockpit of instruments and equipment is often based on the airline's policies and traditions. Among other equipment, you can often choose among the manufacturers of autopilots, electric generators, hydraulic pumps etc. To a large extent the selection takes into account the existing maintenance organization and spare parts availability. It's always a problem when buying a new product on how much to standardize, taking into account existing technology and to what extent to take a chance on newer and more modern equipment. Standardization can be useful to bring down operating costs but can also be an obstacle to desirable development.

K.H. Larsson, head of the project department,

Because the DC-4 did not have a pressurized cabin it could not fly over 10 000 ft, which sometimes could be quite uncomfortable for passengers. Two stop overs, in Prestwick and in Gander, had to be made to fly from Stockholm to New York, and the total travel time was about 24 hours. Photo by Boeing.

The Lockheed Constellation was the main competitor to the Douglas DC-4 and DC-6 products.

was responsible for the technical requirements formulation of the DC-4 aircraft on order. During his stay in America during the war years he had done the groundwork developing an appropriate specification for future Scandinavian airplanes, but it was only after the end of the war and the initiation by SILA of the Atlantic operation that it became possible for SAS staff to travel over to Douglas for assisting with the final drafting of the specifications, contract, and necessary warranty provisions.

The first of the 10 planes ordered landed at Bromma on, 6 May 1946, and all were delivered before the end of 1946. The fleet was divided into seven for the prospective SAS and three for ABA.

Boeing B-17 Flying Fortress, ABA's Felix

In June 1944 SILA had been offered to take over a number of diverted B-17 bombers from the USAAF as an exchange for hundreds of detained crewmen who were then released. Of these planes seven were transferred to Saab for alterations to airliner specifications and a couple were held as reserves and were used for spare parts. The rebuilt version came to be known as Felix. Rebuilding meant that any purely military equipment was removed and the bomb bay was converted into the passenger cabin. The nose section was changed completely and became a space for the radio operator and all radio equipment. ABA's technical organization was responsible for the operations and engineer Carl-Erik Kyle was appointed to be the company's representative in Linköping. Three of the planes were given to ABA and were equipped for 21 passengers with longitudinal seating and four were transferred to SILA. These were fitted with 14 seats in forward-facing rows. Because they would be used on the North Atlantic routes with long flight times, this arrangement provided the utmost comfort. Two of the airplanes were transferred late in 1945 to the Danish airline DDL that would become one of

Sven Gibson prepares for the flight to New York
Photo By Anders Gibson

A letter that was sent on the B-17 on 27 June 1945, which after the flight was signed by the pilots.
Photo Ulf Abrahamsson.

13

the parent companies of SAS. On 9 October 1944, ABA performed the first courier flights between Bromma Stockholm and Prestwick in Scotland, This and subsequent adventurous flights are vividly described in captain L. A. Nilsson's book "Courier flights". After the war ABA used the planes for flights to many destinations in the European route network.SILA made a test flight to Iceland on 13 June 1945, and the first flight to LaGuardia Airport in New York on June 27. SILA made a total of 31 trips to New York City in 1946, before the traffic was taken over by SAS.

In addition to North Atlantic traffic, SILA made a number of flights to Addis Ababa, Ethiopia and some to Rio de Janeiro in the spring of 1946. This attracted much international attention.

One of the ABA's planes, SE-BAM, crashed on 4 December 1945 during a flight between Stockholm and Gothenburg. The entire crew perished.

Employment by ABA

When I was hired by ABA, 2 July 1945, it was mainly because I would help with analyzing the technical issues, in part composed of totally unknown devices and systems that were part of the Boeing B-17 Flying Fortresses taken over from the U.S. Army Air Force (USAAF). The planes had landed in Sweden, diverting there after bombing raids over Germany. They had been hit by anti-aircraft fire, technical problems or fuel shortage. Many of them were relatively or absolutely undamaged and we thought therefore they could be used for civilian use after repairing them. ABA and SILA succeeded to negotiate contracts with the USAAF for a nominal sum of $1 per aircraft. Modifications for future use, among other things, planned Atlantic flights were

The Boeing B-17 and crew at Bromma airport.
Photo SAS.

B-17 flightdeck.
Photo by Anders Gibson.

made in cooperation with Saab in Linköping.

During the delivery of the aircraft from the USAAF a number of flight tests were conducted with selected pilots from ABA, which therefore provided a particular insight into how the airplanes would be handled but all manuals and technical documents were still classified. That is why ABA's technical and operational departments to the best of their ability were preparing the technical and flight-related documentation supporting the planes' use, a very demanding task. There were many electrical, instrumentation systems and radios that were completely unknown to ABA engineers. Thanks to my knowledge from a engineering degree from KTH (Royal Institute of Technology in Stockholm) with a focus on low power technology and subsequent employments during the war in the defense industry and the Maritime Administration, all within the industries of electric instruments and radio, I was considered appropriate to participate in the work on the B-17. Olof Carlstein got the overall technical responsibility for these areas and he led both the engineering office and the workshops that were responsible for the systems. It was under his able and inspiring leadership that I got my first lessons about how they would be managed and maintained.

Director Charles Lignell, who came to ABA shortly after the company was formed, led the technical organization during 1943-46. To him reported Karl-Henrik Larsson, head of project department, which was responsible for the studies and analyses of the types of aircraft that could be of interest to the company, as well as the elaboration of decision making for management in the event of an acquisition. They would also assist the project team with engineering capability, and, above all, to produce documents needed for maintenance and operational teams. One was led by Bo Hoffström which dealt with cases concerning aircraft structure with associated systems and equipment, engine issues and documentation for performance calculations and route planning calculations. Reporting to him also were the drawing and design office. Olof Carlstein led the other group. He had electricity, instruments and radio and also the communication function for flight operations. Bo Hofström's group was called the Engineering Department and Olof Carlstein's was named Equipment Department.

Boeing 377 Stratocruiser

From early 1946 SILA's management realized that competition on North Atlantic routes would be so difficult that the already contracted DC-4 aircraft would not be enough in the future. It would require more modern planes with greater comfort, longer range, pressurized cabins, shorter flight times, and preferably no stopovers.

In February a contract was signed with Boeing for the delivery of four 377 Stratocruiser aircraft. These were meant to be distributed as follows: two to Sweden and one each to Denmark and Norway for a future use of the single company of ESAS, the European SAS, which began to appear in the discussion that has been going on for a long time.

The aircraft should have the range that allowed nonstop flights between Europe and America and offer a luxury that corresponded to what was expected earlier by cruise ship passengers. The plane would be designed as a double decker with standard passenger seats on the upper deck and beds and lounges on the lower deck.

In order to provide passengers with a more luxurious environment than had been common in the past on older aircraft, and while giving them a sense of Scandinavian interior design, a peculiar decision was made to give three planes Swedish, Danish and Norwegian interiors and the fourth plane something like an "international" character.

Architect Sune Lindström won the Swedish, "international", and the Norwegian assignment. (Sune Lindström is best known for the Wennergren Center in Stockholm, "Svampen" water tower of

The Boeing 377 Stratocruiser Photo Boeing.

The Boeing 307 was the first pressurised airliner, which made it possible to fly over the "bad weather". The first aircraft flew in 1938 but only ten were produced before Boeing went over to war production. Photo Boeing.

The lower cabin in the Danish Boeing 377-version with H.C. Andersen motifs on the wall panels. Photo by Boeing.

Örebro and Kuwait Tower in Kuwait City). Most important was the variety of materials and colors for seats, carpets and curtains and other textile materials. Lindström hired the Danish designer Malene Björn to produce interiors for three of the airplanes but not the Norwegian. She chose "folklore" from the county Dalarna for the Swedish plane and searched for someone who was good at this form of art.
She found the artist Hans Prince from Leksand. His paintings were installed in the Swedish aircraft.

When British BOAC later bought the delivery positions from SILA they requested their standard interior, but Boeing insisted that the buyer should inspect the interior because of the "high quality" in the Swedish Interior. BOAC chose to retain the Swedish interior. Boeing later invited its customers to take the form of more colorful design against the previous very neutral schemes, which was thought to be good for motion sickness.

In May 1948, Boeing project leader A. H. Morgan stated in the Boeing Magazine: "Interior design of future aircraft may be governed to a great extent by the experience of SAS. With this styling we can do a great deal more with colors and textures in the future than we are willing to do now."

Malene Björn was also invited to work for Boeing. She declined and instead accepted the task of decorating the 17 Douglas DC-6s SAS bought.

The design of the 377 was based on Boeing's experience from previous airliners of the type 247, and 307 Stratoliner and the successful B-17 and B-29 bombers. The former two had not been a great success. Douglas DC-3 outshone the 247 and the DC-4 likewise the Boeing 307.

The decoration in the Swedish B377 Stratocruiser, Hans Prince, 1945, Dalecarlia inspired painting. Depicted are Archbishop Erling Eidem, Swedish Prime minister Tage Erlander, King Gustav V, the housekeeping minister Karin Kock and finance minister Ernst Wigfors. Photo The Culture museum in Leksand.

Boeing's 247 was considered by many to be the first modern airliner but it was outsold by the Douglas DC-2 and especially the DC-3. Photo by Boeing

As the design evolved, it became pretty clear that Boeing would find it difficult to cope with the range requirement. It depended, among other things on the selected type of engine from Pratt & Whitney not achieving its promised performance. It had the designation R-4360 and was a radial engine with four rows of 28 cylinders and capable of producing 3,500 HP. It was used very sparsely in other transport aircraft installations, so it is difficult to make comparisons.

When an aircraft does not meet the fuel consumption guarantees and thus deteriorated aircraft range and increased operating costs, it is difficult and nearly impossible to determine with certainty the underlying causes. Engine performance can only be determined on engine test stands at ground level and not during normal operation in cruising flight at high altitude. The aircraft's aerodynamic characteristics can only be predicted based on models tested in wind tunnels and this methodology has its limitations, of course. As a result, there are long and difficult negotiations between the aircraft and engine manufacturers, but whatever the outcome of these are, the airlines are stuck with the deficiencies. To a certain extent, they can improve their position by calling for the introduction of appropriate warranty provisions.

When the test flights with the 377 started, it turned out that the fears that arose during the development were real. Boeing also announced that there would be considerable delivery delays.

For SILA, and thus the planned SAS part, the plan for the Stratocruiser was nonstop flights between Sola airport near Stavanger and New York. Traffic to and from Oslo, Copenhagen and Stockholm was to be conducted with smaller aircraft.

When those plans could not be implemented with the deterioration that was revealed, negotiations started with Boeing and other possible operators who did not have the same range requirement as SILA. It turned out that the British company BOAC, which had ordered seven planes, was interested in the SILA airplanes and SILA managed to get the aircraft transferred from the manufacturer directly to BOAC. As a result BOAC received four planes with different interiors and specifications. It all went to SILA's satisfaction and resulted in no major costs. Before that, however, ABA/SILA had managed to establish a liaison office at Boeing in Seattle. Three engineers and a secretary from ABA were placed there and two Americans had also been hired. The task was to complete the specification work and then monitor so that work was done to ABA/SILA's satisfaction. The ABA staff was moved to an office set up at Douglas in Santa Monica, California for similar tasks for the DC-6 acquisition.

The 377 project showed a certain exuberance and lack of judgment from both Boeing and the participating airlines in relation to future long-range operations. Boeing sold only 55 civil 377s but over 800 military versions were built.

Sven Gibson checking out the Boeing 377 flight deck. Photo Anders Gibson.

Parent companies' fleets

At the end of World War II the following aircraft were in the ABA, DDL, DNL fleets:

ABA: 1 Fokker F-XII, 5 Junkers Ju 52, 3 Douglas DC-3 and 5 Boeing B-17
DDL: 2 Fokker F-XII and 1 Focke-Wulf Condor
DNL: No aircraft. The Germans had laid hands on all of them.

At the end of the war, only five of the seven Boeing planes were registered in Sweden. The other two were, in late autumn 1945 transferred to DDL.

ABA

It was apparent that the few airplanes that existed at the end of the war would not be enough to cope with increased traffic and the new anticipated destinations. ABA had lost two DC-3s, which had been shot down by the Germans, and had not had the opportunity during the war to obtain compensation for these.

The B-17 planes and the ordered DC-4 aircraft were not a good fit for all the destinations that would be operated. It was therefore clear that ABA, like many other airlines was looking around for an increase of its fleet, among others, through the purchase of planes of the C-47 and C-53 types, that the American military sold for low prices.

These two types were military versions of the DC-3 and could relatively easily be rebuilt for civil passenger or cargo purposes. ABA first selected the C-53 because these planes had mainly been used for personnel transport and did not have the heavy-duty floor and the large cargo door like the C-47. Acquisition was via the American company Globe Aircraft that specialized in acquiring a large number of these surplus planes and in turn selling them to the airlines, ABA purchased five C-53s and had the Canadian company Canadair in Montreal rebuild them to ABA's specifications.

The planes were delivered in the autumn of 1945 and in early 1946.

Later seven C-47s were acquired in the same way. At the time of the order all C-53s had been sold and ABA had to settle for the heavier variant.

Even later ABA purchased, directly from U.S. surplus inventories in Europe, another two C-47 planes that, after an in-house reconstruction of cockpit equipment, were used as cargo aircraft.

DDL

During the final phase of the war, DDL had also begun probing the possibilities to acquire airplanes for the expected increase in traffic after the war. In

SAS DC-3 flying in DNL, in SAS, Linjeflyg and still flies for The Flying Veterans! Photo By Gunnar Akerberg.

DDL had two Focke-Wulf Condors that were delivered in 1938. The Condors had two cabins, a smoking area with 9 seats, and one with 17 seats. One of the airplanes was flown to London in 1940 and was confiscated by the English, and the other was damaged in 1946 and scrapped.
Photo SAS.

May and June 1945 Director Lybye and Captain Damm had discussions with U.S. authorities about the possibility of buying older used military versions of the DC-3 that were presumed to be available after the end of the war. They were allotted a small number of planes that were in the Mediterranean area, where they went to inspect them and they chose three units but were not allowed to buy them. However, the planes were leased on a five-year contract with deliveries in August, September and October of 1945. The U.S. military did not start its sale of surplus aircraft until later. Unfortunately, the deliveries occurred later than what ABA had succeeded with by acting just one month later.

Traffic on DDL's routes could start only with the existing F-XII and Condor planes. In October 1945 DDL signed the formal contract with Douglas for two DC-4s, which SILA in 1943 had already ordered on behalf of DDL. At the same time, contracts for the supply of three civilian DC-3s for delivery in March and April 1946 were also written. From the 1st of November DDL began operating the two remodeled Boeing B-17s, that had been recently transferred from Sweden under previous plans.

Because there were difficulties for Denmark with dollar allocations for additional purchase of American planes, DDL decided to purchase five Vickers Vikings from the British firm Vickers. First delivery of these twin-engine planes with seating for 24 passengers, was during the last week in 1946 with the others arriving in the summer of 1947. This airplane type, which was a development of a bomber, was not very successful. Only about 100 units were produced and were not long-lived in DDL and SAS service. Two crashed in Oresund. In 1949, they were taken out of service.

During 1945, and the next few years, DDL built up its fleet of DC-3s so by the end of 1946 the company had a total of 16 planes, three of which were of the DC-3D type, purchased new from Douglas, three converted C-53s, two rebuilt C-47s, and eight C-47 cargo planes. In 1947 the company acquired two additional C-47 cargo planes.

DNL

During the German occupation beginning in 1940, DNL, as opposed to DDL, could not operate any flights outside of Norway. From 9 April 1940 to March 1941 the route Trondheim-Tromso-Kirkenes was operated with Junkers Ju 52s, but then all aviation activity ceased.

After the war the Norwegian authorities decided that Norwegian aviation would be conducted by the Norwegian Civil Aviation Administration. (NCAA) The principal question of whether there would be state-controlled or private aviation was not yet decided. The NCAA, which had been established by the exile government in London during the war, ordered in January 1945 ten DC-3s from Douglas, five of which were later was canceled. According to information provided by Douglas no new DC-3s

Vickers Viking cabin with luxurious armchairs. Photo SFF's archives.

DNL had five Short Sandringhams during period from 1947 to 1951. The aircraft were used in Norwegian domestic service and had room for 37 passengers. Four P&W R-1830 engines. Photo SAS.

from the factory were delivered, either to the NCA nor to DNL. Original sources does not give a clear picture of how this order was handled. However, it is clear that the three planes of the C-53 type were acquired and were converted into passenger aircraft by Canadair and delivered to the NCAA quite soon after the end of the war. They were transferred and registered by DNL in spring 1946. It is also clear that three C-47s were purchased and then converted to passenger versions and delivered to the NCAA in the autumn of 1945, and transferred and registered by DNL a year later.

The civil aviation authority had the administrative responsibility to conduct air traffic and operational activity until it was transferred to DNL

The first DNL DC-3 flight took off from Copenhagen on 1 april 1946 followed by flights to London, Stockholm, Marseilles and Rome.

In 1945 DNL had also managed to assemble five useful Junkers Ju 52s out of the residue of the type that remained in Norway after the German retreat. These planes were used only within Norway.

On 8 July 1946, DNL contracted for the purchase of three English Short Sandringham flying boats. These were delivered during April, May and June 1947 and were put into service along the entire long Norwegian coast. They turned out not to be particularly appropriate for the traffic and could only be used during the summer and they were also not economically viable. One crashed after just four months, and a second in the fall of 1948. Two replacement planes were ordered one of which was delivered in April 1948, and the second in June 1949. In May 1950, the third of the original planes crashed. It was decided later to discontinue the operation and in 1951 they disappeared from the SAS fleet.

In 1947 DNL transferred seven C-47s which were registerred at DNL. From the source material that I have access to, it is not clear how the acquisition was done, but it is obvious that at least three of them were previously used by the air defenses. Who

DNL had two Ju 52 on Norwegian domestic routes. Here in an early SAS-decor. Photo SAS.

Thomas S. Falck Jr DNL, Marcus Wallenberg ABA and Per Kampmann DDL signing the SAS agreement in August 1946.
Photo SAS.

rebuilt them as passenger versions is not clear.

The parent companies' combined fleet on 1 October 1950 had the following composition: 12 DC-6, 9 DC-4, 36 DC-3 and 2 Ju52. Three Ju52 had been dismantled during the period 1945-1950, and all three Sandringhams had crashed.

SAS development years 1946-1950

The SAS consortium that was formed on 1 August 1946 by DDL, DNL, and SILA was intended to take care of the intercontinental traffic while ABA, DDL and DNL would continue to take care of the domestic traffic, intra Scandinavian and European routes.

It was quite natural that it was appropriate to coordinate even the latter traffic. At the end of 1947 evaluations started which led to a collaboration for the entire European route network which started on 18 April 1948.

The European common route network operated under the internal designation of ESAS (European SAS). The transcontinental cooperation continued as before under the name of OSAS (Overseas SAS) which, like ESAS was only used internally. Externally all operations were called SAS.

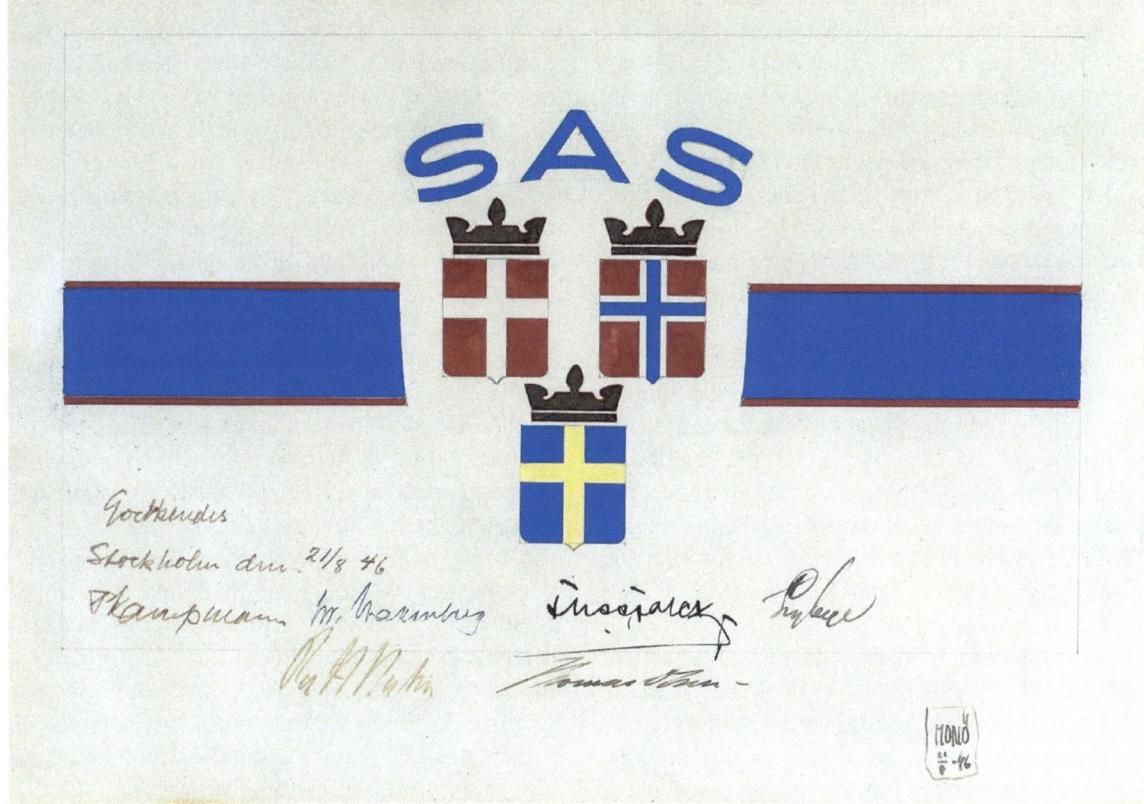

SAS first logo from August 1946.
Photo SAS.

In conjunction with these changes, it was decided that the ABA and SILA would be merged into a company called ABA and SILA would exist only as a holding company for half of the shares in ABA. This change was approved by the Swedish Government and the Board of Directors of SILA on 14 May 1948.

When the operational units ESAS and OSAS were formed, the intention was that they would eventually be combined into one body. It took, however many evaluations and decisions among legal, economic, political and practical experience before this could be implemented. A consortium agreement was signed on 8 February 1951, with retroactive effect from 1 October 1950. The final version of SAS was thereby established.

The rapid growth of the business in the late 1940s led quite naturally to an entire organizational change. In May 1947, Olof Carlstein was appointed as Chief Operating Officer and reporting to the technical director Karl Lignell, and included the responsibility for both engineering offices for supervisory and maintenance workshops.

This meant that I succeed him as head of what was called The Equipment department as well as handling the electrical, instruments and radio cases and operational communication issues. The technical office run by Bo Hoffsten retained its duties. In May 1948, Bo Hoffstrom announced that he wanted to withdraw from the executive duties of his office in order to fully devote himself to the Scandia project, which he led on behalf of ABA, as well as the new engine test stand installation that was his unique design. He would also assist the company management in various analyses which was why he was transferred to the Executive Board.

To my surprise and many others I was appointed as his successor and, at the same time, the two departments merged to become a common technical office which got responsibility for the entire aircraft from the engineering point of view. The group dealing with matters relating to aircraft performance, route calculations as well as weight and balance issues, was however transferred to a newly formed line section which also included all flight operations.

After the merger of ABA and SILA1 the founder of ABA, Carl Florman handed over the leadership to Per Norlin who for a period left the position as head of SAS, being replaced by the Norwegian Per Backe. When SAS finally was formed on 1 October 1950, he returned to the head position in SAS and was succeeded by the former technical Chief Karl Lignell as head of ABA.

As a result of the ESAS and OSAS arrangement and the subsequent formation of SAS, it became necessary to standardize all aircraft in some respects. Very important was the airplane color scheme, because it must be the same for all fleets so that the traveling public would perceive SAS as a unified company. The former OSA planes had ended up with the well-known dragon. It was the result of a contest held by SAS among architects and designers. The jury that would choose the winner had no knowledge of the participants but they chose, funnily enough, Rune Monos proposal.

They did not know that he was already engaged by ABA some time back.

It was also the intention going forward that both aircraft and crews be mixed between the three countries which required the cockpit layout and instrumentation and other things standardized as far as possible and appropriate for the DC-3 types. They became the core of the activities not carried out with DC-4 and DC-6 which was originally quite similar in these respects, but some rearrangements and adjustments were needed even for those.

Completely different philosophies and practices had naturally formed in the four pilot associations (ABA, DDL, DNL and OSAS) that became relevant. A working group was formed with the four units' chief pilots and a neutral chairman who was not a pilot but well versed in the technical points. The main point of discussion was the position of compass, artificial horizon, airspeed indicator, and altimeter. They eventually succeeded and the result of it being, in the pilot language, called "basic tee" meaning that the top horizontal line formed by the airspeed indicator, artificial horizon, and the altimeter. The middle vertical line was formed by the artificial horizon and the compass. It turned out later in talks with aircraft manufacturers and other airlines that this particular configuration had been adopted in most international standards.

SAS first CEO, P. A. Norlin. Photo SAS.

The propeller era

Douglas DC-6

In the autumn of 1946 it became clear that Boeing would be affected both by extensive delays in delivery and performance issues with the Boeing 377. KH Larsson's project team had already followed the development at Douglas that had plans for a successor to the DC-4-called the DC-6.

The designation DC-5 had been used for only five planes that had been built for the Dutch KLM, but production was stopped at the outbreak of the war. Seven military planes had been built with the designation R3D.

Douglas DC-5 was a high wing aircraft with a nose wheel and capacity for 16-23 passangers. It was produced only in a few units and for KLM.
Photo Boeing.

The DC-6 had basically the same wing as the DC-4 but a cabin which was about 7 feet longer. The fin was slightly larger and higher than the DC-4 for maintaining the control of power loss on an outer engine. The engines were substantially more powerful than its predecessor. Again Pratt & Whitney was chosen and it was called the Twin Wasp R-2800 with an output of 2100 hp. The engines were supplied with reversible propellers that could be used at landing or aborted takeoff as areodynamic brakes, which improved both takeoff and landing performance. The airframe was strengthened to accommodate a pressurized cabin. It meant that the plane could fly at significantly higher altitudes and thus increased the range with retained comfort for passengers and crew.

The range, however, was not sufficient for the DC-6 to allow nonstop flight between Scandinavia and New York, so it would basically have the same route as the DC-4 with a stopover in both Prestwick in Scotland and Gander, Newfoundland, at least in the westbound direction. It was still a big step forward with shorter flight time and greater comfort with the pressurized cabin. KH Larsson's project team made a detailed study of the DC-6 and its main competitor, the Lockheed Constellation. They found it to be beneficial for many reasons to select the DC-6 for both SAS and ABA.

On 15 November 1946 a contract was signed with Douglas for the delivery of seven DC-6s for SAS and ten planes for ABA. This was the first aircraft order made in the SAS name since the consortium was formed on 1 August 1946. Three SAS planes would be awarded to Sweden and two each to Denmark and Norway.

The purchase was intended primarily for SAS North Atlantic operation, but the route network was expanded rapidly to include the South Atlantic and the Far East. The ABA aircraft were intended for the major European routes. It was, however, soon discovered that the expected traffic for a large portion of the destinations was not enough. In addition to the encountered difficulties in raising dollar currency to the extent required so after some negotiations it was accepted to transfer four of the ordered, but not yet delivered planes to any other airline. They managed eventually to find an Australian company BCPA (British Commonwealth Pacific Airlines) which took over the four planes.

It was intended that the delivery of the first aircraft would begin in autumn 1947, but they were delayed because of two accidents that occurred in America. All DC-6s were grounded until some design improvements were introduced which took about five months. SAS received its first DC-6 in early May 1948.

When ordering aircraft there are sometimes opportunities on a given aircraft type to select the engine manufacturer. In the case of systems, instruments and radio equipment, there are usually opportunities to choose a large part of the equipment. The same applies frequently to interior arrangements and galley design. A large part of the specification and contract work is related to these areas.

In the DC-6 case, there were two propeller makers to choose from: Hamilton Standard and Curtiss-Wright. Douglas had set up his first option as Hamilton Standard, whose installation meant traditional aluminum blades and a rather complicated, mainly mechanical / hydraulic pitch control mechanism. Curtiss-Wright offered a construction of hollow blades of steel and a propeller hub likewise made of steel and the whole system was much simpler. Propeller control was all-electric and much simpler in structure and function. Along with several others, American Airlines SAS chose Curtiss-Wright.

In practical operation it proved to be a less successful choice. The design of the control gave rise to major operational disruptions caused by the electric rotation speed sensor that was mounted on the engine nosecap, just behind the propeller. It was subjected to severe vibrations it could not sustain in operation. Many modifications were introduced but the result was not satisfactory.

An even more serious circumstance had not

SAS DC-6 SE-BDE, Alrek Viking at Bromma. DC-6 is bigger than the DC-4 but spcifically equipped with a pressurized cabin providing more comfort for the passengers. Still it did not have non-stop range to New York from Scandinavia.
Photo SAS.

been anticipated. The steel blades proved more sensitive to fatigue stresses than those made of aluminum and cracks appeared after a certain time in both the blades and the hubs. Despite thorough and frequent inspections with all the available test equipment, it happened that during a South America flight a propeller tip of about 20 cm broke off and went through the airframe just above the floor and exited higher up on the opposite side. Because of the imbalance that occurred in the engine installation, the engine and all its supports were torn off the wing and ended up in the sea. There was therefore no opportunity to do a complete analysis of the event.

Despite the damage the flight was able to continue to the nearest airport that had runways long enough to allow the landing of a DC-6. It was deemed impossible to repair the damage incurred at the site so Douglas agreed to ferry the plane to Santa Monica, California with a special crew. Ferry flights with just three engines operating are performed from time to time, when spare engines are not available or cannot be shipped within a reasonable time. But to do it with a plane that lost the whole engine installation and thus had significantly greater aerodynamic drag, and to additionally fly such a long route with several intermediate stops is probably unique in aviation history.

Inspection regulations were obviously tightened after this event and surveys started to find safe solutions to this serious problem. Curtiss-Wright came up with proposals for improved variants of the steel blade and hub but SAS chose as quickly as possible to move to Hamilton-Standard's installation that the majority of the DC-6 operators used. The decision resulted in high costs, increased empty weight of the aircraft, and in turn led to reduced potential revenue cargo.

The event provided an important lesson. When it comes to choosing aircraft, engines, and other equipment, it is essential to consider to what extent the solutions will be common among airlines, especially among the influential and the average carriers so that one does not become lonely or just among a few like-minded operators. Early on it is also essential to get access to the operating experience from colleagues; and that the manufacturers be exposed to pressure when it comes to finding solutions to emerging problems. Despite competition between airlines, the technical side usually shares their experiences, both directly and through the manufacturers. This is also partly done through the actions of the regulatory authorities when it comes to serious errors that may affect airworthiness. In particular, the US authorities are very strict in this regard.

During their operation in SAS, the DC-6 planes went through a significant change. At an IATA traffic conference in Nice in 1951, the US airlines, particularly PanAm, launched a proposal that a tourist class be introduced. This aroused strong opposition from many quarters, but it was decided that as of 1 May 1952, a tourist class would be introduced on the North Atlantic. This meant that seat capacity must be expanded in order to make it economically viable.

It could be done either by closer seat spacing, or going from four seats abreast to five. What a difference from the luxury which was strived for on the Boeing 377. The comfort decreased greatly. To implement this change, new seats were bought and to attach them to the cabin floor, new anchor points had to be developed.

Bo Hoffstrom then came up with the brilliant idea of introducing seat attachment rails which enabled the chairs to be moved at intervals of 1 inch with the consideration that there could be requirements later to change the distance between seats. The design he developed was adopted by more and more companies and has since become the international standard. In the DC-6 the rails had to be mounted on top of the existing floor which was provided with an additional floor of light plywood to avoid that someone would trip over the rails. In recent aircraft, including the DC-6B, they are part of the floor so that the top of the rails are flush with the floor.

Another SAS idea that was developed at that time was the introduction of so-called Standard Units for the galley equipment. It was one of the designers in the drawing office, Tord Holm, who in collaboration with the cabin crew and catering staff began to design the appropriate size of the folding tables monted on seat backs and the tray that would accommodate the tableware, food, and drink that was needed to give passengers the service desired. The molded, lightweight plywood tray that was the result of these considerations was made by SILA and was accepted by several airlines and led to many copies being made. When the dimensions of the tray were set, boxes were built that were adapted to fit the trays stacked by six in height with enough distances to fit in glasses and cups, etc. The dimensions of these boxes also proved suitable for other supplies for the galley equipment such as bottles for beverages and much more. They were also an excellent part of the carts that came increasingly into use.

The introduction of these devices led to designing an actual galley that could be simplified and serve as racks for the boxes. Loading and unloading was simplified and also transportation between the catering kitchen and aircraft could be carried out more efficiently than with the older procedures. These ideas have been applied to a large extent by many airlines and galley manufacturers.

Saab 90 Scandia

During the war years 1939 - 1945 aircraft makers had in many countries built up a large technical organization and a very extensive manufacturing capacity. When the end of the war could be seen, it was natural that the extent to which this could be used for civilian production was examined. This was also true for Saab that had great success providing the Swedish Air Force with aircraft.

The American companies Boeing, Douglas, and Lockheed concentrated on large four-engine aircraft and thereby left the field open to those who wanted to find a suitable successor to the aircraft of the DC-3 size class or larger.

From early 1944, Saab produced a preliminary description of a project in collaboration with ABA. Within ABA Bo Hoffström led this work and his counterpart at Saab was Tord Lidmalm. Saab's board approved the project in late February 1944, and it was designated Saab 90 Scandia. The first plane was planned to fly in the summer of 1945, but did not fly until November 1946.

The twin-engine plane was equipped with a nose wheel and laid out for 32 passengers. The engine type was selected as the Pratt & Whitney R-2180, which is half the engine size selected for the Boeing 377. The engine had thus two rows of seven cylinder blocks instead of four. The plane's cabin would not be pressurized thus it would be simple and with a low price in order to reach a large market in areas where competition would be from the pressurized airplanes.

In the US, Glen Martin Aircraft was first to offer the domestic airlines a plane that had the designation 2-0-2, and was also a twin engine plane but with room for up to 40 passengers. It was fitted with Pratt & Whitney R-2800 engine, the same engine Douglas

SAS Saab Scandia with capacity for 24-32 passengers ready for takeoff
Photo SAS.

Saab Scandia SE-BCA
Photo SAS.

opted for on the DC-6. The 2-0-2 also did not have a pressurized cabin. Before they were ready to sign contracts, Martin presented an improved model that would be supplied with a pressurized cabin and designated the 3-0-3. United chose to sign a contract for 35 planes of the type for delivery in 1947 and another 15 in 1948. The flight tests began in July 1947, but it turned out that the plane had stability problems. The measures required to eliminate the errors would be very costly and cause delays.

United canceled the contract and ordered instead aircraft from rival Convair, namely the CV-340, which was very similar to Martin's and had the same R-2800 engine, and additionally had a pressurized cabin. It had completed sucsessful test flights. Martin completed its project, however, and eventually solved the stability problems and introduced further improvements in the 4-0-4. But Martin did not achieve any major successes with the 4-0-4 despite orders for about 100 planes from, among others, Eastern, Northwest and TWA. It became the CV-240 and its successor, the CV-340 and CV-440 that became the dominant DC-3 replacement type around the world, especially in Europe.

To return to the Scandia, the analyses that ABA did showed that seat-mile-costs of the Scandia were more favorable than for the models mentioned above. The Scandia's size was also better adapted to the route network and traffic volumes expected in the planned traffic programs. The simpler plane was obviously cheaper to produce and the Swedish wage level was significantly more favorable than the American. It would also not require as large an outlay of dollars. A large part of the equipment and, above all, the engines had to be paid in dollars.

The decision not to initially supply the plane with a pressurized cabin could possibly have been influenced by the first featured Martin model, the 2-0-2, which was not equipped with one. It may well have been interpreted that other companies had anticipated that there would be a sufficient market for such a plane of this size around the world.

Saab had thoughts of an upcoming version with a pressurized cabin and a visit to Convair in San Diego was arranged to investigate whether it was possible to select a similar installation from the subcontractor AiResearch as Convair had chosen. ABA also had anticipated that there would be a pressurized cabin in later versions and had exercised quite a big pressure on Saab when it came to selecting the R-2180 engine type in order to ascertain that there was sufficient power from the engine to also drive the cabin compressor.

After this explanation of the situation, it is now appropriate to address the ABA / Saab measures. As was mentioned earlier, the project was a couple of years late and the plane flew for the first time in November 1946. Due to political unrest around the partly state-owned SAS's future status, it was not until 28 April 1948 that a contract was signed for the purchase of ten aircraft. The only company besides ABA that ordered the Scandia was the Brazilian company, Aerovias Brasil, which also ordered ten planes. Aerovias Brasi later became VASP

The first of ABA's ordered planes were delivered on 3 October 1950, two days after the final formation of SAS and thus Scandia became a SAS aircraft. In April 1951 another five planes had been added.

The future of the Scandia project was completely changed by the government's intervention. After the 1948 Berlin crisis there followed a major political unrest in Europe in the form of the Cold War. Saab received orders to end the Scandia project and to fully concentrate on the design and manufacture of aircraft for the Swedish Air Force, which required a huge effort from Saab's side. At SAS, it was discovered that the Scandia fleet would be limited to a total of eight planes which led to a renegotiation of the original contract. For the last two planes, the final assembly was done by Fokker in the Netherlands by an agreement reached with them. The same was also true for a part of the planes that were ordered by VASP. The last two SAS planes were delivered in late 1954. Saab tried to persuade Fokker to continue the Scandia project but they abstained because they had already started their F27 project, a twin-engined high wing aircraft with turboprop engines.

The Saab Scandia was structurally in the same class as the American competitors, had good flight characteristics and was much appreciated by pilots for its flight characteristics. There was a feature that caused a lot of concern among the passengers. The engine exhaust pipes ended on top of the wing, in contrast to many other piston-engine aircraft, and this meant that at certain operating conditions large exhaust flames appeared that scared many travelers who believed that a fire had broken out.

Although the Scandia project was Swedish, the fleet was based at Fornebu, Norway, which became the SAS base for twin-engined airplanes in the future. When it was time later to replace the Scandia with the Convair CV-440, all airplanes were sold to VASP which became the sole remaining Scandia operator. It may be noted that the selected engine type was produced in only 65 copies for the Scandia and 10 for a helicopter called the Piasecki XH-16. Spare parts were, however, obtained from stocks of the bigger engine R-4360, which had many common parts, and was produced in quite large numbers, as it was the most-used powerplant on four-engine aircraft.

Douglas DC-6B

In 1948, Douglas had begun planning the continued development of the DC-6. The improvements would include increased cabin length, increased payload, increased takeoff weight and longer range. This was accomplished by increasing the fuel tank volume, and Pratt & Whitney promised more powerful R-2800 versions including, among other things, the introduction of water / alcohol injection that increased power output.

SAS knew of the plans and had started to prepare themselves in case they became a reality. Drawing on the experience accumulated over the procurements of the DC-4 and DC-6, we thought that it might be possible to achieve advantages in negotiations with Douglas if several airlines could coordinate the specifications of their aircraft.

It was then natural to consult with companies that had similar operational and maintenance-related conditions similar to SAS. It was therefore decided that SAS would send me and control manager Lars Tullberg to KLM, Sabena, and Swissair to acquire information. The trip was made in early December 1949. KLM did not show much interest but both

DC-6B Torkil Viking.
Photo SAS.

Sabena and Swissair were more positive. It all resulted in no action but it provided some valuable contacts that could come in handy in the future.

In the previous analyses of the DC-6, Douglas had a strong competitor in the Lockheed Constellation. The investigations made at that time resulted in a conclusion that the DC-6 was superior for SAS. In the new analyses the competition was repeated as Lockheed had also developed their plane.

KLM had already purchased both the DC-6 and the Constellation and at the visit, we got the clear impression that they would continue with that policy. We did not succeed to get any proper explanation except that they considered it important to have competition between Douglas and Lockheed. Sabena had no clear attitude. At Swissair, there were two camps. Within the project group there was a preference for the Constellation but those who were responsible for the daily operation and technical maintenance showed more interest in Douglas. It was difficult to predict what the outcome would be. At SAS, the situation was similar. Those who had their roots in the past OSAS had a certain influence from some Americans that were included in their early organization, a clear preference for Lockheed while those who came from the old ABA side and thus lived with responsibility for maintenance activities rooted for Douglas.

We could also discern ways of manufacturers to conduct sales activities. Douglas almost invariably negotiated with the representatives to whom SAS Management had delegated the task, while Lockheed also sought contact with the higher ranks within the company and also with board members to speak for their product. These bodies could not reasonably be completely familiar with all of the specific circumstances of the aircraft's performance and operating economics!

The data that manufacturers are presenting is of course the most positive that they can achieve. All performance data is presented under the most favorable conditions for flights operated with their own specially trained test pilot. Airlines have in their analyses assumed what the average of their own pilots can perform under normal operating conditions. One example is that in real air traffic there may not always be the most favorable flying altitude from a performance standpoint because of the weather or traffic density during the flight in question. Only the experience of previous operations, for a long time and large numbers of flights, can provide guidance to the correction factors to be applied to the data that manufacturers present. In cases where no information is available, qualified estimates must be used.

What has been said above applies if the aircraft

The Pratt & Whitney Twin Wasp is a 14-cylinder radial engine launched in 1932. More than 175,000 were manufactured, more than any other aircraft engine so far! The engine was used in both civil aircraft and warplanes. Power consumption is 1000-1200 hp, depending on the version.
Photo Pratt & Whitney

DC-6B Hjalmar Viking.
Photo SAS

in question are in service or are in the prototype stage. The problems are many times bigger if the aircraft is only in the design stage. The latter is in fact often the case for the airlines that want to be at the forefront of the queue when it comes to introducing new aircraft types. The leading airlines find themselves therefore in a position where they need to assess manufacturers data based on their own experiences of aircraft and engine manufacturers' past performances. It is also important to have good contacts with the companies' engineers and not only listen to salesmen´s reports.

The development cycle from the first project concepts to the finished product is also long. For the airframe manufacturers it is in the order of five years and for engine manufacturers about seven years. The airlines therefore need to establish early contacts with many technical groups from the manufacturers in order to evaluate the calculations and designs, which later become a reality. This also means that it is desirable for long term continuity among the experts that airlines have in their technical staff.

For SAS, the decision to buy the DC-6B was not so difficult. There were quite rich experiences from the DC-3 and DC-4 and to some extent from the newly delivered DC-6. The good contacts that above all, Karl-Henrik Larsson had established with both American Airlines and United Airlines in particular, came in very handy here because both had been good customers of Douglas. Similarly Douglas's great success with aircraft types in both civil and military production would serve as references.

Regarding Lockheed there were not at SAS or its parent company any direct experience and SAS had not as good contacts with former or previous operators of aircraft built by them. An enquiry at KLM gave no clear picture of how the company looked at a comparison between the two types of aircraft. The calculation and analysis of the Constellation's performance and analysis of structures and engine installations gave no indication that the airplane type would exhibit some advantages over the DC-6B. Another circumstance beyond the technical and operational analysis of the aircraft itself is the major costs associated with a transition from one manufacturer to another when it comes to training of both the engineering staff and the flight crew.

Taking into account all relevant facts it was clear that it would be advantageous for SAS, in an expansion of the long-haul fleet, to purchase the DC-6B. Both Swissair and Sabena also chose the DC-6B for their continued airplane orders while as mentioned KLM chose both types.

In March 1951, the SAS board of directors decided to purchase six DC-6Bs, and after the usual contractual work and specification, an agreement was reached with Douglas shortly thereafter for delivery of the first aircraft in May 1952, and the other before the end of the year. Not long after, the order was extended to cover another eight aircraft to be delivered before the end of 1954. The SAS fleet then consisted of 14 planes. The orders were made after the project responsibility was transferred to my department.

It would later prove that the DC-6B became the most successful piston engine aircraft type and with the lowest cost per seat mile and ton mile. In total 704 planes of the different DC-6 models were built. Even 30 years after the maiden flight of the DC-6 over 130 aircraft were still in service in various configurations. But only four of the archrivals were in operation in 1976.

SAS polar flights

SAS had long been involved with plans for flights over the northern polar regions on the routes to the US West Coast and Japan on the northern route. Many preparations and studies had been done and potential intermediate stops and alternate airports were analyzed; communication means and navigation aids were studied, etc.

It was only when they had access to the DC-6B aircraft was it deemed appropriate to start test flights. It was decided to make the first delivery flight of the DC-6B, OY-KME, from Santa Monica through Edmonton in Canada, and the US military airport at Thule, Greenland, and on to Copenhagen and Stockholm. The flight began on 19 November 1952. This and several subsequent flights are described

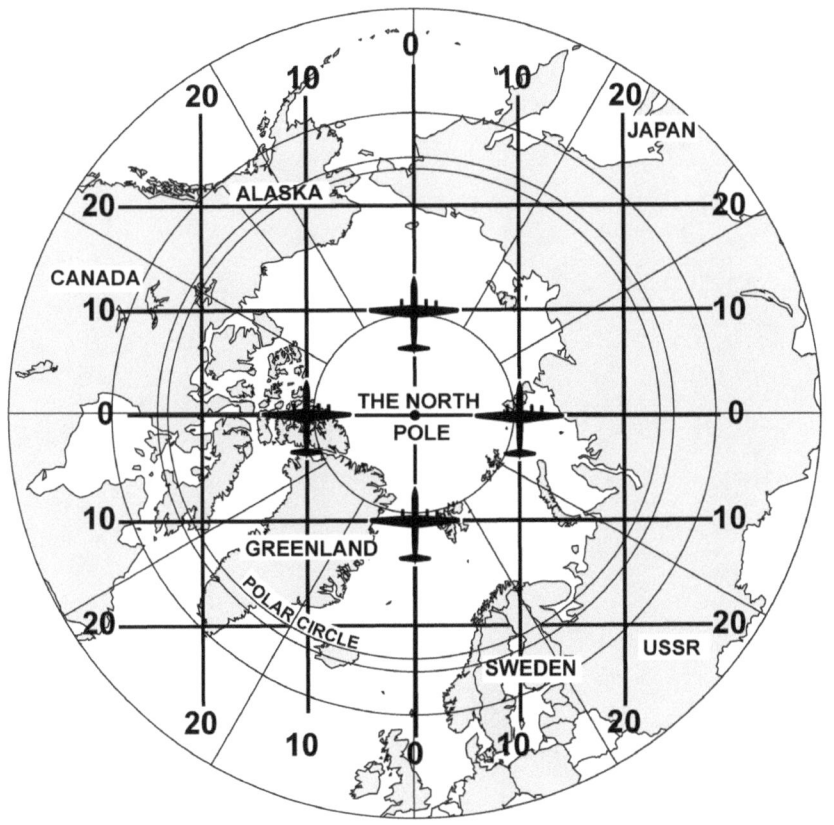

The Polar Grid was developed to safeguard navigation in the Polar area. SAS was awarded the prestigious Christopher Columbus Award for the 1962 polar flight.
Photo SAS and reworked by Hans Kampf.

in many publications so they will not be described in this context. But it may be appropriate to touch on the new instruments introduced in the aircraft to allow for the safety and regularity, as deemed necessary for commercial flight over the polar regions. In particular it is navigating in those areas that requires special equipment.

Since a considerable part of the routes are in the vicinity of the magnetic north pole, which is quite far south of the geographic pole, the conventional magnetic compass becomes virtually unusable. Some radio beacons and other electronic aids were not available then. Satellite navigation was not yet in use and astronomical methods could not be used under all conditions. The solution to part of the problem was a specially designed gyroscope that had such stability that the instrument's drift could be reduced to be less than about 10 degrees per hour

It was felt that the technology had now evolved so far that it would be possible to obtain these instruments. Contact was therefore made with the two leading US firms on the subject, the Sperry Gyroscope Company and Eclipse-Pioneer in the Bendix Group. The latter proved most interested and willing to assist SAS with an instrument that became known as the Polar Path Gyro which had been developed for the US bombing forces. The problem was that it was still surrounded with great secrecy and therefore not released for civilian use.

The Bendix liaison with SAS for many years, Douglas Hembrough, under a big hush-hush arrangement, managed so that SAS could borrow an instrument for the planned delivery flight. The Douglas factory arranged the necessary changes to the aircraft. It is likely that Douglas Hembrough exceeded his authority when he made the arrangement. The whole thing was so sensitive that after the flight the instrument had to be returned to Eclipse-Pioneer by courier, as hand luggage, so that it could not be diverted or damaged during loading for the transfer to Teterboro, New Jersey.

There were three men in SAS who had the major responsibility for implementing the technical and operational actions required so the operation would succeed: the reputed Danish flight captain Povl Jensen, the Norwegian chief navigator Einar Pedersen, and the Swedish instrument engineer Arne Vernblad.

The delivery flight was conducted with Jensen as the commander and Pedersen as navigator and it went without any major problems. This pioneer flight caused a lot of publicity, but it cannot by a long shot be compared with the enormous press coverage that occurred when regular passenger flights between Copenhagen and Los Angeles were inaugurated on 15 November 1954. At that time the confidential classification of the Polar Path Gyro was removed.

Einar "Sverre" Pedersen makes sure of being on the right track.
Photo SAS.

Douglas DC-7 series

Douglas Aircraft's DC-7 series was conceived under rather peculiar circumstances. It started with the engine manufacturer Wright that had developed the R-3350 engine, that was installed on earlier types of Lockheed Constellations, to a new version named R-3350 Turbo Compound. It was equipped

Polar equippment was tested in dificult conditions before the polar flights started. Photo SAS.

with a turbocharger and had 3400 hp or 30% more power than the previous type. By installing it in an improved Constellation with an extended body, higher takeoff weight and greater fuel capacity, and thus longer range, Lockheed could offer TWA an aircraft that could fly nonstop in both directions across the American continent which American and United Air Lines could not do with their DC-6Bs.

In 1951 people tried to convince Douglas to develop an aircraft with these engines but Douglas was doubtful as such a project would adversely affect sales of the DC-6B. In January 1952 however American offered to invest $ 40 million as a payment for 25 planes of the type that came to be called the DC-7. With this contribution to the development costs, Douglas improved the DC-6B through a body extension of 40 inches and installation of Wright R-3350 Turbo Compound engines that had an initial power rating of 3250 hp.

105 planes of the type were built. Of these, 34 went to American, 57 for United, 10 Delta, and 4 to National. Pan Am was not interested because it did not yield any significant improvements in range.

In this situation, SAS got involved in a strange way. We were contacted by National who wanted to investigate whether the two companies could arrange a collaboration for further orders that would mean that National would use the plane during its winter season in which they have an extensive high traffic between New York and Chicago and Miami, while SAS would use them during the summer months when SAS had its high season. This was an interesting idea even though the DC-7 did not have significantly greater range than the DC-6B and thus resulted in the need for stopovers to the same degree. Higher operating costs would be offset by the capital costs, which would be halved with the arrangement.

Talks took place with Ted Baker, the head of National. To our surprise, he ran these discussions completely by himself without the participation of any other employees of the company. The negotiations took place in late February 1954. They did not lead to any result because it turned out eventually that the US aviation rules could not allow an arrangement of the kind outlined.

This sidetrack prompted us to study the plane. It turned out that it would not bring any improvement to the SAS range target. The next phase of the DC-7 development was the DC-7B. The plane was virtually identical to the DC-7 except that it had a higher takeoff weight and extended engine nacelles in the form of saddle tanks on the wing top side that gave it greater fuel capacity and thus better range. But neither could this plane fly nonstop from mainland Europe to New York against the prevailing westerly winds.

112 planes were built of the type and delivered mainly to the US domestic companies, but some went to the PanAm despite the range limitations and to Panagra, a joint venture between Pan Am and another company, Grace American shipping, for South America traffic. PanAm, however, tried to interest Douglas in a further improvement in range. SAS had also made such requests regarding nonstop flights from Scandinavia to New York but also in view of the polar routes to Los Angeles and Tokyo, which were then scheduled to begin shortly.

The designers at Douglas had begun to sketch out a version with increased wingspan by inserting a constant wing section between the fuselage and the existing wing. This would be a fairly simple change but it significantly increased the fuel tank volume; and the inner engines were moved farther from the fuselage thus substantially reducing the noise inside the cabin. They would also extend the fuselage for more seating.

The cost of this type would be higher than those applicable to the DC-7B and there would be significant certification efforts with a new wing ,enlarged rudder, and taller fin to maintain stability in case of engine failure, since the engines were

DC-7C LN-MOD Guttorm Viking. With the DC-7C it was finally possible to reach the US east cost directly.
Photo SFF archive

moved farther outboard. It was not enough that PanAm was prepared to sign an order for 25 planes; Douglas demanded that several companies show a clear interest. The plane would be called the DC-7C and was called "Seven Seas" with a view of the seven seas over which this aircraft type would fly.

On one of my visits to Douglas in Santa Monica to follow the progress of the project, an unexpected event occurred. After an evening, when I had dinner in a restaurant with a close friend at Douglas, he dropped me off at the at the Hotel Miramar, which was the hotel that was most frequently used by airline employees who visited Douglas. I went into the bar to get myself a beer before I went to my room. I had just sat down and had the beer served when someone came and gave me a pat on the shoulder. When I turned around I saw that it was John Borger. He had about the same assignment at Pan Am as me at SAS and was also the person who through many years had the greatest influence by airlines at aircraft and engine manufacturers. I knew him only slightly but had noticed when we met that he was not as communicative and cooperative as most of my colleagues at other airlines. It was not personal but a result of the legendary head of PanAm Juan Trippe who required that his employees be very cautious and restrained in their relations with employees of other airlines. PanAm wanted to keep secret all their plans and always wanted to be first, best, and greatest of the international airlines and be leaders in most contexts.

John asked me to come over to a dark corner of the bar to discuss if we could pull together to bring the greatest possible pressure on Douglas to bring about the plane that we both wanted. Imagine my surprise as the others who sat at the table were Andre Priester and none other than Charles Lindbergh. Priester was John Borger's director and closest to Juan Trippes. It was widely known that Lindbergh worked as a consultant for Pan Am.

It was a strange experience to be together with probably the world's most famous person in the 1900s aviation history and for almost two hours sit and discuss many of the issues relating to aircraft projects. It was soon apparent that range was the most important requirement. I asked cautiously if they intended to contact other European airlines. Then came an imperative for me to continue discussions which implied total secrecy from my side. It must not be revealed so that Juan Trippe would know talks had been conducted with rival airlines on this matter. BOAC was unthinkable for they were engaged in the Bristol Britannia; KLM were both a Douglas and a Lockheed customer; Air France was also an operator of the Constellation. SAS was the only reliable Douglas operator also showing unusual ambition through the planning of polar routes.

The next important question was how many planes we intended to acquire. I announced that the first order in all probability would include seven planes with an option for an additional seven, which thereby would replace the existing 14 DC-6Bs. I was therefore satisfied that Olof Carlstein's desire for a uniform fleet would materialize.

At detailed further discussions on the plane's performance, I reported that the SAS requirement was to be able to fly nonstop in both directions across the North Atlantic from the three Scandinavian capitals, and to the US West Coast with one stop, and to Tokyo as well with a stop in Anchorage.

PanAm did not mention, oddly enough, SAS New York routes but mentioned Hamburg and probably to Frankfurt, Amsterdam, and Paris. As to the last destination, it felt historical to listen to the man who in 1927 flew alone in a single-engine plane for 34 hours and now discussed the aircraft, which would make the same trip with over 100 passengers in 8-10 hours and also be able to do the same distance in the opposite direction.

DC-7C Magnus Viking at Bulltofta. The aircraft type ended its service in SAS on domestic routes.
Photo Sven Stridsberg.

The continued discussions touched on other specification issues of the engine, its power rating and other airplane performance. They did also discuss the plane's lifespan for the first operator. The upcoming transition to jet propulsion meant perhaps a rather short time until the aircraft had to be traded to other less demanding operators or converted into cargo aircraft.

We parted from this most interesting rendezvous with yet another appeal from PanAm that this meeting certainly would not get passed on to anyone and that SAS would not inform Douglas of their demands until at least a week elapsed.

Douglas and the rest of the world would get the impression that it was PanAm who introduced this aircraft and all followers were just that.

I have not informed anyone earlier than now about these circumstances. True, I have told some close friends and relatives that I met with Charles Lindbergh but provided no details on when and how. One thing that struck me during the strange evening was the question of whether this encounter was just a coincidence or if it was somehow planned. I have thought about it many times over the years but I have not wanted to ask John Borger at some of the occasions we met in recent years, as has happened several times in different contexts. I have had a feeling that it could be embarrassing for one or both of us. However, I have come to the conclusion that the whole thing was planned. What was discussed was so important that it could hardly be a coincidence that might determine whether the meeting would take place.

One can possibly speculate that a meeting would be arranged one or a few days later but that coincidentally came to take place as it did. The only alternative explanation I can see is that the Douglas man I had dinner with was involved in the scheme and that he also made the same vow, so Juan Trippe by other channels might know about it. Anyway, all other involved persons are now deceased so I consider myself to be able to break confidentiality without anyone being harmed.

Charles Lindberg visited Scandinavia in 1933 and met both representatives of the DDL in Copenhagen and ABA in Stockholm. They discussed future opportunities to open flights between the United States and Europe. Neither DDL nor ABA saw any opportunities at the time as they lacked the appropriate aircraft.

After PanAm and SAS each presented their respective requirements and Douglas had been able to analyze them and PanAm had given the clear message that they would order twenty-five planes, and SAS had stated that it almost certainly intended to order at least seven planes and probably another seven later, Douglas decided to launch the project.

As a result, SAS started to analyze the aircraft in detail. It was less extensive than a normal evaluation because most of the design elements were well known from the DC-6 and DC-6B. Most systems were also similar. The audit was completed then by preparing one SAS specification that led to the modernization of some installations in the cockpit, which included the introduction of weather radars. Furthermore a contract proposal was drafted so that the final negotiations with Douglas could be accomplished during the festivities at the inauguration of the polar route to Los Angeles in mid-November 1954.

The order would include eight planes instead of the seven stated earlier. It was also the view that later there would be another six ordered. This was done and the SAS fleet then came to consist of 14 planes, thus replacing the DC-6Bs which would mean a rational operation from an economic standpoint.

Charles Lindbergh in front of his Lockheed 8 Sirius "Tingmissartoq", NX-211, during Charles Lindbergh and wife Anne's visit to Hagernas 4 September 1933. From left Unnerus, P.A. Norlin, Sven Rydin, Carl Florman, Dir NK Ragnar Sachs, Arvid Flory, Charles Lindbergh, Gabriel Hedengren, Westerberg, unknown, Elis Nordqvist, unknown, Huss, Ernst Roll, Burém Sparre and K.G. Lindner. On the wing Tord Ångström and Karl Lignell. Several of the persons in the picture would later have important positions at SAS Photo from a donation by Erik Bratt to the SFF archive.

The result was not quite what was expected. A purely "clinical" comparison between the DC-6B and DC-7C showed that the unit cost of the DC-7C was slightly higher than the DC-6B but this would be offset by the lower operating costs that arose when one could eliminate the costs of intermediate stops for only fueling.

This was true of US routes and the polar route to Tokyo, but not for the Far East southern routes, where intermediate stops were made at the places where SAS had traffic rights. This meant that the operating cost of these lines was slightly higher for the DC-7C than the DC-6B. Swissair also acquired the DC-7C for the Atlantic routes described but employed the DC-6B for the Far East!

Another factor which greatly came to affect operating costs were the frequent engine disruptions. The last R-3350 model, which was installed in the DC-7C, with an initial rating of 3,400 hp, proved to be a development that had gone too far in improving performance. The result was frequent engine replacement, which of course was particularly costly when they occurred along the route network with delays and aircraft ferry flights as a result. The DC-7C got to share with the Boeing 377 Stratocruiser the playful name "the world's best three-engine airplane," but for the airlines, it was certainly no joke. The Boeing planes had the final version of the Pratt & Whitney R-4360 piston engine.

In spite of the top management of Douglas being hesitant, and showing some caution at the launch of the DC-7C, the program became a success for the company. As stated previously 105 DC-7, 112 DC-7B and 121 DC-7C aircraft were sold, thus totaling 338 planes. These planes were the last piston engine airplanes that Douglas built for commercial aviation.

Among other clients for the DC-7C was KLM, which abandoned its Constellations, Alitalia, and BOAC, which replaced its Britannia. To definitively demonstrate its superiority as the best long-haul aircraft Douglas arranged with SAS help a record flight which was supervised by the FAI (Federation Aéronautique Internationale), an organization that maintains all records in aviation. It was the delivery flight on 17 November 1956 with the last plane, LN-MOE. The plane was transferred first from Santa Monica where it was manufactured to the airport in Long Beach where there were longer runways and where Douglas factories had installations that could cool the fuel to -20 degrees C before it was loaded into the plane's fuel tanks. In this way one could get more fuel by weight. It is the weight of fuel that defines the energy content, not volume. The crew consisted of Douglas chief pilot Jack Armstrong, SAS chief test pilot Anders Helgstrand, (later director of Sterling) a flight engineer, whose name I have forgotten, and a representative from the engine manufacturer Wright, and myself.

The flight went largely by a great circle route and we landed at Bromma after covering a distance of 5217 nmi, with a flight time of 21 hours and 44 minutes. Because the winds were more favorable than estimated there was, before landing, enough fuel left so that the plane would have been able to reach Helsinki and maybe even Leningrad, as the city was then called, but SAS's press department wanted the landing to be made at Bromma as planned. Both the distance and time records are likely to hold up today for piston-engine aircraft, but the distance record was later overtaken by a jet.

It may be mentioned in this context that SAS operated three additional DC-7C aircraft that were purchased or leased from other airlines. These were

Picture: Pratt & Whitney R-2800 Double Wasp, an 18-cylinder- radial engine used in at least ten key civilian and military aircraft during the 1940s and 1950s. Around 125,000 engines were manufactured with power output between 2,000 and 2,500 hp.
Photo Erik Prisell.

Inspection of the first SAS DC-7C.
Photo by Birger Holmer.

SAS DC-7C Rolf Viking. Photo SAS.

SAS LN-KLB. Convair 440 Metropolitan was an appreciated workhorse on the short routes for 20 years. Photo SAS.

converted to freighters. From the outset, Douglas designed the DC-7 series aircraft so that they could relatively easily be converted into cargo aircraft.

When the project was launched it was realized that jet-powered aircraft would be introduced after quie a few years and then it would be necessary to convert a considerable number of passenger planes. Out of the 14 Douglas-purchased planes, seven were used by SAS for only four years while the other seven remained in the fleet for about ten years.

Convair series: CV-240, CV-340 and CV-440 Metropolitan

As has already been mentioned several aircraft manufacturers started after the war in 1945 to study the possibilities for launching new aircraft to replace most of all, the Douglas DC-3 and DC-4. Convair in San Diego was one of the companies that wanted to build a replacement for the DC-3. The Convair airplane was based on a specification developed by the American Airlines that requiered a plane for 40 passengers, equipped with a pressurized cabin and powered by two engines of the Pratt & Whitney R-2800 type, i.e., the same engine type as for the DC-6.

On these premises Convair drew up a proposal, which was designated CV-240. American Airlines accepted it and Convair started the design and manufacture of the plane without producing a prototype which was met with some amazement among airlines. The plane flew for the first time in March 1947, and the first delivery to American entered service in June 1948. It quickly became a huge success and was built in 176 copies for the airlines and not less than 414 military versions for the US military.

Among the European customers were KLM, Sabena and Swissair. SAS was not included because they had already invested in Scandia. As previously reported an ABA study showed the unit costs of the Scandia were more favorable than the CV-240. But the absence of cabin pressure, the troublesome engine problems and the sudden closure of the project became an obvious disadvantage for SAS.

Neither could SAS participate in the cooperation started by Sabena, Lufthansa and Swissair called the BENESWISS-agreement which involved helping each other with technical services and parts supply not only in their home bases but also on common out-stations on their routes. Their early experiences of this would prove fruitful in the establishment of the cooperation which later evolved to a much greater extent between SAS and Swissair and was later also joined by KLM and the French airline UTA. Sabena, however, was outside of the latter arrangement because they chose Boeing to supply the transition to jet planes.

As a result of the success of the CV-240 Convair developed the model by extending the body, enhancing the range and installing the more powerful R-2800 engine that was also used in the DC-6B. At the same time, a new flap system and an integrated folding door / staircase in the front of the body were incorporated. The new model received the designation CV-340 and 212 planes were manufactured for airlines and 102 for military use in the United States. The first plane of this type was put into service during 1952.

Convair was not content with the success and launched a further improved type in 1954 which originally was designated CV-340B, but later on SAS's request was changed to CV-440. This version had the same dimensions and engines as CV-340 but had increased takeoff weight and a modified engine nacelle that resulted in the engine exhaust and cooling air being carried over the wing upper surface in a rectangular enclosure instead of cylindrical pipes as in previous models. The nacelles were also provided with sound-absorbing material to reduce noise levels.

CV-440 Metropolitan.
Photo Sven Stridsberg.

In 1955 it became increasingly evident that SAS would not survive the competition, not only in Europe, but also in the Scandinavian market and domestic flights with the DC-3 and Scandia, which of course did not have pressurized cabins. It was not until the late summer of 1955 before SAS seriously engaged in studying the Convair planes. It was mainly the new SAS president Henning Throne-Holst who demanded quick action.

A trio that consisted of the chief engineer Olof Carl Stein, chief legal counsel Erik Norman and I were tasked to quickly prepare the ground for a board decision. There was not time to do a normal aircraft evaluation with the help of the necessary specialists in the relevant fields. The aircraft type was well established in the market, it had a very good reputation and performance data could be verified by companies that already operated the CV-240 and CV-340. Those polled all felt that one could trust the Convair data.

Our first assignment was to inform Convair that our boss demanded that the plane should get the designation CV-440 and the commercially viable name of Metropolitan. The requirement was accepted by Convair without any protest. In only one working week, the team that was sent over to Convair both successfully defined an SAS version of the plane and drew up a contract proposal, a record in the history of SAS. This was facilitated by Convair's very knowledgeable and easy to work with staff, both regarding technology and law, and that could take quick decisions. The organizations of such as Boeing, Douglas and Lockheed were equally or more qualified in many areas but they were larger and had longer decision paths and were thereby more cumbersome.

The specification was based largely on the DC-7C work previously undertaken by all stakeholders involved and the results could be used as appropriate. This was true, as an example, for the design of the flight deck.

When the group arrived home it was met by great satisfaction from the route network and sales departments but got pretty big criticism from the technical and operational groups who complained bitterly that they had not been involved. It may be that when buying an airplane it often happens that certain conditions change from the time when a specification is established until the plane is delivered and that some changes need to be introduced. It also happens that some modifications are so expensive that it is advantageous to make them in-house after delivery. They are usually called Post-Delivery Modifications (PDM). Curiously the PDM paperwork for the CV-440 became less extensive than for any other aircraft delivered during this period.

The first order of eleven aircraft with an option for a further twelve was signed in August 1955. Of the twelve options only nine were exercised. The first flight of the plane took place in October 1955, and the first delivery to SAS at the end of March 1956, an unusually short time between order and delivery dates.

Convair made 153 Metropolitan planes of which more than half were used by European airlines. The aircraft was highly appreciated both by passengers and by the SAS staff. They were used for domestic, Scandinavian and European traffic, and were kept in SAS operations for nearly 20 years. Linjeflyg chose Convair as a replacement for the DC-3 and bought a total of 23 used aircraft.

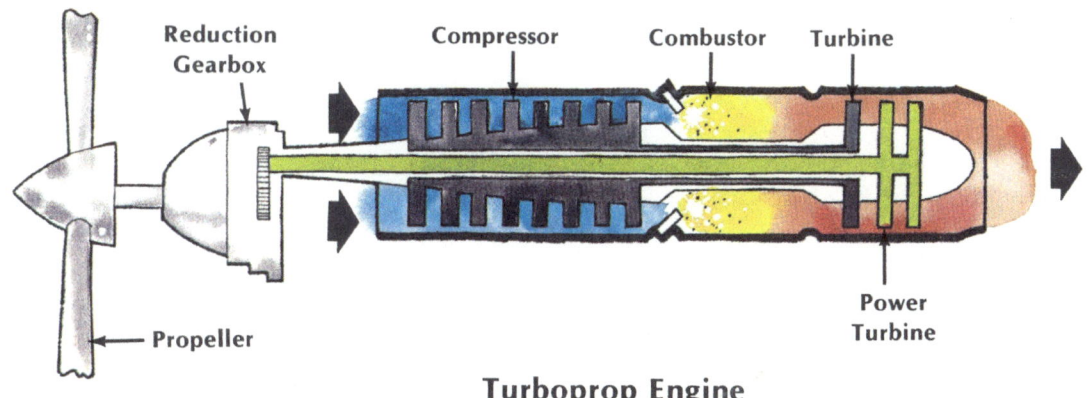

The Turboprop engine was developed in the 1940s. The purpose was to reduce the jet engine's high fuel consumption by extracting thrust by a propeller via a gearbox. Engines for the most common turboprop aircraft are in the range of 2,000 hp to 5,000 hp.
The new European transport aircraft the Airbus A400M has 4 turboprop engines with 11,000 hp each.
Photo General Electric.

Turboprop Engine

Turboprop Aircraft

In the previous sections, some aircraft, which were competitors to the planes SAS selected, were briefly reviewed. However, it is appropriate to outline briefly a different type of aircraft namely those with turboprop engines. These included mainly the Vickers Viscount. As soon as this aircraft was launched in 1948 it attracted a great deal of interest from many directions. Turboprops could be an appropriate transition from piston engine operation to pure jet propulsion. At the time the Viscount was launched it was thought quite generally that the pure jet engine was too fuel consuming to work as a commercial airliner.

The fact that the reputed engine company Rolls-Royce manufactured the Dart engines for the Viscount contributed to the interest. SAS analyses of the aircraft, which was made when the Viscount had flown a few years, showed however, that there would not be any better operating economy than with the CV-440 or DC-6B on the routes that would be affected by a possible Viscount purchase. There were also technical objections in some areas but they were not of the nature that they had decisive influence on the evaluation of the aircraft type.

Another Vickers plane studied was the Vanguard, which was much larger, with longer range than the Viscount and fitted with a Rolls-Royce engine, the Tyne. This plane could not offer better financial performance than existing or ordered SAS planes. Viscount sales totaled 439 units in three different versions and thus became a successful product, while only 44 Vanguards were manufactured.

A third aircraft was also studied – the Bristol Britannia, which was built for the long distance routes of the British airline BOAC. It was fitted with turboprop engines of Bristol's own manufacture. Bristol was of course hoping that it would get widespread use as an alternative to the DC-7C and Super Constellation. SAS's preliminary investigations revealed that it would not provide any improvements compared to the DC-7C.

For some reasons, unknown to me, the former SAS CEO, Throne-Holst, took an interest in the Britannia. It led to him to want a visit at the factories in the city of Bristol in England. It was a tad puzzling since SAS had already signed a contract for the delivery of eight DC-7Cs. He wanted me

Vickers Viscount LN-FOM owned by Fred Olsen Flyselskap A/S was painted in SAS colors for ad hoc leasing to SAS.
Photo Sven Stridsberg.

to come along as a technical advisor. The trip was conducted in spring 1955, and it led naturally to the participation of many of Bristol's top executives. During the trip back Throne-Holst asked numerous questions of me that I understood almost as much as a graduation oral exam for me rather than an effort to analyze the airplane characteristics. He did not disclose his impression of the Bristol presentation. This was the only visit he made to a manufacturer during his time as CEO.

One result of the visit was that it was agreed that Bristol would conduct a demonstration flight to Bromma at the beginning of 1956. It was carried out on 23 March and the purpose was of course that the most relevant units within SAS would get acquainted with the plane. A representative group of SAS staff with Throne-Holst at the forefront boarded the plane but when the engines were started one of them failed, despite strenuous efforts.

Everyone left the plane and the senior management of SAS was invited by Bristol for lunch in the airport restaurant. Just when it was over, one of the accompanying mechanics came up and gave notice to Bristol's sales manager that they had solved the problem, and all were invited to board the plane. Then he made the disastrous mistake of saying that the problem was that "a failing-25-cents switch had caused the mishap." Throne-Holst responded directly: "Do you believe that I will buy an airplane that causes an hour delay because of a failing 25-cents switch. "

He gave thanks for the food, got up and went back to his office without taking part in the flight. His interest in Britannia died on the spot. A 25-minute demonstration flight was conducted, however, with all other invited guests. The Britannia was not a commercial success, which of course meant that even BOAC bought the DC-7C.

Another turboprop aircraft became the subject of a rather extensive study namely Convair's proposal to replace R-2800 engines on the CV-440 with Rolls-Royce Dart engines. Both SAS and Linjeflyg were subjected to a major sales campaign from Convair. It was not an issue for SAS to extend the life of the CV-440 fleet and Convair chose to instead propose a modification of the existing plane. SAS came to the conclusion that a conversion would not give any improved operating results during the relatively short time such a plane would fit into the SAS routes, given the already approaching jet era. Now in retrospect one can conclude that the assessment of the CV-440's remaining lifetime at SAS was underestimated. The plane came to stay in the fleet for almost 20 years!

For Linjeflyg the situation was slightly different by reference to the average shorter flight time that applied to their network and it was judged that entry into the jet age would occur somewhat later for them.

The redevelopment plan then failed, as SAS and Linjeflyg could not come to a joint decision. This contributed to some extent that Linjeflyg instead somewhat earlier invested in the Fokker F-28 jet.

In America, Lockheed had started a project to meet a set of requirements from American Airlines regarding a turboprop-powered aircraft that would complement the Boeing 707 on such routes which were not considered economically appropriate to the 707. The result was the Lockheed Electra, a plane that was to be ordered mainly by American and Eastern. It was equipped with four Allison turboprop engines. SAS analyses showed that the plane could not show any advantages in relation to the types of aircraft that were or had been ordered. Certain hesitancy for most people was also to bring in one fairly unknown engine provider. The aircraft was at first quite successful among the relatively few companies that ordered it but after some time some major difficulties occurred. Under certain operating conditions it encountered strong uncontrollable oscillations and vibrations in the engine mountings and the whole engine installation was destroyed, in some cases ripped off the wing and caused crashes.

Bristol Britannia.
Photo Sven Stridsberg.

SAS CEO H. Throne-Holst inspecting the Bristol Britannia.
Photo Birger Holmer

The jet age

de Havilland Comet

As with the turboprop aircraft the first jet airliner, the de Havilland Comet was a subject of SAS studies. The Comet came into being as a result of the report of the so-called Brabazon Committee, set up by the UK government in 1943 to draw up guidelines for their own airline industry activities after the war. It led, among other things, to the design of the above-described English turboprop aircraft.

The assignment to construct the first commercial jet plane was awarded the de Havilland. The work was initially done in a quite secret mode and the information to the outside world was limited about what was going on. Since the British airline BOAC ordered fourteen planes in 1947, the secrecy eased and materials became available so that airlines could begin to study it. Among the early stakeholders were PanAm, Canadian Pacific Airlines, Air-India, the French company UTA, Panair do Brazil and LAV from Venezuela.

A more detailed presentation to the aviation world and the public did not come until the plane was displayed at the Farnborough air show in autumn 1949. By the then available information SAS found that it would not be a profitable operation using the aircraft. The range was too short to fit the North Atlantic operation. If SAS had put the plane on that route, the necessary stopovers would eat up most of the reduced flight times that would arise on the routes. Visits to the factory or comprehensive technical evaluation were not done.

There were also some technical objections to the plane. In particular it was the engine installation. To install two engines so closely together in the wing root on each side of the body would be an intrusion in one of the most difficult areas available when it comes to finding a satisfactory design. Should a fire occur in an engine, or a blade failure occur in the compressor or turbine, fire or uncontained parts could pose a major risk to the adjacent engine and both wing root as well as the cabin structure. SAS found in consultations that many other airlines had similar views and both Boeing and Douglas stated that they could not accept such a design for a commercial aircraft.

BOAC put the Comet into European service on 2 May 1952 and later the routes to Asia. On 10 August 1952, a Comet, totally unexpected, arrived at Bromma Airport in Stockholm which granted an opportunity for many to inspect the plane from outside and some selected people to go through the cabin and take a look into the cockpit.

The reason for this visit was that the plane was to fly to Helsinki to bring Prince Philip back from visiting the ongoing summer Olympics. On the way, the plane would pick up some dignitaries from the British Embassy. I was invited to come along and that way got my first experience of a flight on a jet aircraft.

It started with a climb to 28,000 feet and then a direct descent to landing at Helsinki's new airport. The plane naturally aroused great attention and also

de Havilland Comet visiting Bromma and SAS. de Havilland Comet was undoubtedly a beautiful aeroplane but stood no chance when the Douglas and Boeing types entered the market
Photo by Sven Stridsberg.

the four passengers were watched with wonder when we walked on the red carpet that had already been rolled out to later be walked on by Prince Philip. The return journey to Bromma was made with a Scandia and took more than twice as long and was a clear indication of what was at hand for the introduction of jet propulsion.

In its first operating year Comets were hit with three total losses, nothing however in scheduled operation. In the first, no one came to harm, in the second one person was killed on the ground and in the third the entire crew was killed. The accidents were considered to be caused by pilot error but one should probably consider the design of the control system was a contributing factor. The rudder servo driven system was designed to reduce the load for the pilots. The artificial feedback was not resolved in a satisfactory manner and did not give pilots the right feeling for what loads the aircraft was subjected to. These shortcomings could to some extent be compensated by training and experience, but it was important that the problem was solved by system changes, which also occurred in later versions of the plane.

Two more serious and catastrophic crashes occurred in January and in April 1954, both off the west coast of Italy. One plane ended up at about 65 meters depth, but the second of more than 1000 meters. Enough remnants were picked up of the first plane to determine the probable cause and in both cases it was possible by autopsy and investigation of salvaged and washed up corpses and belongings to get a complete picture of what happened.

Both aircraft had been destroyed by explosive decompression, i.e. the fuselage had been split open due to material fatigue at the cabin windows or other openings in the fuselage. Although the Comet had undergone extensive testing to show that the strength of the structural elements were satisfactory, they had not been enough. These facts were well known among experts, both theoretically and technically, but greater care was obviously necessary. What happened meant that the entire aircraft industry came to pay more attention to material fatigue. The aircraft specialist press handled these circumstances largely correctly, but in the public media, it often seemed as if Comet was hit by newly discovered technical problems.

As a result of the Comet accidents authorities started to require tests of the whole pressurized fuselage in water tanks. Such a tank was manufactured for the Comet in order to define the material breakdown process. To simulate the fuselage fatigue conditions, by cyclically pumping it up to the current cabin pressure and then reducing it to zero, would result in an explosion of devastating dimensions when it splits open. By immersing it in a large water tank and varying the internal water pressure, there is no risk when it gives way. It is also significantly faster in this way to implement several tens of thousands of cycles than if it is done with air. This regulatory requirement has significantly made development programs more costly for new aircraft types. As they gained experience of the test samples, they have essentially been simplified and become less costly.

In retrospect it may be mentioned that SAS and many others pointed out that the cabin skin in the Comet was significantly thinner than, say, the DC-6B, even though the Comet had twice the cabin pressure to be able to operate at a cruising altitude of 30,000 feet.

After a long flight ban the Comet was redesigned to a version named Comet 4, which was built in fifty units but all did not enter into service. PanAm never completed their previous orders and options. BOAC put their Comet 4 on routes over the North Atlantic on 4 October 1958, a few weeks before PanAm started their Boeing 707 operation at the end of the same month. Some argued that PanAm therefore assumed that the English would be the first to receive the bulk of the expected criticism of the noisy jet traffic.

You may wonder why I have written so much about Comet, a plane that SAS never acquired. The reason is that I wanted to highlight the problems that easily can arise in large leaps in development that could lead to both large delays and costs. The lessons learned from Comet influenced to a large extent the entire aviation industry and also the supervisory authorities.

The choice between the Boeing 707 and Douglas DC-8

The studies and analyses made of these aircraft types were the most extensive that up to then had been performed in SAS's history. Colleagues in several other airlines have mentioned that the same was true for them. Ever since the de Havilland Comet project was launched, the other major aircraft manufacturers studied the possibilities to construct a plane that could compete with the Comet. The company that early and, most wholeheartedly, got involved was Boeing as opposed to the others who had no profitable production of larger aircraft at the time. Immediately after the war ended in early 1945, Boeing sent a delegation, which among others included their head of aerodynamics, George Schairer, to Germany to review part of the German research results in his area of expertise. Namely, there were indications that the Germans were at an advanced stage of their research. Boeing found very interesting data on the swept wing designs and this gave reason to study this area.

In September 1945, Boeing had already come so far that they had begun to analyze the potential of designing a bomber project, the XB-47, with a wing with 35 degrees sweep. The intention was to improve performance at speeds approaching the speed sound, i.e. in these contexts, usually denoted by Mach 1.0. In September 1947 the first prototype of the XB-47 was already prepared for ground trials before the first flight took place on 17 December of the same year, the forty-fourth anniversary of the Wright brothers' first flight.

Early in test flights, people noticed a stability problem that could occur with severe oscillations in mainly the rudder and aileron systems. These are usually called "Dutch- roll." The name is derived by a known aerodynamicist Dr. Jerome Hunsaker who suggested at a lecture on the phenomenon that the aircraft's movements were similar to those he had seen Dutch skaters perform when they were skating on the canals in Holland. The phenomenon could prove to be of great importance in the design configurations of wings, rudders, and aircraft systems of aircraft with swept wings.

Another circumstance which gave Boeing great experience for future use was the design of the engine installations and nacelles, which were attached to the pylons under and in front of the wing.

The B-47 had six engines, four of which were in twin nacelles and two in separate pods. The later larger bomber, the B-52 with eight engines in twin nacelles per pylon gave Boeing further experience in this type of installation. This would prove important in the development of the 707.

Boeing had good experiences regarding tanker aircraft with large orders from the Air Force for the propeller-driven KC-97, the military version of the Boeing 377 Stratocruiser. They forecasted that there would be a need for jet-powered tankers that would better suit air refueling of the large amounts of fighters and bombers with jet engines that became part of the Air Force arsenal. By utilizing the experience from the B-47 and B-52 they could derive a modern jet-powered tanker plane.

In April 1952, Boeing decided to invest $16 million of its own funds to build a prototype which became known as the Boeing 367-80. The plane generally was called "Dash 80." At the design phase they took into account of course the possibilities to develop it into a commercial aircraft for both passengers and freight.

It was a low-wing plane with four engines mounted on pylons on a wing with 35 degrees sweep. The fuselage had a cross section of 132 inches, the same as the upper deck of the 377. The plane was built in a separate workshop and was kept secret as best they could. There were some information leaks, of course, but they seemed not to worry about potential competitors.

When the plane was presented to the world on 15 May 1954 it aroused an enormous interest. The presentation of the Dash 80 resulted in a need for both aircraft manufacturers and airlines to review and possibly revise their plans for the future. The English were engaged in improving their Comet for the upcoming Comet 4 version. Lockheed continued to invest in the Electra turboprop plane and felt that

May 14 1954 the Boeing 367-80, called Dash 80 was rolled out in front of thousands of Boeing employees. The aircraft is now on display at the National Air and Space museum site at Dulles airport outside Washington DC. USA. Photo Boeing.

Boeing had embarked on a too risky project.

At Douglas, however, it was feared that its hitherto dominant position as a supplier of commercial aircraft could be threatened if the Dash 80 was developed as a passenger aircraft. The leading technicians were convinced that you immediately have to bet big to get ahead of Boeing. But Donald Douglas was more hesitant. He felt that they should continue to build and earn money on the successful propeller planes still being ordered in large quantities. There were forces within the company that argued that they should await developments that were likely to lead to a need for a twin-engine jet aircraft. But pretty soon even Donald Douglas was convinced that the competition from Boeing must be met. The engineers continued their studies of how a competing plane would be configured, but it was not until the beginning of June 1955 before Douglas formally informed the aviation world that an aircraft called the DC-8 would be built.

Let us return to Boeing and activities during the past year. It began with the decision to work with the US carriers and PanAm took the lead when it came to the design of the passenger version. It was obvious that the cabin diameter of the Dash 80 at 132 inches, would not be enough for a future passenger aircraft and Boeing had already decided that the KC-135 tanker that was developed from the Dash 80 prototype would have a diameter of 144 inches, which would allow 6 seats abreast with an acceptable width of the aisle. To build the production version as economically as possible, Boeing counted on being able to work with the same jigs and tools that applied for the tanker plane. But the negotiations for this arrangement led to delays of several months before it came to a mutually acceptable solution. In the meantime Douglas opted for a cabin diameter of 147 inches for its DC-8.

To compare the two aircraft interiors, United had built a mockup where half the cabin length consisted of Douglas's proposal and the other half of Boeing. United found for them, that the Douglas proposal was best by incorporating a wider aisle which gave an airier impression. When Boeing realized that Douglas would gain an advantage it forced a change of mind.

Boeing had now changed the name of the new type of aircraft to Boeing 707. Boeing had previously used numbers as Model 40, Model 80, Model 247, Model 307 and Model 377 but switched to the designation 717 in a tanker aircraft based on the Dash 80 after which the 700 series became the standard.

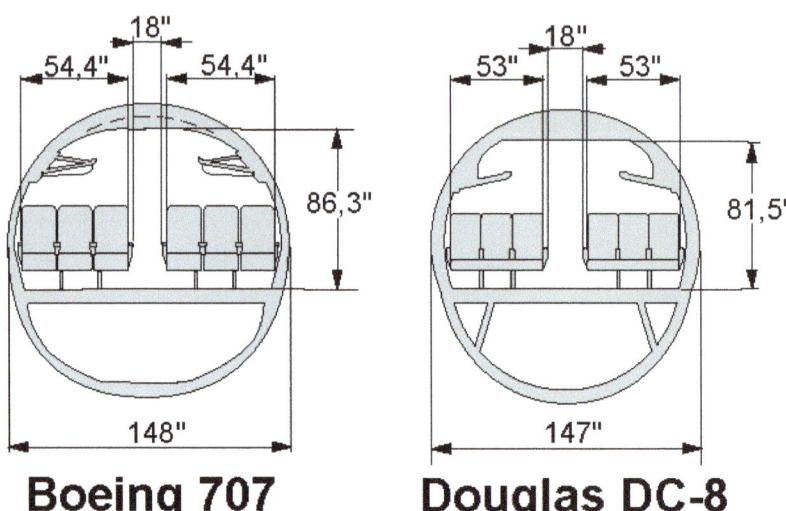

Cabin Cross-sectional comparison between the DC-8 and 707.
Drawing Hans Kampf.

Boeing went on to call the prototype the 707 during further testing.
Photo Boeing.

To outdo Douglas it was decided that the Boeing 707 would get a cabin diameter of 148 inches. It was realized that one must suspend the ideas of combining the structures so that they could satisfy both military and civilian customers. The experience of the KC-97 and Stratocruiser spoke for itself. The agreement it had signed with the Air Force on jigs and tools had herewith no meaning and costs to build the 707 would increase significantly.

While Boeing was working on adapting the 707 to the airlines' preferences, flight tests continued with the Dash 80. It turned out that the plane had the same tendencies as the B-47 and suffered from Dutch roll. To reduce these tendencies a device was introduced called a "yaw damper" but test pilots were still not entirely happy with the result. It would later prove that additional actions were required. Skilled test pilots can control the situation but you cannot assume that airline pilots in general can manage all possible situations.

During the late summer and autumn of 1955 SAS technical and operations departments were very busy with the DC-7C and the CV-440 introductions and further development of the polar flights which were extended to also include Tokyo. At various visits at Douglas in Santa Monica, we followed of course the Douglas DC-8 activities with great interest but no direct evaluation was done. Both Douglas and Boeing were active with numerous visits in Stockholm by sales staff that made their presentations of the planes.

At the airline associations International Air Transport Association (IATA) Annual General Meeting (AGM) in New York on 13 October 1955, PanAm announced that it had ordered 20 Boeing 707s and 25 Douglas DC-8s. Then all airlines got very active. Shortly thereafter, United announced that they had ordered 40 DC-8s and American Airlines responded with 50 Boeing 707s.

Now it became urgent for SAS to seriously study the two manufacturers' products. A group that varied between ten and twelve people from relevant departments had to spend most of November and December 1955 to study the two projects at Douglas in Santa Monica and at Boeing in Seattle. The group was led by the chief engineer Olof Carlstein and included, among others, Counsel Erik Norman, chief pilot Povl Jensen, aerodynamic and performance specialist Gunnar Antvik, and myself.

The Civil Aviation Authority airworthiness expert, Tord Angstrom, also participated in the work. It was he who later would issue airworthiness certificates for aircraft that SAS would possibly acquire. Although there is an agreement between the authorities in most countries that their respective Airworthiness should be accepted internationally, it should still be useful to authorities to get a good understanding of what such a big shift that the introduction of jet propulsion for passenger aircraft meant. In this case, Tord Angstrom also had great knowledge of, above all, structural issues and especially fatigue strength, an area which of course had special significance because of the Comet accidents.

The first version of the 707 that was offered to airlines had the designation 707-120. It was the model that Pan Am and American ordered. It had a maximum takeoff weight of 247,000 lb, and was powered by four Pratt & Whitney engines, which initially had the military designation J57. Later it

SAS chief pilot Povl Jensen finds himself comfortable in the 707 cockpit.
Photo by Birger Holmer.

was called the JT3 for civil versions. The predicted performance let PanAm expect to be able to fly New York-London non-stop in both directions and thus, successfully compete with BOAC's upcoming Comet 4. The Boeing plane also had higher cruising speed than the Comet.

SAS estimated that the 707 was not of interest, because a nonstop flight to New York could not be done in both directions with sufficient revenue cargo. A stopover for refueling would greatly eliminate the time savings that would occur in comparison with non-stop flights with the DC-7C. It was judged that a competitor such as Pan Am, would argue in the same way.

Both SAS and many other companies estimated that Boeing would come forward with improved versions shortly and SAS decided to conduct a detailed analysis of the plane when new material became available. Boeing had a big lead over Douglas through the experience gained by the construction of both the B-47 and B-52 that had swept wings and pylon-mounted engine installations. This knowledge had been used extensively in the construction of the Dash 80. Because the plane could indeed be considered a kind of prototype for the upcoming 707, SAS was invited to let three people participate in a demonstration flight.

The Chief Pilot Povl Jensen, the performance specialist Gunnar Antvik, and I were chosen for the mission. The aircraft was not certified for anything other than tests by Boeing and a few demonstrations, consequently we were provided with parachutes that had to be strapped on for the entire flight. The aircraft was fitted with a special tunnel just behind the wing that in the bottom had a hatch, which could be opened outwards so that the occupants could easily leave the aircraft in an emergency.

It was a very peculiar experience to participate in this flight. After a briefing of about 40 minutes the flight started with Boeing's legendary chief test pilot Tex Johnston in the left seat and Povl Jensen in the right seat. As the plane reached the appropriate altitude they changed seats and Povl got to do the maneuvers he wanted. He performed a landing and a takeoff. All went to everyone's liking and it was clear that Povl's handling of the plane impressed Tex Johnston. Later Johnston let us know that Povl's ability and way to calmly and quickly assimilate and handle the aircraft was among the best he had experienced from any pilot who had no experience in big, jet-powered planes with swept wings.

Throughout the flight Gunnar Antvik was completely occupied with reading interesting instruments and making notes that could be used to verify the information provided about the Boeing plane's performance.

I tried to get an idea of how a flight of this kind of plane would be perceived by passengers. We

Birger Holmer and Gunnar Antvik examine the 707 in detail
Photo by Birger Holmer.

were fully aware that the 707 would differ in many respects from the prototype but it gave at least a good insight into the major changes that were under way at the time of transitioning to jet propulsion. Our specialists studied their fields and received briefings of drawings, models, mock-ups, and parts that were already defined and manufactured. They found no significant deficiencies or material weaknesses except in two very important areas. The one already mentioned tendency that the plane could enter a Dutch roll, even within the normal speed range. Boeing could convincingly present evidence that this would not also happen to the 707-120. Subsequent experience would show that this concern was justified.

The second area was the wing structure. Both SAS's own experts and above all Tord Angstrom were very critical of the essential elements of the structure. Most were anticipated problems with material fatigue. Even here it would much later prove that this was correctly judged.
Generally we got the impression that at Boeing the aerodynamics staff had the strongest influence on the design solutions when it came to wings, rudders and flaps and engine installations. They defined the configurations and then the structural engineers were left to do their best to solve the mechanical construction.

During the visits to Douglas in Santa Monica we were met with equivalent presentations of the DC-8 aircraft, which at first glance appeared to be a twin of the Boeing 707. However, there was a significant difference: the DC-8 wing had a sweep of 30 degrees compared to 35 degrees for 707. This led us to examine more closely what experience Douglas had in swept wings with jet propulsion. In Santa Monica, there was no personal experience but at the Douglas plants in El Segundo and Long

Beach, both suburbs of Los Angeles, there was some. There an airplane called the A3D Skywarrior had been built, a twin-engined bomber destined for the US Navy. The plane had a sweep angle of 36 degrees and the engines were mounted on pylons in the same way as the DC-8 and 707. It had flown for the first time in late October 1952.

In Long Beach they had been commissioned to design a new twin-engine aircraft called the B-66 Destroyer, which had 35 degree sweep. It had an engine installation as very similar to that chosen by Douglas for the DC-8. The B-66 made its first flight in late June 1954. Another interesting fact was that the US Air Force forced Boeing to let both Douglas and Lockheed build the B-47 under license to increase production capacity and from a safety point, spreading the business. This gave the two companies the opportunity to have a detailed knowledge of Boeing's general design methods and of course get detailed insight into the plane's flight characteristics. These three factors had certainly influenced Douglas in the decision to choose a 30-degree sweepback to achieve the desired flight characteristics under all conditions.

In the case of the other aerodynamic design of wings, rudders and flaps systems, both companies differed. The companies had slightly different philosophies. Douglas decided early in its history not to build their own wind tunnels because there was good access to the tunnels of various types in the Los Angeles area where they could rent time. There were tunnels including one at the California Institute of Technology (Caltec) but also NASA and others had wind tunnels in the area.

In the Seattle area, there were not these opportunities and it was deemed impractical and expensive to use tunnels far from their own operations. Boeing therefore built their own wind tunnels and they could decide over their capacity and availability. Boeing had a clear advantage when it came to quickly resolving problems that arose. The perception the SAS group got regarding the two companies' technological expertise in the aerodynamics area in general was that they were fairly equal, but you still got the impression that the aerodynamicists' opinions outweighed the specialists in structure more at Boeing than at Douglas where they were more equal.

After obtaining the desired information on the Dash 80 and the model 707-120 that was under construction, the SAS Group proceeded to do a more detailed analysis of Douglas plans showing three variants of the DC-8 plane.

First came the DC-8-10 which had a maximum takeoff weight of 257,000 lb and was equipped with the Pratt & Whitney JT3 engine, same as the 707-120. It was this type United ordered. Later came a version with the designation DC-8-20 which was fitted with an engine which initially had the military designation J75, which at that time was classified, but later got the civil designation JT4, also from Pratt & Whitney. The thrust of the JT3 engine was increased by almost 40% to 15,000 lb. This version was added primarily to reduce runway requirements at high average temperatures. Finally came the DC-8-30 version, which had the same body and wing as the previous models but with some minor improvements. It was also fitted with the J75 (JT4) and was offered with a takeoff weight of 275,000 lb. It was this version that would become the Intercontinental model and was the only model that was interesting for SAS.

It was an odd problem. Douglas and of course, Boeing had gained access to classified performance data, weights and dimensions etc. for the engine, to be able to make presentations of the aircraft with this engine type. The condition was, of course, that they could not reveal anything about the engine data they received. SAS and all other interested parties were then in a position to completely accept that the aircraft manufacturer had interpreted them correctly. SAS specialists' detailed technical survey of all this

DC-8-62 clearly showing the low nose position
Photo
www.Scanliners.com.

material gave no reason to highlight something that was not acceptable to SAS. Douglas's choice of a 30-degree sweep angle was obviously a reason for a debate and Douglas emphasized strongly that they made it with respect to the desired flight stability under all operating conditions, and accepted that the plane thus lost maybe 5-10 knots cruising speed in relation to the 707. An unfavorable impact on operational economy, Boeing claimed, but Douglas did not.

In the cabin, people noticed that Douglas kept quite large windows and the distance between them had been based, at that time, on quite common dimensions with regard to the distance between seats. Boeing had chosen significantly smaller windows and distances between them so that passengers would have ample opportunity to look out at other seat pitches.

Another interesting observation it may be necessary to mention. In a lot of drawings and brochures it seemed the DC-8 stood slightly on its nose, i.e. the nose gear was slightly shorter than the main. The explanation given was that the main undercarriage length was determined so the air intake of the engine would have a certain minimum distance to the ground to avoid the "vacuum cleaner effect" while taxiing on the ground that would lead to stones and other debris that could be there, to be sucked into the engine and cause great damage to them. To further reduce the risk the engine intake forefront was fitted with an outlet from the engine compressor that would give an air swirl down to the ground that would mitigate the vacuum cleaner effect. Another reason, which was raised, was that at landing the nose should be lowered toward the runway as soon as possible after the main touched down. Thereby reducing the wing angle of attack and thus its lifting power so braking performance was improved. A fourth reason was that by this arrangement the nose wheel weight was reduced. These explanations were accepted, of course, but it turned out much later that the main motive was another. Based on past experience with the DC-4, DC-6 and DC-7 series development, Douglas was counting on that even the DC-8 would see one or several body extensions, which of course also happened. At such extensions obviously Douglas wanted to have large margins so that the tail would not hit the ground during rotation during takeoff or with a high angle of attack at landing. These circumstances were not mentioned during the contacts that SAS had with other carriers or by Boeing. The 707 series had from the outset less "ground clearance" than the DC-8 and Boeing could not follow when Douglas later launched the extended versions DC-8-61 and DC-8-63.

After obtaining the available data the DC-8 group continued to further study the 707. It had in fact been claimed that Boeing had new versions of the 707 in mind as a response to Douglas's DC-8-30 launch. Because PanAm had ordered 25 DC-8s and only 20 Boeing 707s they had indicated that Douglas was preferred rather than Boeing. One of the reasons was that the DC-8-30 had higher payload and longer range. PanAm felt that the 707 needed a larger wing to become competitive.

This led to a Boeing proposal to enhance the range by building a section at the wing root that would move the original -120 wing outboard by six or seven feet in a similar way as was done with the Douglas DC-7C. Within Boeing, this led to a prolonged debate and the end result was that they decided to construct a new wing for the version that came to be known as the 707-320. This plane would also be powered by the J75 so that it became competitive against the DC-8-30.

At the time, in mid December 1955, when SAS would determine whether the order would go to Boeing or Douglas, work on the new wing had not progressed further than that so SAS had to make its assessment based on the structural reconstruction of the 720-wing. With the wing's new aerodynamic design Boeing intended to reduce or preferably eliminate the tendency for Dutch roll that the 120-wing had. It seems strange that no major effort had been made in this regard in the design of the -120 wing when they were well aware of the problem from the Dash 80.

On 10 December 1955, Olof Carlstein was requested to go back home to see SAS president Throne-Holst who announced that he wanted to implement an order before the end of the year and preferably before Christmas. This led to our having to take a provisional position at the time. The result of the talks was that on the purely technical evaluation the two alternatives were virtually equal, but with three significant exceptions.

SAS first DC-8-33 here showing the big noise mufflers at the engine exhaust
Photo SAS.

Two 707-320B were selected as VIP aircraft for the US government and remained in service until 1992. 707-320B had compared with 707-120 an all new wing with an increased span of 14 feet, wing area increased by 26 % and the fuselage length by 8 feet, but was still slightly smaller than the DC-8-62. Boeing manufactured 581 aircraft of the 707-320 type
Photo Boeing.

The first was the unresolved problem of Dutch roll that Boeing had not addressed in a satisfactory manner. The second was the fatigue life of the wing of the 120 model was not expected to be of the same class as that of Douglas, who could base their designs on the good experience from their DC series. Both SAS's own experts and Tord Angstrom were completely convinced of this. The third factor that was important was that SAS's own and others' experiences from many years of operation with Douglas aircraft had given great confidence in Douglas's ability to develop their planes and give good support to aircraft in service, it is called "Product Support" or "After Sales Service," Boeing's performance in this regard from previous civilian aircraft was not on the same level.

Another factor that influenced SAS opinions was the fact that PanAm at this stage seemed to prefer Douglas. Similarly, United had decided to use the DC-8 but despite this had to endure fierce competition for one year from, among others, American and TWA who ordered the 707. SAS had traditionally enjoyed particularly good relations with senior engineers at United and therefore could share their views on the choice between the two manufacturers. Although Eastern, known as a very critical aircraft purchaser, had decided on Douglas and also the European airlines Lufthansa and Swissair.

The message Olof Carlstein brought home was that everyone in the group preferred Douglas. The rest of the group stayed another few days in Seattle,

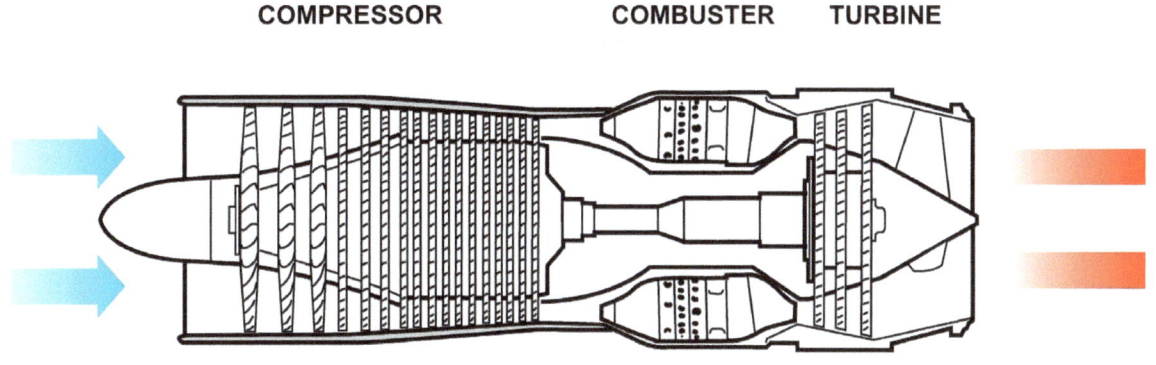

The jet-engine´s very simple principle: the air sucked in through the intake is compressed and heated up in the combustion chambers and the reactive force in the exhaust propels the aircraft forward. Part of the energy is used in the turbine, which powers the compressor.
Picture Hans Kampf.

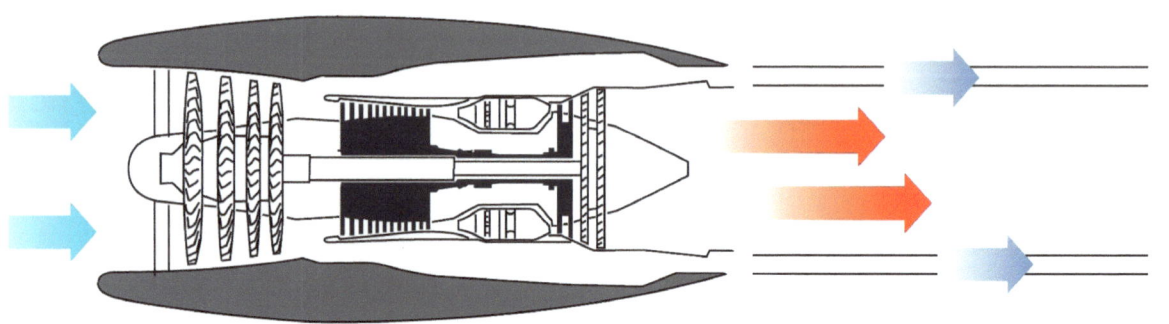

In the fan engine the compression is performed in two sections. the air not led through the engine core is channeled in the by-pass to the exit where it is mixed at the exhaust with the hot gases that have passed the core and the combustion. The effect is a quieter and more fuel efficient engine.. Typical thrust for the first fan engines is 17,000 lb. Picture Hans Kampf.

as the examination of the 707 was not completed, and SAS did not want to give the impression that no decision would be taken before the evaluation was completed. The group had obviously orders to immediately contact the main office in case something new of a significant nature would show up. This did not happen and on 20 December 1955 a contract with Douglas was signed in Stockholm regarding the purchase of seven DC-8-30s with options of a further three planes.

The seven firm aircraft orders were intended to serve the routes between Scandinavia and North America, and the polar route to Japan. New York and Los Angeles were already included in the route network and the planned extension to Montreal, Chicago and Seattle. The three option aircraft were planned to be used for routes to South America and Africa and the Far East southern route when traffic needs motivated the use of such large jets. The delivery time was set for the spring of 1960 and the price was $ 5.4 million each. The contract was defined by the plane in Douglas's then current basic specification of the -30 model with some modifications.

By then we had insufficient time to prepare an SAS specification. One of the most important changes was the maximum takeoff weight that had been debated vividly. At the launching of the DC-8-30 it was set at 275,000 lb. We requested an increase partly to provide sufficient margin to the range at full load, and to manage an anticipated increased empty weight. It is very difficult to calculate the empty weight of an aircraft that is only defined by drawings and other similar information. Experience from previous aircraft designs gave reason for caution in this regard. SAS succeeded in raising the takeoff weight to 287,500 lb. and requested even higher weights but Douglas argued that it was not possible to go higher. The matter had been brought right up to the top management on the technical side, namely Arthur Raymond, Senior Vice President of Engineering.

Another very important aspect was the engine selection. The Douglas specification prescribed the still-secret Pratt & Whitney J75, but an additional clause gave SAS the option to choose an engine that Rolls-Royce had launched and which was named Conway. Both Douglas and Boeing had left the engine selection open but had not at the end of 1955 provided sufficient information so that an assessment could be made by airlines. Neither Boeing nor Douglas showed any enthusiasm at this point. It could be that both companies were completely occupied with the final definition of current models while engaging in an intense sales campaign. It could also be related to their desire to promote a national interest. Another factor could be that the ability of airlines to choose another manufacturer would put extra pressure on Pratt & Whitney to provide both manufacturers and airlines favorable conditions. It could also be that the US authorities would speed up the release of declassified information on the J75 engine, so their own industry would not lose production.

At the time of the SAS contract signing in late December 1955, the DC-8-30 had a maximum take-off weight at that time of 287,500 lb. and any SAS attempt to further increase it had not yielded results. Well into the New Year 1956, we were surprised to learn that Douglas, in connection with attempts to win an order from SABENA, had given in and promised to increase to 295,000 lb. so that SABENA would choose the DC-8 and not the 707. Despite this, SABENA selected the Boeing option.

At the beginning of 1956, Douglas had orders for 98 planes from seven companies and Boeing had orders for 73 planes from six companies, but then the wind changed. PanAm never bought more than the first 25 DC-8 planes. It is said that this was because Douglas did not achieve the promised performance, but it is also said that Boeing also did not achieve its goal with the first series of the 707. PanAm orders to Boeing consisted of only six of the -120 type, while all others were of the -320 version.

Between 1957 and 1961 Boeing sold 172 planes of 707 type while Douglas sold only 47 planes. It's hard to find a comprehensive explanation for this. The performance of both types was so similar that the

PanAm was the first Boeing 707-120 operator. On 26 October 1958 PanAm opened commercial jet operation across the Atlantic. The inaugural flight PA114, started in New York via Gander to Le Bourget Paris. The return flight stopped at Keflavik for refueling. Travel time including the refueling was 9 hours compared with 20 hours on the Stratocruiser on the same route. Boeing 707-120 did not have nonstop range for New York-Paris. Nonstop range was achieved later when the 707-320B version was introduced.
Photo Boeing.

differences that existed could hardly be decisive. It appears that Boeing had more interest and resources through banks and other influential bodies to assist the airlines with the financing of purchases and perhaps had been more amenable when it came to agreeing on price or other contractual conditions. Donald Douglas was, with his ancestral Scottish background, more careful in his actions, saying that the banking relationship he used served the company's aims and proudly declared that it is the airline responsible for ensuring their own financing! At the end of January 1956 the secrecy regarding the Pratt & Whitney J75 engine was lifted which officially became known as the JT4. It then became possible to compare the two engine types. In the SAS technical organization, there was at that time no propulsion engineer with good knowledge regarding jet engines. I do not know if any discussions on the possible use of consultants were conducted. There was, in the Air Force and the Swedish aerospace industry, access to skilled technicians who could have assisted SAS in this matter. It was determined, however, that myself and MSc in engineering, Knut Jonn from "Operations Engineering" would visit

The first JT4 engines emitted a lot of smoke.
DC-8 aircraft.
Photo Boeing.

the two manufacturers, Rolls-Royce and Pratt & Whitney in early February of 1956.

The trip went first to Rolls-Royce in Derby in England, where we were received as if we were real "big shots" with accommodations in their guest house Duffield Bank House. At dinner on the day of arrival senior manager Denning Pearson (later Sir Denning) participated, along with chief engineer Adrian Lombard and C. Lovesey, his closest employee. All three were also present at the lunch the following day. The technical review was carried out mainly by Lombard and Lovesey. The Conway engine was developed primarily for military bombers and for the planned a four-engine passenger plane, the Vickers VC-10, which had two engines mounted on either side of the tail, like the Caravelle. It also had hopes that even the DC-8 and 707 would be provided with the engine. As mentioned both Boeing and Douglas had made it possible for airlines to choose the type of engine.

On the Conway engine Rolls-Royce had obviously applied all the lessons gained from its previous engines and, in particular, the Avon engine which was used in the Comet. They presented however, a new development in that it was provided with an arrangement of two concentric shafts, each driving both a compressor and a turbine. The low-pressure compressor at the front also had a fan, which means that some of the air is not passed on to the high pressure compressor but fed into a duct inside the cowling of the engine and into the exhaust. This method led to an improvement in fuel consumption and also reduction of noise levels by the hot gas stream from the turbine, which was surrounded by cold air flow with lower velocity. The engine type came to be called a fan engine or by-pass engine. We also talk about the by-pass ratio i.e., how much of the total amount of air that enters the engine air intake that only passes through the fan. For the Conway this factor was 0.3.

The presentation of the engine in general gave a very solid impression and produced great respect. A tour of the workshops did not give the same impression, and this was also true of the resources in terms of development laboratories and test stands. In comparison to what we have seen before at US engine manufacturers it seemed almost primitive.

We received of course a lot the technical and performance data that could be studied at home later. The journey then continued to Pratt & Whitney in Hartford, Connecticut in USA. There we were more at ease because of previous visits over the years which led us to a greater extent meeting technicians at slightly lower level than was the case in Derby. We had 18 years of experience from a piston engine operation to fall back on when it came to assessing Pratt & Whitney's ability to perform on jet engine programs designed for airline requirements.

DC-8 demonstration flight withTed Conant, Douglas 2nd in command
Photo via Birger Holmer.

The review of the JT4 engine constituted largely an account of how the experience of the JT3 applied to the larger JT4. It was not a radical change but basically the same engine as the JT3 but at a slightly larger scale. It had been developed to primarily improve the B-52 but also to later fit civilian aircraft and there was already operating experience to fall back on. We also did a review of their workshops and test facilities for fresh observations to compare with Rolls-Royce. Even here we received lots of material that could be studied at home.

In general it can be said that the comprehensive performance data for engines are not very educational for airline technicians as they generally do not have the skills to transfer the information to aircraft performance. It is the latter that is the airline's competitive basis.

After returning home, we made a summary of our assessments and recommended that SAS would obtain the JT4. There was no major discussion on this matter, but management decided to accept our conclusion. SAS management unexpectedly showed lukewarm interest to further discuss the issue. Maybe it was because SAS would become the first company to choose the Conway if that were the case. It turned out that it was only in May 1956 that Trans Canada and Canadian Pacific decided in favor of the Conway engine. Alitalia also chose it. For Boeing it was BOAC that first chose Conways for their order of 15 planes, but the order also came later than the first group of customers. Even Lufthansa later ordered 707-320s with Conway engines. Of the first 152 DC-8s built, 32 were equipped with Conway engines and no more were ordered. During the time that elapsed between the early aircraft orders in the years 1955 and 1956, and until 1958-59, deliveries of planes with many changes and improvements were made on both the 707 and DC-8. At Boeing the main concern was to complete work on the new wing for the 320 model. This led to a total redesign of the wing both aerodynamically and structurally. SAS had reason, at a much later date, to re-examine the wing and could then conclude that the objections that SAS

The early engine installation on the DC-8-33 with pylons that are attached high on the leading edge of the wing
Photo Boeing.

had regarding the 120 wing had been resolved to the satisfaction with the new wing.

The objections SAS and several other airlines had against the "Dutch-roll" phenomenon of the Dash 80-plane, and would probably be found on the 707-120, had from Boeing's view been pushed back by chief test pilot Tex Johnston with the assurance that the problem could be eliminated by proper training of pilots. His assessment was accepted by Boeing's senior management and even by the United States aviation authority. This problem was tragically evidenced during a training flight with American Airlines while shutting down an engine to practice an engine failure. The plane entered into a "Dutch roll" and went onto its back, crashed, and all on board were killed. A few months later it happened to Pan Am in a similar event on a training flight near Paris. Also this time the plane rolled onto its back and an engine was torn off. The pilots managed to get control of the plane and land with the three remaining engines.

Even Air France was subjected to such an adventure, but also with the successful completion of a landing. The fourth case affected Braniff Airlines on a flight in the Seattle area. This time three of the four engines were torn off, but a Boeing pilot managed to gain control of the plane and implement a crash landing. Four of those on board survived, but four died.

These events did not get any big publicity when no paying passengers were affected. But it naturally led to quick action of Boeing and the regulatory authority. Tex Johnston changed his mind and Boeing leadership announced that it would incur the costs of implementing the modifications required. The cost of the entire program for both delivered planes and those under production amounted to about $ 150 million. Among the measures was a noticeable imcrease in the size of the rudder, the size of the extented fin, increased servo assistance, and the yaw damper received greater authority. A tail fin was also installed under the tail section of the fuselage.

It is interesting to note that the British authorities had even before the accidents required that changes needed to be made for them to be able to certify the plane that their own companies purchased.

Jack Steiner, 727 program leader and later for the 737 was one of the great characters at Boeing.
Photo Boeing..

Tex Johnston, who was a well-known pilot in the industry, became famous for being a little reckless. In connection with an aerial display over Lake Washington in Seattle for 300,000 spectators, he made a barrel roll with the Dash 80 prototype. He flew past at an altitude of 3000 ft with a speed of around 390 knots, pulled up into a pitch angle of 35 degrees and conducted a full 360 degrees roll, to the entire Boeing management's surprise and consternation. Tex turned around and made another barrel roll. At a later meeting Boeing boss Bill Allen was very clear what he thought of the maneuver: "Do not ever do it again!"

It may be mentioned in this context that a review of the literature provides information that a pilot in the US Air Force tried to make such a looping with a KC-135 (military version of the 707) around 1957 which resulted in the two outer engines being torn off. The pilot was able to land the aircraft.

When test flights with the DC-8 began on 30 May 1958, it was found that Douglas had difficulty in meeting its promised performance. Fuel consumption was a few percent higher than indicated. An extensive modification program was started, including, among other things, major weight savings, a demand for greater thrust from the engines, and increased fuel capacity, etc. The result was that the maximum takeoff weight increased from the contract's 287,000 lb. to 310,000 lb. for the SAS DC-8-30. By all measure taken several of the promised performance parameters were restored, but fuel consumption was not significantly improved, resulting in slightly worse operating costs than anticipated. The increased takeoff weight also meant increased landing fees because they are based on takeoff weight. Douglas was hit hard by all the changes. It has been indicated that the costs amounted to about $200,000 per plane.

Boeing also had to do modifications and had difficulties in meeting the promised guarantees and one wonders what the reason was. It seemed as if Boeing had been a little too optimistic when it came to transferring the results from the Dash 80 test flights to the production version. The data the airlines received from Boeing had probably, in one way or another, reached Douglas, so that during the entire evaluation process they claimed that whatever Boeing can do, Douglas shall able to accomplish, with the exception of the various factors connected with the chosen different wing sweep angles. Douglas was fully aware that Boeing had some advantages but also some disadvantages as discussed above.

I want to emphasize that we did not get the idea that there was direct industrial espionage. As an illustration of that position, it may be of interest to touch on some facts concerning the US aircraft engineering community. The leading engineers of both companies belonged largely to the same generation. Three universities dominated in America in terms of education of aviation engineers at a high level. They were the Massachusetts Institute of Technology (MIT) in Cambridge, Cornell University in New York State, and the California Institute of Technology (Caltec) in Pasadena.

This means that most of the top aviation engineers at both manufacturers and airlines had a very similar education and many contacts and friendships from their college days were maintained as they circulated among the various companies. Transitions from one to the other company did occur also at a high level but in very few cases; and they probably did not have any decisive importance. The fact that Douglas used outside wind tunnels may have led to a greater risk existing for information leaks from Douglas to Boeing than vice versa.

It is a common practice in America that the leading engineers gives lectures before the various engineering fellowships and they talk about their companies' progress in relevant areas. Thus, as an example, Jack Steiner, gave a lecture in Seattle in autumn 1954 on the upcoming introduction of jet aircraft in which, with quite a bit of detail, he outlined the progress that Boeing had made with the Dash 80. Steiner had a very prominent position in Boeing hierarchy with regard to the 707. After the lecture, he liberally invited participants to get a closer look at the plane. It provided, among others, several Douglas specialists the opportunity to study the plane both externally and internally without opening hatches or otherwise, to study the details. This openness was certainly prompted by

Joe Sutter 747 program leader
Photo Boeing.

Donald Douglas Sr hands over SAS´s first DC-8-62 in May 1966.
Photo via Birger Holmer.

Boeing believing itself to have a huge advantage over everyone else.

Another source of information transfer was obviously all the airlines groups alternately visited the two producers. It was inevitable that the questions asked in many cases were prompted by information provided during the visit of the competitor and it was not difficult for those who would respond to guess what the reason for the issue could be.

Another aspect of the problems that can crop up during a technological leap forward such as the transition from piston engine operation to jet propulsion, can be illustrated by the manufacturing and certification rules that must be issued. It turned out that the US Federal Aviation Agency (FAA) regulations did not address the then current technology issues. A strange thing occurred when the FAA found itself forced to transfer responsibility to Boeing, the writing of parts of the regulatory framework that would apply to their own products.

It was Joe Sutter, chief aerodynamicist for the Boeing 707 at the time, who steered this work. He later became head of the Boeing 747 project. According to his own information the work was done in cooperation with the FAA, the Civil Aeronautics Board (CAB), the Airline Pilots Association (ALPA) and the airlines. I have never heard anything about the creation of rules in such a strange way. It seems that no other aircraft manufacturer had the opportunity to influence the inception of the regulatory provisions.

It's likely that the airlines and pilots who got involved belonged to the company that ordered the Boeing aircraft. I remember that senior technicians at Douglas became very upset when they understood what the application of the rules would mean for the DC-8. The resulting degradations were not deemed necessary if differences which existed between both companies' designs had been considered.

There is no reason to criticize Sutter and his colleagues at Boeing who were certainly acting in the best of intentions to achieve a safe and economical product. The fault lay with the authorities that in the absence of their own competence should have made sure that the rule making had a broader review.

Joe Sutter states in his book that the procedure was not satisfactory but that flight safety did not suffer as a result.

During the period until their first deliveries both manufacturers were engaged in designing the planes for the various airlines' own specifications but also in making general improvements.

One area that had received increasing importance was noise control. There was increasing pressure from many quarters calling for noise abatement measures. Many different solutions were proposed. They covered in particular complicated exhaust nozzles, which also had to be combined with the thrust reverse system, which made the problem even harder to solve. Most devices meant both weight increases and degraded performance.

For SAS it was necessary to specify what was needed in the cockpit to adapt it to SAS operational standards and philosophy. In the same way, as mentioned in the previous section, it concerned in particular instrumentation, radio equipment and navigational aids and associated control panels. Furthermore, galley arrangements adapted to the standards of service that SAS had developed. Finally, cabin decor, color selection for walls, ceilings and hat racks, carpets, other textiles, and seats designed in accordance with SAS ideas. As a consultant in this field Throne-Holst hired well known Danish architect Finn Juhl, who among others, become internationally known through his assignment to design some parts of the UN building's interior.

Douglas decided not to produce a prototype but instead go direct to the production series aircraft and agree with some of the first clients to use their aircraft for flight test with arrangements regarding payment for this. The production would take place at the factory in Long Beach because hangar space and runways in Santa Monica were not sufficient for an aircraft of the DC-8 size. Existing hangars and workshops in Long Beach had to be supplemented with additional buildings which included a new headquarters for a total cost of $ 20 million.

The assembly of the first plane started on 18 February 1957 and "roll-out" took place on 9 April 1958. "Roll-out" is a ceremony that can be compared with launching of a ship and usually takes place with great pomp and ceremony. The first flight took place on 30 May 1958 and on 31 August 1959, the DC-8-10 was awarded its airworthiness type certificate. Delivery of SAS's first DC-8 took place on 31 March 1960.

The DC-8-62 had almost the same length, wingspan and Max Takeoff Weight as the Boeing 707-320B. SAS's most common configuration had 154 seats.
Photo SAS.

SAS-Swissair-cooperation

SAS traffic and sales departments had for some time thoughts of collaboration purely regarding traffic with any company in Central Europe. Soundings were made which resulted in Swissair being the most appropriate, both in size and location in Europe. A shared interest was found that under certain conditions, daily connections could be offered passengers on some routes. Neither company had the basis for such an offering on its own to South America, Africa and the Far East. A collaboration of traffic and sales activities could make this possible. Work with the plans progressed, but the pace seemed not be as fast as desired.

Since both companies only bought a few DC-8s, it would be desirable to have a technical collaboration so that they could arrange one maintenance system with a merger of the two fleets. It would be unduly expensive if each company would have established a complete organization for maintenance. SAS had seven planes on order and three options while Swissair had three plus two. Even if the options were exercised and more were acquired eventually they would still be rather small fleets. SAS had the opinion that it needed at least a fleet of about 15 planes to establish a profitable operation.

Given the size of the DC-8, new hangars were needed for both the daily supervision and space for a maintenance dock, large spare parts stores, new workshop equipment, and test facilities.

Swissair DC-8-30
Postcard by SFF.

The idea was that you could borrow aircraft from each other during the maintenance checks and for other possible needs; so the aircraft had to be virtually identical, except for exterior decoration and interior materials and color scheme. If the flight deck instrumentation and other installations were equal, one could also use a common flight simulator. Travel and accommodation expenses would be modest in relation to the purchase and operating costs of an additional simulator.

When the plans were discussed in both companies, it was decided to appoint a delegation of two men each to see if it was possible to accomplish uniformity of the aircraft specifications. It was SAS flight operations' Povl Jensen and I and my counterpart Armin Baltensweiler from Swissair and their chief pilot von Tscharner that got the task.

Both SAS and Swissair had at that time reached a long way to individually determine desirable amendments to Douglas's basic specification. Only the titles of the committed or planned "Change Orders" occupied two A4 pages. It turned out that the differences between the two companies' lists were not particularly large and in good cooperative spirit and with good assistance from Douglas, we managed to reach agreement. On 3 April 1958, a document was signed, which defined a common specification for the SAS and Swissair DC-8 fleets. With this arrangement in place, additional efforts speeded up the other measures that were needed to further strengthen the comprehensive cooperation agreement established between the companies.

Caravelle

During the summer 1952 a few events occurred that had some influence on SAS's engagement in the upcoming transition to jet propulsion. The British company British Overseas Airways Corporation (BOAC) started on 2 May 1952 service with the de Havilland Comet, as mentioned earlier.

On 10 August the same year quite unexpectedly a Comet came for the first time to Bromma and at that time I was invited to fly onboard on a flight to Helsinki, as mentioned earlier. It was my first flight with a jet-powered commercial aircraft and gave, of course, a foretaste of what was to come.

A week later the doorman at the entrance to the SAS headquarters phoned me and announced that there was a Frenchman at the entrance, who wanted to meet the technical management of SAS. He had not made any advance notice of his visit.

It so happened that I was the only one available that day because it was still vacation time.

Into my room came a man who introduced himself as Jean Gelos and who spoke pretty broken English. We had to do the conversation in English because my knowledge of French did not allow the possibility of using that language.

He represented a company in Toulouse called the Société Nationale de Constructions Aero Nautique de Sud-Est (SNCASE). The only piece of data that he brought was a big drawing that covered almost the entire desktop and it represented what in aviation language is called a three-view drawing. Such a drawing shows an airplane in the three projections from above, from the front, and from the side.

The plane was designated SE-210 Caravelle. It had a totally new concept with two jet engines mounted near the back of the fuselage just forward of the stabilizer, which in turn had been placed a bit higher up on the fin so that the gas flow from the jet engine exhaust went under the stabilizer.

The plane had a swept wing and a cabin that would accommodate about 75 passengers. The nose section was the same as for the Comet. They had reached an agreement with de Havilland that they would provide the structure to reduce costs. The nose section and cockpit are very costly in both design and manufacturing. The engines would also be the same as for the Comet, namely Rolls-Royce Avons.

The purpose of the visit was to hear about SAS's potential interest in such a plane. The answer was that SAS with interest would follow the possible development of the project, but there was need for far more detailed information about the plane's design as well as performance data prior to any further interest being communicated. In late October 1952, airlines had apparently shown sufficient interest in the plane that the French authorities decided to support the project.

In early November 1952, I visited for the first time the factory in Toulouse for a closer look at both the plane's design and to study what resources the company had to implement the project. The engineers involved in discussions gave a very knowledgeable and solid impression but I thought they seemed to have limited knowledge and experience in the design and manufacture of commercial aircraft. Existing

Caravelle LN-KLH.
Photo SFF

hangars and workshops seemed fairly modest in order to succeed with such a large project. It was stated that a large building program would be started as the French government had announced that not only design but also the production of two prototypes were given the green light. In February 1953, the head of the company Georges Hereil, stated that he received preliminary permission to go ahead with the two prototypes, but it was not until July 1953 before the formal permission came.

The prototype, 01, was completed in April 1955, and the first flight was conducted on 27 May the same year. In early July I again visited Toulouse to study the structure and witness the second flight of the prototype 01. The general impression of the company and the aircraft remained good but I felt, however, uncertain whether they would manage such a large and transformational project.

In March 1956, it was time for a smaller group from SAS to obtain a closer acquaintance with the plane. SAS had been promised to test fly prototype 01. The group consisted of three captains, Sven Forsberg, Fridjof Giørtz, Göran Lind, Gunnar Antvik, and me. The visit was to everyone's satisfaction and the pilots were very happy with the plane's flight characteristics.

Somewhat later in the year, two SAS executives got the opportunity for a demonstration flight from Paris to Rome during conditions that simulated a commercial flight. They had hired flight attendants from Air France and equipped the plane so that it could serve a fine French meal. Both SAS directors were fully convinced that the Caravelle could be an excellent aircraft for the European routes. The plane had the right size and performance that was appropriate for the task.

On 2 October 1956 the prototype, which had now registration F-BHHH, came to Bromma for a demonstration flight for a large part of SAS management. The result was that an even larger circle inside SAS was able to express opinions if this type of aircraft would fit in perfectly in SAS plans, to as early as possible transition to jet propulsion also for European traffic.

At this time, the French Government decided to merge SNCASE with SNCASO (Société Nationale des Constructions Aéronautiques du Sud-Est) to strengthen mainly manufacturing capacity. The aggregate company was named Sud Aviation. Large building plans for hangars and production lines were reported. The misgivings I stated earlier could thus be eliminated.

After further contacts between SAS and Sud-Aviation's management it was decided that SAS would undertake a major evaluation of the Caravelle. Because our engineers were still very busy with everything that had to do with the DC-8 preparations, it was not until the end of May 1957 before it could begin. Since the review related to a company that was virtually unknown in Scandinavia and had limited experience of previous airliners, it had to be more extensive than those of previous audits and had to cover a larger scope than usual.

The last week of May 1957 and the first week of June a group of up to 15 people under the direction of Knut Hagrup who was then director of operations, was assigned with this mission in Toulouse. Olof Carlstein or I did not participate because we were both busy with the DC-8 preparations. Carlstein also had other urgent tasks because of the new

Caravelle's flightdeck was typical of its era
Photo Hans Norman, www.scanliners.com.

engine workshop at Linta, Bromma and the large hangars and workshops at the airport. I had to travel to Douglas for critical specification issues for the current DC-8.

The Working Group submitted a preliminary report on 8 June 1957 and a full report a few weeks later. Both reports indicated that the Caravelle was a perfectly acceptable plane for the intended routes and Sud Aviation had, or certainly would have, the resources needed to manage the project. After the management reviewed the reports the board was informed of the situation, contract work and specification writing started, led by Olof Carlstein, Chief Legal Counsel Erik Norman, and me.

Sud Aviation had on SAS's request developed both a French and an English version of the contract. It was argued that if it came to a legal dispute, the French version would prevail, over SAS's wish, that the English would be the standard. It was reasonable that the discussions about this would lead to favoring the French. Because SAS's knowledge and experience in French legal language and legislation was limited one had to find a way out. The contracts SAS concluded after the war in buying aircraft had been with American English language and US law as the basis. The solution to the problem was that SAS engaged an independent French law firm that specialized in interpretation between French and American legal languages and the news was that SAS could feel safe with the translation. That French law would apply just had to be accepted.

In parallel with the contract work in progress the definition of the SAS specification was done based on all the experience gained while working on the definition for Douglas planes. No difficulty was encountered getting any amendments or additions that we wanted introduced and the cost would be included in the price. Other technical factors were more significant than previous aircraft purchases. It was important to clarify the requirements that SAS asked for regarding documentation and scope of post delivery services. Because Sud-Aviation could not demonstrate previous experience of such support for commercial carriers, we had to provide a detailed account of SAS's requirements regarding manuals, service bulletins, parts supply, a service representative at the maintenance base for the plane, etc. In other words, what is called the "after sales service" and "product support". SAS desired that the scope of this would have the same standard as Douglas and other American manufacturers provided to the airlines. Only Air France was a customer at the time when SAS was prepared to buy the Caravelle and it did not seem like they just as clearly had made such requests. It can be explained that it could be easy, so to speak, at home, to hire Sud Aviation for assistance when required. SAS got the sense that our requirements in these respects "Americanized" Sud Aviation for the benefit of their sales efforts in both Europe and America and other countries. When all those issues were sorted out, it was time for SAS to place an order at Sud Aviation.

On 28 June 1957 the prototype F-BHHT flew to Copenhagen with Georges Hereil and several of Sud Aviation's management for a demonstration flight for the SAS board of directors and the management people who had not been at the earlier Bromma demonstration. After completing the flight of over 1.5 hours the plane returned to Copenhagen after which the members of the board who wanted to be at the contract signing, together with SAS president Throne-Holst flew to Paris for the signing of a an order for six SE-210 Caravelles and 19 options. SAS was thus the second airline after Air France that ordered the Caravelle. In the aviation world, it was considered that Air France was an obvious buyer and therefore regarded SAS order as a sensation and a confirmation that French manufacturing of commercial aircraft was established.

To coordinate the cooperation that was now required between SAS and Sud-Aviation a representative was appointed, based in Toulouse, supplemented with a small number of inspectors who supervised the production and assembly of the airplanes. As chief representative director, Lars Tullberg was appointed, who for many years had been the leader of all the SAS technical control organizations. In addition to all his other qualifications, he had the advantage of mastery of the French language. It was particularly important in France where "Aviation English" was not so commonly used as would been desirable. The French are all very proud of their language and it is important that foreigners show respect for that.

Based on experience gained from the SAS aircraft constructed in warmer climates than the Scandinavian, it was required that winter tests would

Caravelle assemblyline in Toulouse. When the last Caravelle was delivered in 1972, 282 aircraft had been manufactured.
Photo by Mikael Öqvist

Sud SE-210 Caravelle III LN-KLH.
Copyright: Gustaf Persson.

be conducted for the Caravelle. The prototype 02 therefore spent time in both Stockholm and especially Luleå to be tested under realistic conditions at ground level. Samples of low temperatures at aircraft cruising level where the outside temperature could be down to minus 55 degrees are taken routinely.

The tests were performed according to a program created by SAS. They took place at the end of the month of January and early February 1958, and resulted in only minor changes and adjustments as needed for some installations.

On 18 January 1958, Finnair signed a contract with Sud Aviation for the supply of three Caravelle and became the third customer.

The first aircraft, which were delivered to SAS on 13 April 1959, had the type designation Caravelle I and registration LN-KLH. Captains Carls and Fugl-Svendsen flew it. In the initial training flights and practice flights were flown to some airports that later would be used. The first scheduled flight with passengers was made to Beirut 26 April 1959. SAS thus became the first airline to put the Caravelle in operation.

As a comparison, the DC-8 was ordered in December 1955 and entered service in May 1960, the Caravelle was ordered in June 1957 and went into service in April 1959! Before the year was over, six of the aircraft ordered had been delivered and put into service. Later the planes confirmed from the options were delivered as type III and were provided with Avon engines with greater thrust than those of the type I plane. The six delivered Type I aircraft were later modified to Type III. Altogether, SAS operated 21 Caravelles during the years 1959-74. Under the agreement with Swissair and Thai International, SAS leased four planes to Swissair and eight to Thai at different times.

It is not an exaggeration to claim that the SAS order for the Caravelle was a breakthrough for the French aviation industry's success regarding the production of commercial aircraft. That they were well established in the case of production of military interceptors was generally known.

That SAS involvement was of great importance for the French nation was manifested by awarding Olof Carlstein, who had been the driving force in the SAS commitment, the Legion of Honor by the French government.

SAS Caravelle LN-KLH at Bromma.
Photo SFF

A total of 282 units in different versions of the Caravelle were produced and it then attained the number that many manufacturers used to think was needed to reach a desired financial results. Douglas entering into an agreement with Sud Aviation to represent them in the US also demonstrated the success; and possibly to manufacture the plane in their facilities if enough interest was shown from the domestic airlines. Douglas gave some support to Sud Aviation in the design of the wing to the Caravelle.

There was, however, only United that completed their plans for introducing the Caravelle on the American continent. After a consultation with SAS, United ordered 20 planes. Also TWA ordered 20 planes but subsequently canceled the contract. Douglas also withdrew later from their commitment when they decided to rather invest on their own, DC-9, project.

Both Sud Aviation and the airlines that bought Caravelle did eventually learn that the Rolls-Royce Avon engine did not fully meet expectations regarding its reliability or the economy. Possible alternatives were therefore examined. General Electric offered the aft-fan engine CJ-805 and had installed it in a modified Caravelle III, but the version was not met with any response by airlines.

Pratt & Whitney was more successful with its JT8D, which later came to be used extensively in both Boeing and Douglas aircraft. The Caravelle 10B, as the type was called, was powered with the P&WA engine, was purchased by several companies. The Danish airline Sterling was among the earliest customers and ordered in stages no less than 34 airplanes!

SAS initially showed quite a high interest level in the version and had informally been told that Finnair wanted to investigate whether there were prerequisites for making a joint order with SAS and organize some cooperation. These ideas were welcomed by SAS who wanted to tie Finnair closer to the Scandinavian co-operation and rather cooperate than compete wherever possible. Negotiations on the technical front were carried out pretty far in the case of a joint purchase but after some time SAS pulled back.

It had at the time of the establishment of SAS for political reasons been impossible, read here Russia, to include Finland.

New information had been received from Douglas on the new DC-9 project configuration and performance. The analyses showed that the plane would have a better outcome both operationally and financially than the Caravelle 10B and development opportunities were greater for the DC-9. The main reason for this was that the wing of the Caravelle was not sufficiently advanced aerodynamically compared to the DC-9. There had been significant progress in the field since the wing at the Caravelle was designed in the early 1950s.

SAS decided to invest for the future in the DC-9 instead of the Caravelle. Finnair was of course disappointed that SAS changed its mind and SAS regretted that it missed the opportunity to establish closer cooperation with Finnair. The Swedish side of SAS had, since the time several years before the war and during the war, good contacts with mainly the technical side of Finnair.

Although Finnair bought some Caravelle 10Bs, they a few years later also bought the DC-9. It may be added that its partner Swissair that already taken a decision turning to Douglas planes also influenced SAS. In their case, they were also affected by an accident involving a Caravelle in September 1963 in which 80 people died. It happened near Zürich after a takeoff from Kloten Airport and created a huge upset in Switzerland. It was not caused by a malfunction of the plane according to the accident report, but could have been avoided with a more rigorous application of existing operational rules. SAS also experienced an accident where all on board were killed. It occurred in January 1960 during an approach to Ankara in bad weather. The accident report could not provide a reason with great credibility but there was no indication that it was due to technical issues so the event had to be attributed to human error.

During the latter part of the 1960s a number of similar accidents occurred, headlined as "Controlled Flight Into Terrain," CFIT.

This triggered ideas on how similar accidents could be avoided in the future and some of the SAS experts, captain Karl-Eric Ternhem and engineer Arne Vernblad, developed a solution to the problem.

The FAA introduced in 1974 a requirement that "Ground Proximity Warning System" GPWS must be installed in all large commercial aircraft. The system was patented by the then Sundstrand Company and one of their engineers was attributed to having invented the system. Ternhem and Vernblad, who

A planned cooperation between Douglas and Sud-Aviation that never took off
Photo Douglas.

were the real inventors of the solution, were however acknowledged by the Swedish Aeronautical Society, which awarded them the silver medal in 1974 for their foresight and a solution that saved many lives.

The Caravelle became very popular among passengers due to the low noise level and the absence of vibrations that had been troubling the piston engine airplanes. A lot of pilots who found it easy to fly and with good flight characteristics also appreciated the plane. The Caravelle served in SAS until September 1974. The Caravelle fleet had then accumulated approximately 500,000 hours in the air during over 440,000 flights. The Caravelle must be considered to have resulted in a very successful introduction of jet aircraft in SAS's history.

The low noise level in the cabin did not however help in terms of noise from starting Caravelle's engines on the ground. SAS flew with the Caravelle from Bromma, leading to strong protests from residents around the airport, which also was the start of the reaction that still pops up in connection with Bromma.

When SAS in the late 1960s wanted to operate with the DC-9 from Bromma many studies were made about the noise around Bromma, which is described later in connection with the DC-9 purchase. Noise problems entailed a need within SAS to increase our knowledge in the field and it resulted in a strong involvement and participation by SAS in both the airline and government organizations, which at the end of the 1960s worked out the first international regulations on environmental requirements via ICAO. See also the chapter regarding environmental requirements, page 179.

Convair CV-990 Coronado

As mentioned earlier, both SAS and Swissair, in the preparation of contracts for the DC-8, ascertained options for future purchases of aircraft for operations to South America, Africa and the Far East. When the time began to approach to complete these plans and convert the options to firm orders, the companies first made their own market studies to avoid the partner influencing them at an early stage. When they were finished a meeting was arranged to see if it was possible to arrange a common understanding of the expected traffic evolution. It proved to be simple because perceptions were very similar. The DC-8 was deemed to be an aircraft too big for the job with excessively high operating costs.

The two companies' projects departments were then asked to investigate whether there were any suitable alternatives. The requirements were that the aircraft would have between 80 and 100 seats and allow nonstop flights on the route from Lisbon to Rio de Janeiro which was the most demanding route in the planned service area.

The investigations conducted by then accessible documentation led to two types of aircraft that could be considered, the Boeing 720 and Convair CV-880. After visiting the two producers during August and September 1958, closer studies of the planes led to the conclusion that none of the offered versions of the planes would meet range requirements with the margins required.

The Boeing 720 was a version of the 707-120 with a shorter fuselage and significantly lower takeoff weight but otherwise based on the same design as the original and SAS therefore did not need a new detailed study. Swissair offered their conclusion with a rather limited study. The reservations that SAS had at the evaluation of the Boeing 707-120 with regard to the wing structure and the presence of Dutch roll persisted until further notice.

Boeing invited us to a demonstration flight on a delivery-ready 707-120 belonging to one of the early operating companies. We gratefully accepted the offer because it gave us the chance to experience a 707 for the first time. Previously it was the Dash 80 on display. In addition to SAS and Swissair pilots there was a pilot from a third company on the flight. It did not develop quite as Boeing had anticipated. The third pilot, in the left seat, happened during the approach to enter into a Dutch roll and we fluttered around over the rooftops of the area surrounding Boeing Field in a very disturbing way until the Boeing test pilot shouted "my controls" and assumed command. In order not to embarrass the pilot he had waited as long as possible to take over command in the hope that the "third" pilot would clear up the situation.

The aircraft we flew had not yet been modified under the measures mentioned in the DC-8/707 evaluation. The modification should reasonably have been even more important for the Boeing 720 given that with a shorter body the rudder gets a shorter moment arm to operate.

Regarding the wing structure there was nothing to add at this time (autumn 1958). Concerns expressed by Tord Angstrom and SAS structural specialists in the autumn 1955 came true after several years of operation with both the 707-120 and 720 which underwent a large and expensive repair and modification program after cracks appeared in the wings.

Convair had opted for a slightly smaller plane than the Boeing 707 and DC-8 but with a similar basic configuration, i.e., swept wings and four engines mounted in front and below the wing on pylons. The engines were General Electric CJ-805s, a civilian version of the successful military J79 used in many fighters. The cabin was designed for about 100 passengers and thus corresponded to both the SAS and Swissair wishes.

When the aircraft was launched, it had the designation CV-600 Skylark. The number 600 was chosen considering that the plane's cruising speed would be 600 miles per hour (mph), which was higher than that for the 707 and DC-8. Only one month after the launch, TWA ordered 30 planes and Delta ten.

The eccentric billionaire Howard Hughes, who controlled TWA, had stipulated that Convair could not deliver any planes to other US carriers for over a year after TWA received delivery of the bulk of its ordered aircraft. His well-known unpredictability meant that the program might not have the stability that was desirable. He also contributed in that the designation was changed to CV 880. It was partly an allusion to the successful piston engine aircraft CV-240, CV-340 and CV-440 of which SAS was the genesis. In addition to orders from TWA and Delta, Convair also got an order for four each from the Brazilian and Argentine airline.

The SAS / Swissair Group's detailed examination resulted in the plane being able to be approved technically and performance-wise with the exception of the range that did not meet the group's demands. Convair then responded by offering a further development, which was designated CV-880M, which had a higher takeoff weight and additional engine thrust. Swissair then signed a contract for delivery of five planes and SAS for two. It may be noted that both SAS and Swissair during these analyses and negotiations met engineers at Convair, who were well known from the piston engine time and they made a very solid impression. The organization was smaller than that of Boeing and Douglas and thus faster to answer questions and provide data required for our assessment.

During the time we spent in San Diego to analyze Convair's offering a singular event occurred. One day I got a phone call from Jim Kennedy, head of Pratt & Whitney's international sales, who asked to meet with me in the utmost secrecy. He came over from the East Coast to San Diego and stayed at a hotel not frequented by aviation people. We met there without anyone else knowing it. He asked me if I somehow could assist in delaying a decision to buy planes from Convair by a couple of months. I refused, of course, such a procedure and suggested that he turn to Swissair that was the leading partner in cases involving Convair projects. He said it was not possible but did not specify the reason why.

I asked about the reason for this strange request. He could not tell me about it except that Pratt & Whitney in a few months would inform the aviation world of big news.

Now in hindsight, it is easy to see that the big news was that Pratt & Whitney would announce its decision to develop its JT3 engine into a fan engine with the fan section in the front. The engine was renamed the JT3D. It was at this time known that General Electric had a project to develop the CJ-805 engine with a so-called aft fan, CJ-805-23. The project was far ahead of Pratt & Whitney, who also expressed great doubt regarding the fan motors and almost ridiculed those who conceivable thought differently. This seemed almost deliberate misleading advertising. A Boeing 720 with that engine would provide the same or better performance than that of the developed model Convair CV-880M.

Why the secrecy? One possibility may be that the JT3D engine was primarily developed to be installed in the B-52 bomber to significantly improve its performance and that P&W wanted to prevent the competition becoming aware of this earlier than desired. The civilian market had to wait. If these thoughts are relevant, it is strange that, if the

SAS and SWR visiting Convair in San Diego 1958. Volrath Holmboe on the left and Birger Holmer on the right side.
Photo by Birger Holmer.

The Coronado flight deck is inspected by Birger Holmer SAS and Bertoni from SWR. Photo by Birger Holmer.

civilian side of Boeing knew about these plans, they could at least have indicated to us that there were expectations that the 720 could be significantly improved.

Convair and General Electric had high hopes that even United would choose the CV-880 but their order for 20 planes went instead to the Boeing 720. The first flight of the CV-880 was made in late autumn of 1958. About half a year later, the first CV 880M was airborne. During these flights, it turned out that not even this version achieved the stipulated range requirement. SAS / Swissair then faced a big problem. Would you try to cancel the contract with Convair and consider a purchase of 720s, which at that time could be offered with Pratt & Whitney engine JT3D, or would you accept Convair's proposals to change to the developed version of the CV-880, which received the designation CV-990, which was equipped with General Electric CJ-805-23.

In discussions with two independent US law firms that specialize in this type of problem, both indicated that an attempted cancellation would not be successful because Convair offered an alternative that could be considered acceptable. It stressed, however, that the SAS / Swissair Group found itself in a favorable position regarding price discussions in this situation.

The big stumbling block with the CV-990 was that it would nevertheless be more expensive and probably have higher operating costs and cause delivery delays. After long negotiations, it was

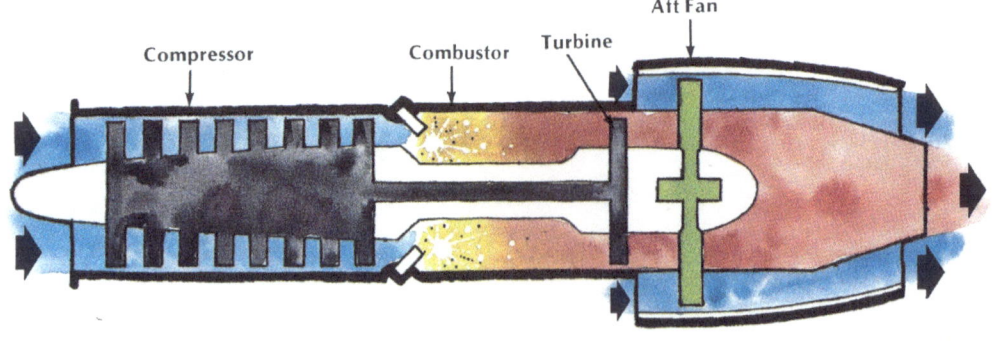

Aft Turbofan Engine

General layout of the General Electric "aft-fan" engine.
The aft-fan principle did not become a successful configuration
Picture General Electric.

decided that the group would accept Convair's proposal. SAS managed to cut the price and also got Convair to set a minimum guaranteed price for a smaller number of DC-7Cs that SAS would offer for sale when the CV-990 was delivered.

I can not avoid thinking about what would happen if the secrecy on the JT3D had been lifted a few months earlier, or if SAS / Swissair for some reason delayed the decision to purchase the CV-880M. The order could possibly have ended up with Boeing.

Swissair increased the orders to seven aircraft but SAS retained only the two CV-880Ms as ordered. It was planned that two of the seven Swissair ordered would be leased by SAS. American Airlines ordered 25 of the CV-990s and TWA placed an order for 13 planes. Deliveries to Swissair and SAS were promised in the period from March to July 1961.

The CV-990 had a longer cabin which allowed for up to 140 passengers; the wing was larger and with a more advanced aerodynamic design and equipped with larger flaps. The CJ-805-23 engines with an aft fan had significantly greater thrust than the original engine. In addition, increased fuel tankage, significantly through the Convair-mounted aerodynamically designed "anti-shock bodies" on the rear of the wing in line with the engines for aerodynamic reasons but also to increase fuel capacity. These changes meant that the CV-990 could operate at higher Mach numbers than both Boeing and Douglas aircraft. All these changes resulted in a sharp increase in both the empty weight and the required takeoff weight.

When test flights began two big problems appeared. There were vibration and oscillation tendencies, so-called flutter, which was linked to the aerodynamic design of the engine pylons and their structure. This area has created problems for most of the aircraft designers who have chosen pylon mounted engine installations on the wing. They must be properly designed aerodynamically to provide as little drag as possible, be strong enough to support the heavy engine installations, transfer the thrust force from the engine to the wing, and still have just enough flexibility not to transfer all bending and gyroscopic forces to the wing in turbulence and in turns at large rudder deflections.

Airlines usually have no in-house expertise in this difficult field and SAS had help from Saab's flutter expert, Dr. Wittmeyer, when it came to assessing Convair's measures and maybe even comment on the appropriate corrections to overcome the problems. The modifications to the wing and pylons that were necessary to eliminate the problems caused substantial delays in deliveries.

Now another problem was added. SAS's poor economic situation led to management changes. When the incoming manager Curt Nicolin worked to rehabilitate the airline's economics, obviously investment was a key area and it hit the CV-990 immediately. He went to San Diego himself to negotiate the cancellation of the two SAS planes and succeeded with it. I do not know how it was resolved but the result was that the sales guarantee for the DC-7C planes disappeared. It is possible that the fact that Swissair expanded its order from five to seven planes saved the situation but meant that the atmosphere between SAS and Swissair deteriorated for some time.

The planes were delivered in late 1961 and early 1962. The planes Swissair leased to SAS came in February and April 1962. One used by SAS was returned to Swissair early in 1966. The second was leased out by SAS to Thai International and it also was returned to Swissair early 1966.

The CV-990 eventually became a technically and operationally successful product but at high acquisition and operating costs. The aircraft was the fastest of the subsonic aircraft and highly liked by pilots and won great acclaim among the passengers. For Convair the CV-990 was a large loss-generating project; it was not possible to sell more than 37 planes, which meant that Convair closed down marking the end of their era within the airline industry.

Swissair as "leading airline" had announced a competition within the company to find a suitable name for the aircraft. Convair had proposed that the name would ideally begin with the letters C and O as well as N, if possible, because the name would be connected to Convair. I do not know to what extent this was forwarded to those in the Swissair who managed the competition. Swissair would of course appoint the winner of the contest but the name would be approved by Convair and would be announced at a cocktail party that Convair's sales manager held for Swissair and SAS delegations.

The "anti-shock bodies" on the inner trailing edge of the wing helped maintaining the higher speed of the Coronado relative to the DC-8 and 707.
Photo SAS.

Armin Baltensweiler, Swissair managing director, would first inform Convair's Jack Zevely about the outcome of the contest. This was done silently and somewhat secluded from others in the party. It was obvious that the winning proposal did not receive Zevely's immediate approval and he apparently told Armin that he would ponder for a moment on the matter. He sauntered around the room and eventually came over to the corner where I stood together with only Convair people. He asked me if I had any suggestions but did not mention any name Armin suggested. I replied Coronado and gave the reason.

Coronado was the name of the Spaniard who were the first Europeans who came to California by sea from the south and then colonized the area. In his honor, two small islands located just outside of San Diego has been named the Coronado Islands and the Spanish name can be interpreted as the "crowned". It would well suit the world's fastest commercial aircraft. The proposal won his immediate liking and he wandered around for a while in the room so Armin could not imagine where the idea came from. He then managed to convince Armin it was a better idea than his.

It was never said what the winning entry from Swissair was. There has been a "diplomatic silence" surrounding this thing.

DC-8 development

Finally Pratt & Whitney announced that it would produce a fan engine. It was an improved version of the JT3 engine that received the designation JT3D and had significantly better performance than the basic engine that was installed in the earliest versions of both the 707 and DC-8. It was even better than the JT4, which was installed in the later models of both aircraft. Boeing launched both the 707-320B and 720B with the new fan-engine, and Douglas chose to call their plane the DC-8-50.

In all three planes the installations worked such that the air flow from the fan was ejected immediately behind the fan in two large almost half-moon shaped gills which left room for attaching to the pylon and for the accessories that were driven by the engine.

SAS analyzed both Boeing and Douglas projects given that the plane might achieve performance that enabled nonstop flights to and from the US West Coast.

It was found that neither of them could handle the task. Because SAS has chosen the Douglas DC-8 for their first order, it was natural to turn to them to see if it would be possible to further develop the plane so that it met customer reqirements. Any orders would include only a few planes to begin with and it was not considered reasonable to change suppliers for such a small number of planes.

Douglas showed great interest and began studying a variant of the DC-8-50 which came to be called the DC-8 Long Duct. The idea was that you would configure the engine installation so that the airflow from the front portion was led into a cylinder-shaped duct that surrounded the rest of the engine and the gas stream from the turbines at the exhaust nozzle. It was estimated to have a more favorable aerodynamic design of the whole unit and would also improve the reverse thrust function because the entire fan air and hot gas flow could be reversed. Furthermore, the enclosing cold and slower air flow shielded the hot and noisier gas stream even better so that the total noise level became lower.

The results of Douglas was so positive that SAS ordered two planes with the new designation. It was later shown during testing that Douglas could not live up to the promised performance and the order had to be canceled. As compensation Douglas, on favorable terms, offered to lease out three DC-8-50s to cope with the SAS capacity needs. One of these planes was delivered as a cargo version. SAS received at a later stage an opportunity to purchase the plane. They arrived in 1965 and 1966 but did not last long at SAS. The two passenger jets were transferred to Scanair during 1970 and 1971, and the cargo plane was sold to KLM.

Coronado taking off
Photo www.Scanliners.com.

Douglas DC-8-50 with new engine installation.
Photo Boeing.

SAS and Douglas celebrate the 10-year anniversary of SAS polar flights. PA Norlin, Marcus Wallenberg, Donald W. Douglas SR, Donald Nilsson and Knut Hagrup. Photo by Birger Holmer.

Douglas DC-8-63 with "long duct" and "cut-back" pylons. Compare the picture on page 51.
Photo Hans Norman.

The DC-8-50 was in 1962 the first [transport] aircraft to cross the sound barrier when a Douglas aircraft did this during diving.

Based on the experience gained while working with the DC-8 Long Duct project Douglas was interested in continuing efforts to further improve the plane to meet the wishes of SAS and was under a high degree of SAS pressure. During the long and intensive studies and negotiations, in which the head of Douglas civilian production, Jack McGowen, and his sales manager Harry Deer spent several weeks in Stockholm, in various stages, we finally found a solution.

According to Douglas, the DC-8-62 was conceived by these men in a hotel room in Stockholm. From SAS Volrath Holmboe, was our specialist in aerodynamics and performance with his experience from his time at the Saab aerodynamics department. For example the changes to the engine mounts (undercut pylons) gave a predicted reduction in drag of about 5%. At one point, the discussion ran so hot that Jack burst out: "I am the one that runs Douglas not Volrath." The solutions accomplished meant that the Long Duct engine nacelles improved further, brand new pylons with more favorable aerodynamic design was introduced, wingtips extended by almost one meter each, the body was extended by six feet, and fuel capacity was increased by about 800 gal, and the takeoff weight was 335,000 lb. For the final negotiations Donald Douglas Jr., who succeeded his father Donald Douglas Sr., came to Stockholm as head of the entire Douglas Group. In the first stage, SAS ordered four planes, later complemented by another six so that the entire fleet were made up of ten planes.

During the entire duration of the DC 8-62 studies, Boeing was not inactive. SAS was offered the latest version of the 707-320B but it could not show any better data than Douglas.

In the autumn of 1964 a new factor appeared that had to be analyzed and assessed. Rumors began to go around in the aviation world that Douglas's finacial situation was not completely stable. Discreet soundings were made in the banking world and in Washington. SAS Chairman Marcus Wallenberg decided to attend a ceremony that Douglas invited us to in mid November, to celebrate the 10th anniversary of the opening of SAS polar route to Los Angeles, and to inquire about the finacial situation. SAS's new CEO Karl Nilsson and I got in this context the opportunity to visit the management of the US Air Force who had the highest responsibility for the purchase of materials. We were therefore flown up to Air Force Edwards Air Force Base in the California desert and met there with several generals. They assured us that the Douglas Group had such great importance for the US Air Force and space efforts that there was no need for concern that any financial problems would not get a satisfactory solution. They showed us an amazing openness, both during discussions and at a short tour of the base. We even got up close and walked around and studied the super-secret SR-71 reconnaissance aircraft. Our visit had apparently been prepared for me by unknown influential people.

When Douglas developed the DC-8-50 series, the US domestic airlines issued requests for a much longer fuselage so that passenger and cargo capacity could be increased considerably and thus lower the seat and ton-mile costs. Here Douglas had a huge advantage over Boeing. As mentioned earlier, Douglas set the dimensions of the landing gear so that it would be possible in the future to significantly extend the fuselage without the tail hitting the ground during rotation and lift-off during takeoff or during landing at high angle of attack. The vertical tail had also been made smaller than Boeing's for the same reason.

With the improvements in performance that the series DC-8-50 brought about, the companies' requests could now be met, with a certain sacrifice in range, which suited several domestic companies well on many routes. The result of these design

features was the DC-8-61 with the fuselage extended over 36 feet in relation to the DC-8-50. And 88 planes were built of the model. After the DC-8-62 became reality through SAS efforts, it was natural that the model was lengthened in the same way as the DC-8-61 and it was designated the DC-8-63.

In September 1965, SAS signed the first order of two DC-8-63s, which were mainly used on the New York route. The plane could be laid out for up to 259 passengers in economy class, but SAS chose initially to configure it with a smaller number of seats in order to offer greater comfort.

In the spring of 1966, it became necessary to possibly buy more aircraft. It was then a complicated situation for several reasons and I was asked to attend a board meeting in early June to describe an investigation that my department made for SAS management and to answer questions.

What was most problematic was that it was known that Boeing had plans to launch a so-called wide-body aircraft, the Boeing 747, and the board wanted to hear what information was available about these plans. I first presented briefly what I knew about the airplane configuration and then

The DC-8-63 was more than 32 feet longer than the Boeing 707-320B and had very low operating costs per seat. SAS airplanes had 200 seats, in a 2-class version. Douglas manufactured 174 aircraft of the DC-8-62 / 63 type
Photo SAS.

Donald Douglas Jr. congratulates B. Holmer at roll out of the DC-8-63 for SAS's efforts in the development of the DC-8-62 / 63.
Photo by Birger Holmer.

The Boeing patent for the 747 concept.
Photo Boeing.

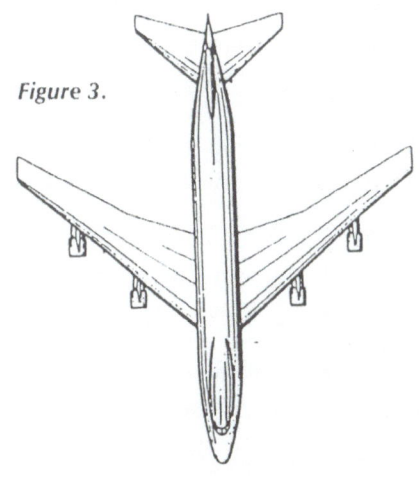
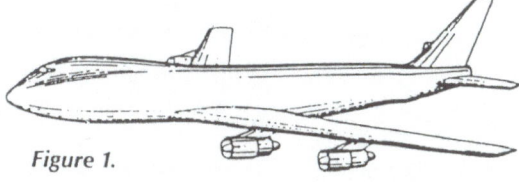

stated which companies had shown an interest in it. I knew it was just PanAm, Lufthansa and Japan Airlines that demonstrated significant interest. Boeing had hinted that it required at least 80 firm orders or clearly written intentions in acquiring a certain number of planes before Boeing was willing to move from project studies to detailed design activities. I judged that then (June 1966) there was not sufficient evidence that Boeing would go further than to continue with studies and that the situation would not change for the rest of the year.

What I did not know was that PanAm chief Juan Trippe at a meeting shortly before July 1965 gave Boeing boss Bill Allen a "Letter of Intent" on a

Delivery of the last Douglas DC-8 to SAS in May 1972. From left Ivar Shogran of Douglas, Captain Egon Ericsson, Birger Holmer, and Ted Conant and Jack McGowen, both from Douglas.
Photo Douglas.

purchase of a number of 747s. This was extremely secret and even within Boeing it was known only by a very small number of people.

That, however, gave Allen a basis for allowing the project work to become more extensive. The document was replaced on 1 April 1966 with a contract which contained a definition of the plane with price and delivery dates, etc. but it was still a secret. It contained a clause which meant that unless Boeing in August of that year had started the detailed design work Boeing would have to pay $ 10 million to Pan Am. It was perhaps that clause that allowed Boeing in August 1966 to announce to the outside world that it had launched the highly ambitious 747 program. Boeing had received a patent for the 747 concept.

At that time I did not have any clarity to what extent Lufthansa and / or Japan Airlines had contributed to Boeing announcing its decision. Although there was a commitment on their part, the number had not reached 80 orders. Anyway, my statement to the Board did not even last for three months!

The outcome of the Board meeting was that SAS added another four DC-8-63s from Douglas. The last of these planes, which we received on 13 May 1972, with registration SE-BDL and Douglas serial number 556, became the last DC-8 produced. In total 107 DC-8-63s were produced. SAS later bought two used DC-8-63s from Eastern Airlines to meet the traffic demand. They were rebuilt to SAS standard

The tug of war between Boeing and Douglas with the 707 and DC-8 was won by Boeing regarding the number of aircraft sold. Boeing sold 1010 planes, while Douglas sold 556. With the DC-8-61 and DC-8-63, however, Douglas won the battle to produce planes that had superior operating costs per passenger-nm or ton-nm, which certainly affected Boeing's decision to launch the 747.

Douglas realized now that the time had come when it was impossible to stick to a cabin width with just six seats across and thus began planning for their own wide-body aircraft, the DC-10; and interrupted the DC-8 series to concentrate on the DC-10. Douglas cut up all the DC-8 production tools to highlight that no more would it be manufactured.

It is interesting to note that both companies indicated that their programs did not provide great economic gains. It was the other aircraft types, military planes or missiles that accounted for the companies' positive operating results. In Boeing's case, it was, among others, the 727 which was the big profit generator.

In the beginning SAS showed no specific interest in the 747 and I got the impression that the Board was mostly interested in assessing the competitive picture of the companies that might buy the 747 early, rather than in the short term need to order 747s.

Short and medium range jet aircraft

Aircraft with turboprop engines such as the Viscount and Lockheed Electra were conceived in the 1950s. Of these the Viscount became popular with many orders (439) including in the US while the Electra had to settle for a fairly moderate success. SAS's acquisition of the Caravelle and its early success sparked plans of other manufacturers to offer jet-powered aircraft for those route distances.

One of the earliest projects was the de Havilland

BAC1-11 in SAS colors SAS leased in ad hoc capacity while waiting for the DC-9 deliveries. Photo Sven Stridsberg.

Caravelle III SE-210, SE-DAF at Gothenburg old airport Torslanda 1974. Photo Sören Hörlyk.

Trident, with three tail-mounted Rolls-Royce engines. The plane had been able to become a serious competitor to the Boeing 727. British European Airways (BEA), however steered the manufacturer to adapt it to their needs and the result was that the aircraft size was decreased and it proved less attractive to the rest of the market. BEA had no need for the range that most other companies demanded.

Among the early twin-engine planes was the British Aircraft Corporation BAC 1-11. The plane was, at the design stage, bigger than what eventually was manufactured. Even in this case BEA's views had the similar effect with the result that the plane did not get the design that the major airlines wanted. It was however a greater success than the Trident.

One can see through history that both BEA and BOAC had too much influence on the UK aviation industry with regards to designing the planes for a larger market.

Boeing wavered long between different proposals with two-, three- or four-engined versions. The airlines that were most active in America were Eastern and TWA both of whom wanted a three-engine plane, whereas United wanted four engines. American remained cautious because they had invested in the Electra. After many long negotiations, Boeing finally convinced all four companies that a three-engine plane was the best solution. In this way Boeing conceived the 727 which was originally planned with an engine that Allison would produce in partnership with Rolls-Royce.

Above all Eastern insisted that it would be a Pratt & Whitney engine and so the JT8 program was launched. It would become the most common engine in many civilian aircraft. Later the JT8 was, in a developed version, also selected to power the Swedish Saab Viggen fighter aircraft.

SAS did extensive studies on both the Trident and 727, especially of the later 727-200 which was a larger aircraft seating up to 189 passengers, but found that the size did not fit SAS's route network. The Caravelle size correlated better with SAS wishes. If the traffic demand could be satisfied with a twin-engined plane, there was no reason to use a three-engine that offered higher direct operating costs, because the contemporary operating regulations required three pilots for the three-engine plane while the twin-engine could be operated with only two. Interestingly, the original design of 737 flight deck was based on three pilots.

The Boeing 727 was unique, with an advanced wing design with leading edge slats with constant chord along the span, and Krueger flaps closest to the fuselage. The trailing edge had a triple slotted flap system that first moved straight back resulting in increased wing area, and with increased extension gradually increased the angle of deflection. The principal leader behind the 727, Jack Steiner, was a very qualified aerodynamicist which, among others, is apparent from the wing design.

During 1965-66 four serious accidents occurred with 727s, three in the US and one in Japan, all of which had its origin in crews who were not properly trained to cope with some of the airplane characteristics during approach to landing.

The well-utilized aerodynamics of the 727-wing meant that lift over drag (L/D) with fully extended flaps and normal approach speed was about 1:5, i.e., the aircraft aerodynamic drag was very high in the landing configuration and with engines idling the descent rate was around 2,500 ft./min. The engines had a "spin-up" time from idle to full thrust in nearly eight seconds. Pilots who came from propeller aircraft to the 727 were accustomed to obtaining direct effect on the wing's lift capability from the propeller slipstream when increasing engine thrust. The delay from idle to full throttle with the 727 did not allow time for the pilots in these accidents to arrest the aircraft's large sink rate when they made the approach from a higher altitude than the normal approach procedure prescribed.

Douglas DC-9

As already mentioned SAS decided not to invest in the later models of the Caravelle but turned instead to the Douglas DC-9.

Just one year before the DC-8 flew for the first time, Douglas started plans for a new aircraft for short and medium haul routes. Like other manufacturers Douglas had also studied alternatives with two, three, or four engines. A model that was called project 2000 and was a mini-DC-8 with four engines. The idea was that you could use many common components, but the slimmed-down DC-8 project did not attract interest among the airlines.

After examining a partnership with Sud Aviation, in the form of agency or licensed production of the Caravelle, they found that it was not an attractive prospect for the future and therefore decided to invest in their own version of a twin-engine plane with tail-mounted engines like the Caravelle. Thanks to Boeing and the dominant US companies' efforts, there was also a suitable engine, the JT8D, which Sud Aviation had also chosen for its Caravelle development program.

In early April 1963 Douglas decided to start the DC-9 series by offering the DC-9-10 version with room for 80-90 passengers. It had a maximum takeoff weight below 80,000 lb., which at that time was a limit for flying with two pilots. The limit was soon thereafter changed.

The cabin cross-section consisted of two segments of a circle one above the floor of the passenger cabin and one at the bottom for luggage and cargo. Cabin width was planned for five seats abreast. The Caravelle had, in the SAS layout, 81 seats and the DC-9-10 tentatively 85. With the "double-bubble" configuration the DC-9 could carry considerably more cargo than what was possible with the Caravelle, which had a pure circular cross-section. The cargo compartment volume in

Boeing 727 with a complex high lift system, flaps on the wing trailing edge and slats in the wing leading edge.
Photo Boeing.

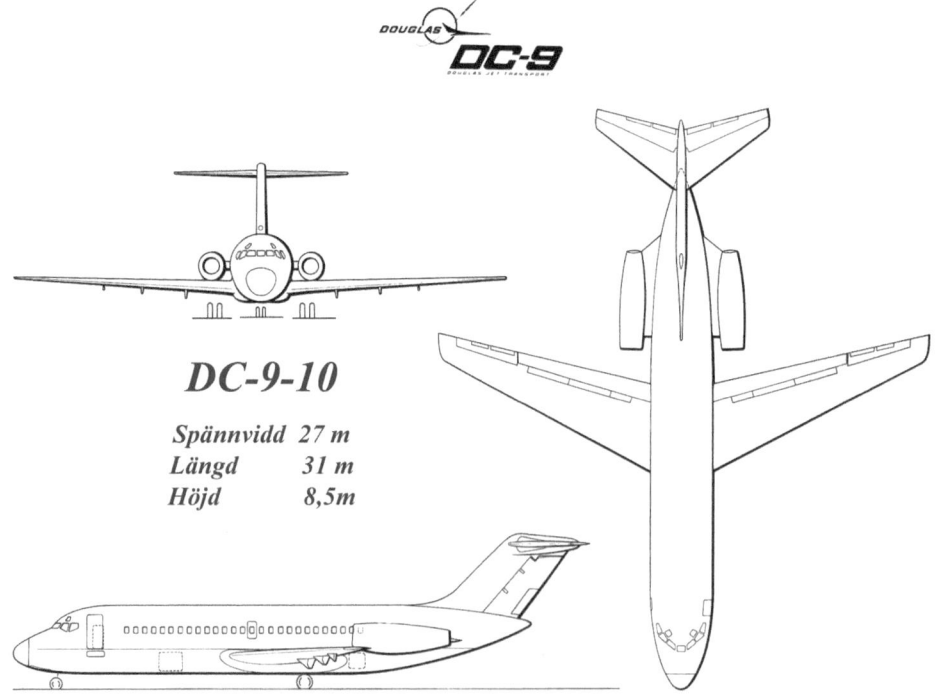

DC-9-10

Spännvidd 27 m
Längd 31 m
Höjd 8,5 m

DC-9-10 3-view plan.
Photo Douglas.

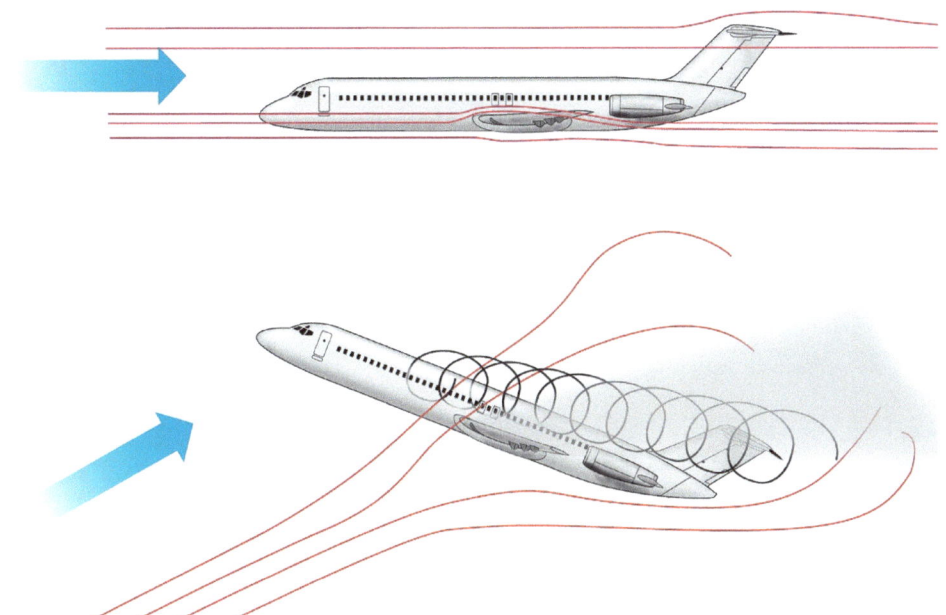

The airflow around an aircraft in normal mode and in "deep stall" are very different. In deep stall, an abnormal flight mode at high angle of attack, the aerodynamic effectiveness of the horizontal tail section is affected by wakes from the wing, fuselage, and the engines. Aircraft with tail-mounted engines and stabilizer located on top of the fin, the so-called T-tail are the most vulnerable. BAC had an accident during a test flight, and the Boeing 727 had a serious incident when an FAA pilot during a test succeeded in getting the aircraft in this mode. The Boeing test pilot saved the situation. An MD-80 crashed after that type had been in operation for many years. Nowadays a "stick shaker" and in some cases a "stick pusher" are required in the control system that warns pilots long before they risk entering into a "deep stall".
Picture Hans Kampf.

the DC-9-10 was 600 cu. ft. compared to just under 400 cu. ft. in the Caravelle. The DC-9 also had a big cost advantage over the Caravelle as two pilots flew the DC-9 versus three in the Caravelle. The DC-9 had a T-shaped tail like both the Boeing 727 and BAC 1-11, and had built in passenger stairs.

Sales were initially quite sluggish. The first order was placed by Delta Air Lines and was followed shortly thereafter by KLM; and Swissair bought five planes to replace the Caravelle leased from SAS. Douglas built a total of 137 DC-9-10s.

Douglas had initially counted on a fuselage that could be extended and after a fairly short time offered a version that was designated DC-9-30. It was extended by 15 ft. relative to the DC-9-10 and the number of seats could thereby be increased to 115 in an all tourist class version. The wingspan was increased by 4 ft. and was provided with wing leading edge slats to improve performance during takeoff and landing. In addition, a later version of the JT8D engine was installed that had greater thrust. The DC-9-30 generated much greater interest by the airlines and not in the least from SAS and Swissair. Because Swissair had acted earlier than SAS purchasing the DC-9-10, and SAS had not been involved with the evaluation, SAS had to do its own analysis of the DC-9-30 and compare it with other options. Swissair considered their studies for the purchase of the DC-9-10 were sufficient to predict the DC-9-30's performance by extrapolation.

SAS's decision to make its own study should not be seen as any underestimation of the analyses Swissair had done but rather a need to submit an internal report to SAS management and Board of Directors, so that someone would be responsible within its own company.

Among the alternatives to the DC-9 were the Boeing 737 and the BAC 1-11 that were considered too small and having too little development potential to fit as a replacement for the Caravelle. The conclusion was based on analysis of available documentation.

The BAC 1-11, however, became interesting because it suffered a serious accident during test flights in that it was exposed to a flight situation that now was called "deep stall". The aircraft was, like the DC-9, equipped with a "T-tail", i.e., the stabilizer and elevator were mounted in the top of the fin. At very high angle of attack, the elevator and stabilizer are being subjected to large air wakes and vortices from the wings, losing lift and pitch control. Above all, it was necessary to increase the span and area of both the stabilizer and elevator and to introduce a "stall warning system" i.e. a device that gives an early warning to pilots of an impending deep stall.

SAS management decided that I, with a group of experts, would make a quick visit to BAC Weybridge outside London to collect the latest information about the BAC 1-11 accident and the necessary countermeasures before an SAS evaluation team traveled to the US West Coast to study the Boeing and Douglas projects. The visit gave information that was valuable when it came to discussing this phenomenon later with Douglas and questions regarding what modifications Douglas had introduced on the DC-9. In part, Douglas grew the span of stabilizer and elevator, and introduced direct control of the elevator. The BAC 1-11 accident gave many lessons to the entire aircraft industry.

Before the working group departed for the US, a study of available documentation of the DC-9-30 was performed and in discussions with SAS management, CEO Karl Nilsson had stated that the work should focus on getting the aircraft further improved with regard to passenger numbers and thus lowered seat- and ton-mile costs.

SAS specialists visiting Douglas for the evaluation of the DC-9 under Birger Holmer's leadership (standing in middle). Photo by Birger Holmer.

When examining the mechanical design of the wings and body with accompanying installations such as rudders, flaps, landing gear, and engines, etc., the relationship with the former Douglas planes was striking and did not give rise to any concern. Engine location was an innovation for Douglas civilian planes and was studied carefully considering fuel supply, fire fighting possibilities, electric generators, hydraulic pumps etc. The tail section was, as mentioned, extra carefully analyzed and Douglas presented the extensive wind tunnel tests and that countermeasures were the same, as on the BAC 1-11. They had been introduced on the DC-9-10 and tested with good results.

In 1965 Ulf Abrahamsson was hired by the project organization, reporting to Volrath Holmboe. He participated in the analyses of the data that BAC provided as one of his first tasks.

The DC-9-10 had already flown for the first time 25 February 1965 and an opportunity to participate in a demonstration flight with such a plane. The demonstration had a positive outcome. The type got its airworthiness certificate in November 1965.

Regarding Karl Nilsson's wishes, the group succeeded in convincing Douglas to further extend the body by 6 ft., which permitted the number of seats to be increased to 125 in a single tourist class. Fuel quantity was increased by about 570 US gallon and the maximum takeoff weight to 114,000 lb. The plane was equipped with Pratt & Whitney JT8D-11 engines with 15,000 lb. of thrust. This variant of the DC-9 was given the type designation DC-9-40 and had as a consequence slightly shorter range and slightly longer runway requirement.

Douglas promised to forward documents to SAS headquarters so that a contract could be established before the year 1965 had ended. The delivery time was slightly longer for this version than was the

The last four DC-9-41s were delivered without painting, only SAS decor, to save weight.
Photo SFF archive.

The Douglas DC-9-40 prototype, painted in Douglas colors, during a test flight over the passenger ship "Queen Mary." The first flight was on 28 November, 1967 and was delivered to SAS in May 1968 as the DC-9-41, with registration SE-DBX, "Arnljot Viking." It was sold in 1991 to Northwest Airlines and registered by the FAA as N750NW, later registering it for Delta Air Lines.
Photo from John Thinesen's collection.

Ulf Abrahamsson, Volrath Holmboe and Birger Holmer discussing different projects
Photo Ulf Abrahamsson

case had SAS, like Swissair chosen the DC-9-30. A lease of the DC-9-30 from Swissair offset this. The DC-9-40 first flew 28 November 1967 and was delivered to SAS 29 February 1968.

The first order covered 10 planes and over the years SAS bought 49 planes of this version.

The last four were delivered in 1979, just at the start of the fuel crisis. In order to reduce the aircraft's empty weight it was determined that they would not have any exterior paint. The empty weight was reduced by about 440 lb. and SAS could report some fuel savings. The fuel crisis meant that the airlines did not uplift excessive fuel loads. SAS developed a special planning program for fuel loading on the critical points and that was running every day. Every opportunity to save weight was investigated.

The four aircraft were painted later with the new decor that was established in 1982 for the entire fleet. These four DC-9-41s were special in another respect. They were namely the first airplanes with hat racks that had doors that were closed before the takeoff and therefore allowed even heavier luggage to be taken on board in the cabin. Douglas had changed its specification. It was a clear improvement for the passengers and SAS decided before delivery of these aircraft that the entire DC-9 fleet would be converted to this standard. The new type of hat racks had become standard in the industry.

Boeing 737

Before SAS took the decision to buy the DC-9 we studied the Boeing 737 option. This project had started about two years later than the DC-9 and had been initiated to address the threat from Douglas.

The 737 had the same cabin cross-section as 707 and 727, which had six seats abreast as opposed to five in the DC-9. This did to some extent affect the assessment of 737. An experience from previous planes with five abreast, was that passengers if possible, avoided sitting more than two in the rows which have three abreast. This means that the third seat was needed when the passenger load factor exceeded 4/5 i.e. 80%, but in the plane with six abreast the third seat be must used when it is more than 4/6 or 67%. One can thus offer a higher average comfort in a plane with five seats abreast.

The reason that passengers react in this way must be that the person sitting at the window has to bother two people to get out into the aisle to visit the toilet or for any other reason. These factors are discussed further in the accounts of wide-body aircraft.

Another factor of great importance was the location of the engine. There had been long discussions at Boeing before it was eventually decided to place them close under the wing. This meant that the engines compared to the DC-9,

BAC 1-11, 727 and others came very close to the ground and were thus exposed to a high risk of loose objects, which unfortunately can be found on airport ramps and runways, being sucked into the engine inlet. During winter conditions snow and ice chunks will be sprayed up from the nose wheel and can get into the inlet. You cannot reduce these risks by extending the landing gear and passenger loading stairs because that would impose excessive weight increases.

It was interesting to hear Jack Steiner, presenting another important reason for the selected engine placement. He was chief designer for the 727, which has three tail-mounted engines. If this caused some disadvantages a two-engine aircraft should be slightly easier to handle. His argument was about the situation when someone wanted to extend the fuselage to provide more rows of passengers. One can then mount two equal sections on each side of the wing without disturbing the balance.

As far as is known, neither the 727 nor DC-9 have been affected by any major difficulties in this respect when their bodies were extended in stages. Neither he nor anyone else expressed any views on the fact that with the chosen location there were no complications due to a T-tail. The SAS Group found no reason to raise any arguments on these issues since there were no means or desire to change the configuration that Boeing selected.

The 737 project was not surrounded with much enthusiasm from the beginning and Boeing chief Bill Allen was doubtful for a long time. It later transpired that the Board was pushing and not wanting to leave the field open to Douglas. A preliminary startup notice had been given 14 November,1964 and a final Decision of 1 February 1965.

The first order for 22 aircraft came from Lufthansa on 16 February that year and the first flight was made 9 April 1967, thus far later than when the SAS Group had completed its evaluation of the plane.

In weighing all of the arguments presented by the study of the three options BAC fell away at an early stage and there were only the 737 and DC-9 left. In the choice between them it should be remembered that in the DC-9 case there were delivery-ready aircraft to study and test fly, while for the 737 there were only documents, drawings, presentations, and references to earlier Boeing aircraft.

Their recommendation was that SAS, like Swissair would order the DC-9 and continue the good cooperation with Douglas.

So very long afterwards (40 years), it may be appropriate to mention that the first series of the 737, which received version number -100 was not

The DC-9's interior, now with the new overhead bins with doors. A happy bunch of hockey players as passengers.
Photo Hans Boethius

737-100 during testing. The blow-in doors on the nacelles open at takeoff to ensure sufficient air to the engines at low speed and close when the aircraft climbs up in the sky.
Photo Boeing.

The Boeing 737 is a good example of profitable projects; it started with the Boeing 737-100, which was followed by the 737-200 and 1125 aircraft produced for these models until the 1980s.
Photo Boeing.

Cabin cross section of the Boeing 737 and Douglas DC-9
Drawing Hans Kampf.

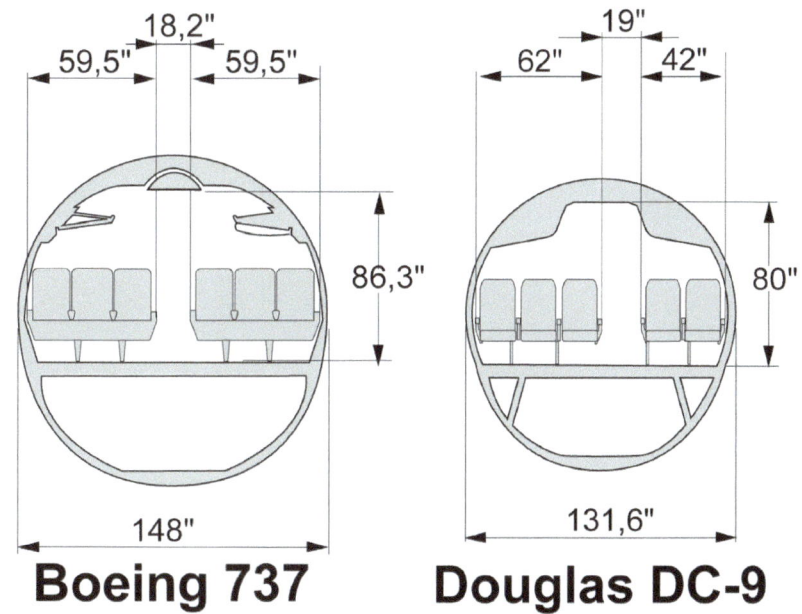

an entirely successful product. One big drawback was the reverse thrust device not giving the braking effect expected and this affected takeoff and landing performance. The shortage was not observed from the drawings or other data but first appeared in test flights. The reason was related to the chosen placement of the engines tightly under the wing.

Although Boeing worked very hard to overcome the problems it took a long time before they mastered the situation and it was also expensive for them.

At Lufthansa there was a very big disappointment over this shortcoming and the plane had quite a few teething problems that took a long time to correct. An initial extension of the fuselage was launched after a fairly short time and received the version designation 737-200 and it was a clear improvement. Later versions changed the engine installation fairly radically by moving the engine forward so that most of it is in front of the wing leading edge and mounted on a standard pylon. Boeing showed great ability to develop the type further with later versions of the 737 that came to outflank DC-9 developments.

Since SAS made the decision to purchase the DC-9-40 and confirmed to Swissair that it wished to continue cooperation with both current and ordered aircraft, it became necessary to establish common specifications in the same way as applied to the DC-8 and Caravelle.

It was then evident that Swissair on some points deviated from the norms established for the DC-8 and Caravelle when they designed the flight deck configuration for their DC-9-10. This was natural because SAS at the time of Swissair's DC-9-10 purchase had plans to continue with the developed versions of the Caravelle. When the idea now again was to borrow or rent aircraft from each other, it became necessary to organize a standardization.

In mid-January 1966 working groups from both companies got together at Douglas in Long Beach in an attempt to accomplish this. The working group consisted of both pilots and engineers specializing in instrumentation and control panels as well as radio and navigation equipment. The situation was delicate. Swissair could be criticized for having been a tad willful and SAS to have been slow to engage. After a time the mood lightened and it was finally agreed in a spirit of cooperation.

The end result was a configuration that only in a few small details differed from the agreement previously developed for the DC-8 and Caravelle. Douglas made a good effort by providing the participants with the necessary technical information for the discussion.

DC-9-33 cargo aircraft. Photo SFF's archives.

Douglas had also found SAS / Swissair configurations represented the most elaborate arrangements and that they could be used as good proposals when they presented the specifications to customers who had their own equally thoughtful views on how the flight deck should be designed.

In the context of negotiations on the DC 9-40 there were two delivery positions reserved for a later ordering of the freight version of the DC-9-30. The cargo volume of 4100 cu. ft. in the plane was in fact sufficiently large so as to attain maximum available load weight before the space was filled at the most common density of cargo. During the review of the fuselage, the group had also studied the structure of the cargo floor area and the design of the cargo door, which was hinged at the upper edge, and its locking mechanisms. Further information was requested about the current design weights and performance. The version was designated DC 9-33AF where AF stands for All Freighter. Everything in the outcome was positive and SAS confirmed somewhat later an order for the two planes. The first was delivered 31 July 1969.

SAS also had a need to find modern aircraft that could operate on several Norwegian domestic routes where performance on short runways was required and also very good climb performance, given the surrounding mountainous terrain. It was found desirable to combine the best properties of the DC-9-30 and DC-9-40 with the shorter fuselage of the DC-9-10 version.

Douglas made an analysis of the proposal and presented a new version that had the advanced wing of the DC-9-30 and -40 together with the more powerful engine and the short body. They sent a representative to Stockholm who outlined the version and submitted performance data that were reviewed. The study showed good results when applied on the Norwegian domestic network and SAS president Karl Nilsson became very enthusiastic regarding the solution.

During the same time period Linjeflyg had informed SAS that there was also an interest in modernizing its fleet and that it wanted to study the BAC 1-11. SAS had early found that the plane did not fit as a replacement for the Caravelle in European traffic but perhaps it could be used for the Norwegian domestic traffic. It was decided by SAS and Linjeflyg management that a joint evaluation of the BAC 1-11 would happen.

A fairly large delegation from both companies traveled in early July 1966 to Weybridge. SAS analysis showed that the plane did not have the performance required and Lineflyg also wanted to study other options from, e.g. Fokker. The DC-9-20 was not of interest to Lineflyg as it was too big and expensive. Upon returning home we found out that Karl Nilsson already decided to buy ten DC-9-20s.

SAS chose the DC-9 thanks in part to the fuselage stretch Douglas offered at the end of the negotiations.
From staff magazine Inside SAS.

A large group of specialists from SAS and Linjeflyg visiting BAC Weybridge in 1968 for the evaluation of the BAC 1-11.
Photo Ulf Abrahamsson.

It was obvious that Karl Nilsson during negotiations with Douglas managed to achieve very favorable prices, delivery times and other conditions.

This occurred despite the fact that Douglas must have realized that sales opportunities to other airlines of the special SAS version were not so good.

A long time afterwards, one can ask whether the SAS study of the BAC 1-11 was primarily intended to put pressure on Douglas. At the same time the SAS delegation gave also good support to Linjeflyg that in turn put increased pressure on Fokker and possibly others that were of interest.

In addition to SAS's acquisition of 49 DC-9-40s, only the Japanese company TOA Domestic ordered 18 planes. In the case of the DC-9-20 SAS became the only customer. In the negotiations with Douglas Karl Nilsson had decided that the DC-9-20 plane would be provided with the same galley that applied for DC 9-40. The reason was that he wanted the flexibility to use the DC-9-20 on other routes than the Norwegian domestic routes in the event of a shortage of DC-9-40 and be able to put them on other destinations in cases of temporary lower passenger demand.

Operating costs for the DC-9-20 were significantly lower than for the larger plane, particularly as SAS chose to reduce the certificated maximum takeoff weight of 100,000 lb. to 87,000 lb. thus saving on takeoff and landing fees. Would SAS wish to change the use of the plane and a need to increase MTOW, it only required a new airworthiness certificate.

An increase in maximum takeoff weight of 100,000 lb. was conducted soon after the type had been in operation since the benefits of the flexibility in traffic planning were greater than considering additional costs in landing fees. The DC-9-20 became popular on the thinner routes with their lower hourly rate compared to the DC-9-41 and with the ability to fly long distances.

In contrast, we overlooked another circumstance. In the specification of the DC-9-40 SAS had provided weights of the galleys that came from the Nordskog company (a Swedish descendant) in Miami and weights for everything that was loaded in the form of food and beverages and tax free goods-- the latter was quite heavy! Douglas had

Douglas test flies the first DC-9-20 aircraft.
Photo Boeing.

this information when it came to design the fuselage sections that must be placed in front of and behind the wing to get the right balance on the plane. Now it was not possible to extend the body but instead to place the wing right in relation to a defined length. DC-9-10s were designed for other conditions.

In the absence of data from SAS on different galley weights Douglas proportioned the percentage applied to the onboard catering load with the relationship between the number of passengers in both types. That this was inappropriate the designers could not know. On the Norwegian domestic routes SAS did not intend to serve more than morning coffee and a cake at the beginning of the day and only light refreshments during other parts of the day, and Tax-free sales could not be sold on the domestic network.

As a result of all this the wing of the DC-9-20 was misplaced. This was recognized too late in the manufacturing process that it was impossible to correct at a reasonable cost or delay. What would you do instead!? First, it was suggested that SAS would impose restrictions on loading the cargo holds. The next suggestion was to use ballast in the form of sandbags. The Station department in charge of the management of the proposals rejected them with force. That left only to install solid ballast in the form of lead ingots.

There was room in the nose wheel well to install these. It also had the advantage over the other two proposals that would result in a smaller overall weight increase as ballast in the nose had a longer moment arm to operate on. Douglas was contracted to install the mounting brackets for 440 lbs. of ingots that SAS would install after delivery.

It was in both SAS's and Douglas's interest that this failure would not get any further dissemination. All preached with emphasis how important it was to save weight when constructing and operating aircraft. That they managed to keep it all fairly unknown in Douglas appeared to be that the brackets that were installed were fitted with empty holes! The Douglas story was that there would be equipment mounted needed for navigation in the narrow Norwegian fjords. For Norwegian technicians and other personnel who for various reasons could see these installations, it was impossible to tell some fairy tales. Since it was known that it was I who was primarily responsible for aircraft specifications, I have suffered much shame for this omission.

What can you learn from this event? Well, when an airline becomes the only buyer of a particular aircraft type, there is a high risk of false specific amendment proposals not being addressed. Admittedly the issue here concerns a type variant but it may still be of great importance.

Anyway, the DC-9-20 was a successful type that was upheld highly by both passengers and above all of the pilots. The plane had performance that was not much different than the first generation of jet-powered fighter aircraft. SAS had some plans to use the DC-9-20 at Bromma and conducted analyses of the noise issue with the help of Bo Lundberg, director of the Aeronautical Research Institute, FFA and noise measurements. The DC-9-20 was certainly quieter than the Caravelle that SAS previously used at Bromma, but the reaction from residents around the airport became strong and SAS chose to abstain. Linjeflyg tested the idea of buying the DC-9-20, likely influenced by SAS, but decided not to go that route. In 1968, the Government also issued a prohibition order for jets at Bromma.

The establishment of the McDonnell Douglas Corporation

As already mentioned, there were rumors that Douglas had financial problems. The soundings made by SAS gave the result that there was no cause for concern. When negotiating the purchase of the DC-9 the question came up again and it turned out that there were reasons to monitor progress and find out what was behind the rumors.

One must go back to 1958 to find out what has happened in the earlier and so successful company. Donald Douglas Senior had turned 66 years old and wanted to withdraw from the direct management of the company and transfer it to his son Donald Douglas Jr. and serve as chairman. The system of a retiring President attaining the post of chairman is a topic that is vividly discussed in the

Donald W. Douglas, Sr. leaving Douglas.
Photo by Birger Holmer

management philosophy. There are both advantages and disadvantages but it easily becomes more problematic when it comes to the father and son or other family members.

In Douglas, it was not particularly advantageous. Shortly after the decision, five of the highest managers who were directly reporting to Donald Douglas Sr. left the company. They were all 7-20 years older than Douglas Jr. and had worked for Douglas Sr. for a couple of decades or more. Douglas Jr. had worked at several locations in the company and was known as a light-hearted and jovial person but had not demonstrated leadership talents of the same quality as the father.

Among the great and difficult tasks he had to deal with was to bring order to the production of the DC-8 in the new hangars and workshops in Long Beach, south of Los Angeles. During the WWII Douglas had a large production of military C-47 aircraft in Long Beach. The decision to relocate was taken by the previous management and was caused by the existing buildings in Santa Monica being too small for the manufacture and assembly of the DC-8. In addition, the airport's runways were too short and the noise of the jets would be unacceptable because the airport was in the middle of a housing area.

Douglas chose Long Beach that had a major airport. The buildings belonged to the Air Force but Douglas bought them and built more hangars, which were large enough for the assembly of the DC-8. In addition a new headquarters was built and all operations were moved from Santa Monica. The new management made a major transformation of the entire manufacturing process using new modern methods of organization. They also engaged sub-suppliers to a greater extent than previously. The Vietnam War meant that the load on the entire defense industry grew significantly, material availability deteriorated, and delivery delays occurred in many stages. This affected Douglas greatly. DC-9 sales were initially quite slow but suddenly they took off and resulted in a huge demand for the plane.

It was to a great extent Jack McGowen's credit that sales of the DC-9 took off. There was only one catch. He sold them cheaply and in more quantity than the manufacturing capacity could cope with. If the low price was due to poor cost control or other factors, they were not disclosed. The labor shortage caused by the war meant that many employees did not have sufficient training and had to be retrained which led to the so-called "learning curve" development was not as expected.

Jack McGowen had, since he was hired by Douglas in late 1930s, made a brilliant career and served, when SAS first came into contact with him, as the responsible project engineer for both the DC-4 and DC-6. When his boss Jim Edward went over to the sales area, McGowen also became responsible for the DC-7 series. He had later senior positions in the coming regime. SAS benefited from the favorable pricing of the DC-9 types Karl Nilsson negotiated so skillfully. One may wonder if SAS unknowingly contributed to worsen Douglas's

Jack McGowen Douglas, and SAS CEO Karl Nilsson after hard negotiations. Photo SAS.

financial predicaments.

To improve the situation in the financial accounting provided to banks and authorities Douglas Jr. had changed the depreciation method for development costs. Previously Douglas accounted for them the year in which they arose. Under the new regime, they would be distributed on the number of years it was estimated that the aircraft type in question would be in production. All the factors mentioned above and surely many others contributed to Douglas in the fall of 1966 ending up in an acute liquidity crisis. Negotiations with the company's banks did not yield any result, especially because during several months they had been very concerned about the development in accordance with information that came to their attention. They refused to issue the necessary credits.

Then there was only one way out, to seek help from any other organizations. The reputed investment company Lazard Freres in New York was commissioned to examine who could be interested. Lazard sent a delegation to Douglas in late November 1966, and by December 9 made it clear that Douglas had to merge with another company and get a new management. Lazard found five companies that were interested namely: General Dynamics, Signal Oil, North American Aviation, Fairchild-Hiller and McDonnell Aircraft.

Their quotes submitted on 2 January 1967 were reviewed by Lazard who dropped General Dynamics and Fairchild-Hiller as they had no capital immediately available in the amounts required. North American had capital and willingness to assist with the people for a new company management. Signal Oil had equity but could not assist with the necessary managerial personnel.

It thus became a contest between North American and McDonnell. From the point of view of Douglas, North American was a benevolent partner, but its director JR Atwood, who at one time was employed as an engineer at Douglas, did not want to invest the capital necessary until the US authorities approved the merger. McDonnell was willing to take the risk. Thus only McDonnell Aircraft remained. It was not particularly welcome in Douglas.

Earlier, in 1963, Douglas Sr. and Jim McDonnell met to discuss a possible merger of the two companies. McDonnell had in fact bought 200,000 Douglas shares and suggested that his company would buy up Douglas. Donald Sr. suggested he would do the opposite and in his opinion, McDonnell had no skills to run a company that manufactured commercial aircraft. While Douglas, had experience of both types of aircraft. Discussions were evidently of a nature that they parted on bad terms.

When McDonnell in the first week of January 1967 made his presentation to the negotiations committee, he announced that he then owned 300,000 shares of Douglas and intended to immediately buy a million and a half and that he would let his trusted manager David Lewis take the lead of Douglas activities. The offer could not be refused and Douglas held on 13 January 1967 a board meeting at which McDonnell's offer was unanimously approved.

It is amusing to note that the two companies were founded and run by men with Scottish ancestry.

Donald Douglas Jr. undertook to call McDonnell and inform him of the decision and spared thereby his father losing face and being confronted with Jim McDonnell.

James (Jim) McDonnell belonged to the same generation as Douglas Sr. and had also received his aeronautical training at MIT a few years later than Douglas Sr. He was active in aeronautical companies but did not form his own firm until 1939, much later than Douglas.

The venture was named McDonnell Aircraft Corporation and was resident in St. Louis Missouri and principally engaged in the design and manufacture of fighter aircraft for the US Air Force. The main aircraft at the time of the merger was the Phantom II, which was produced in the thousands.

The "new" McDonnell Douglas Corporation (MDC) headquarters remained in St. Louis and as mentioned, David Lewis was contracted to manage operations at Long Beach. He appointed Jack McGowen to be his right-hand man. Donald Douglas Sr. received the title of "Honorary Chairman of McDonnell Douglas" but he never participated in any board meetings. Donald Douglas Jr. had to move to St. Louis to work in "corporate management" directly under "Mister Mac," as Jim McDonnell preferred to be called. He did not last long there, but moved back to the West Coast when he found a suitable job.

David Lewis was a business leader of the highest standard and he quickly got both production and sales to run in an excellent manner so that the banks got their money back in good order. He also started the DC-10 program and worked in a very efficient and pleasant manner.

Drop-out rates and the changes in its senior management had affected SAS relating to favorable prices for the DC-9 and negatively in terms of delivery times in the short term. It was feared that long-term strategies and plans would deteriorate, as senior people with long experience were not available. The technical competence appeared to be unaffected by the turmoil in the leadership. In the discussions and negotiations that took place during the time between SAS staff and Douglas engineers, vendors, and contract people, nothing worrying was noticed. It was a clear indication of the inherent strength of a company that could work as well as it did while it underwent such radical changes.

Supersonic aircraft

Concorde

The reason that the Concorde is included is not that SAS had some thoughts of buying the plane. However, there was reason to understand the plane sufficiently enough so that it was possible to assess the potential competition from airlines that might buy it. It could also be that any company would be interested in linking SAS as a "feederline" and in that case SAS ought to know the plane's capabilities. Ever since experimental aircraft performed flights with speeds above the speed of sound, which of course is usually called Mach 1, it became natural that aircraft manufacturers began to study the possibilities to construct an aircraft with such speed capability. One of the first initiatives to start a project was in England where they established a committee named "Supersonic Transport Aircraft Committee," which had its first meeting on 5 November 1956. It issued a report 9 March 1959, which recommended the development of a medium-haul aircraft with a range of 1500 nautical miles (nm) and a cruising speed of Mach 1.2 and a long-haul aircraft with the range of 3000 nm and a speed of Mach 1.8. Development costs for the smaller plane were estimated at 50-80 million pounds and for the other plane, 75-95 million pounds.

At the Paris Air Show in June 1961 Sud-Aviation showed a model of the Super Caravelle, a four-engine supersonic aircraft with seating for 70 passengers and a range of 2000 nm. This sparked discussions between the French and English governments who both felt that they should work together in Europe to meet a probable American competitor.

On the engine side, there was quite quickly an agreement between English Bristol Company, who already had an established engine named Olympus, and the French engine company, SNECMA to cooperate in the development of the English engine.

On the aircraft side, an agreement was more sluggish. It was only in November 1962 that an agreement was reached between the governments and the two companies Bristol and Sud-Aviation to collaborate on the design and manufacture of Concorde. It was possible to arrange this only because they planned for two production lines, one at Filton in Bristol and one in Toulouse! That it would be a complicated and expensive project was obvious especially as supervision would be done at the government level as funding would be made through national budgets.

A number of committees were established at different levels. The technical work was led by Dr. Archibald Russell on the English side and by Lucien Servanty on the French. In June 1963 the definition of the aircraft had already progressed so far that PanAm signed an option for six planes which meant that a few other US airlines also signed for options. It was taken for granted that BOAC and Air France would order the plane but they showed a rather cool attitude in the beginning. Since both companies were under state control, one can assume there were tactical political considerations behind this. Among other option holders were Lufthansa, Sabena, and Japan Airlines. In total 74 options were signed. SAS abstained.

The big question for the producers was the cruising speed they would go for. Mach 2.2 was selected, so they could build the plane with known aluminum alloys that could handle temperatures up to about 250 degrees F. If one goes higher, one must use steel or titanium. They considered it too risky to go up to Mach 3 even though they were also

Air France Concorde
Photo Air France

concerned that the Americans might do so. In May 1964 the definition of the plane was completed that would accommodate 118 passengers and have a total load of about 27,000 lb. It would have four-engines and have an empty weight of about 135,000 lb. and a take off weight of 385,000 lb. They hoped to sell 240 planes! Development costs were estimated at 200 million pounds.

What were SAS's views of this project? So much information had then become available that one could make a theoretical analysis. The completed calculations showed everyone that it would require greatly increased ticket and cargo prices to achieve a satisfactory operating economy. It should be emphasized that a purchase price for the Concorde was not available to SAS but had to be estimated to the best of our ability. The study, and ongoing contact with mainly the French part of the Concorde, clarified that a detailed evaluation of the plane was not an issue for SAS. The decisive factor was of course that SAS studies clearly showed that the Concorde would not be able to fly between Copenhagen and New York with a reasonable load.

The difficult question about the "Sonic Boom" was not addressed because SAS was not engaged in the Concorde project. By contrast, Bo Lundberg, FFA, did a large study called "Speed and Safety in Civil Aviation" that created a lot of attention throughout the aviation world.

The first flight was made on 2 March 1969. In conjunction with the air exhibition in Paris in June 1973, SAS was invited to participate with three people in a demonstration flight and I was one of them. The flight took off from Le Bourget and went straight west. The first 25 minutes took place during ascent and at subsonic speed until the plane left the coast near the island of Jersey after which it accelerated from Mach 1 to Mach 2 during the subsequent 25 minutes. The speed was maintained for 40 minutes under a wide turn out over the Atlantic until it was reduced to below Mach 1 at the coast. The landing took place after a total flight time of 124 minutes. You could always follow her speed on a large Mach meter, on the front cabin wall. The flight was felt to be much like an ordinary trip on a jet. The noise and vibrations were also roughly similar. The cabin had the same cross section as the Metropolitan and had four seats across. Because it was more than twice as long it gave a pretty tunnel-like impression. What surprised me most was that it took so long to accelerate from Mach 1 to Mach 2. You almost got the feeling that the engines were the weakest link.

PanAm canceled their options in January 1973 and most of the others followed PanAm shortly thereafter. According to what has been said they got their deposits back. Air India, Japan Airlines, and Lufthansa dropped their options at a later time.

Concorde lands with the lowered nose section
Photo Air France.

Eventually only Air France and BOAC remained. Their respective governments probably influenced those actions. Air France received four planes and five were delivered to BOAC.

No official price for the Concorde was specified when the options were signed in 1963 but it is said to have been of the order of $12-13 million. A current price for 1973 was reported to be approximately $65 million. Development expenditure was originally estimated at 200 million pounds, which in 1974 had grown to more than 1 billion. Concorde was put into service 21 January 1976 on the London-Bahrain route with a flight time of four hours and six minutes.

In 1960 the Russian aircraft manufacturer Tupolev received a contract to develop a competitor to the Concorde. The Tu-144 first flew on New Year's Eve 1968 shortly before the Concorde. One Tu-144 crashed during the Air Show in Paris in 1973. After another accident in 1978 the aircraft was used for a period of transporting mail and packages.

The project had unfortunately a tragic end when a Concorde, taking off in Paris on 25 July 2000 suffered an accident and all 109 aboard and four people on the ground were killed.

U.S. SST project

In April 1961 the international airline cooperation body IATA held a conference on supersonic aircraft. The conference took place before the English and French governments announced their decision to start the Concorde project. A number of experts from aircraft manufacturers, engine companies, and airlines showed papers in which they presented their views on the possibilities to design and manufacture supersonic aircraft. All suggested it likely that it would be only in 1970 or shortly thereafter that it would be possible to deliver them. Opinions differed, however on whether you should aim for Mach 2 or Mach 3 aircraft.

Because the English and the French decided to start the Concorde project, President Kennedy announced in May 1963 that he would help to start an American project. It became not his privilege to pursue the plans, but his successor Lyndon Johnson who in 1964 began the mission.

The US Federal Aviation Administration, FAA, was appointed to lead the project and it was estimated that development costs would amount to about $1.5 billion. The government would bear the brunt of the financing. It attracted a lot of criticism that it did not choose anyone from the airline industry that had experience in the design and manufacture of aircraft. The criticism was mitigated, however, when the head of FAA announced that Bill Magruder had been appointed to manage the business. He was a very respected aerospace engineer who served in the Air Force and served as a test pilot at both Lockheed and Douglas.

After inquiries into the aviation industry to identify areas where there were interest, qualifications, and available capacity, Boeing and Lockheed were appointed to individually design a prototype, and General Electric and Pratt & Whitney to develop the engine. The task was to design a plane for at least 150 passengers, a range of 3500 nm and aim at a cruising speed in the range of Mach 2.7 to 3.0. The aircraft manufacturers went different ways. Boeing chose a complicated design with a swiveling front wing with a hinge that would provide a variable sweepback of 30 degrees during takeoff and landing, and 72 degrees at cruising speed. Lockheed chose a double-delta with 84 degrees sweep at the base and 65 degrees at the outer wing. The configuration was very similar to the Concorde's wing, and reminded a lot of the Saab "Draken" (Dragon) configuration.

General Electric chose a pure jet engine while Pratt & Whitney preferred a fan engine. Because of the selected wing configurations, there was almost no alternative to engine placement than under and at the rear of the wing similar to the Concorde. In addition to the evaluation that Magruder and his staff would do, ten qualifying airlines were invited to make their own assessments of the proposed projects.

To our surprise, SAS was honored to be one of three companies outside the US, which showed what a good reputation SAS technical and operational management had in the international aviation world. It probably was related in part to the pioneering efforts SAS had done like the polar flights and launches of the Caravelle, DC-8-62, and DC-8-63 programs. The two other companies outside the United States were Lufthansa and Japan Airlines. (Air France and BOAC perhaps were excluded because they were so involved with the Concorde.)

For SAS it meant a mission of a few weeks of intensive study in autumn 1966, together with the other invited airlines, and with the manufacturers in Seattle, Burbank, Cincinnati and Hartford. SAS analyses resulted in a recommendation to choose Boeing as an aircraft designer and General Electric as an engine producer. It proved to be the same choice as most airlines and also the FAA.

The continued work at Boeing with the prototype design showed eventually the choice of "swing-wing" was too difficult and costly. They were forced to move to a double-delta wing. In the US Congress resistance was growing ever stronger that the US government would bear the costs and the environmental movement was also having a greater influence. This meant that Congress finally stopped the entire operation in March 1971.

Boeing's final draft of its supersonic project. Photo Boeing.

Wide-body aircraft

Boeing 747, often called jumbo jet

The US Air Force announced in the mid-1960s, a competition to build a large transport plane, the C-5A. It would be about twice as large as the existing cargo planes and have a very large body volume. The three major aircraft manufacturers Boeing, Douglas, and Lockheed accepted the challenge and individually made proposals while General Electric and Pratt & Whitney made proposals for appropriate engines.,

Lockheed and General Electric won the competition, which was held in October 1965. All three aircraft manufacturers' proposals were double-deckers with a large cargo door in the nose to unload large vehicles and other military equipment.

Boeing, who helped in the preparation of the draft budget to get the project approved, was obviously disappointed. Boeing, which could not extend the fuselage of the 707-320, felt the strong need to find a solution to meet the Douglas success with their DC-8-61 and -63. Boeing decided to use the experience working with the military project to construct an airliner with a size that could be a commercial success. They did a market survey mainly among their own customers, who received basic data for aircraft with 250, 300, and 350 seats. Virtually all participating carriers preferred the largest airplane.

Hoping to win the competition for the C-5A, Boeing had already in the summer of 1965 appointed a small team of 20 people who began designing an airliner. In August of the same year Joe Sutter was appointed to lead the work in competition with Jack Steiner. Both of these engineers were extraordinarily skilled engineers with extensive experience with Boeing but Sutter was equipped with greater ability to cooperate than Steiner, who had a more dominant disposition. When the news came that Boeing lost the competition for the C-5A, many who worked on the project moved over to Sutter's group.

Many inside Boeing felt that the new plane should be a double-decker style like the 377 Stratocruiser and utilize much of the work on the C-5A military project. They also found support from PanAm where the boss Juan Trippe was a great advocate of the solution. Pan Am was very much involved in the design of the new plane from the beginning. There was also a widely spread view that the new plane would be relatively short lived as a purely passenger jet because the SST plane in a not too distant future would take over transoceanic and other long distance services and that the plane should therefore be planned so that it could be easily converted to a cargo aircraft.

A double-decker creates problems in loading and unloading of passengers and cargo when ramps are needed for easy handling of both decks. One challenge was the emergency evacuation of the passengers on the upper deck. According to regulatory rules, a fully loaded plane shall be evacuated within 90 seconds, which requires the existence of doors and emergency exits with inflatable slides that reach the ground with such an angle that passengers do not hurt themselves on impact. It happens in exercises and demonstrations that participants can get injured.

The competing group inside Boeing wanted a cabin that allowed up to ten seats across and was equipped with two aisles, a configuration that came to be called "wide-body." The width also meant that they could unload two standard containers with dimensions 8x8 feet, side by side, in a combination or all-cargo version of the plane. A pure circular shape of the cabin also resulted in providing a much larger lower cargo hold for spacious containers suitable for mechanical handling. The body would also be designed so that one could have cargo doors on both ends of the body and a folding nose.

The specification for the military C-5A specified that loading would be through a large door in the aircraft's nose which is why Boeing knew how this would be solved. They must, among other things, place the cockpit floor slightly higher than the top of the door's opening. The aerodynamic design of the cockpit had the result that the "hump" had to be extended aft. This gave room for a lounge that was initially considered to belong to the first-class

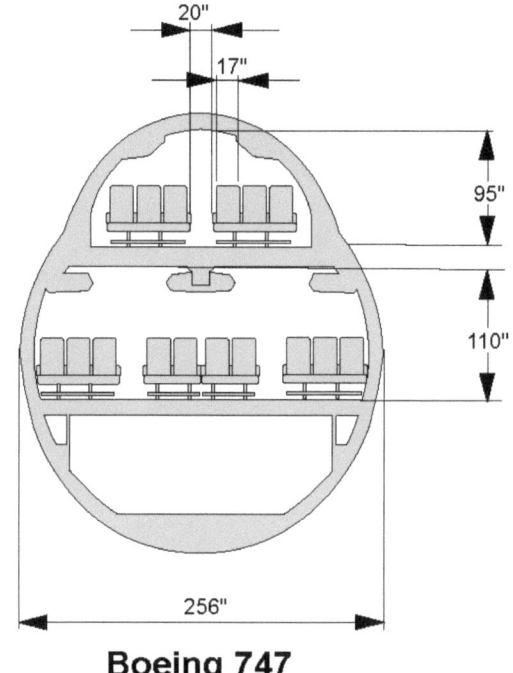

Boeing 747

The cabin cross section of the 747 at the front of the fuselage.
Drawing Hans Kampf.

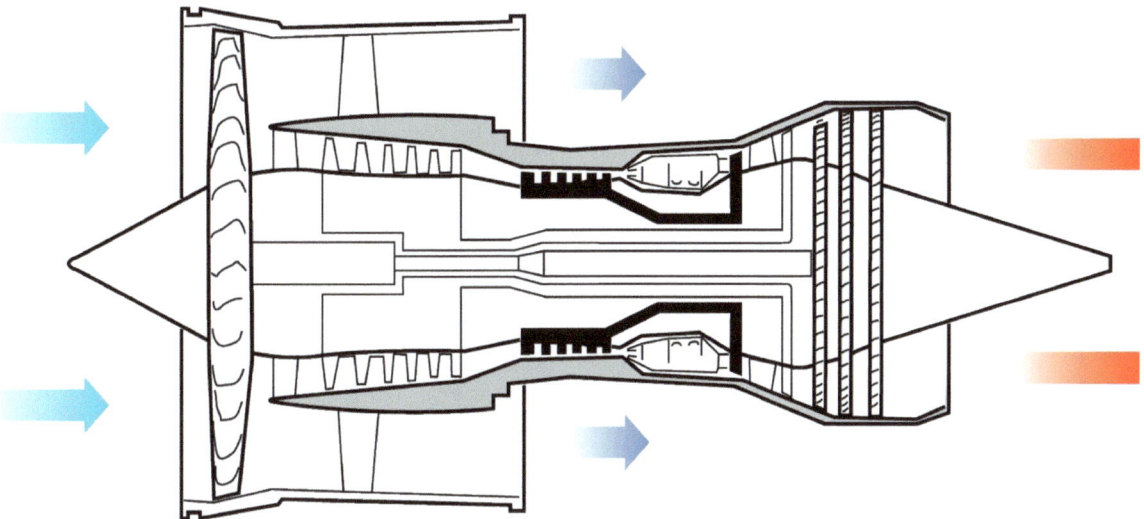

The truly large fan-engines have a much larger "by-pass" ratio than the early fan-engines. It was now possible to design engines with thrust of over 44,000 lb. Today's largest engines deliver more than 110,000 lb. of thrust Picture Hans Kampf.

section of the aircraft's nose, but that could also be used to increase passenger capacity.

The configuration came to be liked by more of Boeing's people but it was felt that they must have PanAm's approval before the design was fixed. Therefore a mockup of wood and plywood was made for each option.

They were made long enough so that they gave a proper perception of the space. Juan Trippe and some of his closest employees were invited to inspect them and they were all convinced that the wide-body option was the best solution. When the project thus gained firmer shape, it became formally designated the Boeing 747.

It turned out much later that PanAm on 22 December 1965 had written a "letter of intent" that involved 25 planes. This was known only by a few people within Boeing and PanAm but it made it easier for Sutter to get the additional resources he requested.

It was also of great interest to decide which engine would be selected. Normally, it is considered that an engine project needs a few years longer development time than an airplane but in this case the time available was also much shorter than desirable. Pan Am had in fact extensively argued that the first plane would be delivered before the year 1969 came to an end. Engine choice would be decided in early January 1966.

Both the General Electric and Pratt & Whitney engines that were proposed were of the high bypass type, i.e., they had a very large ratio between the air flow through the fan section and the air passing through the compressor and turbine. This type of engine could be given a thrust in the order of 50,000 lb. while "low-bypass" engines of the type that was used in the Boeing 707 and DC-8 had about a third as much thrust. It was the development of fan engines, which enabled the 747 program to get started.

General Electric chose a "by-pass" ratio of 8:1 while the Pratt & Whitney stayed at 5.5:1. The GE engine that was selected for the C-5A would be designed for a cruising speed of Mach 0.7, and a lot of other military requirements and it required a rather large revision to power the 747 that would have a cruising speed of Mach 0.85. Its thrust was assessed not to be sufficient for further development in accordance with Boeing requirements. Pratt & Whitney was however completely free in the design of the engine conditions, which was named JT9D, all according to Boeing and PanAm's requirements. On the other hand, the development costs of General Electric were to be paid by the Air Force, while Pratt & Whitney had to undertake the entire investment, which would affect the price of the engine. It took time for Boeing engineers to get the choice of the JT9D confirmed by their management and it turned out to be because a board member of PanAm also sat on General Electric's board!

The next important area to define was the wing aerodynamic design. To meet the requirements PanAm set, namely a cruising speed of Mach 0.85, a sweep greater than the 35 degrees that applied to the Boeing 707's cruising speed of Mach 0.82 was required. There were engineers at Boeing who wanted to go up to 40 degrees but compromised with 37.5 degrees. Boeing said that they learned so much from the experience of the Boeing 707 and later the wind tunnel, that it was envisaged to completely avoid the problem of "Dutch roll" even at the larger wing sweep. To secure good low speed handling during takeoff and landing, the so-called Krueger flaps at the wing leading edge and triple-slotted flaps were introduced. They later became a rather complicated mechanical structure, which resulted in a significant weight increase but gave the 747 extraordinarily good flight characteristics in the low speed range. The flap system had already been proven on the Boeing 727.

Another area that needed improvements was the landing gear because of the high aircraft weights. In supplement to the conventional main landing gear legs with four-wheel bogies that had their attachment points a bit out under the wing, another two were installed in the center under the body slightly aft of the wing-mounted main landing gears. These were also four-wheeled bogies and like the wing-monted they were retracted into the bottom of the fuselage and were covered with doors. The nose gear was conventional with two wheels. The plane then had a total of 18 landing gear wheels and a distributed load on ramps and runways so that it did not exceed the existing type aircraft and thus below the airport authorities' allowed values for existing airports. Boeing could also use the same wheels and tires as on the 707 which simplified tire spare stocks.

In early April 1966, the process of defining the plane's design and specification had come so far that the letter of intent document could be replaced by a contract containing prices and delivery times. The price is said to have been 22 million dollars and Juan Trippe demanded that the first plane would be delivered before 1969 ended. He also demanded that PanAm would get a large part of its 25 planes before any foreign competitor would get their first delivery. Bill Allen made a promise that if Boeing in August 1966 had not started building the 747, Boeing would pay Trippe $ 10 million. This suggests that work of the Sutter group up to April 1966 was regarded as a feasibility study and only then assumed the character of a launched program. Although the contract of April would be kept secret Boeing began to negotiate with airlines that were deemed to be interested in buying the 747 when PanAm fired the starting gun.

Among those contacted were American, United, TWA, BOAC, Lufthansa, and Japan Airlines. When so many companies were informed of PanAm's purchase, information began to leak and there was much speculation about how many orders Boeing needed before the actual manufacturing was launched. The numbers 40, 50 and 80 were mentioned. Prior to August was over, only Lufthansa and Japan Airlines had ordered three planes each! Despite the meager results Boeing started production. This meant that Boeing had only 28 months available to tackle this huge program.

It is usually claimed that aircraft manufacturers need three to five years to develop their product and an engine company should preferably have additional two years of its task. In this case, both should manage it in less than three years!

The incredibly ambitious program became very complicated because Boeing had not sufficiently large hangars to assemble an aircraft the size of the 747. Workshops and offices were not available to the extent needed and construction work was

The engine in SAS's 747 was the Pratt & Whitney JT9D-7 at a thrust of 47 000 lb. Bypass-ratio 5, weight 8,600 lb and fan diameterr 92 in.
Photo Pratt & Whitney.

initially carried out in widely dispersed facilities in the Seattle area.

After an intense search that analyzed places far outside Washington State, even down in California, they decided eventually on the small town of Everett, 30 miles north of Seattle. There was an airfield, Paine Field, a former military airbase which had long enough runways. But the area had to be developed extensively to provide space for the ramps and the large building complexes that would be built.
There was more earth moved than was the case when the Panama Canal was built. Boeing's own land adjacent to the airfield covered more than 1.6 square miles. The large hangar building erected was the largest ever in terms of volume.

Furthermore, a highway had to be built that connected with the existing highway from Seattle; and additionally a rail spur was built that connected with the existing network in the area. It had a slope that was higher than any other main rail in the US. A major reason for these road projects was that Boeing, both for manufacturing and in many cases also design, found it necessary to a far greater degree than previously to use subcontractors for large and bulky parts thus requiring that the transport roads permitted handling wider loads than the then-current standards.

When the design of the plane firmed up, and the facilities needed for the production had been resolved, Boeing started a marketing campaign that primarily was directed towards existing Boeing customers. The domestic US companies showed quite cool interest and many thought that the plane was too big for their networks; and they had already invested in the DC-8-61, which had the appropriate size for the near future. The situation was similar

747's complex aircraft landing gear.
Photo Boeing.

for the foreign airlines that in many cases such as SAS had chosen the DC-8-63 for their fleets. This was mentioned in the "DC-8 release" (internal information) the first week of June 1966 to highlight the likely development of the 747 program in preparation for the forthcoming purchase of some additional DC-8-63s. I was then completely ignorant of the existence of the PanAm letter of intent from December 1965, and their equally secret contracts from April 1966. Boeing had at that time not shown any interest in SAS and no one from SAS had visited them first half of 1966 to possibly be able to snatch up any information about what was going on.

My assessment was that a clear message to start production of the 747 would not come until well into 1967 and that it would take at least three years before the first customer would get his delivery. So it would be opportune to take advantage of some additional DC-8-63s before the competition would make them redundant. As already mentioned, my assessment of Boeing plans was not valid for more than a couple of months!

For Boeing's part, sales were sluggish even after the clear message in August 1966 that the development would be up and running. It was only in the autumn of 1967 that there was some increase in the number of orders. In October 1967 Boeing was able to report that 13 companies had ordered 85 planes. Among the European companies who ordered at that time besides Lufthansa, who decided in the summer of 1966, KLM was now included.

When SAS in December 1967 placed an order of two aircraft the decision was based on market competition assessments. A strange thing occurred in that the purchase of the hitherto most expensive aircraft was made without performing any detailed evaluation of the plane. Only the contractual analysis and performance guarantees had been studied. This does not mean that SAS took some big risks compared to PanAm, whose chief engineer John Borger throughout the aircraft's inception had followed the construction of the 747 in detail. He was widely known as one of the most knowledgeable and influential engineers in civil aviation. He was also a tough person who never left sight of the airline's interest. He almost stayed in daily telephone contact with the technical personnel at Boeing and visited them several times each month.

Because Swissair in early 1968 signed an order for the 747, KLM contacted both SAS and Swissair to find out if there was interest in KLM joining the existing cooperation between SAS and Swissair. The initiative was received with favor from both companies and a high level meeting was held. It was decided that the cooperation would be led by a "Management Group", which consisted of the companies' highest technical managers and some of their closest employees. The group became known as the KSS Group.

The three companies had dealt with their purchases independent of each other but it was decided that they would arrange a common specification of the aircraft so that the technical maintenance could be arranged in the same way that applied to SAS and Swissair and that the work would be distributed in an appropriate way. For the specification work two groups were established, one for interior and galley arrangements and one for the cockpit equipment. KLM's Gerry Lam led the first group and the SAS participant was Karl-Ingvar Segefelt from my department and Bjorn Erichsen from the catering side. I was appointed as leader of the cockpit group in which the participants were Vic Persson and Arne Vernblad from my department and captains Sture Bostrom and Karl-Erik Ternhem from the flight department. From Swissair Captain Ernie Hurzeler and engineer Ernst Bertoni participated. Three captains, Frank Hawkins, Chuck Ramsay, and George Malouin, represented KLM. The first two were Englishmen, and the third was American. As a technician Gerry Lam attended on the occasions when he led his own group.

Work in the cockpit group became a fairly lengthy story. SAS and Swissair were well interacted after the work done on the earlier types of aircraft. KLM had a somewhat different view of both arrangements and responsibilities between the left seat and right seat and this influenced the design in many respects. The whole thing was not helped by Boeing responding grudgingly when we wanted to implement changes to what Boeing and PanAm already agreed to. Boeing constantly had the attitude: "we know what is best for you." We had noticed that attitude in previous contacts on the Boeing 707 and 720 but were not worried, as those cases did not lead to any orders. Our counterpart at Boeing named Ed Pfafman, who had also been described by his manager Joe Sutter as "that stubborn Dutchman," did not facilitate the situation. He had a hard time understanding that what was accepted by the PanAm could not also fit our operating philosophy.

At one of the meetings of the cockpit group in Seattle, we got the opportunity to meet the PanAm chief pilot Scott Flower. He gave the impression of being very authoritarian and unwilling to discuss various alternatives to his own opinion.

The contrast with the open cooperation that characterized our cockpit group's attitude was most evident. It required not less than twelve meetings before the group was done with the specification. They were held alternately in Seattle, Copenhagen, Amsterdam, and Zurich.

The version of the 747 that PanAm and the earliest customers had ordered was designated 747-100. In PanAm's contract of April 1966 the plane had a max takeoff weight of 655,000 lb. It had somewhat later grown to 710,000 lb. The version the KSS Group ordered was designated 747-200B with a max takeoff weight of 714,500 lb. This version was developed because of several airlines' desire for greater range. Boeing introduced additional fuel tanks in the wing center section of the fuselage. The increased max takeoff weight also meant that Boeing forced Pratt & Whitney to supply the JT9 with higher thrust.

Since SAS signed a contract with Boeing in the usual way, a liaison office was established at the plant in Everett. The engineer Knut Jonn, who came from "Operations Engineering," was in charge there. The staff consisted of himself, plus a secretary and a smaller number of inspection engineers that varied according to the different stages of the manufacturing location with Boeing. The main task for them was to supervise the production of the SAS planes, follow the contractual provisions and otherwise be a link between Boeing and all visiting SAS employees. Through their daily contacts with various people in Boeing, Knut Jonn obviously got good insight into Boeing's way of working and could account for the interesting facts both in respect to earlier stages in the advent of the 747 and also current events. The group did not belong to my department but reported to the chief engineer at the headquarters, but was also very helpful in our work.

Boeing had during the design and manufacturing process major problems, mainly in four areas: the wing configuration, increased empty weight, engine accessibility and its function, as well as the cost picture. When the wing configuration was established and its aerodynamic performance was satisfactory it was found in further wind tunnel tests that the spanwise lift distribution was not acceptable and that there was a risk of flutter. An analysis showed that the wing should be twisted about three degrees to eliminate these problems. The drawings had already been forwarded to the workshops and to some ongoing manufacturing shops. A twist of three degrees would mean a redesign of the center wing box through the fuselage and it would be very costly and a significant delay of the entire program and possibly derail the entire project.

When the company management was informed about it they decided to let an independent group led by Jack Steiner design an entirely new wing. He assembled a group of 50 engineers to achieve this in the shortest possible time. Joe Sutter and his aerodynamics and structure specialists worked on his wing design and found that it was possible to solve the problem by only twisting the outer wing about 3 degrees outboard of the outer engine and the Steiner Group could end their work. The solution was named "The Sutter Twist."

As with most aircraft projects the 747 was affected by considerable increases in empty weight during development. It was not possible to extrapolate past experience because of the large difference in dimensions. Boeing had no experience in commercial aircraft of this size. The company management decided to establish a working group of highly qualified engineers who would do a complete analysis of the situation. They managed to trim the weight increases by just over 20,000 lb. and also additional changes that PanAm had demanded became the subject of an audit.

The working group wanted to trim the weight of the triple-slotted flaps installation by 1700 lb. through the transition to a double-slotted flap, but this would have meant an increase in landing speed of at least eight knots. PanAm did not accept the proposed deterioration in slow speed performance. It would violate the contractual guarantees.

The empty weight increases that nonetheless became necessary contributed to the max takeoff weight being gradually increased and that, in turn, required an increase in engine thrust. Pratt & Whitney had great difficulty in meeting the requirements and it resulted in significant delays in deliveries. They could also not meet the promised performance.

In addition to all these difficulties the cost situation become very difficult for Boeing. The Sutter group cost about five million dollars per day, and he was instructed to reduce the staff by 1000 people. He found it impossible to implement and he showed the management team that he instead needed an additional 800 people in order to meet the the delivery times commitments to PanAm.

There was no reduction in personnel, but instead he was allowed to schedule as much overtime as contracts permitted, which of course increased costs. Joe Sutter had more than 500 people employed within his own department and the production workforce was approximately 20,000 workers.

Boeing succeeded despite all the difficulties and with much fanfare arranged a customary "roll-out" on 30 September 1968. A roll-out is usually likened to a ship launch and means that the first completed aircraft of a new type leaves the final assembly hangar and is named while a champagne bottle is thrown against a protective steel plate mounted at the nose of the aircraft to protect the plane against any damage.

Some prominent person within the company or any well-known person in the industry, city, municipality or country usually performs the ceremony. In Los Angeles, it could happen that some famous movie star would be given the assignment.

Attendance tends to include a big part of the company's management and selected groups from relevant departments, representatives of the local political administration, and sometimes even from the government. Important people from the airlines that ordered the plane will of course also be invited. In Boeing's case, among other people, flight attendants in uniforms from the 26 companies, which at this time ordered the 747, were present.

In a perfect roll-out the plane should roll out on its own power if the hanger is formed so the exhaust air and gas flow from the engines do not damage the plant. In most cases the plane is towed by a tractor with a towbar attached to the nose gear in the same manner as is done at airports.

From the outside, the plane looked fully completed but it was far from it. The engines mounted on the airplane were completely unusable and many other installations were not complete. Boeing had set their sights on the first flight would taking place on 17 December 1968 in order to celebrate the 65th anniversary of the Wright brothers' first flight. But the plane was not sufficiently completed, so it forced them to delay the event until 9 February 1969.

Up until the first flight they worked feverishly to get the engine problems resolved and achieve the final assembly of everything that was not ready at the roll-out.

During the taxi tests it was concluded that the rear main landing gear tires were subjected to so much wear and tear on the turns that it was not acceptable; and that it required excessive engine thrust to make the turns that must be performed at airports. Sutter had realized that this would happen and had made a provision to make them steerable but his superiors decided at weight saving campaigns that would not happen. He was nevertheless prepared to make them swivel and could therefore in a rather short time solve this problem.

The first flight was carried out as planned,

Flight attendants from 26 customers attended the 747 roll-out in 1968. The SAS chief hostess Wivica Ancarcrona-Borell represented SAS and stands as No. 8 from the left. Boeing manufactured 830 aircraft of types 747-100 / 200/300. Photo Boeing

although in quite unsuitable weather and got a positive outcome despite a support to a flap broke and caused the flight to be shortened. Flight properties in the low speed regime and landing were very good and won the flight test pilots' appreciation. The concerns that have been questioned about the cockpit's great height proved to be no disadvantage, and the landing was carried out very satisfactorily.

However, in further exploration of the high speed envelope, which is a very troublesome procedure for all flight test engineers, "flutter" was induced, i.e. vibrations and oscillations that are often very difficult to determine, and not easy to correct. In this case it was found in further tests, with extensive instrumentation, that the reason was that self-oscillations of the outboard engine installation and the outer wing had the same or similar frequency range and therefore a natural attenuation.

Natural oscillation of the outer wing is dependent on the amount of fuel in the outer wing tanks but the aircraft has to be approved for all variations of fuel. Boeing would solve the problem for the very first part of the aircraft series by installing ballast weights in the engine pylons but later in the production changes to the pylons design would be introduced that eliminated the problem. The flight test program was delayed around a month because of these events.

Another major concern was the engines from Pratt & Whitney. They produced major disturbances both in increasing and reducing thrust and especially if the throttle movements were made relatively quickly. At a missed approach increased thrust must be available quickly to give maximum climb performance. The phenomenon is called "engine surge." Sometimes loud booms might accompany it with flames ejected from the engine and sometimes the surge causes the engine to stop running.

Another problem was that the engine's outer case, was insufficiently dimensioned such that it did not stay circular which gave rise to what was called "ovalization." That this was not detected during runs in test stands was unrelated to the engine when it was not subjected to the inertia forces and large gyral moment that occur during flight at sharp turns and especially in turbulent weather. The effect was that the turbine and compressor blades abraded on the case in some places and gave rise to glitches in some areas, which caused poor performance so that the promised fuel consumption could not be maintained. Until a redesign could be fitted, engines were fitted with an outer yoke that added rigidity to the entire engine assembly. This resulted in a significant weight increase.

Another major problem arose as Pratt & Whitney could not deliver acceptable engines at the pace required. At one time 17 almost completed aircraft were parked outside the hangars without engines and with concrete blocks mounted to prevent the plane from tipping over on its tail. During the flight test program some 80 engines were discarded or destroyed.

All the problems mentioned above, which resulted in significant delays and the use of maximum allowed overtime, left Boeing in great financial troubles and the entire company was very close to bankruptcy. Revenues from other successful programs were not enough to offset the enormous costs the 747 productions caused. But with the help of the banks and pulling together their own resources, Boeing did overcome even this predicament. It testified to a great inherent strength of the company and its management.

The PanAm contract required Boeing to deliver the first aircraft before the end of 1969. It managed to get the Certificate of Airworthiness on 30 December 1969 but delivery could not be made until a week into 1970. PanAm would start its first revenue flight on 21 January 1970, to London.

SAS and the KSS Group had decided to delay purchase of the 747 until the improved 747-200 version with more range became available. The 747-200 flew for the first time on 11 October 1970 and was certified on 23 December the same year. KLM became the first airline to put the type in service at the beginning of 1971

SAS's first aircraft was delivered on 22 February 1971 and had the serial number 114. The aircraft had of course a Viking name, which quite naturally was "Huge Viking!" The second plane was delivered on 12 November.

The SAS version could carry a maximum of 396 passengers and additionally about 20 tons of cargo. The rather late deliveries to SAS meant that the early purchasers and Boeing at that time had managed to gather valuable experience during the past period and it served SAS well. No major operational or technical problems had been revealed in addition to those already mentioned regarding the engines. From the point of view of passengers and crews it must be said that 747 was a great success.

As early as 11 February 1970 I had, through SAS New York office, received a freebie from PanAm for a trip to London. Because of fog in London the flight was diverted to Frankfurt so it resulted in a flight time of eight hours. The general impression from the trip was very positive. You get a completely different perception in a wide-body aircraft ; the presence of two passenger aisles and galley placement in the middle of the plane makes it possible for passengers to move about more in the plane. I was seated next to the windows and quite close to the galley. The only negative experience was that during turbulence I heard cracking and creaking sounds that came from somewhere. A request was made to Boeing to explain what this phenomenon

747 in SAS colors LN-AET Bjarne Viking. Photo Johan Ljungdahl.

was. It took a long time to find the cause and to come to terms with appropriate countermeasures. It was the attachments of the rear overhead bins and pantry sections to the fuselage that gave rise to them. They had not noticed this during the test flights since the units were not filled with their contents at that time. The fuselage is subjected to the asymmetric forces when the wings move during turbulence.

The first SAS aircraft was put into service 1 April 1971 on the route to New York and the other in December of the same year. It soon became clear that the 747 was not the ideal plane for SAS. It was too big for the number of passengers who from northern Europe could be channeled via Copenhagen to New York and return. Freight traffic showed a clear tendency to increase sharply and then Boeing developed a Combi version of the plane that became attractive for SAS. A small delegation from the company therefore traveled to Seattle to get acquainted with this option. It resulted in an SAS order of two aircraft with the objective to sell the two pure passenger jets.

Douglas DC-10

As already mentioned, there was great activity among manufacturers of aircraft and engines and airlines in the late summer of 1966 when it became clear that Boeing had started the 747 project. Boeing, Douglas, Lockheed, and General Electric and Pratt & Whitney had all participated in the competition for the military C-5A program that Lockheed won. All wanted to now use their experiences from that exercise also for civil projects. Douglas and Lockheed saw opportunities to develop new planes when the new big engines would become available. Rolls-Royce who did not participate in the C-5A project now saw a chance to get into the scene.

Many proposals, including double-deckers, saw the light of day but pretty soon it was clear that the solution would be a wide-body aircraft. A man who played a major role in this context was Frank Kolk, project engineer at American Airlines. He had in 1966 drafted a proposal for a plane that would have such a large cabin width that it could have a seating arrangement that allowed for two passenger aisles and seats for 250 people, have a range of approximately 2,000 nm, and designed for subsonic speeds. So it would be a much smaller plane than the Boeing 747 and would be a better fit for domestic services in the United States. There were also requests for takeoff performance that would allow traffic from LaGuardia Airport in New York that has both short runways and weight restrictions because some of the runways are built on piers in the water.

The plane came to be called Kolk´s Jumbo Twin. Douglas called it the DC-10 Twin, which was early evaluated including by Swissair which, however chose other solutions. Frank Kolk's proposals came to play a big role when it was time to launch the European Airbus project.

In America now Lockheed and Douglas started to prepare their proposals. They both came, however, to the conclusion that it was better to go for a three-engine plane that seats about 300 passengers and with considerably longer range than Kolk demanded. Several of the US domestic companies had requests for planes that could make Chicago-San Francisco,

McDonnell Douglas DC-10 Twin, a short-lived project. Illustration MDC

New York - San Francisco or Miami-Los Angeles nonstop. Moreover United wanted to have planes that managed the route from Denver to the West coast, which demanded good takeoff performance because of the airport's location at about 5,400 feet altitude and high summer temperatures. The close proximity of the Rockies also demanded good climb performance.

A crucial factor was that many organizations and groups at that time were reluctant to have only two engines on aircraft that could carry over 300 passengers over long distances and high terrain.

It first started with serious plans by Dan Houghton at Lockheed immediately after Lockheed had lost the competition to build the American SST in early January 1967. They tried initially to meet Kolk's idea of a twin-engine airplane but soon, as has been said, realized that it was best to go for a three-engine project, the L-1011. It took Douglas considerably longer to come to a decision. This was due largely to major organizational problems in connection with the merger with McDonnell. In late June 1967, however, McDonnell Douglas would announce the DC-10 project's launch.

The big question for both manufacturers was how to place the third engine. Lockheed decided to do the same as Boeing had done with great success on the 727, and also de Havilland with the Trident; i.e. build it into the tail section and employ an S-shaped air intake duct from the top of the fuselage down to the centrally located engine. Unlike the 727 and Trident planes the other two engines were positioned in front and below the wings on pylons in the same way as four-engine jet aircraft. The large and heavy high-bypass engines would have created excessive balance problems if tall were mounted at the tail. Douglas chose to place the third engine in the vertical tail section, with the air intake lower edge slightly above the fuselage. The solution required large reinforcements in the vertical tail section causing weight increases, but it was felt that the engine operating conditions were more important.

Both Lockheed's solution and Douglas's obviously resulted in big difficulties for engine maintenance and engine replacement. After the aircraft manufacturers had selected their configurations a feverish activity started at the engine companies. Pratt & Whitney was initially somewhat neglected, because it was well known in the industry that they had big problems in meeting Boeing's requirements. The choice was thus primarily between General Electric and Rolls-Royce, who now saw a chance to break into the American market in earnest.

Rolls eventually managed to win at Lockheed and became the only alternative on the L-1011. Boeing had refused Rolls-Royce because of their reluctance to accept the composite material Hyfil, chosen for the fan blades, and the perception that Rolls was not living up to adequately giving the airlines good product support.

Some of the domestic airlines tried to persuade Lockheed to select General Electric but this would have meant a substantial modification of the tail, since the GE engine was considerably longer than the RR engine. A change would have become very costly and would have shortened the passenger cabin by two rows of seats.

Douglas decided to choose General Electric's CF6 as the first engine option but was also willing to discuss the other engines. With the chosen engine placement they could without great difficulty install any of the three engine options. In many places, there was reluctance towards GE. The company's experience in civil engines was not particularly extensive and the GE engine in the Coronado was not impressive. A careful analysis of the engine and above all the possibility of further development were judged to be of great importance.

Among the US domestic airlines, they had hoped that the results would be better if they all chose the same manufacturer for both aircraft and engine. A certain amount of cooperation between airlines took place for once, but in the end individual analyses were conducted. To an unusual degree banks, finance companies, and even governments were involved. First to announce its decision was American Airlines, who chose Douglas but left open the engine question to see what others decided. United followed soon after and chose the DC-10 with the GE engine, followed by American's choice of GE. In contrast, Eastern, Delta and TWA chose the Lockheed L1011 with Rolls-Royce RB211 engines.

Such was the situation when SAS began to seriously study the possibility to procure aircraft in this size class. It worked in cooperation with KLM and Swissair in the same way as for the Boeing 747, with the addition that the French private airline UTA (Union de Transportes Ariens) wanted to join the group, which was well received.

The four companies would together make a joint order at the same time. One of the working groups established would conduct the common evaluation and prepare a specification that would apply to all. SAS again had the presidency of the group. Through much of the work that had been founded in collaboration regarding the Boeing 747, it went much easier and quicker this time.

KSSU Group, as it now was called, drew up its demands and a significant difference relative to the US requirements was a need for more range. KSSU required at least transatlantic range between the relevant capital cities and SAS wanted above all to reach the US West Coast, given that wide-body aircraft had to eventually replace the DC-8-62. The other KSSU companies also gladly saw that the range needed to be increased so that it became possible for longer nonstop flights. This led to a big competition between Lockheed and Douglas to meet these requirements. The long-range model that Douglas offered was designated DC-10-30 and had engines with greater thrust, enhanced fuel capacity, and some improvements in the wings.

Lockheed had major concerns because Rolls-Royce did not have the same opportunity to increase thrust on the RB211 as GE had with its CF6 and it took several years before Lockheed could offer a long-range version, the L-1011-500. The evaluation of performance gravitated therefore to Douglas's advantage. In the design audit the two planes were roughly equal, but the L-1011 was, as it would prove later, in some respects better but the differences did not receive enough attention from the KSSU Group. Some facts will be reported later.

During the specification work, the group greatly emphasized the flight deck equipment about which we were met at both companies with much greater understanding of modernization than we were met with at Boeing. Lockheed was also far more advanced in this area than Boeing but also, in relation to Douglas, were better in some respects. An American Airlines representative made the following statement: "Lockheed's avionics are the best in the business." Avionics is the sum of all electronic installations that are in an airplane.

The KSSU Group had intended to supplement the Douglas basic specification so that it was equal to or better than the L-1011's in these respects. We managed what was required, including something that came to be known as Area Navigation System. The flight could be pre-programmed from the control panels in the cockpit and implemented from takeoff to landing using the navigation instruments. The pilots' main task was to ensure that everything was carried out according to plan. In this way, it reduced their workload.

Furthermore, a registration system called "Aircraft Integrated Data System", AIDS, an installation that, from sensors in different parts of the aircraft, recorded desired parameters from up to 200 measuring points. The system was in

KSSU was estabilshed in 1969. Photo SAS.

addition to the so-called "black boxes" (which are in fact orange) that authorities require and which record the parameters needed for the investigation of incidents but above all for accident investigations. Recordings from AIDS are primarily intended to provide information on disruptions and malfunctions from different systems of the plane to facilitate troubleshooting. These and other enhancements made in the KSSU specification resulted in the most modern cockpit at that time.

One last big meeting was held in Copenhagen with the participation of people from the top managements and delegations from both Lockheed and Douglas. It was Douglas who won the competition, and with four companies performing jointly, prices and other contractual conditions became favorable. Shortly thereafter a small group from the four companies flew to the air show in Paris together to on 6 June 1969, announce KSSU's decision to sign orders and options on a total of 36 DC-10-30s.

For SAS there was at that time only a question of options, but Douglas wanted from a PR point of view, considering that it was a cancelable order, not to have to reveal that one of the companies was not yet ready to sign a binding order. The reason for SAS's position was that the capacity needs for the next few years were covered by the DC-8-62, DC-8-63, and the quite recently purchased Boeing 747. Of these options two were converted to firm orders in the fall of 1971, and three more planes somewhat later. SAS's own fleet then came to include five planes. After consultation with SAS Thai International also ordered two aircraft conforming to the SAS specification.

A consequence of SAS's actions was that SAS had to surrender the presidency of the specification group to Swissair, which according to the terms of the KSSU cooperation became the "leading airline" for the DC-10 and had primary responsibility for the maintenance of the DC-10 fleet; KLM took care of the overhaul of the CF6-50 engines. SAS participated in the ongoing specification work on the same terms as the other companies.

The first flight of the DC-10-30 was made in June 1972, and the first SAS plane flew in September 1974 and was delivered on 5 October. Another followed in November of that year and the other three in 1975 and 1976.

DC-10s suffered two catastrophic accidents that came to reduce both the airlines' and the passengers' confidence in the aircraft type before it could be restored. The first occurred in March 1974, before SAS received any deliveries. It was an aircraft from the Turkish company THY that, after takeoff from Paris during the climb around 13,000 ft. altitude, experienced an explosive decompression when the rear cargo door blew open because its locking mechanism was not completely secured. The result

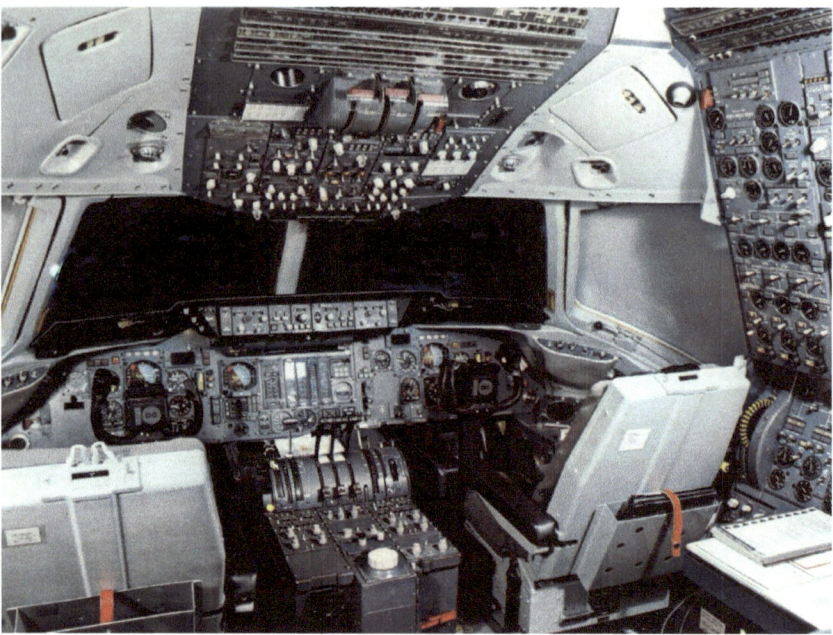

DC-10-30 Flight Deck. Photo SFF's archives.

was that the cabin floor gave way, the rudder lines to tail control surface became inoperable and the plane crashed with 346 fatalities.

The reason appeared to be that the latches had not been fully engaged when the cargo door was shut. This in turn was because they had not been inspected after an improper adjustment by the company's maintenance department. Loading staff in Paris had difficulty closing the door and had used excessive force to get the closing handle in the fully retracted position. It was noted by the accident investigation that revealed that one of the push rods that was included in the closing mechanisms had been damaged because of this. Douglas instructions and a sign at the handle pointed out that only hand pressure was allowed at closing. What good did a sign in English do when the staff could not read English!

It was further found that the electrical warning in the cockpit that pilots would check before start was based on the handle being in the right position and not that the latches were properly engaged.
A similar event, with a broken cargo door up at about 13,000 ft. altitude, had occurred at American Airlines in June 1972 but without failure when the pilots managed to land the aircraft in spite of very serious damage to the aircraft. Even in this case force had been used so that the pushrod had been deformed. Douglas had after the incident recommended the installation of a guide for the push rod to prevent deformation. The US Federal Aviation Administration, FAA, unfortunately had not issued any mandatory requirements (AD note) that this modification should be incorporated.

In the Paris case it proved that the modification had not been introduced to the Turkish plane despite Douglas's inspection documentation showing that this was the case.

SAS DC-10 had 260-280 seats, a significant increase in passenger capacity compared to the DC-8-63 and also increased freight volume. Douglas made 446 DC-10 aircraft.
SFF archive.

Douglas's own organization received strong criticism for these events and the FAA had to endure very harsh accusations for not intervening stronger after the first incident. The accident and incident showed that the cause was improper maintenance and operation of the ground staff. It could have been avoided with a better design so that the indicator in the cockpit had been based on the locking rod's position and not the handle's.

This had apparently not been noticed by the airlines at their audits, nor by the authority. Even the KSSU Group had missed this deficiency. A seemingly relatively small error that had a huge impact.

The second accident affected American Airlines in May 1979, i.e. after SAS had taken delivery of its first two planes. During a takeoff from Chicago the plane just before lift-off lost one of the wing engines that was torn from its mounts. The plane became uncontrollable and crashed and all 273 on board were killed.

The investigation quickly showed that the wing engine mounts were damaged before the accident happened. American had, like a few other companies, adopted a different procedure for engine replacement than what Douglas prescribed. Instead of using the fixtures and procedures that Douglas described they had carried out the engine replacement using a forklift pushing the four ton engine package from below into the mounts to save time, instead of having the engine package hanging from above and fitting it without external loads. With this handling the mounts in the attachment were damaged and cracks emerged that reduced the strength. When the engine was torn off it damaged the hydraulic system so the leading edge flaps on the same side retracted, creating an asymmetric situation that the pilots could not master. Furthermore stall warning also disappeared and the pilots thought they had only lost thrust from the engine and could not see from the cockpit that it had departed the plane.

The accident led to the grounding of the DC-10 for 38 days until all the aircraft had been inspected and repaired. Because none of the European companies had used the wrong maintenance method, inspections were carried out faster and with the help of Swissair, which is responsible within KSSU for the DC-10. As a result, the European authorities accepted that the ban time could be reduced with respect to these airlines.

The circumstances surrounding the above accident led to a special commission being established in the US to examine the circumstances of the case in detail because even the US authority was subjected to harsh criticism for not intervening at an early stage in order to eliminate the shortcomings revealed.

The DC-10 became the subject of an analysis, which came to be more extensive than for any other plane. The aircraft was compared quite naturally with the other two wide-body planes of the same design generation. The analysis was particularly concerned with hydraulic and flap systems. Both the Lockheed L-1011 and Boeing 747 had four independent hydraulic systems while Douglas had three. Caravelle also had three independent hydraulic systems. Furthermore, the Boeing 747 and L-1011 had mechanical locks for the flap systems in the extended position, while the DC-10 was dependent on hydraulic pressure to keep flaps in position. The two other planes had hydraulic lines placed on the back of the rear wing spar, while the DC-10 had them at the front of the front spar, where they were more vulnerable to damage if an engine would be dislodged.

The conclusion of the very detailed audit was that Douglas designs got full approval and the DC-10 was considered to be equivalent to the others in terms of safety. Although this time the airlines and the FAA got more critique than the manufacturer.

The two accidents have been reported to illustrate some of the types of problems that an examination and evaluation of aircraft may be dealing with. The struggle between Douglas and Lockheed can be illustrated, e.g. by the fact that Douglas eventually sold more than 400 DC-10s, most of which were long-range versions of the DC-10-30 while Lockheed's sales figures ended up with about 200 planes. Douglas later sold about 60 KC-10s to the USAF as air refueling aircraft.

Lockheed had to withdraw from the civilian market mainly because Rolls-Royce could not maintain its planned program for the RB-211 because the company was forced into bankruptcy and was nationalized. A contributing factor was the problem Rolls-Royce encountered with the Hyfil blade that they had chosen for the engine. It turned out that they did not pass the ingestion test when ice and birds are thrown into the engine and therefore had to turn to titanium blades, which resulted in an increase in weight of 550 lb. per engine. Another factor was that Rolls-Royce could not increase the thrust of the engine until late in the program, which is why Lockheed could not offer a long-range version of the L-1011 in time. Lockheed also failed to meet its promised fuel burn performance.

The airline cooperation group within KSSU caused the aviation authorities of the countries concerned to establish a corresponding group, NSSF, (Netherland, Scandinavia, Switzerland, France) in order to create common rules for the maintenance and operation of the KSSU planes. NSSF also carried out a joint type audit of the DC-10-30 during the period 1970-1974. The Safety Authority in Sweden designated Ulf Abrahamsson to represent the Scandinavian authorities. As part of the DC-10 type review, NSSF conducted several visits to MDC. The disastrous consequences of a loss in pressure in a DC-10 cargo hold for any reason, was pointed out by NSSF. Earlier MDC was aware of the seriousness of this possibility but deferred to the FAA which approved the DC-10.

Boeing saw that interest in the so-called Tri-jets was large and studied a minor 747 variation with three engines, two under the wing and a third engine in the tail, similar to the 727 configuration. The project was discontinued after a short time. In contrast, Boeing made a special version, the 747SP with a 46 ft. shorter body, which was designed for the really long range but was sold only 45 units. The short body required a significantly taller fin.

Boeing 747 SP with accommodations for 285 passengers in a three-class configuration. Photo Boeing.

Airbus A300

Sud Aviation had initially success with the Caravelle, which was the first jet that proved suitable for short- and medium-haul traffic. It was, however, later superseded by the DC-9 and Boeing 737. The reason was that the latter planes had more advanced wings and more dependable and economical engines in the form of the Pratt & Whitney JT8D, compared to the Rolls-Royce Avon that existed on the Caravelle. Sud Aviation later developed a Caravelle version that was equipped with the JT8D but not even that variant could withstand competition from Boeing and Douglas.

It was natural that Sud Aviation then studied a replacement. Efforts resulted, among others, in a project called Galion but it did not create any great interest. In this situation, Sud Aviation became interested in Frank Kolk's specification for a twin-engined widebody aircraft with high-bypass engines as already mentioned in the DC-10 section. In the US, this resulted in the development of the three-engine DC-10 and L-1011.

Sud Aviation now saw the chance to take advantage of the option that Kolk outlined and started, under Roger Beteilles' management, to study the project that later became known as the Airbus. In the meantime, people in England established a commission, headed by Lord Plowdon, which would study the European aircraft industry's future role. It submitted its report in December 1965, and emphasized that the British operations should be coordinated and concentrated to a greater extent and that cooperation should also be established with companies on the continent, especially with France and Germany. The manufacturing industry began to undergo major structural changes with a strong consolidation that reduced the number of manufacturers of large commercial aircraft significantly.

In the US Convair had already ceased its airliner

production in the 1960s. Lockheed had difficulty competing with Boeing and Douglas, and in 1983 delivered the company's last civilian aircraft, a Lockheed L-1011 TriStar. During most of the 1970s it was also unclear how the Airbus consortium would develop and if the English industry could retain its own development skills, at least for regional aircraft. Netherland's Fokker was still independent, but a rapidly growing regional aviation market did however, lead to several new manufacturers being added, among others, French-Italian ATR, Embraer of Brazil, Spanish CASA, and the Swedish Saab. The trend among engine manufacturers went in the same direction and there were now really only three manufacturers of large jet engines: Pratt & Whitney (PWA), General Electric (GE) and Rolls-Royce (RR). It resulted in the aircraft manufacturers now often quoting their large aircraft with three engine options. For airlines it meant separate negotiations with the engine manufacturers.

General Electric and SNECMA of France jointly established in the early 1970s a partnership, named CFM International, to develop an entirely new engine family, the CFM56. The engine has, after the usual introductory problems, been a great success. Eventually this caused Airbus Industrie to be established in May 1969 as a Franco-German organization for the development of the A300 aircraft, a wide-body aircraft for about 300 passengers, optimized for short- and medium-haul traffic.

In the beginning England was not part of Airbus Industrie but Hawker Siddeley Aviation still got the responsibility to design and build wings for Airbus. It was felt that the company was clearly the best of all possible options.

France was responsible for the technical and industrial coordination while Germany took care of the fuselage and the cabin furnishings. In terms of engine choice General Electric emerged victorious with the CF6-50 engine. An agreement was made with Douglas to purchase the entire engine installation design including the pylon from the US company. This choice was certainly influenced by European airlines who, at the time, had ordered the DC-10 with the GE engine. It was estimated that it would be easier to sell the plane in the United States if it was fitted with American engines. General Electric had also reached an agreement with the French engine company SNECMA that they would be involved both in the design and the manufacture of some parts of the CF6 engine. This agreement came about despite the fact that Pratt & Whitney owned 11% of SNECMA!

There was however in the beginning quite slow progress in raising any greater airline interest in the Airbus. There was also a slight hesitation in French government circles, who had the responsibility for the Concorde project being completed. They wondered if Sud Aviation, which at that time had been renamed Aerospatiale, had the resources to even play a key role in Airbus Industrie. To Roger Beteilles´ aid came Henri Ziegler, who was a very experienced technician with great confidence in many French quarters, including the government and together they succeeded in continuing with the Airbus plans. During the period up to the end of 1977 they had sold only 38 planes to four companies from the start of deliveries in 1974. But the new management team worked tirelessly and continued the production. At one point 16 unsold completed planes were lined up at the Toulouse airport.

In the spring of 1978 the tide turned and the completed planes were quickly sold. A contributing factor was the rapidly rising fuel prices and increased competition, which required larger and more fuel-efficient planes and only Airbus had something to offer for short- and medium-haul traffic. By the spring of 1979 over 250 planes had been sold, including 20 to Eastern, the first US customer.

SAS and Airbus

In the spring of 1977, SAS became interested in Airbus. The reason was that traffic on some routes had increased to such an extent that we began flying two DC-9s almost in parallel on routes like Stockholm - Copenhagen, Stockholm - Oslo, Stockholm – Luleå, but especially Copenhagen - Paris and Copenhagen - London. It was easy to show that it was financially and operationally advantageous to have a fuel-efficient plane on these routes which was twice as large. It saved on flight crew costs, including on the pilot side, the most expensive category of personnel. Congestion in the air and at airports increased and it was thus easier to get the coveted slots.

After an extensive investigation a contract was signed in December 1977 for two aircraft and options of a further ten planes. Through the cooperation that already existed within KSSU it was decided that it would be desirable to also seek a common specification for this aircraft since all intended to procure Airbus equipment. The same specification group, already established for the DC-10, was commissioned to implement one for the

The number of manufacturers of large commercial aircraft in Europe was reduced to one company, Airbus, and included the German, French, English and Spanish industries. Picture Ulf Abrahamsson.

Airbus A300 SE-DFK.
Photo Johan Ljungdahl.

Airbus. At that time SAS also received the chairman role, thanks especially to the long experience SAS had when it came to cooperation with the French manufacturer.

The basic specification that the work was based on had the designation A300-B2 but there was also a variant called the Airbus A300-B4, which had a slightly different wing box, which could be utilized for a large center tank that essentially would extend the range of the plane. SAS chose the body of the B2 version with the B4 version wing but without the installation of the tank arrangement. This addition could be implemented later if the need arose.

In the contract SAS had reserved the right to optionally select a different engine type than than the General Electric CF6, i.e., the same as in the case of the DC-10-30. SAS management, on the New Year 1978, took advantage of this possibility. It was the beginning of numerous complications. In the negotiations for the coming KSSU cooperation regarding Airbus aircraft, it was determined that KLM would be responsible for the maintenance of the CF6 engine. With SAS's departure from this plan it was perceived an unfair act and it was not considered appropriate that SAS would retain the chairmanship of the specification work which was then transferred to Swissair. But otherwise the work continued unchanged.

Before the decision on the engine selection I had done what I could to prevent this development but I was gagged and had to keep quiet about my idea. The background to the decision was that the engine maintenance for SAS engines would be at SAS Linta shops where all Pratt & Whitney engines for KSSU's Boeing 747s were overhauled. Concerns about the work situation at Linta outweighed considerations of collaborative partners and operating economy.

To possibly avert this development General Electric offered at no cost to supply all necessary equipment to SAS Linta that they could also perform the CF6 engine overhaul. This offer by GE was viewed with disapproval from KLM's side.

My resistance was caused by, among other things, the fact that the JT9D engine was considerably heavier than the CF6 and had higher specific fuel consumption. In addition, the choice of another engine meant a later delivery and required extensive test flights. Certification and development problems would cost Airbus more than 190 million francs.

Unfortunately all this caused big problems. Airbus had bought the entire engine installation from Douglas and GE with the associated pylon. It was found from test flights that problems arose with the JT9D engine installation. Airbus contacted Douglas to get assistance from the chief aerodynamicist Dick Shevell to solve the problems.

There was another factor contributing to the SAS management's decision. Pratt & Whitney had

Bengt Rehn signs the delivery documents for SAS's first A300 Snorre Viking, 1980 in Toulouse. Photo Ulf Abrahamsson.

launched another improvement of the JT9D engine for the 747, a version that received the designation JT9D-7Q. SAS was interested in installing it on their 747 aircraft. The engines on SAS planes had the designation JT9D-70A and could be modified to the version JT9D-59 that would be installed on the Airbus. It virtually only needed modification of the engine mounting points and a different positioning of the auxiliary components. By ordering new engines for the 747 planes and transferring the existing 747 engines to the Airbus this would be a beneficial program.

An agreement was signed with Boeing to install the new JT9D-7Q engines on two 747 aircraft. SAS also decided that out of the eight options for the Airbus two would immediately be switched to firm order positions. SAS planning assumed that additional options would be changed to firm orders. So SAS ordered engines from Pratt & Whitney for the additional 747s but when the expansion plans for the Airbus fleet were later not excercised, some engines were canceled with hefty cancellation costs.

New CEO

In August 1978 Knut Hagrup left the position as SAS's CEO. Carl-Olof Munkeberg took over and he had to, among other things, take care of the cancellation of engines as mentioned above. Munkeberg started to introduce business class on longhaul flights and implemented it on the DC-10 fleet with a section behind the first class cabin. It can be said that he started the big change that would come later when Jan Carlzon in1981 took over as CEO.

The first A300 delivery took place on 14 January and the second on 10 March 1980. In Toulouse SAS had, as technical representative and control manager, Bengt Rehn, who also had a presence there in connection with the purchase of the Caravelle. Delivery negotiations were protracted; as SAS aircraft with JT9D engines did not comply with the performance guarantees. Fuel consumption was found to be about five percent too high. SAS demanded that Airbus commit to making the changes necessary to achieve the right level.

When Jan Carlzon in 1981 became CEO of SAS the traffic policy was changed radically. The idea to replace the duplicate DC-9 routes with the Airbus was given up directly. DC-9 flights were distributed more evenly across the day and there were more direct flights between Stockholm and Oslo and the European metropolises. Passengers would not be bothered with the stopovers in Copenhagen and thus in many cases avoid having to change aircraft. The Airbus epoch was therefore quite short at SAS and then because the aircraft had the odd JT9D-59 engine, it became very difficult to sell and was therefore transferred as a first step to Scanair.

Before this occurred and deliveries of the ordered aircraft, SAS actively participated in the specification and negotiations with the Airbus consortium. The KSSU Group strove to apply as much as possible of the work that occurred for the DC-10 to standardize especially the cockpit so pilot training and flight operations would be simplified. The group was also trying to include relevant parts of new technological developments that had taken place in the meantime.

What was most interesting was a further shift to electronic instrumentation and introducing what is known as "fly-by-wire" to transmit commands from the levers to the rudders electrically instead of the usual rudder cables. The KSSU group, however, entered into this work too late to influence the design of the systems for the A300.

The KSSU group, however, had an interest to draw up a specification even for later versions of the Airbus, with a shorter body and smaller wing, which came to be called the A310. For this variant the KSSU Group played a not insignificant role when it came to implement the new features and additionally providing an even more extensive digitization and application of electronic instruments in the cockpit.

For Airbus the development, the manufacturing, and extensive sales meant that the company took a decisive step into the international aviation industry. SAS demands that Airbus should adjust their standards and procedures for the international market gave good returns for both the Caravelle and the subsequent Airbus types.

SAS is probably the only international airline that had a technical director, Olof Carlstein, who was awarded the Legion of Honor for his contributions to French aerospace industries.

The DC-9 regained a favourable position in the fleet to match the new strategy of the new CEO Jan Carlzon
Photo Lennart Berngard

Reflections by Birger Holmer

Some general reflections may be in order regarding the evaluations, specifications and contract designs that were made during the period between 1945 and 1981 as outlined above. In the case of an aircraft evalution there were hardly any lessons to be learned from the available literature, text books and syllabi or teaching, at for example, KTH in Stockholm.

In 1945, even the teaching of Aeronautics was a subdivision in Shipbuilding technology. There was one Professor in the subject and some assistants. However, some eminent engineers had been educated whom primarily Saab and the Air Force employed. The emphasis in teaching had for obvious reasons, been in the design and manufacture of aircraft and not for evaluation and operation. A large part of the engineers in aeronautics were graduated from the school of Mechanical Engineering, and had supplemented their knowledge in the aeronautical field through self-study and specialized courses.

Of the leading engineers in ABA, as the war neared its end, there was only one Master of Science, namely KH Larsson and he was graduated as a mechanist. The others, Charles Lignell, Bo Hoffstrom and Olaf Carlstein had lower engineering degrees. All, however, were highly talented and highly experienced in aircraft operation and they had together developed methods for how to conduct audits of interesting aircraft projects for the company.

Faced with the imminent enlargement of air traffic they had during the last year of the war begun to recruit a number of engineering graduates with adequate training but also several engineers in various fields of technology. When I got to ABA in mid-1945, there were people with extensive knowledge and experience that one also had quickly to acquire.

In addition to these assets one could, from reports and presentations that flowed from the manufacturers' sales engineers and the brochures they handed out, create a good basis to supplement and develop the skills and methods that already existed within the company.

There were neither in Sweden or Scandinavia any other companies with similar or higher skills that could offer opportunities for exchanges of these problems. On the European front initially the competitive situation was an obstacle for further discussions. In contrast, we found that it was easier to discuss with the US airlines that only operated domestic flights and had no plans on Atlantic traffic.

K.H. Larsson had during his long stays in America during the years 1944 and 1945 fostered good contacts mainly with United Airlines. He worked out an agreement with United's chief engineer Bill Mentzer that an ABA engineer would get the opportunity, during about two months, to visit the United technological base in San Francisco and follow in detail the process of preparing for deployment of the DC-6 into service in 1947.

I was lucky enough to be chosen for this mission and got my own desk at their engineering office and free access to all the information I asked for. The collaboration with their engineers at many different levels became very instructive. There was only one small catch. I could not bring back any materials of original issue and not make copies of the documents but needed to transfer all information to my own notes. The result of this long visit became among other things, a good insight into how a large and influential airline operates; good technical information and important contacts for future use. It may be mentioned that ABA / SAS came to play a similar role when it came to the German and Italian efforts to reestablish themselves in European airspace after the war. They did not feel welcome in the former war-torn countries. But with the Swedish neutrality and liberal attitude it was arranged that, the technical director of Lufthansa, Dr. Kressner, got to spend a few months in Stockholm to study our organization and methods. In the same way Ernesto Eula of Alitalia came to stay some considerable time at Bromma.

Cooperation between international airlines.

In general, the technical cooperation between international airlines is stunningly good, but it had a little sluggish start. The International Aero Transport Association (IATA) was formally introduced in 1919 to coordinate the participating companies' common interests.

The work was interrupted during World War II but was revived after the war ended. It was then that the scope was widened and came to include a "Technical Committee" that would protect companies' common interests among each other, the authorities, and manufacturers. IATA became an airline industry parallel to the state authorities' organization, "International Civil Aviation Organization" (ICAO), a body under the UN. The intention was to coordinate joint operational rules for civil aviation operations. Both IATA and ICAO placed their organizations in Montreal, Canada so that they could work together. In the media and in the public eye IATA is often perceived as a price cartel, but its role has been, among others, coordinating traffic and economic aspects in order to facilitate that passengers will be able to travel on flights that need the participation of two or more operators to complete the desired trip.

In addition to these areas, IATA has been of

great importance in coordinating the technical, operational, economic, and legal aspects of air transportion.

One area that has received particular importance is the safety of aviation in all its forms. It is an area in which airlines, manufacturers, and authorities have a strong common interest. This has greatly influenced airline efforts and has been the basis for the openness and accommodation that has been proven in most cases. As this spirit has been spread it has opened the doors between the technical departments of airlines. The competitive situation has been ignored in these areas and handed over to the commercial departments.

Manufacturers have jumped on this trend and often invited large groups of airlines to conferences and symposia as they talked about their products and plans in order to get some other airlines' views on the proposed solutions to common problems or trends at an early stage.

Furthermore, some attempts have been made to establish collaboration between some airlines that had common interests. As mentioned above in the DC-6B section, SAS made early reconnaissance trips to KLM, Sabena, and Swissair. It did not lead to any result but shortly thereafter just three of the companies' established limited cooperation for the Convair 240/340 aircraft. When SAS and Swissair much later began collaborating with the DC-8 and later the Convair Coronado, it was followed shortly thereafter by the Caravelle. Only a few years later, the time was ripe to extend it to include the Boeing 747 for the KSS Group and later extended to include also UTA when it came to the DC-10. Similar arrangements were made for the Atlas Group, which consisted of Air France, Alitalia, Lufthansa, and Sabena. You could learn from each other and develop evaluation methods and specification development. A further point is that the SAS was one of the companies that wanted to belong to the elite among the companies working in the same traffic areas as SAS and thus be competitive with respect to service and reliability. To achieve this, the company had to closely monitor developments in all relevant areas and be prepared to purchase the best available aircraft types. This meant that the company often had to choose aircraft at a time when the interesting plane was only on the drawing boards.

The choice between the Boeing 707 and DC-8 was a good example of that. The Dash 80 was an experimental plane in many respects, but gave a good indication of what could be expected of the final version. The evaluation of Douglas projects was based on sketches and calculations, and experience from previous types. It was, in most cases, only the major airlines venturing into such evaluations while smaller companies delayed purchase until the large companies sold their planes to replace them with even better versions. It was thus the secondhand market at low prices that largely supplied that market with airplanes.

To illustrate the situation, I would like to relate a statement that was made in 1955 by the then fairly new SAS president Throne-Holst when he became irritated by SAS Group spending so much time on the US West Coast to analyze the Boeing 707 and DC-8 before a conclusion was made. He expressed the opinion that it could not possibly be more difficult than choosing the type of car between Ford and Chevrolet. He eventually got better insight into the problem and was an excellent manager to work for during the later aircraft selections.

Criteria and priorities during the evaluation and specification work.

For evaluations of aircraft, engines, and other equipment, the following priorities were followed:
1. Safety in all its aspects.
2. Regularity and availability for airline traffic.
3. Passenger comfort and service.
4. Operational economy

This priority order can appear surprising at first. But if the first three are not met, one cannot expect that revenues and expenses will meet expectations. An airline or aircraft may not see the expected number of customers unless these areas are cared for in a satisfactory manner.

United Airlines manager Bill Patterson made a statement which loosely translated means: "What importance have seat mile costs got if the passengers gather around competitor departures."
Perhaps these were the same ideas of Jan Carlzon when he felt that the Airbus purchase did not give the desired effect on the revenue side.

Safety

The authorities' manufacturing regulations and operating regulations largely control the security but it is the responsibility of each manufacturer and airline to ascertain that they additionally have a policy to develop their own safety philosophy.
It would be too extensive to go into detail on how to do this but a reporting system exists, which among others the US Agency requires, namely that daily reports of errors and incidents that occur both in flight and on maintenance operations on the ground be sent to the manufacturer who, in turn, distributes the information to all known customers of the respective aircraft. In addition to reporting it is required that the manufacturer prepare repair and modification instructions with recommendations or requirements. If necessary, the authority will issue so-called "Airworthiness Directives" (AD), to define within what period of time errors must be corrected. In particularly important cases grounding of aircraft can be ordered. All this documentation

is of course essential reading for the staff involved in the evaluation and specification.

Special attention is also given to published accident reports issued after accidents. Aircraft structure will be examined in detail regarding the aircraft's wings, body, rudders, flaps, and landing gear. In addition to the purely static load conditions the design is scrutinized especially with respect to dynamic forces and fatigue strength.

Two concepts have special meaning in this context, namely the "fail safe" and "safe life." It is important that the structures be designed so that they can function even if some tearing and cracking occurs during operation. The elements that can not be treated so that they can function safely until repairs or modifications are carried out, must be designed to have safety margins for the longevity required, ie, SAFE LIFE. This causes extensive fatigue tests that must be performed and reported for these details. Attention is directed to the attachment points for engines, rudders, flaps, fuselage, and landing gear. Much attention is directed toward the cockpit design and all the instrumentation and controls, as well as the autopilot and navigation systems. Much effort is put into making the design such that the pilot's workload is as low as possible by extensive automation. Autopilots and navigation software allow the crew's attention to be concentrated on monitoring that everything works, so that they only need to manually take control during the most critical flight phases, namely takeoff and landing.

Regularity and aircraft availability

In addition to caring for flight safety, it is required that an airline exhibit high dispatch regularity of the airplane, and that the company obtain passengers' confidence. This requires great attention in many fields including things not directly related to the aircraft and safety.

Furthermore, it is important that everything is done to facilitate the embarkation of passengers and their disembarkation so that the time on the ground between flights is kept as short as possible. The same is valid of course for baggage and cargo. The design of the cabin layout and galleys holds great importance in this context. An airplane can generate revenue only when it is in the air.

Passenger Comfort and service

In assessing a transport aircraft's attractiveness and earnings potential, great importance must be given to the design of the fuselage so that cabin interior and cargo holds are made effective.

The cabin cross-section is of great importance in view of the seat arrangements that are selected. As emphasized above, the outcome will be different if it is "five-abreast" or "six-abreast." For wide-body aircraft, the variations can be considerably more. In general it can be said that it is best to try to arrange as much flexibility as possible since experience shows that interiors arte often changed during the aircraft's lifetime.

Ever since pressurized cabins were introduced, it has been necessary, for strength and weight reasons, that the fuselage has a circular cross section. It usually turns out necessary to select the "doubled-bubble" arrangement to meet all requests, i.e. two circular segments joined at the floor; the upper for passengers and lower for freight and baggage.

In order to vary the number of seats in width and seat pitch in the lengthwise direction, it is necessary to introduce seat attachment rails whose location must be carefully studied. This type of floor rails Bo Hoffström designed for the reconfiguration of the DC-6 in the early 1950s became an industry standard that is still alive and currently has found a footing in the automotive world.

The arrangements of the overhead racks need close attention as they have great influence on the possibilities to meet passengers' wishes to carry cabin baggage which has become increasingly important over the years. The design also has great significance for the aesthetics of the cabin and for availability and accessibility by passengers.

Placement of galleys and their construction is of great importance to enable the level of service and the flexibility required. They should also be easy to load and provide a good working environment for the cabin crew.

It is customary that the aircraft manufacturer defines seats and galleys as "Buyer furnished equipment" (BFE), i.e., it is the customer who buys these directly from the available providers and therefore has full responsibility for their design and delivery to the aircraft manufacturer. It is partly in these areas that the airlines show their individuality.

Aircraft evaluation

It may be useful to briefly describe how SAS analyses and evaluations of airplanes were done during 1950-1970. Among the first documents that aircraft manufacturers presented for the airlines were often a Payload/ Range chart that indicated the aircraft capacity both in terms of number of passengers, freight potentail and range. The graph shows the payload according to SAS's assessment of some long-haul aircraft.

The horizontal lines showing the aircraft's maximum load, is controlled either as a structural limit by the "Maximum Zero Fuel Weight", (MZFW), or a volume-limited load, i.e. the number of seats with a standard weight for passengers including luggage and weight in the cargo holds of a specified density. The calculation also includes a default value for the reserve quantity of fuel, which is always required.

Payload-Range diagram showing the aircraft's cargo capacity in tonnes as a function of range.
Image Ulf Abrahamsson

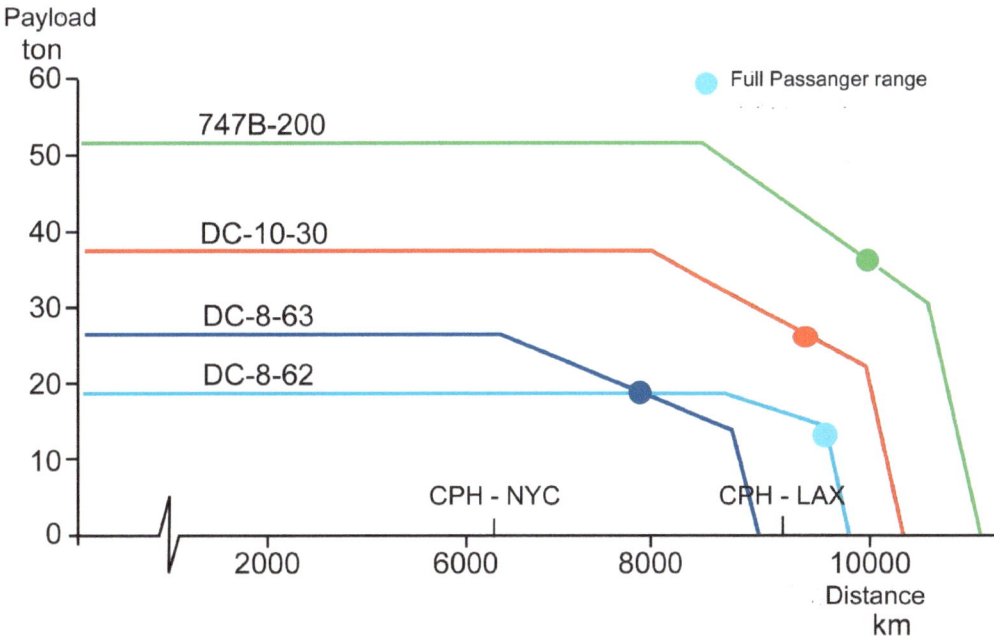

The gently sloping line gives the range limit as it is controlled by the maximum take-off weight that applies to each aircraft type when fuel must replace payload; and the steeply sloping line shows what the fuel capacity limit gives. By reducing the aircraft weight by reducing payload, range may be increased slightly.

The point where the line hits the x-axis is known as the range a type of aircraft can fly with only "a verbal message", i.e. without any payload.

SAS always made its own assessment of input parameters that often differed considerably from the manufacturer's documentation. The large deviation was usually the calculation of the aircraft empty weight where we always had a higher value than the manufacturers, because we added the weight of food and drinks for passengers and the crew SAS operated with. Moreover, the impact of the weight gains that always arise over the years, because of modifications and repairs, were considered.

Fuel consumption also increases due to this but also because of engine wear and in-service deterioration of the aerodynamic smoothness of the wings and fuselage. SAS had to define a realistic result while manufacturers are happy presenting what the type of aircraft could do under the best conditions.

Manufacturers operated in the same way regarding their assessment of operating costs but in SAS calculations obviously the price increases associated with SAS specification changes were accounted for.

The variation of operating expenses with flight time and distance was calculated and presented in the form of curves that showed the cost of the offered seating capacity and freight per flown distance. Costs which SAS included in the calculations were usually in two groups, fixed annual costs like depreciation, interest, and insurance; and variable hourly rates such as maintenance, fuel, crew costs, landing fees, and ground handling. That the curves show higher costs for shorter distances is associated with the many cost elements such as fuel consumption during takeoff and climb to cruising altitude and airport fees, etc. which receive proportionately greater influence. That costs rise sharply when reaching the corner to the right of the payload / range diagram depends on the number of passengers or cargo that must be reduced to make room for more fuel.

The operating costs used in this initial study are somewhat typical or estimated based on past experience. The real cost cannot emerge until the evaluation and specification work is carried out. This is not essential because in this stage the task is to sort out which types of aircraft are suitable for further analysis. It is the manufacturer's task to find the right balance between the plane's maximum takeoff weight, the number of seats and / or freight capacity, and available fuel volume. After an analysis of these

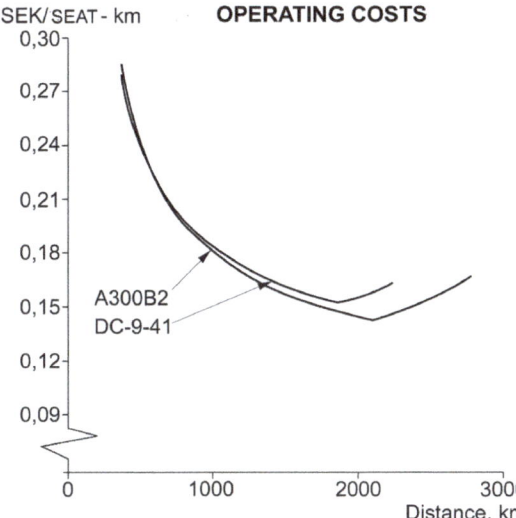

The graph show variable seating cost per km as a function of distance flown for the DC-9 and A300 B2. The DC-9 has almost the same cost as the almost-twice-as-large A300!
Image Ulf Abrahamsson.

basic data it is important to study the plane's takeoff and landing performance so that you can assess the extent to which they can be used at the airports with regard to the length of runways and any obstacles in the airport surroundings for both the regular destinations and the alternate and reserve airports.

After analyzing the factors mentioned above, it was often possible to identify one or two options that warranted a more detailed study. It was infrequent that three types of aircraft qualified for further study. Specialists in many fields conducted these.

The working groups included representatives from aerodynamics, performance, aero structures, engine technology, hydraulics, cabin decor, galley equipment, electrical, instrumentation, radio and navigation equipment, etc., and of course pilots and cabin crew. The number and extent varied of course, given the current circumstances. The starting point was available type specifications, drawings and diagrams, as well as the aircraft themselves or prototypes or mock-ups depending on what was available. Since the airline's job is to transport passengers and their baggage and freight, to a desirable extent it was necessary to seek the comfort and service as required.

Next, it was obviously important that the aircraft types could meet the safety and dispatch regularity required. With regard to flight safety, both international requirements established by the ICAO, agency of the UN and by national aviation authorities, where the US Federal Aviation Administration (FAA) is one of the leading institutions, were considered. The Scandinavian authorities generally adopted FAA regulations, it was the Federal Aviation Regulations (FAR), which guided the SAS assessments. Regarding dispatch regularity it was based on assessments of SAS's own experiences and attitudes.

Later in Europe, joint design and maintenance requirements were developed with respect to the Joint Aviation Requirements (JAR) that replaced the FAR for European activities. The next step in the analysis was to study the cost picture. One of the largest items is fuel consumption and secondly crew costs, maintenance costs, and airport charges. Aircraft maintenance is a very important factor when it comes to maintaining flight safety but it is also important to achieve operational reliability and regularity. One must ensure that all structures and installations are easily available for inspection and control. The need for spare parts for their own inventory management must be assessed and manufacturers' resources to quickly deliver those parts, which, due to size or cost, are not suitable to be kept in storage by the airline. Manufacturer resources to assist the airlines in emerging serious disruptions are important elements. These cases are usually called "after sales service" and have great significance in the assessment of the manufacturers. We also study the need for new test equipment, and engineering and hangar facilities, and also ground equipment to manage the aircraft on the ramp in the form of forklift trucks, ground supply, stairs, and passenger ramps. Loading aids, and the transport of catering equipment must also be analyzed.

Another important factor is the need of training resources and flight simulators. The use of flight simulators has over the years become increasingly important not only for economic reasons but also because they can train flight crew in a variety of emergency situations which are in a way too risky to perform with the aircraft.

An extremely important factor in the assessment of an airplane was obviously if there was access to a prototype or a production aircraft for an extensive test flight.

After all that described above has been taken care of, the next phase of negotiations with the manufacturer begins, namely the preparation of an SAS specification for the plane. It is extensive work to negotiate amendments to the manufacturer's basic specification that SAS would like so that the plane can handle the SAS requirements. It is desirable that as much as possible is done before the contract is written so that you can get bargain prices.

At the actual contract negotiations, of course, the aircraft price and delivery schedule were of the utmost importance, but also the guarantee provisions.

In negotiations with American manufacturers another aspect came into the picture. Because of US antitrust law during this period, all contracts involving aircraft manufacturers and their customers must be presented to the authorities and thus become available to interested parties or persons. This meant two things. Most contracts contained a most-favored-nation clause whereby the manufacturer undertakes not to sell the same product to others under more favorable prices. This meant that the basic agreement contained a price that is based on the aircraft basic specification. For practical reasons, then all specification changes and other revisions and their price were to be accounted for in side letters or change orders. This would lead to an unreasonable burden on the parties involved if they would have to study and evaluate all the changes and additions that could be added between the first contact signing and delivery of the last plane on order. So it was only the "basic agreement" that the authorities had access to.

It may be of interest to note that during the time period reported herein, these "Side Letters" or "Change Orders" have not meant that there were some price reductions, but usually very substantial additional prices. A contract with such accompanying additions could often be an A4 size document that had a thickness of about two to three inches.

In addition many guarantees were entered into these contract supplements and it is neither in the manufacturer's or the airline's interest that other parties know about these. This applies for example to weight guarantees and performance guarantees such as max takeoff weight, landing weight, and operating empty weight. Among the performance data included are takeoff and landing distances, climbing ability, and fuel consumption or range under specified conditions. These data are usually specified with tolerances of a few percentage points. Because the aircraft's cargo capacity will be indicated as a difference between usually quite large numbers, the result can be extremely troublesome if a pair or more of these values are developed in an unfavorable direction. Therefore, a so called Mission Guarantee was often prepared which means a guarantee that a certain amount of cargo could be transported a fixed distance under certain specified conditions. The design and content of these gave the customer a good idea of the manufacturer's confidence in its own commitments.

The legal department led contract negotiations between 1950 and 1960 with the assistance of technical and operational expertise. Because contracts were usually developed in English, the legal department often scrutinized the text with the help of law firms that specialize in the area.

Technical and flight operational activities

In the years from 1945 until the 1960s, SAS technical and operational activities contributed many experiences that influenced the planning of how the fleet development should be planned. It was found, for example, the requirement for a fleet size of about 12-15 planes provided for a rational and economical operation.

The assessment was later revised that the fleet size should be at least 20 aircraft but preferably 30 to obtain the economy and rational operations. The number of spare engines is just one example of factors that affect this. Likewise, for the operational activities, many fixed costs such as in the training of crews that is made because, for various reasons, a change of aircraft type. Large and costly resources in equipment and personnel cannot be charged to a small aircraft fleet with a few units.

An important area that could help reduce pilot costs to the extent possible is to specify the aircraft cockpits so that the instruments, controls, and other installations will be as similar as possible in a fleet of different aircraft types. The question arises whether to standardize on the existing older equipment or to drive development forward and to the extent possible modernize the older types. These problems are reduced if you can stick to a given supplier for the aircraft types chosen for the various route networks.

SAS has largely been able to succeed to a large extent by selecting Douglas planes for their fleet. Every decision has been taken on each type's own merits but there has been a considerable advantage in the outcome of the selections as they have been made. The series DC-3, DC-4, DC-6, DC-6B, DC-7C, the DC-8 types, the DC-9 types, and finally the DC-10 speaks for itself. Around the world you can see companies that made the same selections as SAS, but one can also see many others who have done the same with the Boeing series 707, 720, 727, 737, 747, and 767

Aircraft manufacturers have their own criteria when it comes to decide on the introduction of new aircraft types. The big question is how many aircraft will need to be sold for the manufacturer to achieve the so-called break-even point, that is, how many must be sold for the project to become a profitable business. Manufacturers often stated levels between 300 and 400 planes.

Boeing had great success with the 727-100 and 727-200 and sold a total of 1,832 aircraft. Production ceased in 1984.
A profitable project.
Photo Boeing.

New times
Ulf Abrahamsson

The Jan Carlzon era

In the mid-1970s the underlying framework for international aviation began to undergo major changes. Commercial aviation's early post-war business was heavily regulated by the framework of international agreements within ICAO and IATA. Fares, routes, and to some extent also the products that were offered to the passenger during the flight, were determined through annual negotiations. In addition the airlines got used to having a fairly steady annual growth in demand and the route networks grew continuously with new destinations. This of course steered the planning of the fleets and when the new aircraft were offered by the manufacturers the traditional airlines could usually without difficulty replace and sell their used aircraft at good prices. The annual profit that airlines showed, to a big part, were often constituted by the sale of aircraft.

The US "Airline Deregulation Act" of 1978 was a major step in commercial aviation history. The US domestic aviation deregulation led to a whole new market situation in the US with brand new rules, for better or for worse. Already in 1979 the liberalization had also begun in international aviation, e.g. "Open Skies". This also affected the North Atlantic routes and thus SAS.

The entire operation was altered when Jan Carlzon in 1980 became CEO of SAS.

SAS went from basically a production and cost-driven business to a market-oriented service where profitability and passenger desires, were first. A new organizational structure was established and a large part of the management team was replaced with new staff, most of Carlzon's own age.

Carlzon introduced the concept of "Customer Time." He called the prior era "heroes and engineers' time." Major changes were carried out with about 150 projects concerning all areas of SAS, which would primarily contribute to increased revenues but also to lower costs.

Carlzon also established a new corporate strategy with the main theme that SAS would become "The Businessman's Airline." The strategy called for greatly increased frequencies, nonstop flights to and from many locations, better service in the air and on the ground, as well as significantly improved punctuality. This meant, among other things that the previous approach, where low cost per seat was most important, was now taken over by the highest possible revenue per flight that could be achieved. First Business Class was a new concept.

The organization that was responsible for specification and selection of new aircraft under Birger Holmer's leadership, was kept largely intact

The new CEO Jan Carlzon implemented major changes within SAS. Photo SAS.

until his retirement in 1981. Then I was appointed to take charge of the function, which then involved about 20 persons with experts in the areas of:
• Aircraft Analysis (performance, environment and costs),
• Avionics and electrical systems,
• Payload Systems, i.e. cabin and cargo holds.

A new Central Engineering was established in the technical division responsible for the daily management of all engineering functions within the division, i.e. in addition to the central function at the headquarters, it was also responsible for engineering departments at the maintenance bases. The Project Department was transferred to Central Engineering with me as a manager.

SAS Airline of the Year 1983!

Jan Carlzon's strategy with The Businessman's Airline was a great success. Traffic increased strongly, especially with full fare paying passengers, and in 1983 SAS was awarded "Airline of the Year" by the prestigious aviation magazine "Air Transport World (ATW)." This success led to an increased need for aircraft. A few years later, SAS got another award from ATW, for the "best passenger service."

Jan Carlzon. takes advice from Lars Bergvall, who later became President of SAS Airline. Photo SAS.

SAS received two fine awards from Air Transport World, first as Airline of the Year in 1983!
Photo SAS.

Jan Carlzon gets good advice from SAS's first CEO, P-Norlin Photo SAS.

The SAS planning function "Central Planning Group", CPG, which previously reported long term plans that spanned over 10 years, found new structure led by Nils Molander, SAS's new Chief Financial Officer; and with Hans-Ake Lilja as head of fleet planning. The direct business responsibility for the purchase and sale of aircraft was somewhat unclear for some time.

The CFO, Nils Molander had formal responsibility but delegated implementation to other people until 1984. Then Lars Rantzen was given responsibility for procurement, leasing and phase-out of airplanes and he initially reported to Jan Carlzon but after a time to different people in leading positions.

As an example of the former planning function approach, it may be mentioned that a long-term forecast made by the CPG in 1976 showed a fleet plan for SAS around 1990, which included a long-haul fleet of 24 wide-body aircraft, a short to medium-haul fleet of about 40 Airbus A300 and 34 DC-9. The reality came out rather differently.

The economy

SAS had since the 1960s been accustomed to having a strong production increase every year. The load factor was around 50-55%, which increased around 1980 to about 60%, but the years 1979/1980 and 1980/1981 showed a loss after a long period of profit. Through product differentiation SAS would both secure an increase in the number of full-fare paying passengers while offering marginal pricing of spare capacity. The ambition was to sell as much as possible of the production that was being performed. For the fleet, the change of strategy meant that SAS in part ought to have smaller aircraft, and to make major changes in the cabins of all aircraft. The strategy was implemented first on the European route network, first class was abolished but what came to be called the Euro Class was introduced! As a first step on the long routes flat-bed seats were introduced on the 747 and DC-10 and first class was named First Business Class. Further a number of measures were taken to improve quality, comfort, service, and punctuality.

Some years later SAS also got the ATW award for Best Passenger Service. Jan Carlzon and Sven Heiding, Head of European routes
Photo SAS.

The aircraft fleet 1980/81
SAS's new CEO took over the following fleet:
Long distance: 5   DC-10-30
                 5   747
of which one 747 was on lease and another ordered for delivery in 1982.
Short-medium range: 11   DC-8
                       4   A-300
                      60   DC-9

i.e. a total of 85 aircraft including five DC-8s that were on lease to Scanair. The fleet thus contained a large number of aircraft types that caused major additional costs, e.g. type cost, which included the crew training costs that was required specially in the rotation of pilots between aircraft types, increased spare costs, and organizational costs.

The aircraft had varying ages, the oldest DC-9 plane was made in 1968 but the latest was delivered in 1979. The oldest DC-8 aircraft was manufactured in 1968. According to the old organization planning, phasing out the oldest DC-9 would have begun as the A300s were introduced in the fleet.

Jan Carlzon even got in the "baggage" a qualified technical division with a central function and four overhaul bases, one of which specialized in engine maintenance, the Linta base, and the other with a base in each Scandinavian country. The Arlanda base, responsible for heavy maintenance of the DC-8, was in the process of building up resources for maintenance of KSSU's Airbus fleet, and the construction of a new large hangar at the airport for about $ 8.0 million. The Oslo base was responsible for heavy maintenance of the DC-9 fleet, and the Copenhagen base accounted for component maintenance and inspections. The workshops primarily had SAS as a customer, and within KSSU also Swissair DC-8s.

SAS had until 1978/79 turned a profit for 17 consecutive years, but the results in recent years did not reach the necessary level in order to continue renewing its fleet. For the two 747s that were ordered and delivered in 1980/1981, SAS found itself obligated to take an 18 year lease with US banks to get the funding. This lease agreement entailed, among other things, the aircraft having to be registered in the United States. This meant that pilots and mechanics had to have certificates issued by the FAA. The long lease period limited flexibility in planning and came to affect the fleet for some years to come.

The new strategies and new demands on the fleet.
In fiscal year 1982-1983 the new SAS management determined its strategy for how the aircraft fleet would evolve over the coming years and it had the following form:

"SAS faces the task of replacing parts of 108 of its fleet over the next decade. To be competitive, the new aircraft should be adapted to market needs while being cost effective. SAS markets will require frequent, and many nonstop flights. In domestic traffic and on European routes 60 DC-9 are currently used, of which the oldest was commissioned in 1968-70 and the youngest in 1979. Mid-East, Africa, India/Pakistan, and Greenland are served by five DC-8s. In addition, SAS uses five DC-10s and three Boeing 747s for traffic to North and South America and the Far East. SAS will dispose a number of surplus aircraft: two Boeing 747s, three Airbus A300s and three DC-8s. These will be sold, or pending sale, leased out. SAS currently disposes therefore five types of aircraft. Over time, the fleet could be concentrated in two or at most three types, resulting in economies of scale and lower costs.

In 1983, SAS worked out a plan for the future exchange of primarily the DC-9 fleet. It was based on two basic premises:

• The new aircraft that already can be bought or found on manufacturers' drawing boards for delivery at the end of the 1980s, represent only a further development of the existing planes. Compared with the aircraft which are in use today, there are advantages mainly due to operating cost. It is therefore important to establish that there are currently no aircraft in operation or in the planning stage which give the customer a better transportation product in terms of comfort, safety, and the environment than, for example, the DC-9 that SAS uses today.

• The DC-9 fleet presents no technical or economic restrictions regarding its use in the 1980s.

These basic facts led to the conclusion that SAS was in no immediate hurry to replace the DC-9 fleet. When the change does happen, the new aircraft should as far as possible be designed based on the requirements of customers. The DC-8 medium-range plane can only be used until 1986 when new noise regulations will be enforced at the international level. SAS's long-range routes require, as well as the rest of the routes, frequent and numerous non-stop routes. In the long run, SAS will use aircraft with

Some in SAS dreamed of new aircraft. Drawing SAS.

Original logo-type.

Aircraft being repainted but many thought there should be new airplanes. Drawing SAS.

smaller passenger capacity and longer range than the DC-10 and 747.

The aircraft used today are relatively new and no replacement is currently envisioned. All SAS aircraft are now undergoing a modernization program. Newer technology is being implemented in the DC-9s, modifying the engines whereby fuel consumption is reduced by about five percent. In order to offer passengers more comfort all planes are rebuilt inside. New seats, new textiles, and other details in the interior give a whole new environment in the cabin. The aircraft exterior color scheme also gets a modern styling."

The decision to proceed with the DC-9 was not received positively in all parts of the airline, some wanted new aircraft. But the message from management was clearly a single new DC-9 or equivalent would cost about $20 million. To repaint the aircraft and change the interiors of the existing fleet of about 80 aircraft would cost $10 million and new uniforms for the crews would also cost about $10 million. It was a low price for a "new" fleet and a new SAS look. The strategy demanded changes.

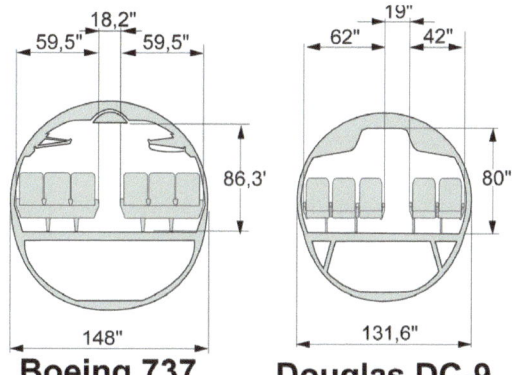

Boeing 737 and McDonnell Douglas DC-9 cross sections
Drawing Hans Kampf.

Airbus A300

The four brand new Airbus A300s that were specified for use on short domestic and European routes did not fit into the new strategy. However, the market was limited to those aircraft in part because of the unique specification. SAS therefore decided in 1981 to invest in a major modification of the aircraft by both increasing the maximum takeoff weight from 313,000 lb. to 326,300 lb. and increasing fuel capacity to attract more interest in the market for aircraft and pending sales and to better fit Scanair's needs. A company linked to Airbus performed the modifications in Bremen. The A300 aircraft were thereafter at Scanair's disposal in parallel with three DC 8-63s.

SAS appointed Bengt Rehn as site manager and controller in Bremen for monitoring the modification. Bengt Rehn had great experience from similar work from the deliveries of SAS Caravelle aircraft from Toulouse and later had similar assignments in connection with the DC-10 modification and MD-80 deliveries.

An A300 was leased to a Malaysia airline in 1983 on a short-term contract. The aircraft crashed however during the approach to Kuala Lumpur where luckily all on board survived. The remaining three A300s were sold to the Danish charter company Conair / Spies in 1986.

McDonnell Douglas DC-9

The new management's strategy and Jan Carlzon's enthusiasm soon created a belief both within and outside the company that persuaded the staff to line up with the big changes to come.

The aircraft underwent a major modification program for increased comfort in the new Euro class. To give full-fare paying passengers the best comfort, a moveable cabin divider was introduced on the DC-9. It consisted of a curtain, suspended, on a special beam which was easily movable. It was positioned before each departure so that the number of seats behind the curtain corresponded to the number of low-fare seats sold and the entire cabin space in front of the divider could be offered to full-fare paying passengers. So they had plenty of space and very rarely needed someone to sit in the middle seat. SAS also increased seat pitch in the front part of the cabin to further improve comfort. The SAS DC-9 cabin with a double and a triple seat in each row had a clear advantage over their competitors who flew 737s, in which cabin you had two triple seats in each row. The 737 seat was clearly narrower than the DC-9's seat. Air France was quite bothered by this and tried in various ways to eliminate SAS's advantage but without much success.

The previous management had started discussions

DC-9-21 in SAS old decor.
Photo Lennart Berngård.

on how the DC-9s were to be eventually replaced; and had realized that the large investment would require that SAS showed strong positive results for several years. Therefore the first measure the new management initiated was a proper investigation of the DC-9 fleet's technical lifetime. The results of the fatigue tests conducted by Douglas showed that the design coped well with 100,000 flights before major steps would be necessary. SAS's oldest DC-9 plane had at the time accumulated about 30,000 flights. Meanwhile, the FAA issued special requirements for "Aging Aircraft"and a number of older aircraft had to undergo extensive modification programs. The requirements on the DC-9 were, however, very limited and consisted primarily of inspections. The economic life was assessed unambiguously as positive, among other things, after the extensive cabin update that was carried out. All aircraft got the new exterior painting, "New Corporate Image."The old SAS color scheme, with the dragon head and the cabin windows simulating shields on a ship, was now completely gone.

It was therefore a natural decision for SAS to continue with the DC-9 and to delay the exchange for a new type. At the same time, however, SAS started a dialogue with aircraft manufacturers on how a future replacement for the DC-9 should be designed. This dialog is described in more detail in a later chapter about the SAS P3 plan, the "Passenger Pleasing Plane".

The new business strategy, focusing on full fare paying passengers, supplemented with discount tickets with a simpler product, a marked increase in the number of frequencies, direct flights on many routes, and simultaneous start-up of new routes, received strong response in the market. The load factor increased and the average passenger load factor rose from the level of around 58-60% to almost 70% during the mid-1980s.

The sharp increase in traffic that resulted from the new strategy soon led to lack of capacity, especially for domestic traffic in Sweden. SAS judged that an increase in traffic of three to four percent per year corresponded to a need for two to three DC-9s per year. Growth in the SAS European Services from 1984 to 1988 was an average of 7% per year. Leasing of several aircraft was especially made to cope with domestic traffic in Sweden.

The management instructed the project organization primarily to quickly procure used DC-9s. To cope with additional capacity when it was needed, it was decided at the Board level in November 1985 to buy five used DC-9-51s, which had previously been operated by Swissair. The decision was met with criticism from the project since the version differed from other SAS DC-9s with a different version of the JT8 engine and it was seen as a somewhat odd bird. In addition the version had significantly higher noise levels than SAS's DC-9-41. Four of the aircraft were sold after about a year, and the fifth was leased to an airline in Hawaii for a long time.

Within the company, among others, the pilot association strongly criticized the fact that SAS chose to continue with the "old" aircraft and it characterized, among other things, the cabin upgrade as cosmetics.

All airlines with DC-9s that could be a potential supplier were surveyed and asked if they had airplanes for sale. Because of the global increase in traffic all available capacity was needed and the answers from the respondents were negative. In one case the answer was "we may well discuss it." The answer came from Dick Spalding, Director of Aircraft Trading at the US airline USAir.

Bengt-Olov Nas, responsible for aircraft evaluation, was sent to Pittsburgh, USAir's home base, in order to gather more information about the aircraft that they were willing to possibly sell and their current condition and specification. The discussions led to USAir offering SAS some DC-9-30s.

At the same time another offer was made on a

DC-9-21 in the new decor.
Photo Hans Norman
www.Scanliners.com.

number of ex-Alitalia aircraft that could be delivered quickly. The deal would be done through an agent from Israel who was also involved in one of SAS 747 leases. A small team under my management went in June 1984 to Tel Aviv to complete the deal. I had with me Bjorn Snellman, our contract lawyer, and Henrik Meldahl who was temporarily responsible for the aircraft purchasing business.

After a day in Tel Aviv SAS management called and told me that during a routine visit by McDonnell Douglas (MDC) sales team, SAS received information that MDC could deliver six DC-9-80s within the same time frame as we could get Alitalia's DC 9-30s, i.e. during 1985. MDC had in fact received a cancellation of the DC-9-80 from Korean Airlines, which made this possible.

MDC had started further development of the DC-9 during the late 1970s and called the new version DC-9 Super 80. The type first flew 18 October 1979 and had an approximately 20% larger wing and a fuselage that had been extended by almost 23 ft. Pratt & Whitney also had a new version of its JT8 engine with a larger fan. Swissair became Douglas's first customer for the Super 80 with delivery in 1980.

Sales of the DC-9-80 were, however sluggish but a new manager in Long Beach, Jim Worsham, who came from the engine manufacturer General Electric, introduced innovation in marketing. He offered American Airlines in 1982 an advantageous lease on a large number of aircraft in which American got the right to return the aircraft after a few years if they did not corresponded to American's requirements. This sparked the MD-80 program.

After an accident associated with type certification, a hard landing with severe damage to the fuselage, one then SAS technical manager stated, "it was fortunate that SAS did not choose the DC-9-80, but had decided to purchase the Airbus A300.."

It now became a priority to start the specification work for the DC-9-80 and to finalize negotiations with MDC. A new engine version called the JT8D-219 was offered. The new version had a larger fan than the DC-9 engine and a bypass ratio of 2:1. This was expected to give a noticeable reduction in fuel consumption and reduced noise. Specialists who, apart from the project, came from operations, technical, and commercial divisions carried out a large part of the specification work in Long Beach during the summer of 1984.

While the specification was discussed at MDC in Long Beach the Olympic Games were ongoing in Los Angeles.

As the leader of the group I had received a telegram from the Chairman of the Board, Haldor Topsoe, which contained a requirement that the specification would be consistent with the Swissair specification for its DC-9-80. At the same time, the requirement that the flight deck of the SAS DC-9-80 would allow us to fly them with the same pilot group that SAS had for the previous versions, to reduce costs. The Working Group decided, however, to make the specification more forward thinking with the limitations that existed. The DC-9-80 had substantially a conventional flight deck without digital equipment.

We also had a clear message from the board that the agreement with MDC for the six planes would not include anything about options. This was with reference to the purchase only being a short-term measure to solve the acute need for airplanes. The normal procedure was otherwise always to put a number of options that corresponded to the number of firm orders for setting the price for any future orders. We negotiated an agreement that included options for several aircraft despite the directives.
In parallel with this the dialogue had been started with the manufacturing industry about SAS's interest of a new aircraft concept, the "Passenger Pleasing Plane," or P3 plane as it came to be called. Some of us now claimed that SAS through its purchase of the DC-9-80 actually started the process of how the

111

DC-9 fleet would be replaced although management with reference to the P3 discussions denied this.

SAS wanted to delay the final decision about the DC-9 replacement, partly because the profitability required in the coming years to create the economic conditions to meet the high investment that would be required, and partly to monitor and influence the technical development so that an appropriate SAS aircraft would be on the market when the replacement would take place. SAS judged that the investment for the exchange of the DC-9 fleet would amount to almost $3,0 billion (1981).

During 1984/85 the decision was taken to buy a total of six DC-9-81s and eight DC-9-82s. The latter version had more range due to higher Max takeoff weight.

SAS chose to place a representative in Long Beach for monitoring the production. Bengt Rehn, who had extensive experience in this type of job, made the move to California. He stated once that the quality of the MDC production in many areas was lower than what should be accepted and he therefore brought this up in an open way with MDC's quality control. We soon received messages from MDC's top management (Jim Worsham) to Jan Carlzon that Bengt Rehn should immediately be called back home. I made a trip to Long Beach to gather facts.

We could soon see that Bengt was right on all the points he had raised and MDC backed off when they realized that Bengt's expertise and experience could be utilized to significantly improve the quality of their production. Bengt got a clear message from me to be a little more diplomatic in the way he communicated with MDC staff, which certainly contributed to the fact that, since then, production worked flawlessly.

The first DC-9-81 was delivered in August 1985 at Long Beach with the presence of the SAS board of directors and executive management. The delivery flight was delayed a few weeks because the engines had problems with oil leaks!

Douglas DC-8

The applicable noise requirements had developed such that the DC-8 would not be allowed to fly after 1985. This led to a project launched in the US for engine replacement on the DC-8. The selected engine was the CFM56. Cammacorp, run by former Douglas Head Jack McGowen, was behind the modification. MDC provided technical support for the engine replacement project.

The type designation became DC-8-70 and about one hundred aircraft were modified. The DC-8-70 was an aircraft with good fuel economy and long range. SAS received proposals but we were not interested since the type would still be phased out. Instead SAS installed in 1984/85 a noise suppressor, "hush-kits," a significantly less costly modification

SAS takes delivery of its first DC-9-80 in 1985. Sandy McDonnell handing over the aeroplane to Jan Carlzon.
Photo MDC.

that made the type pass the current noise regulations and gave SAS phase out flexibility.

It started with three DC-8-62s being sold in 1986 and one aircraft leased to the airline AirPeru. To cope with Scanair's needs after the A300 phase out, three DC-8-63s were purchased for the remaining time. The entire DC-8 fleet was sold during 1988.

Boeing 747

SAS had an excess of 747s as the phase out of the older 747 planes failed and new ones were delivered. Both SAS and Scanair utilized 747s pending phase-out.

In the spring of 1982, SAS was in contact with Nigeria Airways who had shown interest in leasing a 747 (OY-KHA). Nils Molander and I traveled to London on 1 March 1982 for an initial discussion and then a group of four people, Douglas Keith, Bjorn Snellman, Tore Granaas, and I traveled to Lagos to finalize the contract.

Nigeria made great demands on SAS as regards the financial settlement, but also in many other areas. Among other things a facility for viewing movies would be installed in the small cabin on the upper deck, a large number of pilots would be made available, nearly 100 flight attendants were to be trained, the cabin would be rebuilt with a new first class, a number of technicians based in Lagos, Kano, and London would be provided, a complete technical review of the aircraft would be made before delivery and of course, the aircraft would be painted in Nigeria Airways colors.

Negotiations in Lagos were awkward when the only contact with SAS management was on a bad telephone line. We did not mind using our own telephone but graciously could borrow their phone when Nigeria's leadership so accepted! The contract was, however, signed in Lagos, on 12 March 1982 and the aircraft would be delivered on April 1st! It seemed impossible at first thought, but Jan Carlzon had quickly managed to create an exceptionally positive attitude of the staff, and the entire SAS organization backed this really impossible task.

747-200 LN-AET, Bjarne Viking was originally delivered with registration SE-DDL under the name of Huge Viking. Photo Johan Ljungdahl.

As planned, the aircraft was therefore flown to Lagos on time. The last part of the movie equipment on the upper deck had to be installed during the delivery flight by the accompanying technicians from the base in Copenhagen. The problem that the technicians had no visa for Nigeria was resolved by dressing them up in uniforms and they could thus be recorded as being part of the crew.

Our technicians in Lagos and Kano had a difficult start in the beginning. SAS bought a house that would function as their residence.

The house had to be refurbished, which the technicians had to do themselves, and supply with furniture. SAS was forced to send several rounds of paint and furniture as the first deliveries were stolen right after landing in Lagos.

The aircraft was returned after about a year and was then transferred to the owner Air Invest. Nigeria came to lease an additional 747 during different periods. The deal on the aircraft SE-DFZ, a lease-purchase agreement with the delivery of the aircraft during 1987 was special. Nigeria had problems in fulfilling the contract. SAS probably got only the deposit given at the delivery but no payment otherwise.

Nigeria managed to transfer the contract to MDC in return for Nigeria buying the last DC-10-30 that came out of the Long Beach plant. MDC later resolved the agreement with SAS but how the deal between Nigeria and MDC ended is unclear.

In July 1982 the Colombian airline Avianca was the next customer for a SAS 747, LN-RNA. Contract negotiations were concluded in New York with the help of an agent from Israel who later also become involved in SAS's search for used DC-9s. During the contract signing with Avianca a long discussion was conducted internally on the insured value of the aircraft that would be put into the contract. The discussion was conducted by telephone between SAS insurance lawyer Hans Westerstad who was in London and me in New York. We agreed eventually that $50 million was a reasonable value.

Little did we know then that the aircraft would crash, on approach to the airport in Madrid in November 1983 where nearly all on board were killed, and being declared a total loss. Some of the survivors said they had seen flames coming from one of the engines, which created concerns within SAS, having continued technical responsibility for them, but it was soon found that the engines had worked as they should.

It was sad to end our aircraft surplus in this way, with accidents and total loss of both an A300 and a 747 even if the economic result was good.

The two most recently delivered 747s, which were registered in the United States, remained with SAS until 1989 when they were taken over by a leasing company, GPA. They did, however, play a role in the MD-11 deal that SAS was involved in 1986-1987, as will be described later.

McDonnell Douglas DC-10

The DC-10-30 fleet consisted of the five aircraft delivered in the mid-1970s. One aircraft crashed in February 1984 during landing in New York when it touched down far down the runway and the aircraft slid down into one of the water basins around the runway system. The damage was too great to make the repair of the aircraft worthwhile.

Later in the year a decision was made to complete the transition to the single fleet of long-range aircraft, based on the DC-10-30, to reduce the fixed costs associated with each additional aircraft.

Budget airline Laker's 'Skytrain' that for some time competed with the traditional airlines, also on the Atlantic, had gone bankrupt in 1982. Laker had a fleet of five DC-10-30 and a number of A300. The DC-10-30 planes, now owned by the US Export-Import Bank, Eximbank, had parked them in the desert outside Yuma, Arizona. The bank had withheld the aircraft from the market for possible use in the USAF's Air Force One fleet. In the context of discussions with USAir about a possible purchase of the DC-9, it was revealed that the Bank now would be interested in selling the aircraft, and it was first come, first served since all airlines sought more capacity. Henrik Meldahl arranged that a bid was placed on two planes.

One aircraft was almost new with a total flight time of just under 1000 hours. A small group including myself, Bengt Rehn, Carl-Erik Andreasson, and a technician flew to California in April 1984 and inspected the aircraft that proved to be in very good condition. However, the aircraft specification matched poorly with that of SAS's planes.

It did not have the large cargo door for pallets in front of the wing and the flight deck was built on the Atlas (DLH and AF) specification. The forward galley was placed in the aircraft's forward lower cargo hold with an elevator going up to the cabin in order to get more seats in the cabin. The group traveled on to MDC in Long Beach to discuss whether a rebuild was possible. MDC confirmed this and provided preliminary cost data of approximately $ 18 million for two aircraft. MDC showed great interest in carrying out this modification.

SAS management took the decision to go ahead with the deal so the chief financial officer Nils Molander and I traveled on 2 May to Washington, DC to conclude with Exim Bank for the purchase of two aircraft at a price of $24 million per plane. During the summer a detailed specification of the modifications was worked out and the work was contracted to the company Tracor Aviation in Santa Barbara just north of Los Angeles.

In Yuma, there were three additional Laker DC-10s and the technical manager at United Airlines decided quickly that they would buy these without inspection after a brief telephone conversation with me. United was very interested in what we were doing. It may be mentioned that SAS and United over the years enjoyed good relationships on the technical side. Bengt Rehn was given responsibility for monitoring this modification at Tracor.

We were now told that the modifications would cost about $ 15 million per plane! This led to many contacts for two weeks at the management level, between Jan Carlzon for SAS and Jim Worsham at MDC, and the final price was renegotiated to be about $ 10 million per plane.

The implementation of the modifications also had its points. While our modifications would be implemented American Airlines also planned to modify the flight deck of some of their DC-10-30s in the same workshop. It turned out that their aircraft had just the equipment that we needed for the Flight Deck on our aircraft and American could use parts of the equipment that were in the SAS planes. We quickly sent over two people, Carl-Eric Andreasson and Christer Bruce, with freedom to complete a

Ex Laker DC-10-30 modified by Tracor Santa Barbara to SAS specification.
Photo Ulf Abrahamsson.

negotiation with American.

A long dialogue with MDC continued during work on some other equipment, which they regarded as BFE, "Buyer Furnished Equipment", while SAS claimed that MDC had the responsibility. The dialogue was not completed until November 1984, in SAS's favor. SAS then bought another five used DC-10-30 aircraft during the period 1986-1987 including two from Thai International.

The cabin in the original five DC-10s had, in the late 1970s, been rebuilt with a business class cabin behind the first class cabin. Jan Carlzon requested that passengers should have access to a telephone on board which was not common in the early 1980s. SAS managed to convince Stockholm Radio to help install a phone in the front of the cabin and the call could be connected with the help of pilots via Stockholm Radio.

Flights to Tokyo over the Soviet Union were not allowed so the route went around with a stopover in Anchorage, Alaska. The DC-10-30 did not have sufficient range to fly non-stop around the Soviet Union, but Finnair announced that they would fly direct over the North Pole from Helsinki. This was studied intensively by the project organization; including rumors of using cold fuel to succeed.
Jan Carlzon had said to the press that based on the SAS experts, it was not possible, so he was hesitant about Finnair's advertising. This was obviously not well received in Helsinki. Finnair had however the advantage of a shorter route.

SAS searched for various solutions such as installing auxiliary tanks in the body, but the increased empty weight meant that this did not solve the problem. SAS installed, however, a "Performance Management System" (PMS) in the DC-10 to help pilots fly more fuel efficiently. PMS was the predecessor to the "Flight Management System" (FMS) that became standard in next generations aircraft.

SAS had now completed the necessary simplifications to its fleet and could now begin to look ahead pursuing the 1982 fleet strategy.

New aircraft to the fleet

Passenger Pleasing Plane, P3

SAS's strong focus on securing the best product for its passengers in the forthcoming aircraft meant that a dialogue was started with the manufacturers emphasizing that they should put more focus on what aircraft cabins would look like in future aircraft.

We considered that a future DC-9 replacement should be able to offer better comfort for passengers, including avoiding triple seats so that no passenger would have more than one passenger to pass to reach the aisle, which would also be made wider, thus improving the ability to provide excellent service on board. Baggage handling would also be simplified so that passengers could quickly get his or her luggage upon arrival at the destination. The passenger should have the latest technology for communications and entertainment at their seats. Although this was directed primarily toward full fare paying passengers, the idea was that greater flexibility in the cabin design would allow rapid conversion of the cabin to meet different needs. A new concept should also provide for shorter ground stops to increase the utilization of the aircraft. The term "Passenger Pleasing Plane" had been created, or P3 plane as it was also called. SAS sent signals to the aerospace industry that SAS, in addition to development resources in the form of specialists, could even imagine participating in the financing of the development.

Jan Carlzon made a presentation at the Paris air show in 1983, which echoed throughout the aerospace industry. The purpose of SAS was to create an innovation in the development of new aircraft types. Jan Carlzon himself had drawn a simple diagram of how a cabin should look and built a cabin mockup in full scale according to these ideas with a length of four rows of seats.

The cabin cross section was chosen with three double seats (2 + 2 + 2) and two aisles where the width was guided by the idea that two service carts

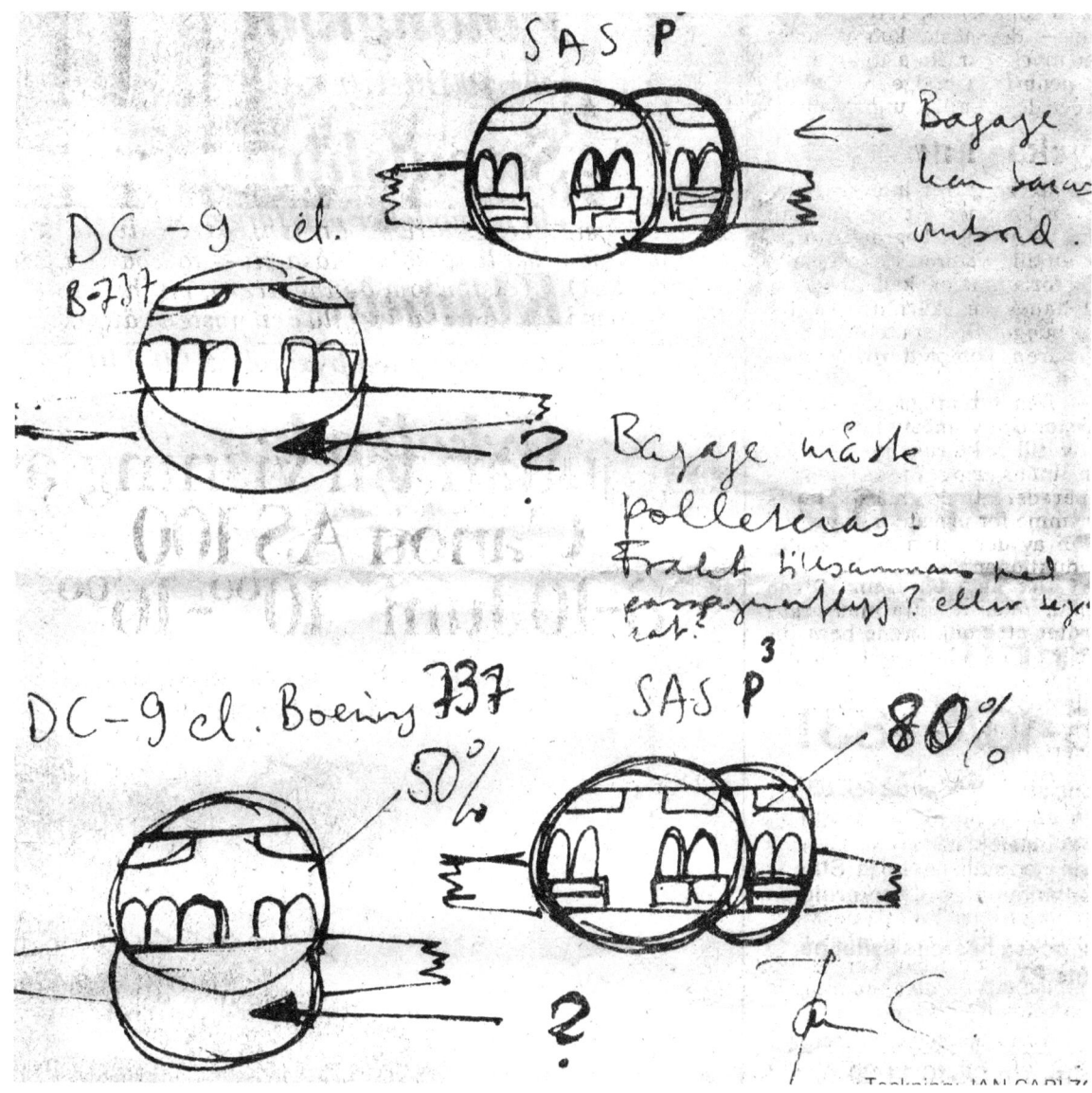

Jan Carlzon P3 plane napkin sketch

could meet or that a cart could pass a passenger standing in the aisle. The cabin width also acknowledged that it could accommodate seven seats in width, i.e. with a triple seat in the middle if an airline wanted a tourist class cabin. The flexibility would be high. Cabin width provided new opportunities for passengers to bring more hand luggage onboard when space became larger by the increased volume in the cabin.

Airbus, Boeing, and McDonnell Douglas responded somewhat different. In cooperation with SAS, Airbus and Boeing built similar short cabin mockups in their development workshops based on SAS drawings; and an intensive dialogue started by fax, telephone contacts, and meetings. Airbus, which was in full swing developing the A320 with planned first delivery around 1987, probably felt that they already had the SAS P3 plane under development.

MDC's DC-9-80, now called the MD-80 after an upgrade of the aircraft type, including increased digitization of the flight deck, also thought that their MD-80 well satisfied SAS wishes!

Boeing however put in a lot of work on the project, while SAS established contact with other airlines outside Europe with the aim to increase interest in rethinking airliner design. Delta Air Lines in the US showed a strong interest while others believed that the operating costs, especially fuel consumption, would make the project unattractive. Boeing did advanced studies of how the cabin cross-section would affect the empty weight and fuel consumption and also developed a special software for these studies and presented it at one of our visits to Seattle in 1983.

Calculations were made for a series of airplanes from 100 seats up to a 200-seat aircraft. The "100-seater" did naturally look quite strange with an unusually short and wide body with wings!

At the same time development of an entirely new type of engine was going on in the engine industry that had many names, such as Superfan, Propfan or UnDucted Fan (UDF)™, which was General Electric's Trade Name on their variant. In 1975 GE had published a document on the "Advanced Turboprop Project," which could provide fuel savings of 30-35%. Fuel prices had risen sharply because of, among other things, the war situation between Iran and Iraq, forcing manufacturers to find new solutions. The leader of the project at GE was Art Adamson, a very colorful person, who had strong backing from Brian Rowe, director of the aircraft engine division.

GE chose a solution with free fan blades directly driven by two separate and counter-rotating turbines that then limited the speed of the turbine where speed was controlled by the fan tip speed. The fan blades had also to be made as light as possible, the engine had to withstand a situation where one or

MD-80 UDF test. Photo MDC.

more fan blades broke off, and the solution was to make blades of carbon fiber composite. They soon realized that noise and vibration could be a problem.

PWA and Allison separately sketched out another solution comprising an engine with front-mounted fans and a planetary gearbox, which had a bypass ratio of 13 to 1 between the turbine and fan blades.

Even Rolls-Royce showed a proposal for a UHB (Ultra High Bypass engine) project with free fan blades, but oriented towards larger aircraft than Boeing's 7J7.

Boeing 7J7

The available engine choices prompted Boeing to see an opportunity to combine these ideas with the work of the Passenger Pleasing Plane project, which got the name 7J7. The young and ambitious project manager Alan Mulally became a good contact for SAS. Besides rethinking of the engines and P3 ideas the project even had a brand new digital flight deck and new systems. A new management team at Boeing with Phil Condit in the lead backed the program. Boeing chose primarily GE's UDF as an engine for the 7J7.

At the outset the plan was to develop an aircraft

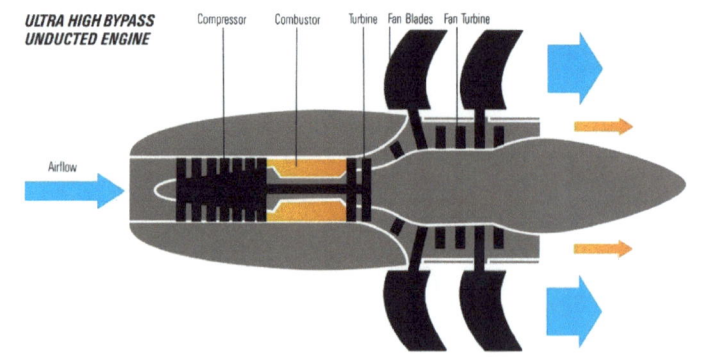

Principle layout of GE UnDucted-Fan, engine Picture General Electric.

The UDF engine is ready for a test run.
Photo General Electric.

40%. The timetable showed that if the program started around 1984, the first aircraft would be delivered in 1994. Something of a risky project, it would probably have to be recognized.

Boeing began early to get international partners both in Europe where Saab could be included, and in Asia. Boeing wanted to reduce their own risk in the project and find a way to meet its main competitor, Airbus, especially in Europe. It may be noted that around the time that Boeing had contact with Saab, they had bought the Canadian company de Havilland Canada whose new Dash 8 was one of the main competitors to the Saab 340! The Japanese companies Kawasaki, Mitsubishi and Fuji were offered 25% of the 7J7 project.

Boeing estimated that 7J7 planes would have a lifespan of 20 years, so for Saab, this could mean many millions per year until their final delivery. Brian Rowe decided early on that a UDF test engine should be test flown, therefore in 1986 a 727 was fitted with a UDF that replaced one of the side mounted JT8D engines. It flew in August 1987. Boeing and GE then confirmed that community noise could become a serious problem and they began to realize that one could find it difficult to meet future noise requirements of FAR 36 and ICAO Annex 16.

for 150 passengers with many of the SAS P3 ideas, planning for deliveries to take place in 1992. The plans were that the 7J7 would replace not only Boeing's own 737 and 727 but also the large DC-9 fleet of about 900 aircraft which were operating. This went well with SAS programming for its DC-9 replacement. The 7J7 program would, in addition to rethinking with respect to the cabin, contain the latest in all fields of technology such as a new advanced engine type, composite materials in the structure, use of aluminum-lithium alloys, and new ideas in most systems.

Boeing claimed that they could offer an aircraft with a total reduction of fuel consumption of nearly

Several airlines had mixed feelings about the project and they were backed of course by Airbus, which saw the 7J7 as an attempt by Boeing to negatively influence A320 sales. In early 1986 Delta Airlines placed an order for 80 MD-88 aircraft from MDC, 30 firm orders and 50 options. Delta had gained assurance of this contract with MDC that they could replace the conventional JT8D-219

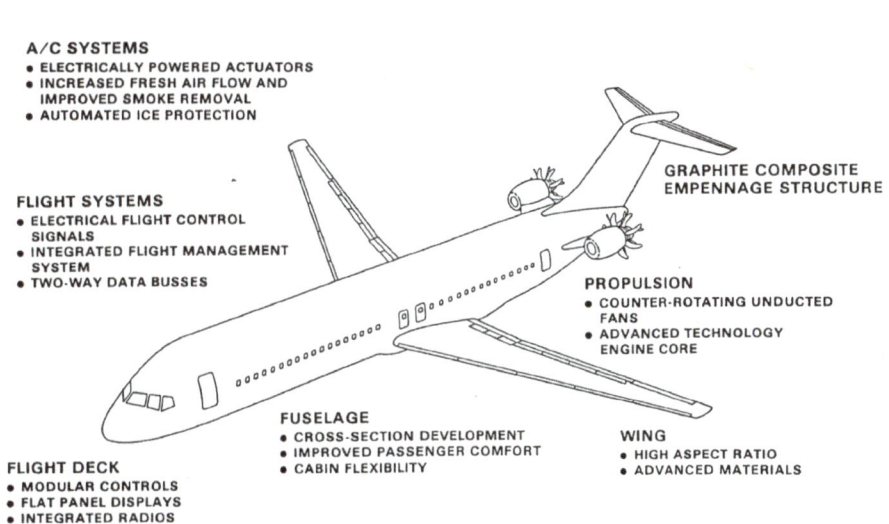

Boeing planned major changes in all systems in its 7J7 plane.
Illustration Boeing.

The UDF engine was tested on both the Boeing 727 and the MD-80.
Photo Boeing.

engines with UDF engines when they were fully developed. SAS stood doubtful, however, to such a solution. Fuel prices had not reached the heights that the 1980 forecasts showed. Now prices were down to more normal levels, which reduced demand for new fuel efficient but expensive designs.

MDC sketched up two new projects, the MD-91X and the MD-94X, also with the new engine type. The MD-91X would be a modified MD-80 and MDC claimed that they could deliver airplanes in 1991 i.e. before Boeing. For flight testing MDC elected equipping an MD-80 with a UDF. This aircraft was displayed at the air show at Farnborough in 1988 where Bengt-Olov Nas, some others, and I had the opportunity to fly on the aircraft. The engine mounting design included a very strong steel structure through the fuselage but the vibrations were still noticeable. Boeing had at most about 1000 engineers employed on the 7J7 project and had put down big money, but announced in late 1987 that the project would be delayed at least a year. The interest of the airlines became less than what Boeing expected. Meanwhile, Boeing began to focus on its 737 program, in which sales had slowed. When Boeing now offered a new version, the 737-300, interest from the market increased. The 737-300 was an upgrade of the 737-200 with a new, modern CFM56 engine. The engine had been available for some time, and as described previously installed in the DC-8-70. Both Boeing and GE began to rethink when the companies saw a growing market with the 737 and accordingly began to hesitate regarding

Final Boeing 7J7 configuration in SAS brand.
Model and photo Ulf Abrahamsson.

One of our employees was an established cartoonist and he showed his view of the aircraft with the UDF engine.
Drawing Bertil Bjork.

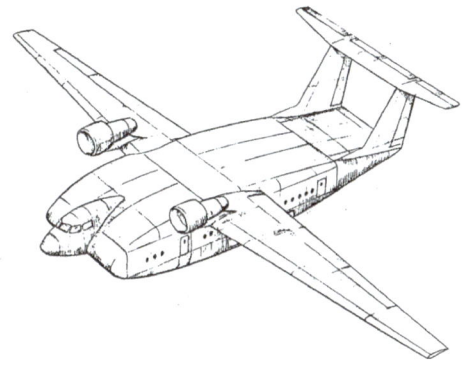

A sketch of Vincent Burnelli concept.

the 7J7 program, considering that it would likely compete with the 737.

The dialogue on the P3 plane and Boeing's 7J7 went directly from the development function, to Jan Carlzon, and the SAS Board. Jan Carlzon became very disappointed when Boeing at a meeting at SAS headquarters announced that the 7J7 project likely would be stopped. Carlzon claimed that SAS had intended to buy more than 100 aircraft of this type. Lufthansa had earlier in a similar manner through its technical director said that they wanted to buy a larger number of 7J7s but it was then probably mostly for testing, to see if Boeing and General Electric were serious. SAS, however, brought along their thoughts and wishes for cabin design in future work with aircraft manufacturers.

Two of the principals behind the 7J7 program, Phil Condit and Alan Mulally, then came to become big names in the development of the long-range Boeing 777 plane. In 2006 Mulally left Boeing and became president of the Ford Group and Phil Condit eventually became CEO of Boeing.

SAS interest in rethinking of aircraft cabins led to an interesting contact in the early 1980s. Olof Palme had a brother, Claes Palme living in Stockholm, who was a lawyer. He contacted SAS management and stated that he knew a person who wanted to show an aircraft design that was brand new and which should be interesting to SAS. It turned out that the person had brought drawings of an old concept, which originated from Vincent Burnelli. The fuselage had a real broad cabin that would help to provide lift. Burnelli had passed away in 1964 but his ideas apparently lived on. We thanked him kindly for information and explained that we were not able to support the project. What connections Claes Palme had, never became clear.

Responsibility for fleet planning in SAS came to be reconsidered during 1984. A new group, "Aircraft Planning Group", APG, was established reporting to Lars Bergvall, director of "Commercial Division." The Executive Board decided that I should be engaged full time but I got strong warnings by Nils Molander, who suggested that I should not accept before the picture of accountability became clear.

APG presented a comprehensive plan in 1984 for SAS management in which the principal behind the plan was a young economist hired by Lars Bergvall. The plan did not lead to any concrete action. In the spring of 1985 several meetings were held on how the fleet planning would be handled and much criticism came up internally. The next part of the question of how fleet planning would be handled came in July 1985 when I had just returned from a trip to the USA and prepared to go on vacation. I got a phone call from Jan Carlzon who announced that I would take care of fleet planning and under my current job as head of the "Central Engineering" in the technical division. An offer I accepted.

The MD-87 with its shorter body demanded an increased height of the fin to maintain directional stability.
Photo Hans Norman, www.scanliners.com.

MD-87 and DC-9-80 turns MD-80

To address the lack of capacity, as mentioned earlier, a decision in 1984 was to buy six DC-9-81s and eight DC-9-82s for delivery in 1985-86. The need for more aircraft increased with the opening of new direct routes and SAS chose to increase the order of the DC-9-80 with 18 additional aircraft for delivery in 1987-1991. Moreover, there was a need for a 100-seat plane that could handle longer distances than SAS's MD-80s. The Fokker 100, Boeing 737-300, and MDC's latest version of the MD-80 series, the MD-87, were studied. The Fokker 100 was interesting not only as a well-developed 100-seater but also because Swissair previously bought the type, and it proved to work well. The MD-87 was a shorter version of the MD-81/82 and additionally with a brand new digital flight deck. It would, however, mean that a new pilot group was needed in SAS as the changes were considered so great that the group that flew the DC-9-20 / 41 and DC-9-80 could not at the same time fly MD-87s. In selecting the most appropriate option it was still felt that the MD-87 was the best option especially as SAS saw an opportunity to create a unified MD-80 fleet by upgrading the flight deck of the 18 DC-9-80s now in the fleet to the new digital standard.

The upgrade of the flight deck for the 18 DC-9-80s was conducted at the maintenance base on Fornebue, Norway, with support from MDC. It was a difficult job in the narrow space in the nose of the aircraft where only one technician could work due to accessibility to the flight deck. The work created great respect in the industry for the base's knowhow. Boeing flew over a 737-300 to Arlanda for a demonstration. The cabin's front section had a layout with a double seat on one side of the aisle and a triple seat on the other side. Boeing wanted to show that the 737 would be able to meet SAS P3 wishes in any case, in terms of passenger comfort.

SAS decided in June 1986 to buy ten MD-87s, and subsequent orders grew the MD-87 fleet to 16 aircraft. The choice of aircraft felt right with respect to the already rather large DC-9-80 fleet and thus keeping type cost down.

The SAS board felt it important and natural to simultaneously notify Boeing about the MD-87 decision to insure Boeing that SAS had continued strong interest in the 7J7. SAS would eventually start the exchange of the large DC-9 fleet, and the 7J7 would be a strong candidate. A letter with this information was therefore sent to Boeing on the day when the MD-87 decision was made.

SAS also ordered two MD-83s, a version with higher takeoff weight and thus more range. The planes would replace the DC-8 on some routes. SAS demanded, however, increased fuel capacity and extra fuel tanks should be installed in the plane's cargo hold. It was a difficult modification that MDC at first was very hesitant to offer. The requirement was linked to the desirability of using MD-83s on a new route, Copenhagen-Jeddah non-stop that needed more fuel capacity. The route to Jeddah, however, was withdrawn after only a short period. The MD-83 was thus for SAS a specific solution that later would cause problems in connection with phasing out the type.

When the MD-83 no longer fitted in, Scanair was seen as a suitable customer for the type to be used for flights to the Canary Islands. Scanair was pretty tough in negotiating and demanded that the auxiliary fuel tanks would be removed to reduce aircraft empty weight, which was done! The standard fuel capacity was still sufficient for Scanair's needs.

Hovercraft, aerostat or boat

SAS services between Malmö and Copenhagen were flown, as long as Bulltofta airport remained, with several aircraft types from the DC-3 to DC-7. Flight time was about five minutes.

When Bulltofta closed and the new airport Sturup opened about 20 mi. from Malmö, SAS saw the possibility of solving the need in an unusual way, and in 1984 started services with a hovercraft accommodating 86 passengers and later with catamarans with capacity for 168 passengers.

It was only unclear whether the hovercraft supervision would be governed by the aviation authorities or shipping authorities. The solution was that Danish Maritime Authority's rules would apply and "flown" by sea captains. The travel time across the Öresund was 35 minutes. When the Öresund Bridge was complete in 2000 the operations ended.

SAS moved for a time to "maritime transport" between Malmö and Copenhagen Airport with hovercraft and catamaran.
Photo SAS.

McDonnell Douglas MD-11

At the board meeting in December 1986 in Copenhagen a recommendation for the purchase of two DC-10-30 aircraft from THAI was submitted to the Board for decision. SAS also had an offer from MDC, which included their taking over the two 747s that were on lease from the US Exim bank, if SAS signed up for options on the MD-11.

MDC had started a new project, the MD-11, a further development of the DC-10 with a stretch fuselage, for about 260 passengers, a new digital flight deck for two pilots, new engine versions, and longer range than the DC-10-30. The wing was basically the same as the DC-10 except that it had been extended with so-called winglets. The MD-11 was also offered in a shorter version for really long distances with room for about 230 passengers and 15 tons of cargo. The project had not officially started, but MDC was expected to "press the button" around the turn of the year.

The two 747s were a problem for SAS and some saw an opportunity to solve it through the MD-11 options. Berfore the meeting the management reviewed the agenda with the chairman Haldor Topsoe. Topsoe stressed during the preliminary meeting that SAS would now start the purchase of new aircraft and that the good results for some years made it possible. I raised reservations because we had not done any analysis of current aircraft but I was then told that I could sit there as museum director with my old aircraft. SAS Vice Chairman Curt Nicolin had during the Board meeting agreed withTopsoe, but the rest of the board seemed somewhat surprised.

The Board decided to buy the two DC-10-30 planes from THAI and to ensure twelve delivery positions with MDC for the MD-11, which was also announced in a press release the following day. In the press release, however, it was stated that SAS bought twelve MD-11s for delivery during the period 1991-1994 for a value of about 10 billion Kr, or about 100 Million USD per aircraft. The price quoted in the newspapers was well overstated and the message created great confusion. Airbus and Boeing were completely taken by surprise. Boeing's representative in Stockholm was called by his bosses in Seattle, who received the information through the news on CNN, and they wondered of course what was going on and blamed their man for not keeping abreast of what was happening within his own area of responsibility. The Airbus representative ended up in the same difficult position with his bosses in Toulouse. Their representative called me on Christmas Eve at noon to discuss how Airbus could come into the picture with its A340, which can illustrate that Airbus was pressed.

He intervened by calling the SAS chairman directly, at the time Tor Moursund, which was not appreciated. I got a clear message to ensure that this was not repeated! Inside SAS were also many who wondered what had happened. We had not done any detailed analysis of the MD-11 when the project was new and we had limited information from MDC. We were moreover also moving at full speed to build up our one-type fleet for long routes with the DC-10-30!

The decision created great interest in the international press who knew that SAS had recently taken the decision to build a single fleet of DC-10s. According to MDC, SAS's position strongly contributed to the decision by MDC to officially start the MD-11 program, since it was now felt that they had enough customers to feel confident about the success of the project.

MDC invited airlines to a kick-off meeting in Long Beach on 31 December1986 in which potential customers like Finnair, British Caledonian, Swissair, and SAS participated. Finnair confirmed later that they were affected by SAS's decision. Swissair chose the PWA PW4000 engine for its MD-11.

The SAS decision was perceived as a confirmation that SAS would continue to invest in long haul services but that it required the continued rationalization within the company. The Head of Operations Viggo Löfsgaard made a statement internally that he felt pleased that SAS has chosen a type of aircraft with three engines and not a type with two engines!

It turned out later that MDC had sent a proposal on the MD-11 directly to our Danish chairman shortly before the board meeting. If anyone else at SAS also had the proposal it is still unclear. Both Curt Nicolin and Jan Carlzon were positive and one can assume that they were informed. That Topsoe acted ought

MD-11 McDonnell Douglas development of the DC-10-30, extended fuselage, winglets, new engines and modernized flight deck.
Photo Boeing.

to be seen against the background that the Danish side always wanted to secure the bulk of SAS's long-haul services originating from Copenhagen with feeder traffic from the rest of Scandinavia.

Immediately after the meeting, I received questions from some board members about how big the investment decision was. Chairman of the board, Tor Moursund, asked later for a separate memo on this. There seemed to be some uncertainty within the board. Formally, SAS now had an agreement with MDC securing twelve MD-11 delivery positions.

As head of airline operations in SAS Lars Bergvall now demanded, in consultation with Kjell Fredheim as business manager for long haul (Intercont), that a larger assessment should be made of aircraft for long distances that were on the market. It should be the ready by 31 March 1987, the date when the MD-11 options had to be converted into firm orders.

The options included in the study were, in addition to the MD-11, the Boeing 767 and Airbus A340. A special team was appointed by me as project leader and some of SAS's most meritorious economists, Carl-Axel Staehl von Holstein and Mats Valinger were included. The group decided that, unusually, we would hire some experts Carl-Axel knew from his time in the US, Dean Boyd and Bob Phillips in the company DFI. DFI was commissioned to do a complete financial analysis that would show how SAS results would be affected by the current options and compared with a DC-10-30 fleet as a reference. They were "locked up" in the offices that the project department had available with clear instructions not to communicate with the outside world without SAS's consent.

Thus SAS launched an evaluation of alternatives to the DC-10-30 even before we established the planned phase out of the DC-10 fleet!

It was a busy time. I delegated responsibility for Central Engineering to a colleauge and worked full time on the project issues. In addition to the analyses of suitable aircraft for long haul going on at the same time we worked intensively with a large study of suitable aircraft for the newly formed SAS Commuter. In addition, I undertook to be acting head of the Technical Division for six months after Christer Nilsson left SAS to become CEO of Linjeflyg. Christer came to SAS in 1985 from Linjeflyg where he was the technical director. We needed now, beginning early 1987, as soon as possible to make preliminary SAS specifications for the four-engine Airbus A340, three-engine MDC MD-11, and the twin-engine Boeing 767-300ER. MD-11 specification required less work as this could be done in cooperation with Swissair, which already had decided on the type and the new PWA-PW4000 engine, while the other two types required extensive and immediate action.

MD-11 had PWA's new PW4000 engine, a version of the JT9 engine. Photo PWA.

Airbus A340

Airbus responded immediately when information about SAS's purchase of the MD-11 was published and soon delivered a proposal for the new A340. It was a completely new version with engines from IAE, the International Aero Engines, a fairly new company formed in cooperation between primarily PWA and Rolls-Royce but with some participation of Japanese, German and Italian engine manufacturers.

The engine had a large fan operated via a gearbox, and a bypass ratio of about 17: 1 and was called "Superfan". You could call it a "Ducted Fan," unlike the aforementioned engine, the UnDucted-Fan, (UDF). IAE had a contract with Airbus, which included certification and delivery of the first engines in 1992.

SAS board members with great technical skills included Curt Nicolin, who really knew jet engines, and Haldor Topsoe, who ran a chemical-technical

Haldor Topsoe. SAS Chairman 1986- 1987. The presidency alternated each year between the three board members representing the private owners, Haldor Topsoe Denmark, Curt Nicolin Sweden and Tor Moursund Norway.
Photo SAS.

Airbus A340, a project under development late 1980s.
Photo Airbus.

Curt Nicolin. First Deputy Chairman of SAS 1986-, 1987.
Photo SAS.

company. We showed reluctance to the IAE engine as it was an untested design. Topsoe, who was very interested in engines and also knowledgeable on the area, called in experts from IAE. The only way to make time for this, was a meeting set up on 25 March 1987 at a London hotel outside Heathrow Airport starting at 07:00 right after the IAE representatives arrived from the US that morning. To the meeting Topsoe invited me and our engine expert at the Linta workshop, Sven-Goran Danielsson. Immediately after the meeting, we estimated that the option A340 with IAE engine was completely unrealistic in the given time frame. In April 1987, the IAE engine project was cancelled and that type of engine has only now around 2015 become available again. The Airbus A340 program was judged to be somewhat uncertain.

In the further analysis A340 was produced with another version of the CFM56, from the French-American manufacturer CFMI. The engine already flew on the Airbus A320 but needed to be developed to cope with the higher thrust the A340 required. Also this engine would be available around 1992. Lufthansa evaluated the same types of aircraft as SAS around the same time. We had good contact with Lufthansa's project department and had some insight into their evaluation of the A340.

Airbus now ran a major campaign to demonstrate the advantages of four-engine aircraft for long-haul regarding the operating costs and safety. MDC acted similarly, applicable to three-engine airplanes. Per Norlin, SAS chief in the early years received a long letter from an MDC employee in which the danger of flying a twin-engine aircraft over long distances was described based on studies that MDC made during 1985. The author argued among other points that the statistics that showed the safety with new engines had been tampered with. It also referred to Lufthansa studies for the Atlantic flights, and that they had concluded that twin engine flights across the Atlantic were not a possibility for DLH. Lufthansa's position was probably linked to the fact it had Airbus A310s, which then did not have sufficient range for the Atlantic flights. The letter was copied to former executives in SAS and Curt Nicolin.

The A340 had the problem that delivery could occur until only around 1992. The MD-11 gave clearly deteriorating financial results in the calculations compared to the other options. The A340 and MD-11 both had the advantage of a bigger cabin cross-section than the 767, which created the opportunity to use part of the space under the floor for the galley and thereby get more passenger seats in the cabin.

Curt Nicolin felt that SAS should furnish parts of cargo space with beds which would provide a good product for first-class passengers. Cabin staff expressed the wish that the space should be used as a rest area for staff. The long flight times meant that rest facilities were required for both pilots and cabin crew.

Boeing 767

SAS now had a confidence problem with Boeing, which of course had read in the press that SAS's acquisition of MD-11 was already firmed up. We then went to Boeing in Seattle with a small specification group and were met with a certain reluctance on the Boeing side, wondering if SAS was really serious. After clarifying for Boeing's management the real situation, we started the work with great enthusiasm even from Boeing employees.

The Boeing option was special because it was a twin-engine aircraft that should manage long over water navigation according to the rules of EROPS "Extended Range Operations". In addition, the first 767 wide-body aircraft was designed to be flown by two pilots and had a completely new flight deck with EFIS, "Electronic Flight Instruments."

Boeing had deliberately chosen a wing design with a large wing area, which, combined with high engine thrust, allowed for rapid climb to flight levels up to about FL 430, 43,000 feet, where the traffic was not so dense. Boeing also invested in new airfoils with slightly greater thickness, which allowed the two wing spars to be separated more. This gave greater volume of fuel that was crucial for Boeing, which saw the opportunity to sell the 767 also for the long haul.

The FAA introduced in 1953 the "60 minute rule" for two-engined aircraft. The rule meant that the flight track for this type of aircraft could not be longer than 60 minutes flying time on one engine from a suitable landing airport. Some routes forced the aircraft to fly detours and were excluded completely from certain routes because of lack of airports along the way.

Jet engines, e.g. Pratt & Whitney JT8D, showed in the 1960s that they had significantly higher reliability than traditional piston engines. The JT8D engine was installed in the Boeing 727, 737 and DC-9, contemporary two- and three-engine airplanes. Thanks to the operating experience the "60-minute rule" was done away with for three-engine aircraft in 1964. It paved the way for the development of three-engine aircraft that was both larger and could fly longer, as the McDonnell Douglas DC-10 and Lockheed Tristar. Left was the twin-engine aircraft that was still limited by the 60-minute rule. Outside the United States the other countries followed the ICAO Annex 6 rules that allowed a maximum of 90 minutes flying time to the nearest suitable airport.

Technological developments led to FAA and ICAO now views that even twin-engine transport aircraft could safely perform inter-continental and trans-oceanic flights if certain additions were made in the design, equipment, and operating rules. The new guidelines came to be called ETOPS "Extended Twin Engine Operations."

The FAA was the first to approve ETOPS guidelines in 1985. The guidelines contained the additional requirements that must be met in order to get permission to fly up to 120 minutes flying time to the nearest airport on one engine.

The basic requirements regarding aircraft was that the engines would have demonstrated sufficient operational safety, include installation of equipment required for increased cooling of avionics, a fire-extinguishing systems in all cargo spaces, and the additional hydraulic motor generator. Furthermore it required the proven operating and starting safety for the APU installation after a long cooling period when flying at high altitude. Even the maintenance requirements were tightened for airplanes that would be flown under the new rules. Boeing experts contributed significantly to this development. Today most of the trans-oceanic flights are ETOPS.

A serious incident occurred in 1983 with an Air Canada 767-200 during flight between Montreal and Edmonton when both engines shut down. The event had an impact on the regulatory framework when several weaknesses were discovered during the investigation of the incident. The root cause was found to be confusion between weight units in kilograms and pounds during the refueling of the aircraft. Air Canada had recently switched to the metric system. The aircraft also had a glitch in the fuel indication system so the pilots did not receive information on the flight deck of the actual fuel supply. Several misunderstandings had arisen but the pilots chose to fly despite this.

Most of the new fine "Electronic Flight Instrument Systems" (EFIS) was knocked out when the generators of the engines stopped and the batteries only managed the basic instruments. The hydraulic systems, which now were run by a "Ram Air Turbine" drove the steering system but with diminishing abilities as the pilot slowed down before the landing. It all ended happily still with a few injuries from the evacuation of the airplane after landing. The captain on board happened to be a qualified glider pilot and the co-pilot was aware of an abandoned military airport nearby used by the Canadian Forces where they could execute a controlled landing after a sideslip when both the speed and height were too high during the approach for landing.

The incident revealed a number of factors that came to influence the design of ETOPS Rules. It later turned out that the technical requirements of ETOPS also resulted in generally better reliability.

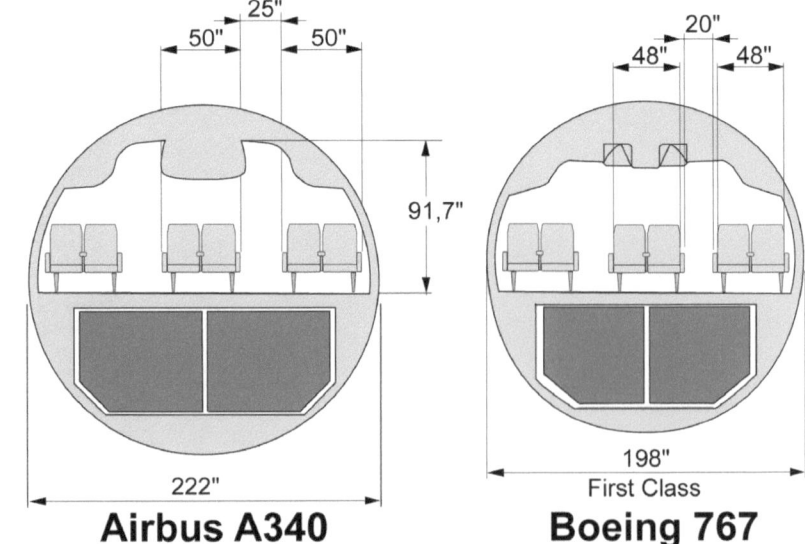

Cabin Cross Section Boeing 767s and Airbus A340s. Drawing Hans Kampf.

Boeing 767 and Mount Rainier.
Photo by SFF.

The choice of a new aircraft for long-haul routes.

A change had taken place in the important Atlantic traffic policy. Several US airlines intended in 1988 to start or expand the number of nonstop flights to various destinations in Europe. In 1986 American Airlines flew 15 frequencies per week to Scandinavia, which was estimated to increase to 52 per week during 1988.

SAS wanted to meet the competition by opening several routes from Scandinavia to the United States. In addition to Copenhagen, direct routes from Stockholm, Gothenburg, and Bergen to several locations in the United States would be opened. This meant that SAS, using planes with better economics than with the DC-10-30, would be able to fly with smaller aircraft. All this gave the 767 option an advantage, which also came out clearly the best in the comprehensive analysis that was carried out. The 767 would also result in significant savings in fuel compared to the DC-10 and additionally reduced noise pollution.

The project organization therefore recommended the Boeing 767 in March 1987 in its report to the management of the airline, called the Airline Executive Committee. Subsequently several high-level meetings were held with Airbus and MDC. MDC chose to give SAS another month to make the decisions but the SAS board chose to defer the decision on the new long-haul aircraft to the board meeting in September.

It now remained to select the engine type and to convince the board and some of SAS's larger corporate customers who had highlighted some concerns about allowing their staff to fly on twin-engine planes. The management also put demands on the Intercont business that it would be able to report annual savings of at least M$ 80.0 in its activities if SAS were to buy new aircraft.

We had three engine manufacturers to choose from, General Electric CF6, Pratt & Whitneys new PW4000, and Rolls Royce RB524. The Rolls-Royce option was droipped early due to increased empty weight and availability timing.

Our internal team of experts, which had been supplemented with former chief engineer at Volvo Aeroengine, Gunnar Broman, recommended the PWA engine.

A big public relations effort on twin-engine flights on SAS long-haul routes started, where I had long phone conversations with directors and government agency people and letters to some Scandinavian companies that were major customers of SAS. In SAS there was also discussion at the highest level and it was not until the board meeting in January 1988 before the board made the decision to buy the 767. In my view, the delay was primarily caused by by Haldor Topsoe, who still wanted Copenhagen as the basis for the long-haul route network in SAS and therefore desired larger aircraft. He was also a strong opponent of flights with two-engine airplanes on the long-haul route network. The Danish aviation authority also showed great reluctance. Topsoe also raised the option to continue with the DC-10 and expand the fleet with the more used aircraft.

The decision in January 1988, was for eleven 767 aircraft of which two would be the smaller version 767-200ER for the Copenhagen-Singapore route.

SAS already had decided in the beginning that each aircraft would have a Viking name and so far it had only been male names. Now it was decided also to use female names. The first 767 aircraft was given the name Ingegerd Viking and delivered in March 1989. The specification of the aircraft now contained a rest area for a pilot as the 767 was flown by three pilots on board on all the long routes. Even the cabin crew rest compartments were two double seats in the rear of the cabin and built in as an enclosure with a door. The inaugural flight from Copenhagen to Singapore became heavily delayed when cabin crew refused to approve the design of the rest area, requiring improved noise attenuating and seals to keep out the smell of cigarette smoke.

Boeing noted that the SAS cabin configuration had the lowest number of seats of all 767 operators (209 seats in the 767-300 and 150 seats in the 767-200). Boeing did not disclose the cabin configurations that their customers have chosen but they provided a list of all configurations. I pointed to the one which had the least number of seats and asserted that it must be the SAS aircraft. Boeing confirmed this! It must be said that the "kitchen" area in the front of the cabin occupied a large area.

When SAS in 1989-1990 built up the 767 fleet the Intercont service area with Kjell Fredheim at the lead could finally establish an effective traffic program with just one airplane type. Thanks to a well-planned traffic program each aircraft could now be used optimally for up to about 16 hours in the air per day! At the same time, SAS had decided to move their traffic from Kennedy Airport in New York to Newark, where Continental Airlines operated. SAS had recently chosen Continental as its US partner. SAS was thus able to offer its passengers from Europe about 60 US destinations with just one change. Big changes that according to Fredenheim involved certain risks but it worked fine. Intercont now managed to show a profit in 1995.

The domestic business area in Sweden, with Peter Forsman in charge, expressed strong desire to get larger aircraft for the Stockholm-Gothenburg route when the number of daily frequencies with the MD-80 was now 16 and increased traffic was considered only to be met by larger aircraft. The project was very hesitant about using the 767-200, which certainly had the right size but was not effective on short routes. A decision was taken in January 1990 to buy two 767-200s for this activity but they could not be delivered in time and the traffic situation changed. SAS requested a postponement of deliveries to 1994-95, which Boeing accepted.

The Boeing 767 soon became a regular airplane type for the traffic across the Atlantic and the higher requirements as required for ETOPS rules, resulted in increased operational safety. The DC-10 fleet in 1987 had grown to eleven aircraft was being phased out now, with rapidly growing 767 deliveries.

The Boeing 767 was well received by customers. SAS decided to discontinue first class on long-haul but instead offered a product called "First Business Class," which our competitors put a stop to. We were not allowed to use the term "First"! The decision was to use the same concept, which was established for the European routes, namely the "Euro Class." SAS desired early on that we should be able to offer flat-bed seats to passengers on long-haul

SAS developed a flexible business class seat for the full fare traveler, Photo SAS

SAS accepting the first 767. From left Ulf Abrahamsson SAS, Neil Standal Boeing, Lars Bergvall SAS, Kjell Fredheim SAS, Borge Boeskov Boeing and Lars Rantzen SAS.
Photo Boeing.

767-300ER delivery from Seattle.
From left, Kjell Fredheim, CEO SAS Intercontinental operations, Inger Rosell Marketing Manager for Kjell Fredheim, Borge Boeskov Boeing, Lars Bergvall head of SAS Airline and Jeff Young Boeing. The journey homeward was delayed due to engine failure.
Photo SAS.

routes. We chose to develop the seats ourselves. Several employees were offered the chance to test the flat-bed seats before the final configuration was determined. A slight complication was of course that when the flat-bed seats were used some seats behind had to move backward to make space. Unfortunately, some times it happened that the seats not stick to the rails firmly, and came off.

In connection with the delivery of the 767 the decision was taken that SAS cabins would get a new color scheme with a gray leather seat cover. It was not long before SAS had to change the decision when both passengers and cabin crew reacted to what some called "the Russian gray." Now the seats were dressed in a nice blue fabric.

Phase out of the DC-9

Noise regulations in FAR 36 and ICAO Annex 16 had been supplemented with a requirement that the phasing out of so-called Chapter 2 aircraft would take place by 2002. The DC-9 could thus not fly beyond 2002. But otherwise there were really no commercial or technical motives to replace the type. Fuel costs around 1980/81 were about 20 percent of operating costs and had decreased significantly so it contributed to the assessment that the new planes that were on the market were not sufficiently cost-effective to cover the massive increased capital costs required. SAS therefore had waited as long as possible to choose the DC-9's replacement.

To cope with the growth in the market, SAS during 1984-1986 bought a number of DC-9-80s, which were converted to the MD-80. At the same time, we noted that interest in Boeing's 7J7 project waned among airlines, and had to realize that we could no longer postpone decisions on how the DC-9 should be phased out. Analyses of available options were carried out in stages during 1985-87, and it felt natural to recommend the MD-80 partly as a DC-9 replacement when the MD-80 fleet already consisted of 26 aircraft.

While SAS evaluated what type of aircraft would replace the DC-9, studies were going on at Linjeflyg (LIN), under Christer Nilsson's guidance, on how the Linjeflyg fleet would best be able to grow to meet its needs. LIN had throughout the 1980s had a growth of almost 9 percent per year in number of passengers. Linjeflyg had traditionally always tried to avoid technical cooperation with SAS and wanted their own solutions when selecting the type of aircraft. The options LIN studied were new Fokker 100, Airbus A320, Boeing 737-500, British Aerospace 146, and MDC MD-87.

In early May 1988 LIN's board of directors made the decision to buy six 737-500s from Boeing with another six options. The 737-500 was a new version with slightly shorter body than the 737-300 but otherwise similar. The LIN configuration had 131 seats. The decision created some concern within SAS management and the board and SAS lobbied pretty hard that LIN should buy the MD-87, but LIN's board with Nils Hörjel as chairman managed to make their own decision. It was feared that with MD-87, SAS would take care of the heavy maintenance and probably at higher prices than LIN could buy on the market. SAS's board signed, in June 1988, i.e. one month after the LIN 737 decision, a contract with MDC for the delivery of 61 MD-80 aircraft of which 24 were firm orders and 37 were options. The order value was about 2 billion USD and deliveries would begin in 1989. The agreement included the ability to later make an engine replacement for UDF engines if MDC launched the UDF program. SAS had previously shown reluctance for this but we felt that the possibility still could be included in the agreement.

Around the same time, as one could read in the press about SAS large order of aircraft, articles could be found about MDC cancelling its agreement with

Saab in Linköping regarding production of wing flaps for the MD-80. The agreement had been in existence for several years and worked well for both parties. MDC explained the actions with the need to reduce costs in the procurement of all their subcontractors. Saab had to return all the drawings, which MDC gave to the new provider, AVCO.

Saab's top management quite naturally contacted SAS to get information and sought support. SAS obviously got criticism from Saab and also from the minister of industry, Tage G Petersson for not having secured counter-trade agreements. SAS raised the issue with Jim Worsham, MDC's president. He offered Saab work with details on the MD-11 program but it did not fit into Saab's production. However, it appeared that MDC had chosen a new supplier that had promised too much and could not deliver the desired product. MDC went back to Saab, return the drawings and conclude a new agreement. SAS also began in 1988 selling DC-9-40s and leasing them back for a while until they were withdrawn from the fleet. In this way securing resale value and even though there were plenty of used aircraft on the market, demand was still high. The manufacturers had difficulty delivering new aircraft in a short time. SAS had sold second-hand aircraft during the period 1986-1988 with gains of around $ million 240.

SAS signs a contract with MDC for 24 firm and 37 MD-80 options achieving an overall order value of about B$ 2.0.
Sitting; Jim Worsham MDC and Jan Carlzon SAS, standing: Ulf Abrahamsson, Glen Hickerson MDC and Anders Claesson.
Photo SAS.

Two happy men after the contract was signed. Ulf Abrahamsson holds a model of the MD-80 with UDF engines.
Photo SAS.

New strategies

SAS evolves as a company

SAS was established as a consortium with an agreement concluded between the three Scandinavian countries in 1951. SAS had a simple structure in which the parent company ABA held three sevenths, DDL and DNL two sevenths each.

In each country, the state owned fifty percent and private interests the remaining fifty percent. SAS Airline conducted the flight operations inside SAS. Later came various subsidiary companies such as SAS Invest, SAS Catering and even Linjeflyg. Under Jan Carlzon's management the organization chart also added several another activities shown in 1987. It shows the situation when the three Scandinavian governments formally extended the SAS cooperation to 2005. SAS International Hotels was included in the ambition of SAS to offer passengers a complete product with accommodations, transportation to and from the airport, and the flight.

Flight operations that early had been supplemented with the formation of Scanair for charter flights, got in 1989 a new branch with the formation of SAS Commuter, focused on traffic in Scandinavia

and northern Europe.

In February 1988, SAS headquarters moved into new premises, Frösundavik in Solna just north of Stockholm City. As a side note, the investment in the fine headquarter roughly equaled the cost of a Boeing 767-300ER in the same year.

SAS ORGANIZATION 1987

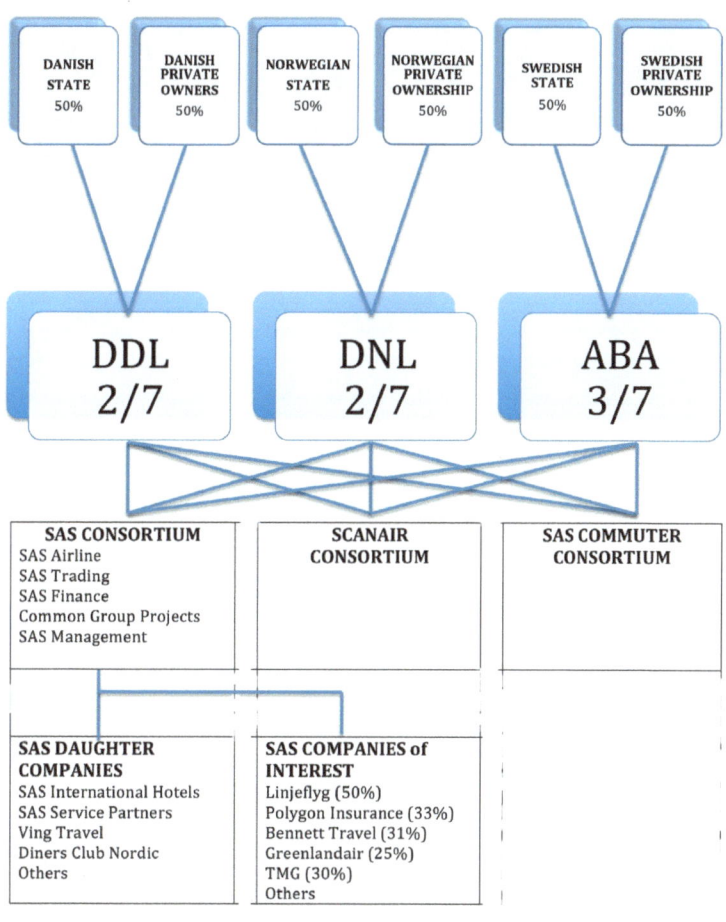

Charter Company Scanair aquires their own aircraft

Scanair, which was set up in 1961, utilized aircraft that were transferred from SAS. It started with the DC-7 and later the DC-8, A300, DC-10, and 747. When SAS had excess planes Scanair even flew with SAS aircraft, and when SAS painted their aircraft in the new color scheme around 1981, Scanair did a similar facelift of its aircraft.

In 1988 Scanair acquired its own fleet of DC-10-10s, which had the capacity for 374 passengers. These aircraft got brand new names taken from cartoon characters like, Bamse and the like. The DC-10-10 was the same size as the SAS DC-10-30 but had lower takeoff weight, which suited Scanair's needs.

When Scanair's operations ceased in 1993, it transferred to the start-up charter company Premiere.

MD-83, registration LN-RMF, Scanair, who named the aircraft "Piff" (Walt Disney figure Chip), took over Torgny Viking from SAS. Photo Hans Norman, www.Scanliners.com.

Airbus A300B4 came onto Scanair's traffic in the summer of 1983 with 295 seats.
Photo: Lars-Inge Grundberg

Scanair DC-10 with 374 seats became the largest aircraft type in the charter business in Scandinavia
Photo Hans Norman
www.Scanliners.com

The ATR 72 was a strong candidate when the SAS Commuter's analysis was done, 1988.
Photo via SFF.

SAS Commuter

Short routes that are flown frequently, i.e. many frequencies indicating a need for relatively small aircraft, characterize SAS domestic traffic in Denmark. In Norway transport by air is often the only possibility, especially in northern Norway, but the customer base is quite thin. The traffic was carried out in cooperation with Widerøe who leased aircraft with crews.

In Sweden, SAS operated mainly on the heavier routes from Stockholm to Malmö, Gothenburg and Luleå while Linjeflyg flew to other destinations. SAS began in the early 1980s, to grow an interest in these other destinations and also some short routes in northern Europe. It was deemed important to be able to offer its own product even in these traffic areas, and feeder traffic was seen as very important especially with the markets in Europenow being liberalize. During 1983-1984 SAS started therefore a special profit center for short and thin routes, named"Commuter Operations Department." COD, with Jörgen Grauengaard as manager.

SAS began by buying four used Fokker F27s, a well established aircraft. The aircraft initially had major technical problems and probably the usual procedures had not been followed with a proper technical review of the aircraft before the purchase. The fleet was expanded, however, by acquiring a further five F27s. Passengers viewed the aircraft however as tight, noisy, and not a product in line with the SAS strategy "The Business Man's Airline." Besides, in addition to serving new markets, SAS also aimed at reducing costs through new contracts for staff in COD.

In 1986 therefore an independent company, SAS Commuter was established as a subsidiary similar to Scanair, who would sell their services to the SAS Group on competitive conditions. SAS launched in 1985-86 a proper evaluation of the aircraft that were on the market with about 50 seats, namely F50, British Aerospace ATP, ATR 42, ATR 72, de Havilland Canada Dash 8-300, and Saab 340, although it was considered too small.

Dash 8 came out well in the analyses. ATR 42's characteristics in icing did make SAS doubtful regarding that type. SAS had the opportunity to do some testing of this problem, and our pilot Jon Ertzgaard could confirm our fears. Jon suggested though that planned improvements by ATR which would be introduced later would eliminate the obvious weakness in the deicing system.

The decisive factor, however, was SAS firm demands on delivery time. A new approach for traffic to Northern Norway had a fixed timetable, starting on 1 May 1990 and the aircraft had to be delivered well before this date. This requirement would strongly control the decision of aircraft for SAS Commuter.

SAS Commuter gets the new Fokker 50 aircraft in 1989,
Photo Hans Norman
www.Scandliners.com

SAS's total needs were judged to be 22 aircraft, and the Board decided in May 1988 to buy 22 Fokker 50 aircraft with first delivery in 1989. The purchase included a requirement that Fokker would buy back the F-27 aircraft. The Fokker 50 fleet was divided into two groups with different cabin configurations, one with 50 seats for the Norwegian operation and one with 44 seats for European traffic.

Hard times

SAS's earnings declined after the sharp upturn in the first half of the 1980s.

Lars Bergvall as President of SAS Airline, raised a warning flag that the 1990s could have a tough start and both Kjell Fredheim, responsible for intercontinental traffic, and Vagn Sørensen, Head of European traffic, saw clear signs of continued decline, and a change in business conditions. The airline's budget for 1990 was missing about M$ 110 and a turn in the planning began to be discerned. Fuel prices had risen in 1991 by 36% compared to 1990 and the year was to become one of the airline industry's most difficult years. The reason was, among others, the war in Kuwait.

Aircraft manufacturers started to feel the airlines' situation, even if Airbus in 1991 showed continued confidence by talking about the need for the "Ultra High Capacity Airplane," UHCA, which would seat 600-700 passengers compared to the current biggest plane of 300-400 passengers . It later became the Airbus A380.

MDC had several new projects on the drawing board. SAS took delivery of its fiftieth MD-80 in 1991, which it wished to celebrate a little extra. SAS therefore sent over a slightly larger group than usual, which also received a briefing of MDC's future plans.

MDC showed detailed information of the MD-12X, a large four-engine aircraft seating about 375 passengers, which would enable the company to compete with Boeing and Airbus. However, we were somewhat skeptical about MDC's ability to launch such a large project.

SAS was forced to launch a major cost-cutting program. One area that immediately was tested was the current fleet plan and contracts with aircraft manufacturers. The necessary adjustments to the traffic program resulted in fewer aircraft. SAS was able to immediately offer a number of its aircraft for sale in a declining market.

A first step was to cancel a number of advantageous options that were included in the contracts with MDC, Boeing, and Fokker. SAS also began to hesitate regarding already contracted deliveries. The MDC agreement included the delivery of 19 MD-80s during 1991 and 15 in 1992; the agreement with Boeing covered the delivery of three Boeing 767s in 1991 and three in 1992. The contract with Fokker included two additional Fokker 50 in 1992.

The MDC MD-12 project that would compete with Airbus and Boeing's large aircraft.
Photo MDC.

The Fleet Development function received a clear message to sell or phase out at least five MD-80s and at least two Boeing 767s, either by sale or lease. Moreover, we would try to delay the delivery of, or in the worst case not receive, contracted aircraft.

Scanair leased two MD-80s, Air Europe in Italy leased two Boeing 767s and Boeing accepted the delay of the delivery of the two 767-200s destined for Swedish domestic routes as well as the three 737-500s that were included in the Linjeflyg agreement. The last DC-10-30 aircraft were sold in a different agreement when the company that bought the aircraft demanded that SAS would buy an MD-80 from them.

A special group for the implementation of sales was within Fleet Development, with Christer Bruce

In the period of tough times, SAS received the fiftieth MD-80. From left Russ Ray MDC, Ulf Abrahamsson, Robert Hood MDC president, Kjell Fredheim, Stefan Obius, John Wolf MDC, and Hank Picard PWA. MDC produced 1180 MD-80 aircraft.
Photo MDC.

SAS MD-80 nr 50
Torkild Viking
September 1991

as manager. He managed to convince Spanair that they needed an MD-80 and we could therefore do the DC-10 sales and meet Carlzon's requirement that the DC-10 planes be sold as soon as possible with a certain profit. We also examined the idea of delaying the phasing out of the DC-9 fleet until 2002, which was the outer boundary of the DC-9-operation in view of current noise rules.

We had a long-term planning for domestic and European traffic that included three size classes: small, medium, and big. Small was an aircraft with about 100 seats, Medium, with about 150 seats and Big ought to have about 180 seats. The focus was primarily on finding a solution for the Small during the second half of the 1990s.

Small, Medium, and Big became well-established concepts in the ongoing fleet planning.

MD-90 and MD-95

In late 1988, as the propfan concepts were sidelined, MDC started the planning for the further development of the MD-80, a project called the MD-90. The biggest change was that the new engine type IAE V2500 would be used. A challenge for MDC was to mount a large and heavier engine on the rear body. The body was lengthened by about 5 feet in front of the wing, in part to create balance and partly to increase passenger capacity. A fully modern flight deck with EFIS would also be included.

During the work with the MD-90 MDC also began to plan for a shorter version, tentatively called the MD-95. It was recognized that ongoing SAS internal analyses of smaller aircraft could be of interest as replacement of the F28 and MD-87.

SAS announced to MDC in late 1991 that it now wanted to renegotiate the delivery program for the MD-80 fleet including the aircraft that would be delivered in the spring of 1992. In addition, a number of options would be cancelled. A first meeting with MDC was held in December 1991 in New York where we argued that SAS intended not to take delivery of ten MD-80s and wished to delay the delivery of three aircraft. MDC could not accept this, claiming that SAS has itself to find buyers. One major problem was of course that the aircraft were already largely completed according to the SAS specification. Everyone realized that this was likely to be very difficult under the circumstances. MDC was hit simultaneously by other airlines with similar problems that also wanted to move deliveries. The dialogue with MDC ended with a meeting in Stockholm in January 1992 at Curt Nicolin's office with representatives from the SAS board of directors, management and Fleet Development.

Before the meeting Fleet Development had examined the basis that existed on the MD-90 and MD-95 projects and since the MD-90 had advanced in its specification, we felt that the MD-90 could be an option for our medium plane (if no other solution existed). The MD-95 was assessed as more uncertain as the specification was very preliminary. Besides, the MD-90 was available several years into the future and we could certainly open a dialogue again later if we so wished. The solution was that SAS entered into an agreement for six MD-90s with delivery around 1996 and thus MDC accepted that SAS would not take delivery of seven MD-80s in the spring of 1992. Some contracted MD-80 deliveries were moved to a later date.

MD-90 cabin mock-up at Frösundavik. From left: Tore Landfald, Sam Drake MDC, Ulf Abrahamsson, Karin Handberg, Jim Phillips MDC (seated), Dan Pemble MDC, Billie Hendrixon MDC, Peter Melander, Joe Zigarovich and Rich Sikora MDC. Photo SAS.

MDC wished we would immediately start the specification work for the six MD-90s, which was a problem since neither management nor any business area in SAS showed an interest in the planes. They were pleased that the problem now lay in the future. There were more pressing problems to solve. MDC made, however, an MD-90 cabin mockup, which was shipped over and placed on Fleet Development's premises in Frösundavik.

In December 1991, an accident involving an MD-81 occurred, the Gottrora crash, in which both engines ceased to function shortly after takeoff from the airport. The accident reason was clear ice breaking loose from the wing on both sides and entering into the engines, damaging the front stages of the compressor, which began stalling, after which the engines stopped. Fortunately, all 129 on board, including passengers and crew survived, but eight people were seriously injured.

In the press one could read "SAS reconsider ordering unfortunate plane." The press linked together the changes that have just been made in the agreement with MDC on the supply of new MD-80s with SAS no longer having confidence in the MD-80, which was of course completely untrue.

SAS acquires Linjeflyg

Linjeflyg was hit as well as SAS by the strong decline in traffic that occurred from 1990 to 1992. The reason was, among others, unrest in the Middle East, which resulted in increased fuel prices, the war in Kuwait in 1991, environmental charges, and the imposition of VAT on travel in Sweden.

The government decided that domestic flights

SAS got three new aircraft types by purchasing Linjeflyg in 1992, Boeing 737-500, Fokker F28 and Saab 340.
Photo Hans Norman, www.Scanliners.com.

Saab 340 in Swedair was part of the Linjeflyg fleet, SAS gained with the purchase of Linjeflyg. Photo Hans Norman, www.scanliners.com.

would be completely deregulated in June 1992 which meant that SAS and Linjeflyg would become competitors. In addition a new company started flying on the Stockholm-Malmö route. The result was 20-30 percent lower prices on domestic flights!

SAS ended up in an awkward situation as half owner of LIN. SAS first sold its share to Bilspedition in 1990, but re-purchased it around the new year in 1992 and purchased one (1.0) percent from ABA. SAS was now the majority owner of LIN and thus assumed LIN's fleet of aircraft, 19 Fokker F28s and 14 Boeing 737-500s, including LIN's leased aircraft, and also responsibility for the current contract with Boeing. In addition to these aircraft it included a number of Saab 340s in Swedair's fleet.

Working groups were set up that would take forward proposals how LIN's organization and airplanes would be integrated into the SAS organization. It was natural to use F28s and 737s because SAS would continue to fly the bulk of the LIN destinations and therefore needed the capacity.

Linjeflyg's decision in 1988 to choose the 737 had consequences for SAS, which now had a new type in its fleet. SAS got an additional total of 51 aircraft in 1992! Some DC-9-41s were phased out and some were leased out. The net increase in 1992 was 46 aircraft and three new planes!

This resulted in a surplus of aircraft and several activities started to change the situation. Swedair's Saab 340 fleet was gradually phased out by leasing to various customers, including to a company in New Zealand, Air Nelson.

Linjeflyg Boeing 737-500.
Photo Hans Norman
www.Scanliners.com.

LIN's CEO, Christer Nilsson, who had left his position as Vice President Technical of SAS in 1987, had a lot of informal contact with me regarding the analyses.

SAS Chairman Curt Nicolin demanded after the decision that Christer Nilsson and I would do an investigation, and that we would explain why we could come to different recommendations. Christer and I agreed to lie low for a while and the matter was forgotten eventually.

We had no idea then that within a few years the various decisions would have consequences for SAS fleet planning. LIN eventually operated nine 737-500s and had contracts for another five. The need for aircraft, however, was less than calculated and some were leased to the Polish company LOT. LIN had three contracted but not delivered 737-500s when SAS bought Linjeflyg in 1992.

Cooperation with other companies

In 1987, Jan Carlzon introduced new targets for SAS and came up with the term "One of Five in 95." The concept came from the assessment that in the 1990s only a few airlines would survive and SAS must have the goal of becoming one of them, probably in cooperation with one of the major companies in Europe. To achieve the goal the strategy "Businessman's Airline" widened and would now be based on commercial passengers' entire service needs, which, among others, resulted in a need to expand the route network. SAS would still provide excellent products, not only for the discerning business traveler, but also for those who sought the best price.

SAS started investing in hotels and other side businesses to be able to sell a total travel package.

The expansion of the route network would be cleared through cooperative agreements with suitable carriers. Several contacts were made with some who already had a connection to SAS such as Thai International and ANA in Japan but also with brand new such as Sabena, British Caledonian (BCAL), Lan Chile, and the US Continental. In some cases, SAS would become a part owner but the main purpose was to build a transport system that would cover all the important destinations that were of interest to the Scandinavian business traveler.

The contact with Sabena was broken pretty soon; philosophies were very different between the companies. SAS and Sabena had also large differences in their respective fleets and therefore no direct advantages existed. Continental had an advantage if one operated at Newark Airport in New York and SAS chose to move their business from John F Kennedy International Airport to Newark to obtain good coordination with Continental's domestic network.

British Airways acquired British Caledonian after SAS had, in late 1987, made great efforts to push through an agreement with BCAL but was stopped by major political opposition in England.

SAS still entered the English market during 1988 by buying a 24.9% stake in the Airlines of Britain Holdings whose largest subsidiary, British Midland, BMI, had a strong domestic network and access to slots at Heathrow airport. The stake did also address coordination of future aircraft purchases.

SAS charter company Vingresor stepped in as 25% part owner of the Spanish charter airline Spanair, a venture that came to be developed further.

In 1987-1988 SAS signed firm orders for 11 Boeing 767s, 22 Fokker 50, and also ordered 24 MD-80s with 37 options. During the same period 14 DC-9s and four DC-10 were sold and all were leased back for a period of between 24 and 36 months. The purpose of the sale was to secure the residual values before the phase-out of the aircraft.

British Midland, BMI

BMI, had a well-developed domestic network amounting to nearly 40 percent of the British market. In addition, BMI's route network was under intensive development in Europe. The group also included some smaller airlines, Manx Airlines, Loganair, and London City Airways. During 1989-1990 SAS coordinated schedules with BMI and gained considerable synergistic effects and a stable foothold at Heathrow, where slots were limited BMI's growth resulted in the need for aircraft and it was natural for SAS to take up the issue of leasing out over-capacity and especially the 737 fleet. Negotiations were completed on a lease of ten years for all the 737-500s, which gradually transferred to BMI and SAS achieved the desired rationalization in its fleet. The decision to phase out or sell the 737-500s created the opportunity to both reduce the number of types and the total number of aircraft,

BMI 737-500, registration G-BVZH was originally delivered to Linjeflyg as SE-DNG
Photo
Augusto Gomez Rojas

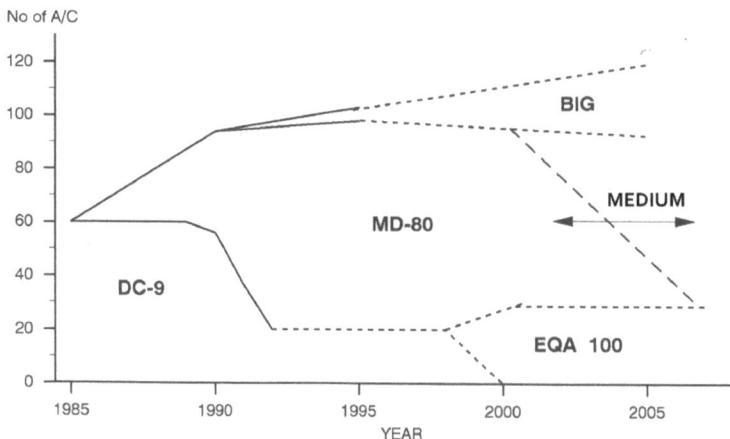

SAS fleet plan as it appeared in 1990 with EQA collaboration on a new 100-seat type
Picture Ulf Abrahamsson.

which were both considered more important than keeping the newest aircraft.

BMI was later to lease a number of Fokker 100s and Fokker 70s where SAS's analyses contributed to BMI's positive evaluation of the type. SAS later increased its stake in BMI to about 35 percent, but eventually sold its holding to Lufthansa in 2009, which also bought the remaining shares. In 2012 BMI was sold to British Airways.

EQA - European Quality Alliance

New agreements were signed in 1989 with Swissair and Finnair, and SAS had now established new hubs in other continents, Europe, and the Nordic countries. The new European group came to be known as the European Quality Alliance or EQA. Austrian Airlines, which had links to Swissair, soon became part of EQA.

EQA was primarily a collaboration of route networks but a group in the four companies also started to highlight fleet planning. Swissair planned for the phasing out of its DC-9-80s around 1994-95. Finnair had a similar situation with their DC-9s.

Although SAS had firmed up the planning for the phasing out of its remaining DC-9s, replacing them with MD-80s, the group agreed to make a move on aircraft manufacturers and requested in early 1990 a joint offer from each of MDC, Airbus, and Boeing for 240 aircraft. The producers were surprised to get a single request for one proposal from four companies even if MDC had been in a similar situation in the late 1960s when KSSU made a joint purchase of the DC-10-30.

The EQA group got a proposal but the dialogue soon ceased when when business conditions began to change.

The request for proposal was based on a common specification developed by the EQA's Task Force. Delivery would begin around 1994 according to Swissair's wishes. It was hoped that, thanks to the large volume, a significantly better offer would be made.

The joint evaluation of the offers came to the following conclusions:

"This joint evaluation has covered the most important aspects of the two family alternatives, MD 90-30 / -40 and the Airbus A320 / 321, respectively. All four airlines have concluded that Boeing has no candidate for an MD-80 replacement while individual airlines definitely included Boeing airplanes in their individual reports as possible candidates The MD-90 family is based on the development of MD-80, which gives certain limitations while the Airbus family is a new product with greater further development potential.

The basic requirements for size and range are better met by the Airbus alternative, while any new airplanes have difficulties in giving improvements in terms of operating costs compared to the existing MD-80 fleet. The large airplanes, especially the A321, give an improvement in seat-mile costs in the order of 5-10%, mainly due to their higher seat capacity. Based on this, the A320 / 321 combination seems to be the favored candidate. The conclusion was also that none of these two programs allow the development of an efficient 100-seater as part of the family.

Finally it is important to fully analyze the present MDC financial situation. Their present situation does indicate that their programs run a higher risk than the Airbus programs. "

The conclusions were later incorporated into the evaluation during future analyses of the appropriate aircraft types.

EQA becomes Alcazar

Within EQA the parties realized that cooperation must be intensified to achieve the desired benefits and they began to discuss a merger to a company with the project name Alcazar, now also including KLM. It turned out not to be an easy task, there were many weighty problem areas. SAS got a new CEO in 1992, Jan Reinås, who took over from Jan Carlzon who now devoted himself solely to the Alcazar project. Several major issues requiring early decisions:

• How would the ownership relationship be established?
• Where would the head office be located?
• Would Austrian Airline with its connection to Lufthansa and linked to the Austrian company Lauda, really be able to stand up to Lufthansa?
• How would Alcazar manage contracts with US partners? SAS had agreements with Continental, KLM with Northwest, and Swissair with Delta.
• Who would become head of the new company?

Alcazar's common fleet consisted in 1993 of a total of 350 aircraft and together the companies flew 38 million passengers. Most likely the head office would end up in Amsterdam, and it was expected by many that Jan Carlzon would be appointed as CEO. He had been a strong driving force for the project, which was already his vision in the late 1980s.

The planning was that Alcazar would be in the air in April 1994. SAS Frösundavik would then likely be closed and many SAS employees would lose their jobs. A consultant report from this period showed no alternatives to the Alcazar and pointed out, interestingly enough, that in the short term SAS would do best to continue as an independent company for the following 3-5 years and later enter into an alliance with Lufthansa or British Airways.

In late 1993, the negotiations ended for several reasons, among others, the difficulty to agree on the most appropriate partners in the US, and that Jan Carlzon had left SAS. Some discussions began suggesting that SAS should be privatized in the same way as BA in 1987, but it never went further than just discussions.

The phase-out of F28 and DC-9

The need to find a good replacement for the F28 and DC-9 became more and more acute. To receive delivery of new aircraft in line with the planned retirement before 2002 required that a decision had to be made no later than the beginning of 1995. A number of studies were conducted during the first half of the 1990s and covered the following types of aircraft: Fokker 100, BAe 146 and our MD-87. The results were presented several times to the airline management.

The Fokker 100, a modernized F28 with a fully modern flight deck and environmentally friendly engines, was well known in SAS through contacts with Swissair that had flown the type since 1989. Fokker also had a new, smaller version, the Fokker 70. A different option emerged when we got the offer to buy the entire USAir fleet of 40 Fokker 100s at a price level of 16-17 million USD per plane, a significantly lower price than the new aircraft but the alternative was soon set aside. The USAir aircraft specification was also quite unique and different from other companies.

British Aerospace had modernized its four-engine, BAe 146, that flew for the first time in 1981, to the Avro RJ and could be delivered in three sizes with 59, 72, and 89 seats in SAS European layout.

We felt, however, that the alternatives in the market did not really met our requirements and we therefore initiated, in cooperation with Lufthansa, a dialogue with Boeing on how they should develop their 737 program. Boeing sought support in the evaluation of their making a completely new aircraft or developing the 737 to something they called 737 NG (Next Generation).

Boeing chose to primarily develop the 737 program with a new and larger wing, a new version of the CFM56, and a limited modernization of the flight deck. Boeing was targeting larger versions than SAS desired for its Small aircraft.

The 737NG had, therefore, both an engine installation and a wing that was adapted for it. Other

A model merger? *Facing strong competition from larger rivals, smaller Eurocarriers are forging alliances among themselves*

Fly SASAUSSWIKLM

Jan Carlzon's plan to create the airline alliance Alcazar through a merger was probably premature. Photo Bertil Ericsson Pressens Picture

A potential DC-9 replacement was the Fokker 100   Photo SFF archive

Another candidate was AVRO RJ-100.   Photo SFF archive

General Arrangement
737-500X

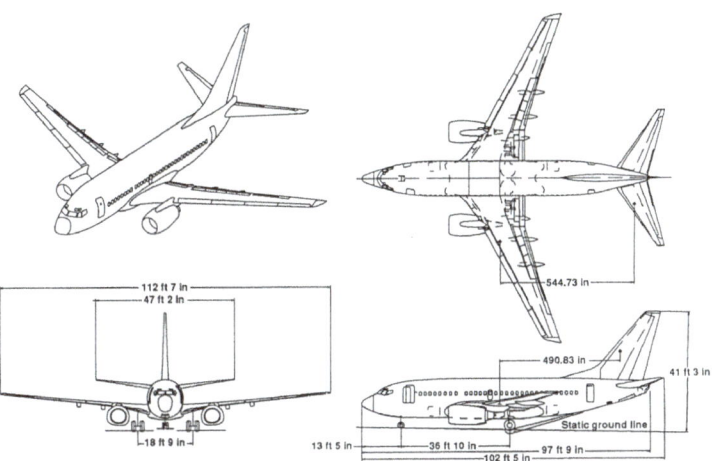

Boeing's development of the 737-500, named 737-500X.
Figure Boeing.

airlines had started to show interest in the 737NG and Boeing offered the larger versions, the 737-700 and 737-800.

Southwest of the United States became the first customer and so began to strongly influence Boeing in the specification of the flight deck with the desire to achieve "common crew" and "common spares" with its existing fleet of 737-300s. SAS avionics expert and the project pilot saw this as a disaster and SAS found generally that Boeing's presentation of the 737NG as "The Airliner of the 2000's" was more marketing than reality.

An airliner of the 2000's should at minimum have the digital avionics products already on the market and which were standard in the 757/767/747-400 and the entire Airbus fleet. In addition it should include as standard equipment the "Enhanced GPWS" Ground Proximity Warning System, which now was on the market. We also assessed that an old flight deck would adversely affect the price in the secondary market. So often Boeing took the position "we can build airplanes and we know what the market wants." Boeing had previously in the 60's claimed, "we know what is best for you!" Our overall experience of rival MDC was completely different as they usually took the attitude "Tell us what you want and we will build it for you."

We had several meetings with Boeing about this without getting an audience for our views.

In 1993 SAS had appointed an internal working group to discuss with MDC how they could develop an alternative to the SAS Small needs. During several meetings at Frösundavik and Long Beach, we proposed to MDC to do something based on the DC-9-30's size, which correlated well with SAS Small aircraft. We showed up with our experts in performance, flight deck, cabin, and maintenance as a working group headed by Bengt-Olov Nas. It resulted in the MDC MD-95 project.

Meanwhile, Rolls-Royce started the development of a completely new engine in cooperation with BMW, the BR715. It was a good fit for the MD-95, which now became a real alternative for SAS.

Airbus announced a new version of its A320, called the A319. The leasing company ILFC officially launched the program at the Paris Air Show in 1993 after an initial order for six aircraft. The A319 was the same aircraft as the A320 but with a shortening of the fuselage by 12 ft. In our investigations the A319 had 116-132 seats (European and domestic).

SAS and MDC project teams during discussions at SAS headquarters Frosundavik on the development of the MD-95. MDC team was urged to think like SAS through the request to "put your SAS hat on."
From MDC in SAS hats from left: Rolf Sellge, MDC's project manager. Rich Sonnenberg Gary Giercsack, Rich Sikora and Fred Esch,
SAS project team from left Bengt-Olov Nas, SAS Project Manager, Tore Landfald, Jan Strom SAS pilot projects, Lars Nilsson, Ulf Abrahamsson, Anna Karin Handberg, Christer Wall, Bengt Nilsson, Hans Gezelius, K. Ness.
Photo SAS,

New CEO of SAS, Jan Stenberg

In the spring of 1994, SAS got a new CEO, Jan Stenberg, who immediately showed great interest in ongoing discussions, both on cooperation with other companies, and on airplanes issues. He set up five necessary steps to create the future for SAS
- Focus on Europe
- Reduce the number of staff
- SAS will gladly cooperate with other airlines but not through mergers
- Parts of the company should be sold out
- SAS will purchase new aircraft

Jan Stenberg engaged directly in a dialogue with Lufthansa, and in the choice of suppliers of small-aircraft.

SAS established a new strategy, which would serve primarily for the measures required for profitability and the basis for the decision on the new aircraf.

Among the goals set were, among others, continued development of the non-stop strategy, focusing on business travelers, and the continued increase in the number of frequencies. The requirement of the fleet was obviously efficiency, flexibility both in terms of number of sizes of aircraft, and opportunities to bring the product to market requirements. The conclusion was a requirement for low operating costs, a small number of aircraft types, preferably a single type for European and domestic traffic, flexibility in the design of the cabin, and the smallest version with about 100 seats i.e. an SAS Small aircraft and one type for "Intercont."

Those responsible for the different route areas did their assessments of the future and on this basis, created a spreadsheet model to find the optimal distribution of the number of aircraft and aircraft sizes for varying traffic growth.

The result was quite clear and visible in the following structural fleet plan arranged by aircraft size in terms of number of seats:

Short- & medium-haul fleet:

Number of seats		1994	1995	2000	2005
"Big"	150-180	1	1	1	20
"Medium"	110-140	66	67	65	44
"Small"	100	44	44	55	55
Propeller	50	22	22	25	25

The assessment was that the need for small aircraft was larger for SAS than for many other large and medium-sized European airlines. The main reasons were
- Relatively sparsely populated home market
- Focus on three hubs instead of one (CPH. OSL & ARN)
- Focus on nonstop service

SAS deemed it possible to achieve profitability with small planes through investments in the business traffic and routes to and from Scandinavia and thus obtain a higher unit revenue than other companies. That the smallest aircraft should be a 100-seat plane was linked to the fact that the the European and inter-Scandinavian traffic consisted of flights with 40-100 passengers, and that SAS after the retirements of the DC-9 and F28, would have the 50-seat Fokker 50 and the 130-seat MD-80. The 100-seat would be missing if no new acquisition was made. Jets with less than 100 seats were judged to provide little opportunity for profitable operation because of the high break-even load factor.

Stenberg also took up the option to postpone the purchase and upgrade the existing DC-9 fleet with noise hush-kits. It would naturally significantly reduce the need for investment but was not a long term solution. It was decided to proceed with the final evaluation of the Small options.

Jan Stenberg took over as SAS's new President in 1994. Photo SAS.

Selection of the "Small" aircraft

We had in early 1994 presented options for the "Small" airplane. Both Boeing and Airbus alternatives were considered not quite optimal in that they both were based on larger and heavier versions that gave higher empty weight and higher operating costs. Boeing's 737-X flight deck was rated as not state of the art which was why this option was not felt to be really good.

But then there was an opportunity for us! Jan Stenberg had invited Boeing's president and wife to that year's Nobel Prize dinner. I had good contact with Stenberg and he promised to convey our views to the Boeing chief. Our avionics expert in Fleet Development, Bengt Nilsson wrote a paper with

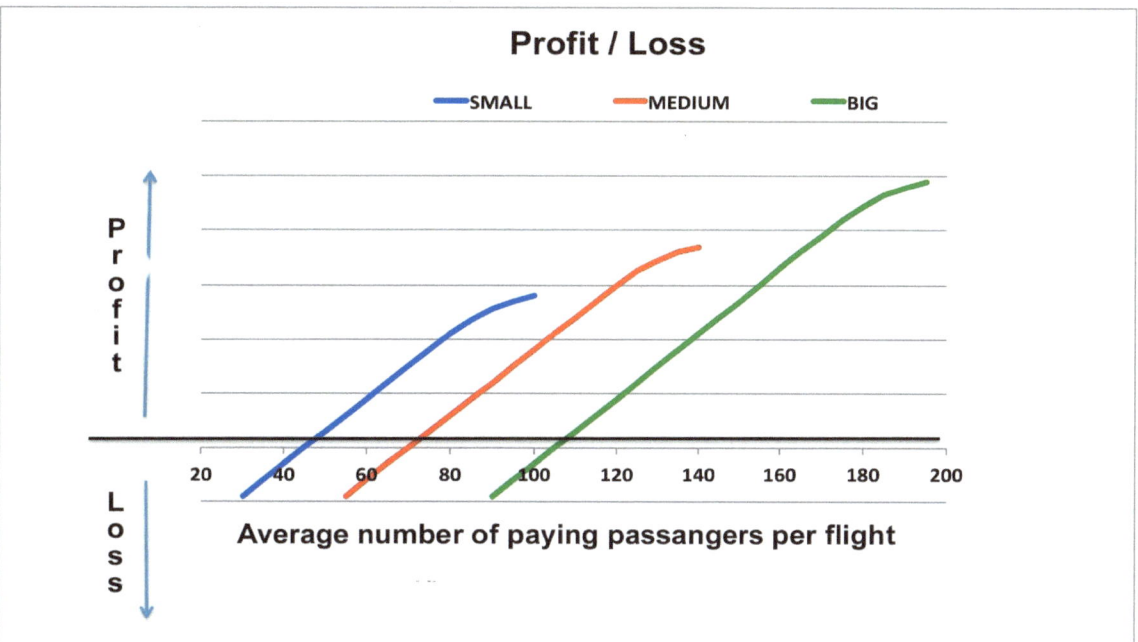

Chart showing profitability for three aircraft sizes with varying number of passengers and a given revenue per passenger. Traffic on weak routes requires small aircraft. Picture Bengt-Olov Nas.

SAS observations, which we left with Stenberg. He had the opportunity during the evening to disclose the contents with the Boeing executive who listened carefully and asked for Bengt's paper. Stenberg's reply that it was written in Swedish was met with the comment that "we will take care of that in Seattle." Then the information entered into the Boeing system at the highest level! The result was that Boeing in early 1995 invited a number of airlines to Copenhagen for a discussion. Participating companies in addition to SAS were British Airways, KLM, Maersk Air, Braathens, TAROM, Southwest, United, American, and a few others. It was obvious that Pete Rumsey, the Boeing 737NG Chief Designer had the goal to convince participants that the planned 737NG configuration was the right thing. SAS project pilot, Jan Strom, and Bengt Nilsson from Fleet Development opposed this view and were strongly supported by the other participants including Southwest! Boeing's conclusion was that "we have heard what you said; we will go home and think about this and will return."

After further contacts, a meeting was held in Bucharest with TAROM airline as the host. Boeing now recognized that they should be marketing the 737NG with a modern flight deck as standard, as per the desires expressed so strongly by our specialists. A great success for SAS and as it would turn out quite right even for Boeing, which now could really market the 737NG as "the Airliner of the 2000's". Boeing's 737NG success well into the 2000s came to show this clearly.

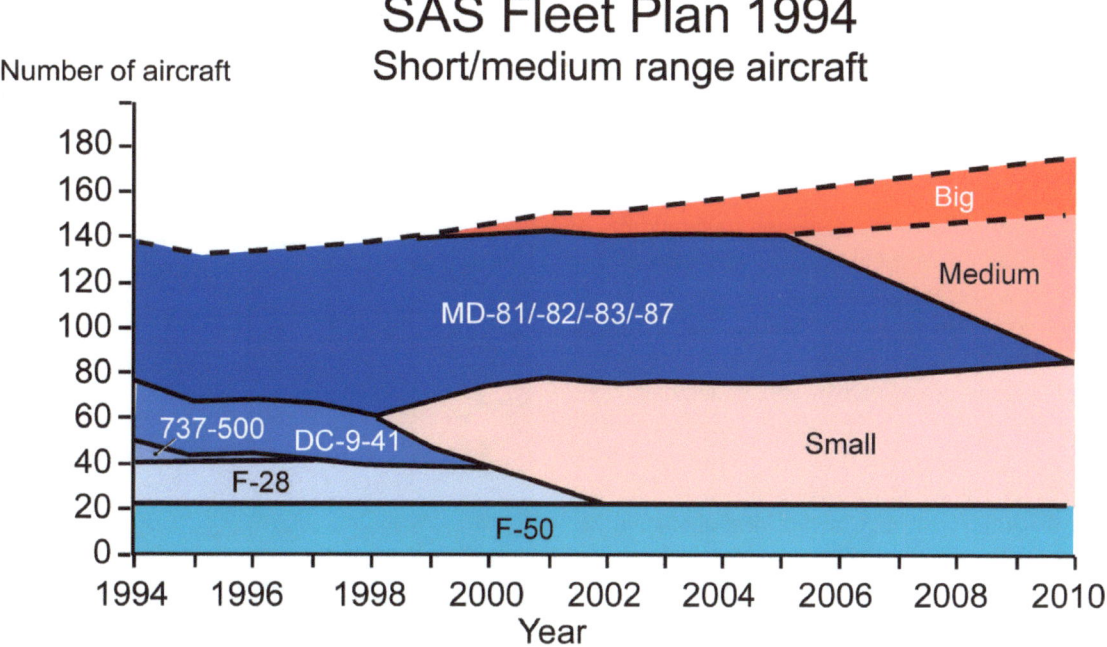

SAS fleet plan in 1994 shows the retirement of F28, 737-500 and DC-9 and phasing in the three new sizes Small, Medium and Big.
Picture SAS.

Boeing finally offered a new version of the 737NG, which they called 737-500X. It had a shorter body but was otherwise the same aircraft as the larger versions. It was an adaptation to the SAS wishes for a small airplane. The wing had a span that was increased by more than 16 ft. compared to the 737-500 but was considerably more modern and more efficient than the wing on earlier versions of the 737. It gave opportunities to fly at higher altitude and at a higher speed than 737-500. The combination of the larger wing and an engine with thrust designed for the 737-700 / 800/900 resulted in the 737-500X having an empty weight that was about 11,000 lbs heavier than the 737-500.

The versions had the same fuselage and thus the same earning capacity, i.e. the same number of seats in the cabin. We were therefore initially hesitant about this solution.

The evaluations took off when Jan Stenberg in the fall of 1994 showed strong interest in the Boeing option. Stenberg took the CFO, Gunnar Reitan, and me to Seattle and made it perfectly clear to Boeing that they would be included in the final evaluation but that they needed to make proper efforts in order to compete. Boeing kicked off directly with the small version, which has now been named 737-600, and it had also decided to modernize the flight deck according to the SAS wishes. The aircraft was now a strong candidate. Since we had not defined any detailed specification I made a phone call from Seattle directly to Bengt-Olov Nas with a request to immediately launch the process.

SAS basic requirements in the evaluation of the new Small- aircraft were:
- Low trip cost and breakeven with 50 passengers per flight
- Range 1000 nm (1852km) with full passenger load and 2,200 lbs cargo
- Comfort level in the cabin equal to or better than SAS's MD-81 version
- Greater flexibility in the design of the cabin
- The cargo holds must be equipped with mechanical handling equipment, the so-called Sliding Carpet
- Environmentally, the new aircraft should be better than the best aircraft on the market (noise and emissions)

The requirement for the Sliding Carpet had a background in the DC-9 cargo holds and MD-80s, which were long and narrow and loaded manually. The loading crew was forced to crawl deep into the fuselage and with a "ceiling" of just three feet. In 1982, SAS contacted a company, Scandinavian Belly Loading Co Ltd., who had ideas about making a kind of sliding carpet and entered into a collaboration agreement for the development of a system that came to be called the Sliding Carpet. A prototype for the DC-9 was developed and demonstrated by the company's production manager Anders Helmner in a room in Helsingborg. The SAS maintenance base in Oslo undertook the technical responsibility. Union representatives participated with interest in the work. A first test installation was made in 1986 in a DC-9 and SAS signed an agreement, with Scandinavian Belly Loading Lund Co Ltd, that covered the entire DC-9 and MD-80 fleets.

The loading of luggage was now considerably simpler; two handlers managing to fill up at the door and subsequently fill the holds at the back as the carpet gradually pulled the luggage into the compartment, driven by an electric motor. No handlers were now needed to crawl into the holds. The final type certificate for the equipment was issued in September 1996 and included the DC-9, MD-80, and MD-90.

So we completed detailed investment and revenue analyses covering the period up to 2015 for all five options: Fokker 100, AVRO RJ100, MD-95, Boeing 737-600, and Airbus A319.

737-700 Flight Deck. Photo Hans Norman, www.Scanliners.com.

Loading of luggage to the Sliding Carpet in the cargo hold.
Photo Telair,

Airbus A320 family, A319, A320 and A321. Photo Airbus.

The Boeing 737-600s were analyzed in different cabin configurations, both with the new flexible seats i.e. five seats across in the Euro class and with the standard configuration with six seats across. The analysis led to the Avro RJ-100 option being deleted, as it was judged slightly too small, with inadequate operating economy, four engines, lower speed, and slightly awkward to unload due to its configuration. The Airbus A319 did not meet the SAS size needs, nor its requirement of operating economy. In contrast, we saw the advantages of the A319 through the link to the larger A321 version, which could meet SAS future needs of the Big-aircraft with 150-180 seats. SAS judged that it was not prepared to compromise on the basic requirements of the Small-aircraft as the number of aircraft needed to be made of this size was large enough to warrant its own type.

Remaining now was the Fokker Fokker 100, optionally in combination with the Fokker 70 and Fokker 130, a project from 1988, when LIN bought new aircraft. Airbus also tried to tempt SAS with a combination of Fokker 100s and A319s. MDC had its MD-95 project and Boeing its 737-600.

In February 1995 SAS invited all five manufacturers and their engine suppliers into final negotiations. A building at Frösundavik that was empty was taken over and we appointed two negotiating groups, one with responsibility for the overall issues such as aircraft price, financing, and delivery times and other conditions, while the other group was responsible for the negotiation with aircraft and engine manufacturers regarding technical questions, support and specifications.

The conditions for the negotiations were favorable, especially with regard to Boeing who just lost a contract in the US where one of the major airlines decided to buy Airbus A320s instead of Boeing 737s. Lufthansa had recently made a similar choice. Airbus had in the early 1990s made several inroads in the US market.

United leased such a large number of Airbus aircraft at a time when Boeing probably felt that the deal was theirs. MDC also had problems with declining sales of its limited product range and Fokker also had problems with their sales.

We put great pressure on manufacturers especially regarding the price of the aircraft. Fokker felt hardpressed and had a hard time getting down to the SAS desired levels but could offer greater price reductions on a first group of aircraft against that which they would receive at a substantial premium for later deliveries. BAe was clearly prepared to meet our requirements. We had also added a new requirement; aircraft manufacturers must submit a residual value guarantee for the aircraft that SAS bought. The design of the guarantee given to suppliers was that it would include a price level for which they were prepared to buy back the aircraft, after a certain time.

We also demanded that improvements needed to

737-600 represents Boeing 737NG family, including a new wing. The new wing has a span of 112 ft. The 737-500 has a 94 ft. span. The body length, 98 is the same between the 737-600 and 737-500. Illustration Boeing.

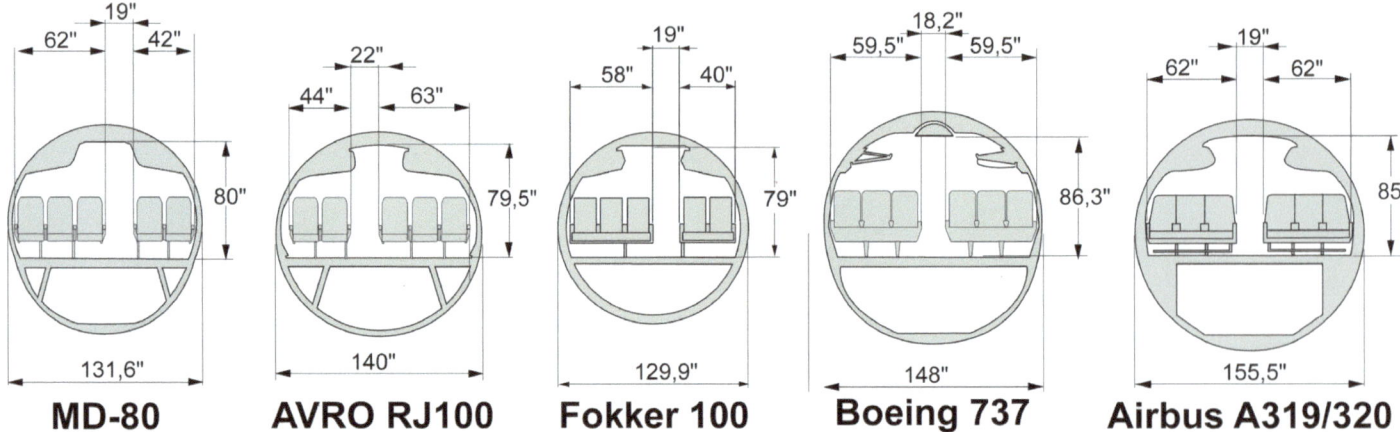

The cabin cross-section of all the candidates for SAS Small aircraft. Drawing Hans Kampf.

be made in the usual escalating formulas that the aircraft price normally included in the contracts. This was to secure price levels on aircraft delivered in the future. When the negotiations were completed (and everyone was exhausted), we found that we had come a long way towards our target and the final evaluation that was made consisted of making a risk value assessment of manufacturers' strengths and weaknesses and their future development. In addition we requested that existing contracts with producers would be renegotiated.

SAS had an agreement with MDC for the delivery of six MD-90s and six options, an aircraft that no one in SAS wanted. SAS had also paid large advances on both of these and with the engine manufacturers for spare engines. That MDC judged an order from SAS to be very important for the company's survival became clear when MDC's newly appointed CEO, Harry C. Stonecipher visited Stockholm just before the SAS decision and then in a rather acrimonious manner wondered why the decision was delayed. MDC judged us as a locked-in client after the great effort SAS made in the development of the MD-95.

SAS also had current contracts with Boeing for the purchase of two Lineflyg 737-500s at rather unfavorable prices and moreover agreement on two 767-200s, originally intended for Swedish domestic services, which were not of interest anymore.

In the late 1980s Fokker had enjoyed a period of financial difficulty but after support by the Dutch government established itself again. In 1993 the German company Daimler-Benz, took over the majority of Fokker through its company DASA, Deutsche Aerospace, but Fokker's future was deemed unsafe. The same assessment was made regarding MDC's civil activities.

SAS buys Boeing 737-600

The conclusion was to complete another negotiation with Boeing that would also contain options for the 737-700 and 737-800 versions.

In the discussion that took place on a Saturday at SAS headquarters were Ron Woodard, Boeing President Commercial Aircraft, head of the Boeing negotiating team, and Jan Stenberg, leader of the SAS Group.

737-600 Letter of Intent signing.
Ulf Abrahamsson, Tom Basachi, Boeing, Jan Stenberg, SAS President, Dick Taylor, Boeing and Ron Woodard, President of Boeing Commercial Airplane Group.
Photo SAS

Boeing got many customers for the new 737 family and increased production rate considerably. Production rate in 2014 was 42 airplanes a month Photo Boeing.

Stenberg also had good contacts with General Electric (part of the 737 CFM56 engine joint venture) and had called on one of their top managers. SAS got good responses to requests for how to handle the old but still applicable contracts. One small problem arose when the Boeing group that was responsible for updating the letter of intent suddenly lost the computer file. We had to sit a long time Saturday night before it was cleared and we were able to sign the agreement. The agreement also included the option to switch to the larger models 737-700 and 737-800. Boeing's program was a great success and production started properly.

We then got approval at the board meeting in March 1995 for an agreement totaling 42 aircraft of type 737-600 and options on another 35 aircraft. We had then increased the number of firm orders from 35 to 42 and thereby got Boeing to accept the deletion of the remaining LIN agreement for 737- 500s, and also the 1992 agreement for two 767-200s. First delivery of the 737-600 was planned for 1998.

The board also decided that the 737-600 engines would be equipped with the new combustion chamber that CFMI offered and which would significantly reduce emissions of nitrogen oxide. It was also decided that 20 DC-9-40s would be equipped with Hush Kits to provide flexibility in the final phaseout of the DC-9 fleet. The Hush Kits safeguarded the DC-9 operation through 2002.
Fokker went bankrupt shortly after they celebrated their 75th birthday. MDC celebrated Douglas's 75th birthday in July 1995 and Birger Holmer and I were specially invited to the 75-year celebration and our then representative in Long Beach, Lennart Ringqvist, who was of course also included. We did not know then that in 1996, Boeing was going to buy MDC, which among other things meant that the MD-95 program survived for some time, now known as the Boeing 717-200.

During the final discussions on the Small aircraft, an internal dialogue was conducted about how SAS would best meet the needs of the Big aircraft and the conclusion was that there existed a solution with Airbus A321 even if it meant another aircraft type. The previous fleet planning involved two different aircraft types to meet the requirement for both domestic and European traffic. The assessment was now that that a good aircraft on very favorable terms was bought, and secured a good replacement for the DC-9.

The new flexible five-abreast-seats, which first were tested on a SAS 737-500, were now installed in the new 737-600 and a couple of 737-800s. After

737-600 in SAS livery used at the time of contract signing. However upon delivery the aircraft, was painted in the new SAS livery, see page 157 Photo Boeing.

MDC celebrating its 75th anniversary with guests from SAS. Birger Holmer, Lennart Ringqvist and Ulf Abrahamsson.
Photo MDC.

just less than a decade had passed the "flex" from six to five abreast in Business class was abandoned to maintain triple seats and six abreast but blocked the middle seat, called "middle seat free," to provide more space for business travelers.

The MD-90 deal is sealed

One consequence of SAS choosing Boeing as a supplier of the Small aircraft was that SAS still had a firm order with MDC for six MD-90s. Jan Stenberg who was not involved in the MD-90 decision thought

MD-95 then became Boeing 717.
photo Boeing.

SAS receives its first MD-90 in Long Beach. Photo MDC.

The extended front body that was necessary to compensate for the new, heavier engines is seen well in the picture. Photo Hans Norma, ww. Scandliners.com

that SAS should rather be selling the aircraft.

I did a limited market survey and found that we could possibly make a sale but at significantly lower prices than SAS would pay to MDC for aircraft. One would then have to take a substantial capital loss of M$ 45-60 in the 1995 financial statements. I suggested that instead we would buy another two MD-90s to reopen the contract and be able to start a new negotiation and fly airplanes for some time. Jan Stenberg accepted the proposal and a dialogue with MDC was launched.

The negotiations in the summer of 1995 became pretty special with Stenberg on holiday in the Stockholm archipelago and I on vacation in the mountains outside Salt Lake City with good friends. Communication with Stenberg was done by fax and SAS finally got a much better agreement with a lower aircraft price. Since the first delivery would happen as early as 1996, we had in a hurry to get the final specification in place and the accompanying modifications implemented on the aircraft.

The MD-90 was at delivery in 1996 the most

MD-90, a new interior with large overhead bins and a new type of hand rail. Photo Boeing.

environmentally friendly aircraft in operation with a fuel consumption which was significantly lower than the MD-80, (30-35%). Noise levels were a total of 24 dB lower than the certification requirements, Chapter 3.

The business managers in SAS now turned around and wanted to use the MD-90.

The cabin for European operation had 141 seats and was of a more modern design than in the MD-80 fleet. New big "overhead bins" were also equipped with practical "hand rails." The front lavatory was wider than the normal standard and even had windows. The noise level in the front part of the cabin was very low, thanks to the new engine and a slightly longer distance from the engines.

The final contract for the MD-90 was signed in August 1995 and was the last thing I did at SAS and my comment when I left SAS was "mission completed." The MD-90 was delivered in 1996, the DC-9 replacement plan was finished, the Small aircraft was in place and it felt safe that Bengt-Olov Nas, who had extensive experience and knowledge in all relevant areas, would stay to push the SAS forthcoming aircraft issues.

The MD-90 contract is signed at SAS HQ Frosundavik in August 1995, from left, Dick Jacobson, Majlis Rosén, Hans Gezelius, Wolfgang Boettger MDC, Bengt Nilsson, Christer Wall, Christer Ek, sitting from left Fred Esch MDC, Ann Gyllenstedt and Ulf Abrahamsson. Photo SAS

Reflections by Ulf Abrahamsson

During my employment at SAS in 1965, I participated under Birger Holmer's leadership in the evaluation of new aircraft for short and medium-haul traffic. The options were former versions of the McDonnell Douglas DC-9 and the Boeing 737. The choice fell on the DC-9. In 1995, i.e. 30 years later, and my last year at SAS, I was a principal in the evaluation of new versions of the same basic constructions, namely, the MD-95 and 737-600. The choice fell on the 737-600.

In both cases it could be argued that the decisions were correct, because they were taken under slightly different conditions. It is also interesting to note that an aircraft type with good basic design usually has a long life with modernizations provided that the development of systems and engines make good progress. For example, the Douglas DC-9-10 was type-approved in 1965 and was followed by versions -20, -30, -30F, -40, MD-81, -82, -83, MD-90, and MD -95. Seating capacity increased from around 85 in the DC-9-10 to about 150 in the MD-90. The latter three versions are still flying.

Boeing's 737-100, the first in the 737 series, also came along in 1965 and was followed by -200, -300, -400, -500, - 600, -700, -800, and -900. Similarly, seating capacity increased from about 100 in the 737-100 to about 190 in the 737-900. Some of these 737 versions are still produced.

The Airbus A320 family, found in the versions -318, -319, -320, and -321, will certainly achieve a similar lifespan.

SAS project organization

Fleet Development had its embryo in a variety of functions in the organization that already existed in 1945-46. Gunnar Antvik then had a small project function and Hans Walther led another function, "Performance Engineering," which both were supported by other departments completing the studies that were needed to make the assessment of current aircraft types. Around 1965 Birger Holmer's "Engineering" department was established, in which a new group, "Aircraft Analysis" was included, under the leadership of Volrath Holmboe.

Birger Holmer hired me in 1965, reporting to Holmboe. Lars Rantzen was working for Hans Walther but moved to Boeing in 1967, during the time when Boeing hired all aeronautical engineers to be found in Europe for its newly established 747 project. Hans Walther became a teacher for Lars Rantzen, me, and Bengt-Olov Nas.

Lars Rantzen returned in 1971 to Sweden and to SAS to replace Volrath Holmboe who moved to "Operations Planning & Control," a coordinating function for traffic planning. Fleet planning was made in the form of long-term plans by a separate central function.

Birger Holmer's department that was then called "Aircraft Research & Development" had besides

Hans Walther with his slide ruler, which was the means of calculus during the 1940s up to 1950s. During the 1960s electronic calculators and even main frame computers were used. In the late 1980s every colleague had his/her own computer on their desk.
Photo SAS

Lars Rantzen participated as head of the department Aircraft Trading from 1985 to 1990, both in the purchase of new aircraft and the sale of SAS surplus aircraft.
Photo Ulf brahamsson

the aircraft-analysis function gathered technical expertise in the fields of instruments, electrical and radio, performance, weight and balance, and documentation. The department included approximately 30 people with the task of putting together analysis, evaluation and specification work for new projects, and to develop performance and weight and balance data for the flight department. The department was soon streamlined into a clean project department, solely devoting themselves to new aircraft.

When Birger Holmer retired in 1981, he left the testament, which described his assessment of the most appropriate placement of the project department especially considering the new organization Jan Carlzon introduced.

Birger Holmer highlighted that: "*For a result orientered organization it will be each division's obligation to optimize their own business. This leads to an even greater extent than today the need of a technical coordinating body in SAS, which is also a technical contact channel to the manufacturing industry, i.e. aircraft manufacturers and suppliers. It seems natural that the acquisition of aircraft, which includes the evaluation and selection of suitable aircraft, its specification and procurement of the same and its airborne equipment, is managed like up to now within a cohesive department and that this function be placed in SAS central leaership.*"

The result was not quite as Birger Holmer proposed when the project department was merged with the Engineering function within the Technical Division to what came to be known as the "Central Engineering" with me as a manager.

Lars Rantzen had left the group for aircraft analysis and assumed responsibility for the SAS procurement of fuel. After some time, also the responsibility for all contracts for purchase and sale of aircraft was also transferred to him. His new function was called "Aircraft and Fuel Trading." Responsibility for fleet planning was transferred in 1985 from the Commercial Division to Central Engineering.

The group that worked with aircraft projects and fleet planning was separated from Central Engineering in 1988, I reported for a few years directly to the CEO Jan Carlzon, and the department was now called Fleet Development. The Fleet Development and Aircraft Trading groups were now in close collaboration, which worked great.

In conjunction with major organizational changes in SAS around 1991, Fleet Development moved to SAS Airline led by Kjell Fredheim. Then, Lars Rantzen moved to London as head of the leasing company Electra Aviation, which was owned by SAS. The function Aircraft Trading was transferred to the Fleet Development group that now also received additional resources in the form of a few qualified accountants. The function now had 18 people in the organization and was composed of additional resources from all divisions of SAS for the Fleet Planning Working Group, "Specification Review Board," and "Modification Advisory Group." The names indicate the responsibilities of each group.

Fleet Development became the unifying function in terms of contacts with the airline industry and the SAS fleet. Fleet Development maintained a large archive of documentation in the form of specifications, performance data, etc., for most aircraft that were on the market. All changes in the fleet and changes in aircraft were managed by Fleet Development.

In comparison with most major airlines SAS Fleet Development was unusual. The others had mostly a pure analysis function for fundamental analysis of aircraft projects but other resources were taken from the line organization. SAS commercial managers had direct contact with the Fleet Development when they wanted to discuss changes in the aircraft fleet, changes in the cabin either to change the cabin-interior or galley. In the same way Flight Operations could also raise questions about the changes on the flight deck and cabin.

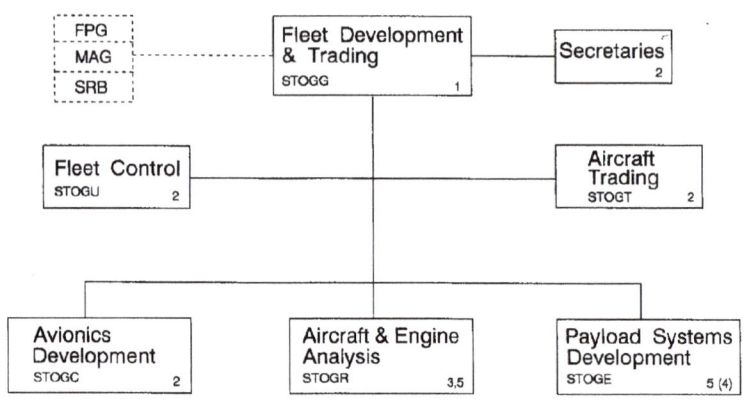

Fleet Development organization, 1991. Picture SAS.

SAS development areas
Passenger cabin

SAS began to focus on cabin issues when Jan Carlzon became CEO and allocated substantial resources to the Passenger Pleasing Plane. Although this did not result in an entirely new aircraft, the manufacturing industry interest in the area increased and experience came to be used internally in the SAS cabin specifications for the 767 and 737. The 767 introduced a "Sleeper Class" with enhanced

Flight Equipment's Flex seats that changed from 3-abrest to 2-abrest quickly changing the cabin from a total 5-abrest to 6-abrest- Foto J. Thinesens

To build an aircraft specification for everyone's wishes was not always as easy as evidenced by Drawing Bertil Björk

There are many views regarding the aircraft specification

recline of the seat back and footrest to provide the passenger with an almost horizontal position.
In connection with the purchase of Linjeflyg, SAS started a development of seats in which one triple seat could be pushed together to make a good double seat with a triple seat on the other side of the aisle that could be stretched out to a wider triple seat, which provided a quick change of cabin configuration. Full fare-paying passengers could then be offered a seat comfort in the 737 that matched the MD 80.

In November 1993, one 737-500 was equipped with a prototype seat made by seat manufacturer Flight Equipment in the forward part of the cabin and tests with the flex concept were carried out over some time. Meanwhile, Boeing committed to develop its own solution using another seat manufacturer.

SAS began to use this seat type in a number of 737s for a few years. Flex seats were replaced eventually by conventional six abreast seating.
The cabin crew started early to express wishes about some kind of handle (handrail) installed along the hat racks. When flying in turbulent air, this would help staff during serving and movement about the cabin. Handrails eventually become standard on all planes. Similarly, SAS was in the 1980s in a leading

role in the increased space for hand luggage even in the smaller aircraft. Passengers soon became accustomed to being able to take quite large bags with them into the cabin.

Cabin Cross Section
Another reflection that feels natural to make is how the cabin cross-sections of different aircraft types have been developed. SAS spent considerable resources in the early 1980s in connection with the discussion with the aircraft manufacturers of the P3 plane. In retrospect, one cannot help but reflect on what results the efforts got.

In the mid-1980s Airbus's A320, was the first to incorporate a wider cabin, for short- and medium-haul aircraft, than what the industry had done before. The passengers in the A320 really got the same standards of available seat width for each passenger that was available in DC-9 & MD-80. The A320 has two triple seats while the DC-9 standard was a triple and a double seat.

Boeing used the standard established with the 707 in 1958, which was later used for the 727, 757 and 737. All three types have the same cross section above the floor. Boeing's cabin cross section is living, in other words, still after 56 years (2014) and has been flown by SAS since 1992, in the 737 from Linjeflyg, and later in the 737-600 / 700 / 800. It is still used in the next 737 versions.

MDC's cabin cross section has now in 2014 flown for 48 years and at SAS for 45 years! SAS made the last MD-80 revenue flight on 25 October 2013 but the cabin cross section can be found in the Boeing 717 (MD-95), which is still in operation in the airline Blue 1 in the SAS system. Blue1 is a Finnish airline owned entirely by SAS. Blue1 was the first airline that became a regional member of Star Alliance. The company was formerly Air Botnia.

Some manufacturers chose their own cabin width. BAe with their BAe-146 and later Avro RJ, which is wider than the DC-9 / MD-80 but is used both with five or six seats abreast. The Fokker F-28, Fokker 70, and Fokker 100 had less cabin width.

Airbus established its cabin standard for large aircraft with the A300 that became operational in 1974; a standard used in the A310, A330, and A340 and has now attained the age of 40 years.

This confirms that when a manufacturer intends to build a new aircraft, the choice of cabin cross-section is of great importance and requires a certain vision of the future. One might think that the SAS vision in the early 1980s did not leave any major footprints but the fact is that the industry put more focus on passenger needs as a result of Jan Carlzon's idea.

Flight Deck
SAS technical and operational departments already had in the 1950s, highly qualified personnel, who performed pioneering work in several areas. One example was in 1954 when flights to Asia and the US West Coast began via the northern polar regions; and along with some manufacturers developed the navigation equipment that was required.

Another example is the effort SAS made after the crash in 1960 when a Caravelle on approach to Ankara flew into the underlying terrain, CFIT, "Controlled Flight Into Terrain." SAS participated actively in the development of the so-called Ground Proximity Warning System (GPWS). See the chapter on the Caravelle.

Another area where SAS went their own and unusual way was in the mid-1980s when we installed an "Area Navigation System," RNAV, in the DC-9 fleet and in the oldest 18 MD-80s to fly more direct and provide shorter routes, saving flight time and fuel. SAS chose newly designed RNAV systems for General aviation, adapting the software to the airline standard which by our testing was approved by the avuation authorities. The DC-9 system worked such that it also could fly automatically via the autopilot.

Performance documentation
SAS had early need for reliable data for operation under winter conditions. The documentation for takeoff and landing performance in snow and ice on the runways in the 1950s was uncertain and in some cases non-existent. SAS, with Gunnar Antvik and Hans Walther in the lead, made certain during 1950-60 that tests were conducted which led to the airports being equipped with accurate measurement techniques and equipment to quickly determine the current friction on landing runways. Aircraft manufacturers began to introduce performance data for operation on wet and slippery surfaces in their manuals. Gunnar Antvik got a nice international award for his efforts and Hans Walther received many assignments at other airlines teaching about performance issues.

Working environment for loading of aircraft
The DC-9 and MD-80 had cramped cargo holds as described earlier. SAS was instrumental in the development of Sliding Carpets that are still sold to other airlines.

Technology developments 1946-1995
Engines
Development has gone from propeller to jet engine and further from the pure jet to fan engines with increasing fan dimensions. The engines were eventually even controlled digitally. Furthermore, this changed maintenance systems to more "on condition" and the industry achieved significant increases in engine running times between overhauls.

When SAS would start flying the Caravelle in 1958 resources for engine maintenance at the Linta workshop were established. SAS had information from the Air Force's experience with the Avon engine, which indicated on-wing time of around 200 hours but in SAS, with a completely different operation, the engine would have running times around 2000 hours between overhauls. The big engines for the 747, DC-10 and 767, worked so well that the removal of engines was often made either to rotate spare engines or that fuel consumption started to rise due to wear. The engines could remain on the wing up to 15 000 -17 000 hours.

The increased reliability of the new big engines became a major contributing factor that the operations with two-engine airplanes are now standard

B-17 Flight Deck. Photo by Anders Gibson.

Piston engine from 1950, the PWA R-2800, which produced 2,500 hp and used on, among others, the Convair CV-440. The engine weighed about 2,400 lb. and had a diameter of 44 in. Photo PWA.

Boeing 717 Flight deck. Photo Boeing.

General Electric GE-90 with a thrust of more than 110,000 lb. Diameter of 11.4 ft., length 24 ft. The fan blades are of composite materials in which each blade is 3.9 ft. long and weighs 49 lb. Photo GE

for a majority of long-haul flights.

The largest aircraft like the A380, however, for obvious reasons, have four engines.

Flight Deck

From lots of different clock–like instruments to computer displays and from control via cables to the fly-by-wire systems. Boeing has been somewhat conservative in the introduction of the complete fly-by-wire system while Airbus A320s have already introduced a new philosophy in the design of the flight deck.

Meanwhile, the navigation has gone, from land based radio beacons via inertial navigation using gyroscopes, to satellite navigation, which also resulted in the airspace could be utilized more efficiently and safely. When SAS started flying long-haul routes after the war the flight deck was staffed with five people, two pilots, a flight engineer, a radio operator, and a navigator. Now the active crew is typically two pilots but on very long distances includes a third relief pilot.

Aerodynamics

The trend is clearly shown by a comparison between the wing of the Caravelle from the late 1950s and wings of the 727 and DC-9 from the early 1960s. The clearest is the increased sweep angle required to fly at higher Mach numbers. The high-lift devices on Boeing 727 and MDC DC-9 were also a step forward which gave excellent takeoff and landing performance despite significantly higher wing loading. DC-9-40s had , for example, a wing area, which was 63% of the Caravelle wing, the maximum take-off weight was about 15% higher and it cruised at about Mach 0.78, whereas the Caravelle flew at Mach 0.65. The Boeing 727 had a very sophisticated lift system, both on the wing leading and trailing edges. The background was that Eastern Airlines had stipulated that their 727s must be able to land and take off with a full load at the former La Guardia airport with a runway length of almost 5 000 ft.

The wing development continued with so-called

winglets, which were first introduced on the MD-11. The wings became significantly more effective without increasing the real span. The Airbus A320 initially had small winglets called wing fences, but now has significantly larger variants called "sharklets" on their aircraft, similar to the "winglets" Boeing has on its 737 aircraft.

Engine and aerodynamic developments enabled us to introduce the development of larger aircraft and aircraft that could fly longer distances. The graph shows the payload-range for a large number of aircraft from the DC-3 to the Airbus A380 and clearly indicates the enormous progress made. For reference, we have used half the circumference of the earth, which is about 10,800 nm.

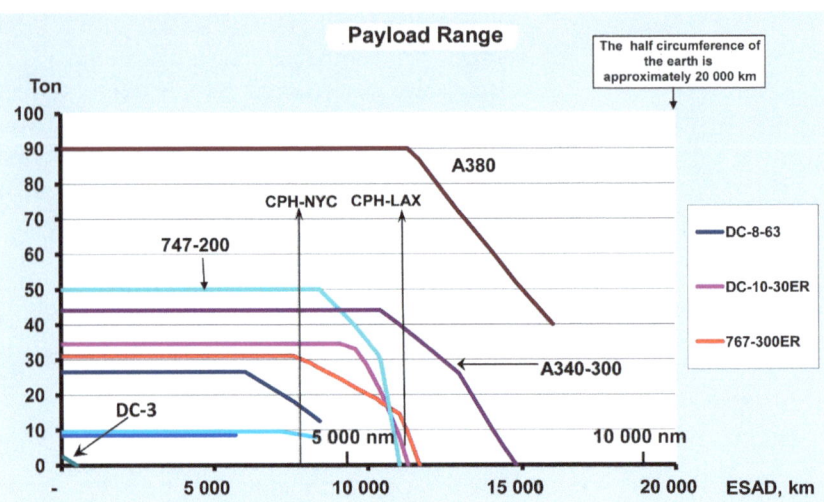

The graph shows the evolution of the aircraft's payload and range (ESAD =Equivalent-Still-Air-Distance) from year 1930 DC-3 to year 2000 with the Airbus A380.
Picture Ulf Abrahamsson

Boeing BBJ with winglets, which reduce air drag and thus fuel consumption by up to 3-4% on the Boeing 737. Photo Boeing

Price development

The entire process of selecting a new SAS Small-aircraft was in many respects unique. It will, in future aircraft purchases, hardly be a situation where the buyer has a competition between five aircraft manufacturers, and as many engine manufacturers. It certainly does require considerably more work in all analyses but of course gives opportunities in negotiations with manufacturers.

Many ask the question what the costs are of the different planes are that SAS bought. Comparisons may be made with some caution. The contracts with aircraft manufacturers usually indicated a base price based on a basic specification to which should be added the cost of the changes that each customer has requested, such as higher design weights, greater thrust from the engines, the design of the cabins or flight deck etc. In addition, the price is usually given with reference to a given point in time from which the asset will be escalated in price up to the actual time of delivery. The escalation is usually controlled by the consumer price index of materials and labor as specified by indexes in the country of manufacture. In the case of contracts for a large number of aircraft to be delivered over a longer period, this implies that the price of the first aircraft and the last may differ significantly.

SAS's first DC-9 in 1966 cost about $ 4 million, the first 747 in 1969 about $ 21 million, the DC-10-30 around $25 million, 767 in 1989 $60 million and the 737-600 delivered in 1998 almost $ 24 million.

When SAS bought 737-600s, rates of $17-18 million appeared in the press but that level was with the airplane in the standard version and without escalation until the delivery date. In negotiations with manufacturers, of course, there is an ambition to get the lowest price, however it is wise to first ensure that the product meets the specifications.

An early philosopher John Ruskin (1819-1900) expressed this in a very sensible way:
on Prices:
" It's always unwise to pay too much, but it's worse to pay too little.

When you pay too much, you lose a little money that is all.

When you pay to little, you sometimes lose everything, because the thing you bought was incapable of doing the thing it was bought to do.

The common law of business balance prohibits paying a little and getting a lot, it cannot be done. If you deal with the lowest bidder, it is wise to add something for the risk you run, so if you do that you will have enough to pay for something better. "

It is not always the price that will determine the choice of product. Aircraft price developments over time shown in the chart compare price per seat from the DC-3 in 1935 to the Airbus A380 around 2005. Boeing has an open account of their aircraft prices. List price for a standard aircraft in 2014 , a
737-700, for example, costs $78.3 million and a 767-300ER costs $191.5 million. Behind the price trend is a fantastic technical-operational development that produced major advances within areas like accident risk, operational safety, environmental characteristics, ability to fly direct non-stop flights to almost all destinations, and not least the ability to fly in all weather conditions. The product as delivered to the passenger in the form of cabin space and available services onboard has also evolved considerably.

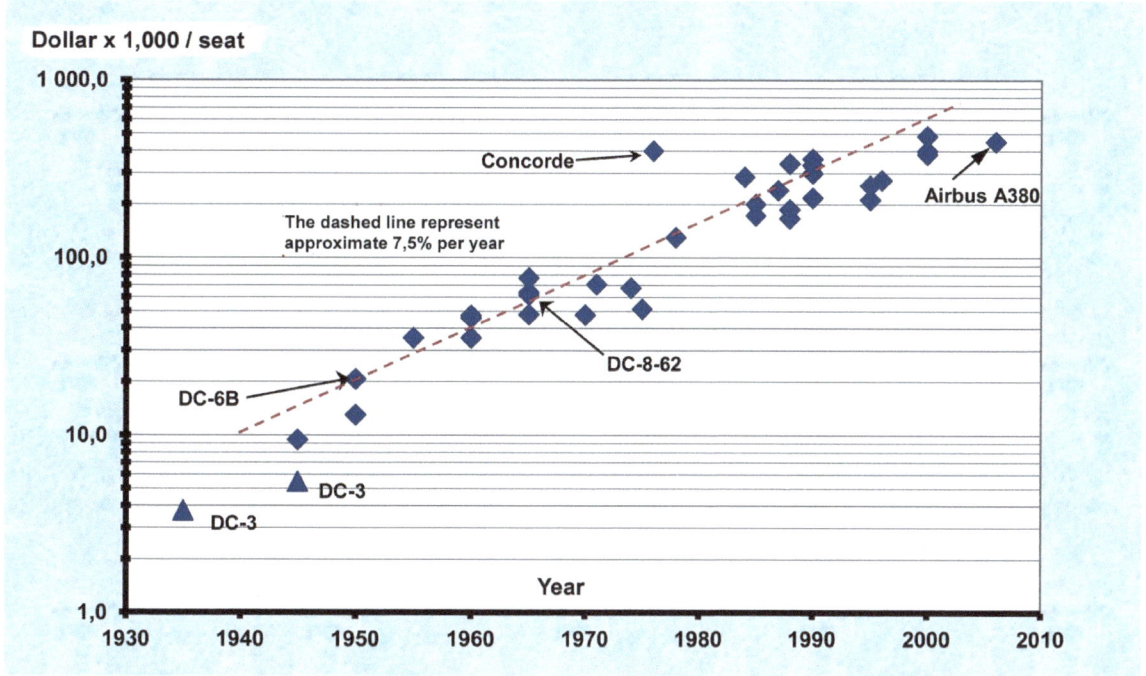

Price evolution of aircraft from 1930 to 2010, price per seat in a standard configuration.
Picture Ulf Abrahamsson.

SAS decisions viewed in retrospect

Generally, one should be wary of post-purchase assessments of decision-making. They must be valued on the basis and values that were available when decisions were taken. Most of them can probably even at a current valuation be assessed as good.

One way to assess the correctness of the decisions may be to see how long the types remained in SAS.

Aircraft	Period	Years
Douglas DC-6/7	1948-1967	19
SE-210 Caravelle 1	958-1974	16
DC-8-62 / 63	1966-2002	21
DC-9	1967-1988	36
Boeing 747	1971-1988	17
DC-10-30	1974-1990	16
Fokker F 28 (LIN and SAS)	1973-2001	20+8
Airbus A300	1980-1986	6
MD-80	1985-2013	28
Boeing 767	1989-2002	13
Boeing 737-600/700/800	1998-	16+

The Airbus A300 was clearly a less good decision while the DC-9 and MD-80 stand out as clearly correct. The first propeller aircraft had consistently less time in the fleet, but it can be explained by aircraft development being fast, including demands for increased range while traffic greatly increased over time and thus the need for larger aircraft.

The decision in 1978 to buy the A300 was taken on the conditions that drastically changed within in a few years as a result of deregulation and the new management philosophy with direct flights and more destinations. The new philosophy was natural with the major changes in the market that began to occur in the 1970s. The A300 came to be phased out within the airline after only three years, when it was transferred to Scanair after reconfiguring at great expense to handle longer distances but was sold after six years in the Group.

The choice of PWA JT9Ds for the A300 still has to be assessed as wrong. SAS was the first and one of very few airlines that chose this type of engine for the A300 and Airbus had to assume very large costs for rebuilding the engine installation and additionally paying for recertification of the aircraft. Airbus could not meet performance guarantees as fuel consumption was 4-5 per cent higher than anticipated and the relationship between SAS and Airbus was not the best for some time afterward. The JT9D engine was initially not adapted to short distances with flight times of about one hour. In recent Airbus aircraft types, however, the PWA engines worked well.

Likewise, the choice of PW4000s for the Boeing 767 can retrospectively be assessed as something daring. PWA often had trouble to meet fuel burn guarantees and the GE engine had more operational experience which perhaps should have been valued more as SAS would start to fly under ETOPS rules.

SAS's 767s worked perfectly except for one occasion when two planes almost simultaneously encountered problems. One could quickly isolate the problem to a faulty maintenance task by Swissair that was responsible for the PW4000 engines. It was later shown that when SAS wanted to reduce the number of 767 aircraft, it was more difficult to lease out or sell 767s with PWA engines than aircraft powered by GE engines.

The period 1996 to 2016   Bengt-Olov Nas

1996 long term fleet development plan

After a few intense years evaluating the DC-9 replacement and procurement of the 737-600, many in SAS, and maybe even externally, thought that nothing would be done regarding new airplanes for a long time to come.

Planning, development and acquisition for the exchange or growth of larger aircraft fleets occur, however, over a long period.

After a period of internal discussions about what in the fleet needed to be addressed next, the following information was given to the SAS board meeting on 19 November 1996:

?*The following studies are currently being conducted.*
1. *"Commuter" study*
2. *"Long Range" study*
3. *"Big" study*

Commuter study

During the first half of 1996, a preliminary study aimed to investigate whether new turboprop aircraft can provide improved operating economy relative to the SAS Fokker F50 fleet was conducted. However, it has been found that replacement of the F50 with only another new 50-seater does not provide any improved economy.

SAS currently has 19 Fokker F28s and four DC-9-20s with 65-75 seats. When these aircraft leave the fleet in 1999, there will be a lack of capacity between the 50 seat F50 and 100-seat DC-9-41, and the coming 737-600.

Markets with an average load of 35-55 passengers per flight cannot therefore be served profitably. SAS has currently (1996) about 80,000 flights per year with such loads.

During the pilot study, it was found that there are 70-seat turboprop aircraft on the market, which in combination with the 50-seater, can fill the gap between 50 and 100 seats. Preliminary calculations indicate that a combination of 50- and 70-seat turboprop aircraft gives a positive financial outcome compared with only the F50 in combination with a 100-seat jet (737-600).

In line with SAS's strategy, to reduced the number of aircraft types in the fleet for cost and efficiency reasons, the aircraft types that offer families of the 50 and 70-seat versions were studied.

Family refers to two or more versions that are so similar technically and operationally that they can be flown mixed by one pilot group in the same way SAS operated DC-9-41 and DC-9-21 or MD-81, -82, -87, and -83 with the same crews. Thus, they enable the efficient use of pilots (economies) and great flexibility in the planning of aircraft capacity. Two producers who market versions of these categories are Aero International Regional AI(R) with the ATR 42 and ATR 72 aircraft, and Bombardier Regional Aircraft Division (BRAD) with the Dash 8 Series 300 and Dash 8 Series 400B. During the evaluation the project team found that only the ATR 42 and ATR 72 currently met the "family" requirements. The Dash 8 Series 300 and Dash 8 Series 400B in their present models are not sufficiently similar from the pilot point of view. BRAD therefore is studying opportunities to modernize the Dash 8 Series 300 to the Dash 8 Series 400B standard.

The pilot study also compared the jets in seat capacity of 50-80 seats. These are the AI(R) AVRO RJ85 and Canadair Regional Jet CRJ and CRJ-X.

All jet candidates have higher operating cost and do not give the positive economic outcome like the turboprop options. The premise has been that SC must operate all options at SC's cost levels.

The 1994-1995 "SMALL" study found that 70-80-seat jets, such as Fokker F70 or AVRO RJ85 break-even load factor would be too high (> 70%) with SAS Airlines cost levels.

Proposals have been requested from AI(R) and BRAD on the ATR 42, ATR 72, AVRO RJ85, Dash 8-320, Dash 8-400, and CRJ CRJ-X.

The quotations are being evaluated. The initial price valuation indicates that the feasibility study's conclusions remain, namely that in the short term a positive economic potential can exist in a combination of 50- and 70-seaters including SAS Commuter's F50. In spite of a family concept is not achieved it would be an advantage having 70 seaters in the fleet. Type cost for a new aircraft is included and studied, especially in the SAS Commuter environment.

The ATR 42 and ATR 72 were rejected in 1987 because of weaknesses in the de-icing system and criticisms of the flight characteristics under severe icing conditions. SAS decided to acquire the F50, The de-icing system is now improved to an acceptable standard. Further evaluation on whether the ATR flight characteristics causes a higher risk than other turboprop aircraft is undertaken.

"Long Range" study.

By closing the Los Angeles destination and the opening of Osaka, SAS shifted the center of gravity of the intercontinental traffic to the east.

SAS 767-300ER fleet is partly payload-limited on the longest routes such that the aircraft cargo volume at times cannot be utilized. Six of the aircraft leases expire starting at the end of 1998. The extension of these leases by up to two years is possible.

With the above background a pre-study is

conducted to take stock of the market and evaluate whether a change from the 767-300ER can provide some benefits for SAS.

The candidates on the market meeting SAS requirements are:

Type of aircraft	number of seats
Airbus A340-200	198
Airbus A340-300	246
Boeing 777-200	268
McDonnell Douglas MD-11	248

All candidates are larger than the 767-300ER except the A340-200, which is about the same size. The others will have about 240-270 seats in a two-class arrangement with SAS demands regarding comfort and service standards.

Cargo volumes under the floor give 9-13 tons more than the 767's capabilities.
The above-mentioned candidates have better range than the 767 and can fly SAS's longest routes without load restrictions.

Currently profit analyses are done to evaluate whether there is a market for the larger capacity and that it provides revenues that can offset the operating costs of the larger aircraft and new investment.

Provided that the analysis indicates a positive outcome, the study is planned to continue during the first half of 1997 requesting proposals, and the development of a business case in the second quarter

"Big" -study

The Short- and medium-haul fleet needs an aircraft with 40-50% greater capacity than the MD-80 on destinations like London Heathrow, Amsterdam, Frankfurt, Brussels, Paris, the Scandinavian triangle CPH-OSL-ARN, and some domestic routes. The 767-300ER is used to London today because of slot limitations. The 767's capabilities is, however not used optimally in this operation and operating cost per seat is higher than for the MD-80. Normally a larger aircraft will result in lower seat costs.

Parallel to the "Long Range" study the market has been reviewed for suitable candidates with 180-200 seats in a two-class layout similar to the 130 seats we have in the MD-80.

Based on the 737-600, which will be flown with 5-abreast in the Business-Class it has been assumed that the narrow-body candidates should have five-abreast in the Business-Class. It is also the standard that Lufthansa will offer business customers in the A321. This requirement means that there is only one candidate that gives +40-50% more seats. It is the recently launched stretched version of the 757, the 757-300. The candidates studied are:

Type	seats: Euro.	Domestic
Airbus A321	150-170	**198**
Boeing 737-800	131-149	**180**
Boeing 757-200	163-186	**214**
Boeing 757-300	**201-228**	**259**
Boeing 767-200	**209**	263
Boeing 767-300	**242**	281

(seat capacities in bold meet SAS requirements)

Technical and operational advantages may be achieved with certain combinations of the Long Range aircraft and Big.

In the Airbus A340-300 scenario and A321, which has the same configuration of the cockpit, operational advantages may be achieved in practice. The Boeing 757 and 767 have identical cockpits, and a few airlines fly both types with one pilot group. The prospects and potential benefits to SAS are currently being investigated."

The Board took note of the studies and gave the go-ahead to continue further *development* of the fleet according to the needs highlighted.

Ulf Abrahamsson retired after the 737 procurement. The project organization Fleet Development reported to the commercial part of SAS and Vagn Sørensen. He appointed Kurt Kühne as head of the Fleet Development succeeding Ulf Abrahamsson. I continued with responsibility for the evaluation and as overall project manager in the studies of the aircraft fleet.

Beginning in 1997 a new generation 737 emerged with the models 737-600, -700, -800, and -900.
In 2011 Boeing launched the fourth generation, 737MAX, with next-generation engines.
In July 2012 Boeing received an order which marked the 737 family's sale of more than 10,000 units!
The first 737-600 was delivered to SAS in September 1998. SE-DNM, Bernt Viking. Photo Hans Norman, www. Scanliners.com.

767 replacement

SAS 767-300ER with Mount Rainier, Washington, USA in the background. Photo Boeing.

The Boeing 767 was purchased in 1988 with Jan Carlzon's strategy of frequency and nonstop in mind. Towards the end of the 1990s, however, competitors on the long haul routes had renewed their fleets with A340s, A330s, and 777s, which were more modern and cost-effective. The competitors captured the market with larger aircraft. SAS's 767 fleet had comparative higher unit costs (US $ / seat-nm) both because of SAS's general cost structure and the size of the aircraft. It was additionally payload- limited on the longest flights. Long haul had for years been losing money, except in 1995, and the challenge was to try to find viable alternatives or shut down.

In spring 1996 a pilot study was therefore set up to review the market, establish requirements, and develop a preliminary estimate. Alternatives that were studied were in principle all "wide-body" aircraft on the market.

What the manufacturers could offer was, from McDonnell Douglas the MD-11, Boeing 777-200IGW and 777-300, and Airbus's A340-300, A340-500, A340-600, and A330-200/-300.

Given the market conditions, unit costs, and traffic growth it was considered that the capacity should be increased by 30-40% relative to the 767-300ER, i.e. to 260-300 seats. New, larger aircraft resulted in improved "Payload Range," about 40% higher payload capacity, 40-60% more seats, 20-25% higher operating costs per flight, but 15-20% lower unit cost. The new aircraft also provided larger and built-in flexibility with respect to the interior, and could allow for coordination with partner airlines. For the study, a project group and a steering group were set up. Fleet Development led

Boeing 777. Photo Boeing.

The MDC MD-11 was not a successful program, because of missed performance guarantees at the introduction. Only 200 aircraft were built, of which 137 were for passenger transport. Many MD-11s have been converted into cargo aircraft. The last commercial passenger flight took place 26 October 2014.
Photo Hans Norman
www.Scanliners.com.

the project in the customary manner, in consultation with all relevant departments through the project. The 1997 pilot study recommended an acquisition project, but with conditions of cost efficiency improvements of the SAS long haul network. The candidates were specified in order to establish conditions for evaluation and proposals.

Proposals were requested from Airbus, Boeing, and McDonnell Douglas. Offers for engine support were collected simultaneously from CFMI, General Electric, Pratt & Whitney, and Rolls-Royce.

Used aircraft were also evaluated, but at this time there were no options on the market.

MD-11 had already been a candidate during the procurement of the 767-300ER. Now, 10 years later, it was not as modern as the Boeing and Airbus alternatives. In 1996 McDonnell Douglas tried to launch the MD-XX, an extended and improved version of the MD-11. The MD-XX was in terms of size larger than SAS's immediate needs and therefore not so interesting. When Boeing bought McDonnell Douglas in 1997, the MD-XX project was cancelled and we drppoed MD-11 as candidate.

Given proposals and the operating expenses, the first calculations of profitability showed it would be difficult to achieve the cost savings and efficiency needed. Different SAS departments were thus under pressure to contribute. One of the larger items was the operational, i.e, pilot and cabin crew costs must be lowered so the management could justify a change of aircraft to the board.

Revenue assessment was very sensitive in the analysis, particularly cargo revenue. Roughly 15% of revenues came from freight so it was important for the result. With 767 the available freight was often limited because of the airplane's volume.

With the 777-200 and A340-300 long haul capacity was increased by 30-40% and cargo weights would be the limiting factor in case limitations occurred. Range was not limiting with the new aircraft without the maximum load that the aircraft was approved for. This could mean that flying with full passenger load the quantity of cargo became limited. When the selected type subsequently went into service this problem turned out in such a way that more tons of freight were sold than any flight could take and palettes with cargo sometimes had to be left behind until the next flight. This meant that volume was left in the cargo holds, which could not be utilized, and a loss of freight revenue.

In late 1998 negotiations were well advanced but at the end of the year, Boeing announced a general base price increase on all their products. Despite the fact that SAS had a preliminary negotiated deal, Boeing raised the price of their 777-200 offer. It was of course not received positively, but it was still a relatively even "race" between Airbus and Boeing.

The slightly larger 777-200 seemed to be more efficient to Asia, which on average meant longer flights, while Airbus had an advantage with the lighter A330-300 on Atlantic routes with

A330-300.
Photo Airbus.

The A340-300.
Photo Hans Norman
www. Scanliners.com

the relatively short flights to the US East Coast. During the evaluation a comment from Air Canada played a role. At one point I asked the Air Canada Star Alliance representative why Air Canada had chosen the A330-300 and not only the A340-300. The answer was; "The Other types seemed to be too much of an airplane for the North Atlantic."

We studied the combination of A340-300s and A330-300s in more detail because both types have very high technical and operational similarities. They are essentially the same aircraft with the difference that A340-300 has four-engines and the A330-300 two. Aircraft structures and systems, except the engine-related, are more or less identical. The cockpit is also identical except for the engine-related systems and instruments. Therefore, the idea was that a pilot could fly both types.

With relatively small fleets, the number of pilot groups is a major cost issue. Maximum take-off weight is significantly higher on the A340-300 than on the A330-300, which meant that the A340-300 has a greater range than the A330-300, which was needed on the longest routes. The A330-300 with two engines and lower weights is more cost effective on medium haul routes such as to the US east coast.

An option with two different 777 variants was also studied: a lower customized max takeoff weight for the North Atlantic and a higher takeoff weight for Asia. The "light- MTOW" variant of the 777-200, however, gave only marginal efficiency gains.

After a final update of proposals and analyses in December 1998 Airbus was chosen for the purchase of eight A340-300s and four A330-300s and a number of options. Because of the requirement to ensure cost efficiency final negotiations were delayed about a year before SAS management had sufficient evidence that savings would be made and the final contract was signed late 1999.

Airbus contract signing. Jan Stenberg, SAS CEO and Christopher Buckley, VP Sales Airbus and SAS and Airbus negotiating teams Photo SAS.

"Big" a recurring need

SAS had since the mid-1980s defined the capacity requirements of the European fleet in Small, Medium and Big categories, which would cover the needs and meet traffic volumes in an optimized way. Based on the DC-9-41, which in the '80s was the backbone of European and domestic traffic, and had 110 seats in the European version, Medium was defined at about +30-40% and BIG an additional +30-40% relative to Medium . Differences between categories could theoretically be defined so that they could cover the entire market demand from 100 passengers per flight to about 200 with the best possible profit margin.

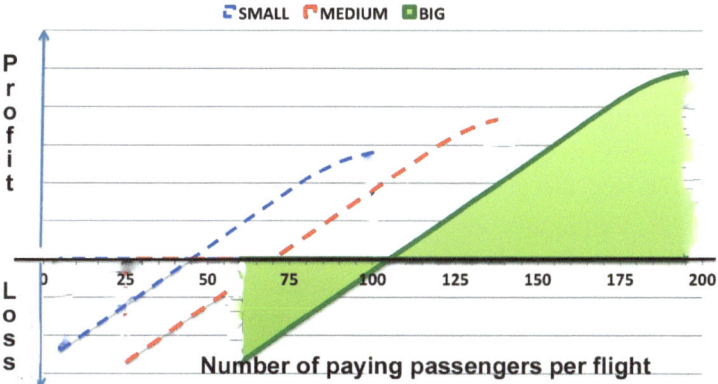

Profit-loss chart, show number of passengers required per flight so the Big-aircraft will be economically viable. The picture also shows how the combination of different sized aircraft optimally covers the market.
Picture Bengt-Olov Nas.

Boeing 757-200.
Photo Boeing.

The MD-80 did fit the Medium definition, but SAS had nothing in the BIG-category.

Small   100 seats   DC-9, 737-600
Medium 130-140 seats MD-80, MD-90, 737-800
Big   170-200 seats   ?

Traffic volumes that demanded the Big existed primarily on routes to major European airports such as London Heathrow, Frankfurt, and Paris. Periodically, there was also similar volume of traffic on the Scandinavian capital triangle segments, mostly Stockholm-Copenhagen.

For a short period one 767-300ER was allocated specifically for Scandinavia to London Heathrow. Therefore the aircraft was re-certified temporarily to a considerably lower max takeoff weight to minimize costs. Landing fees at European airports are charged relative to the max certified takeoff weight. Only flying Scandinavia to London, the high max takeoff weight that gave the 767 its intercontinental range was not needed.

In parallel with the 767-replacement study a Big-study commenced. The largest European aircraft that SAS had was the MD-90-30 with 141 seats. Thus it was not qualified as Big.

Commercial requirements were set up as follows:
- 160-180 seats in a two-class arrangement with possibility of up to 80% Business class.
- Cargo Capacity, three tons in addition to full passenger load.
- Range to meet Europe's major destinations.
- Service and comfort would be based on the t hen two-class concept.
- Flexible interior.
- Lower unit costs than the MD-80 and MD-90
- 50 minute maximum turn-around on the Scandinavian triangle CPH-OSL-STO.
- Meet SAS environmental objectives and strategies.

Available from manufacturers and the second-hand market were A321, 757, 767, and 737-900.

The first analyses limited the study to the so-called "narrow-body" or "single aisle" types for cost reasons. The 767 which is a "wide-body" could not compete in terms of operating cost with the smaller aircraft on the relatively short routes. For a "wide-body" to financially give better results it also needed revenues from the larger freight capacity. In the relatively short European routes with multiple frequencies per day, these freight volumes were not available to the correct level of revenue. Other European airlines had previously experienced this problem with the A310 and A300 the shorter European routes.

There were two main candidates; A321-200 and 757-200. The concept of flexible and relatively large Business class gave a capacity of 154 to 178 seats in A321-200s and 156-179 seats in 757-200s. In relation to the types' actual size and capabilities in a single-class system, it was a rather low numbers. A relative major cost item is the ground handling of aircraft. This applies to activities such as loading and unloading of baggage and cargo, maintenance of toilets, water, and cleaning. These were studied carefully and the question of how long of a turn-around time would be required compared to the smaller aircraft. An important advantage of differences in size of the fleet is the ability to schedule the "right" size to the current traffic needs, so-called demand-driven dispatch. If the larger aircraft needs longer turn-around it defines much of the network planning and scheduling affecting the whole system.

The working environment in ground handling had for a long time been a big issue, especially at Scandinavian airports. For this reason, SAS had earlier developed and implemented tools to improve the work on the apron. One example is the so-called Sliding Carpet that was installed in the cargo holds to facilitate loading and unloading. Noise levels around the aircraft was another area.

The prospects for the main candidates were slightly different. Airbus A321-200s already had a container system as a customer option, while the 757-200 body cross section, which is smaller, is not suited for containers. It could however be equipped with a sliding carpet or a telescopic bin system for handling baggage and cargo in the hold. One difference remained; if a mechanized system was chosen, namely that the 757 would still be loaded manually from the ground to the system onboard while the A321 containers are loaded in the terminal. Both candidates were considered to be able to barely cope with the 50-minute turn-around time.

When this important part of the study was discussed a letter arrived from the Danish authority regarding working environment, which indicated that it was considering to set the maximum amount (lbs) a loader could lift per day. The amount discussed would require that the number of handlers had to be tripled if such a rule were to be introduced. It thus became untenable not to equip the aircraft with some form of mechanized loading system.

In March 1999 it was decided that the 757 was not a realistic option. Boeing's offer was not sufficiently interesting and the 757 gave no cost advantages. As a new type with a separate pilot group of about 50 pilots, a new type cost would be incurred. Once the 767 been replaced, no pilot commonality benefits remained. Handling and turn-around was considered to marginally meet our requirements and any stricter regulation of the loading staff working environment could create issues and unforeseen costs.

Boeing decided in October 2003 to close the 757 production due to declining interest. Left in the competition were 737-900 and A321-200. The 737-900 had a great advantage in terms of similarities with other 737NG aircraft, which had started to be phased into the fleet. 737-900s were specified with 140- 162 seats which marginally qualified it as Big. The 737-900 was at this time somewhat limited in its load capacity and range because of performance weaknesses. Estimated unit costs were not clearly better than A321-200 and capacity (162)

is not really in the Big class.

The choice was therefore the Airbus A321-200. The order resulted in eight firm delivery positions and four options.

Airbus A321.
Photo Hans Norman
www. Scanliners.com

Big becomes Medium

After four aircraft were delivered in 2001-2002, and entered service, there came a decline in traffic volumes and profitability. SAS reorganized in 2003 into four business units: SAS Denmark, SAS Norway, SAS Sweden, and Intercontinental.

Aircraft types and allocation to the new internal companies needed to be reviewed and there was a discussion whether the A321 should or should not stay in the fleet. Copenhagen eventually became their base along with an MD-80 fleet. The number of A321s was now considered to be too many so discussions with Airbus were raised about a version switch to one of the smaller models. With the size difference being considered appropriate to current market needs, the choice fell on the A319-100.

In the meantime, a cabin configuration project had concluded that all SAS aircraft should be converted to an increased number of seats to obtain better unit costs. The A321 was reconfigured to 193 seats and the A319 was specified with 141 seats. Capacity difference between the A321 and A319 was thus good with the Small, Medium, and Big principle. Four A319s were delivered in 2006 under the original contract. To celebrate SAS´s 60th anniversary, one aircraft was painted in the so-called retro painting with the original Viking color scheme.

A319 in SAS retro color scheme
Photo Hans Norman, www.Scanliners.com.

To the left, A320 offloading ULDs
Photo Bengt-Olov Näs.

Engine selection

CFM56-5C4 engine for A340-300.
Photo CFMI.

Throughout the evaluation of aircraft types SAS had negotiated with the respective engine manufacturers with regard to technical support, warranties, and concessions for the engines in question.

A separate evaluation group had been established with Christer Wall, Bo Moller and Staffan Elmen representing the engineering department, Jan-Olof Johansson of the purchasing department of technical support, and myself for the Fleet Development and Project Manager for the engine selection. The group evaluated engines for both the A330 and A321.

Technical division engine selection team at Pratt & Whitney Hartford, Conneticut. From left: Christer Wall, Staffan Elmén, Magdalena Adams Pratt & Whitney and Bo Möller.
Photo Christer Wall.

Airbus A330-300

When the aircraft choice was made and the contract signed, there was still plenty of time to choose the engine type. The A330-300 was offered with three engine options; General Electric CF6-80C6, Pratt & Whitney PW4173, and Rolls-Royce Trent 772B. For the A340-300 there were no engine options, it was offered only with the CFMI CFM56-5C4. Airbus was neutral in the election but we had very useful discussions with the Airbus power plant group on the different advantages and disadvantages. On this occasion the Trent 772B and PW4173 were clear market leaders. The GE engine had not yet been certified for the A330's maximum

PW4000 Pratt & Whitney's test center in West Palm Beach, Florida, United States.
Photo Pratt & Whitney.

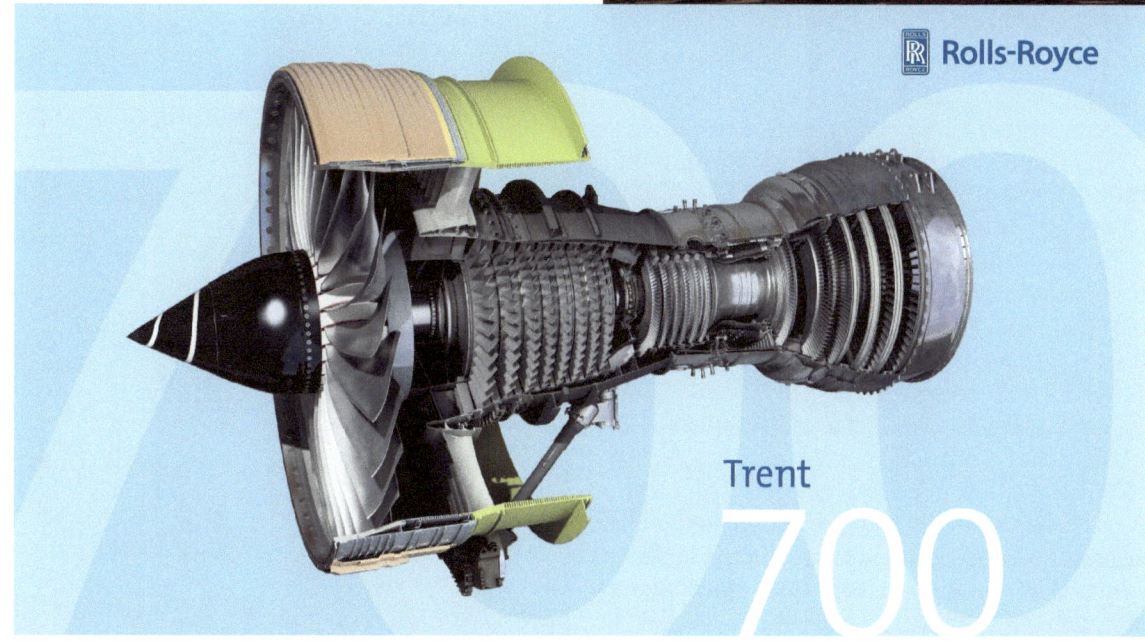

Rolls-Royce Trent 700.
Picture Rolls-Royce.

take-off weight, which meant a big disadvantage in range and payload compared with the competitors. Certification of the maximum takeoff weight would only happen a few years after our contracted aircraft deliveries. In practice, this meant that the PW4173 and Trent 772B became final candidates fairly early.

SAS now had a well-established environmental policy that basically demanded that the development of the fleet should lead to overall improvements in emissions and noise.

The PW4173 had been certified with relatively high emission values for nitrogen oxides (NOx). With SAS demands for continuous environmental improvements, these values did not meet SAS desires. Pratt & Whitney, however, had an improved combustion chamber under development, which showed much better values. It was however not planned for the PW4173 in the period concerned, but to meet SAS demands for continuous environmental improvements, Pratt & Whitney eventually changed its plans and offered the improved Talon combustion chamber for the A330-300 with the PW4173.

Cost estimates showed an even race between the two engine candidates and both producers made big efforts to get SAS as a customer. SAS had for a very long time been a major customer of Pratt & Whitney, but had very limited experience with Rolls-Royce. The operations department testified that there were some minor performance differences that could provide some more operational flexibility with the Trent engine. Some pilots had flown with a charter operator to become familiar with the A330.

Rolls-Royce was finally selected as the supplier and the Trent 772B. After the choice was made the final negotiations on the support contract followed. The contract signing took place at Rolls-Royce in Derby, England, 12 September 2001, the day after the 9/11 attacks in New York and the Pentagon.

Airbus A321

Both the 757 and the A321 were certified with two engine types. When the 757 was dropped, it was only the A321 which required an engine selection. On the 737NG there was only one type, the CFM56-7B, while A321-200 could be ordered with CFMI CFM56-5B or International Aero Engines V2500. At the engine manufacturers a special competition arose because IAE on this occasion was a so-called Joint Venture (JV) between Pratt & Whitney, Rolls-Royce, Japanese Aero Engine Corporation and MTU in Germany.

For the engine choice for the A330 Pratt & Whitney and Rolls-Royce competed but on the A321, they collaborated and competed with CFMI. Even if manufacturers were organized so that the business cases would be operated independently, we heard concerns from Pratt & Whitney about information leaks and thus competitive advantage

because the Rolls-Royce staff seconded to work in IAE was placed inside Pratt & Whitney in Hartford, Connecticut, where IAE had its engineering and sales department.

This did not concern us directly but an unusual situation had arisen in connection with personnel changes between Rolls-Royce and IAE, which as we in the engine selection group had to deal with. The differences between the CFM56-5B and V2500 were nominally small, but the producers had the opportunity to give SAS various levels of support and discounts on engine price. CFMI had probably hoped that SAS would choose the 737-900 because it was already addressed in the agreement written for the ordered 737-600.

IAE was more eager to close the deal, which was clearly reflected in their proposal, and the choice fell on the IAE V2500 engine for the A321. SAS already had V2500s on the MD-90.

Installation differences between the body mounted engines on the MD-90 and wing mounted on the A321 are so big that benefits of using common spare engines did not exist. At the component level, however, there were similarities that could provide benefits, albeit small, during the overhauls.

A330-300 with RR Trent engines.
Photo Hans Norman

SAS signed the Rolls-Royce Trent support contract with Rolls-Royce in Derby, England, 12 September 2001. From left: Christer Wall, Bengt-Olov Nas, Sue Newsam, RR, Jan-Olof Johansson and Charles Cuddington, RR.
Photo Christer Wall.

Bigger Commuter fleet

SAS's Commuter fleet consisted in 1996 of 22 Fokker 50s (F50) with 17 based in Copenhagen and five in Tromsø, northern Norway. The Commuter fleet mainly fed traffic to the main system and was used to some extent to increase frequency in the "off peak" hours on some routes. The Fokker 50 was a reliable aircraft, but its capacity represented a relatively large gap to the other types, which mainly flew from Kastrup, Denmark. SAS therefore wanted to evaluate a commuter aircraft with larger capacity. A study was started with what was then available on the turboprop market with a view to replace the F50. Only one type was in production with larger capacity, the ATR 72. Bombardier planned, however, to launch a further development of the Dash 8 family with approximately 70 seats.

In the regional aircraft market, there were two manufacturers of turboprop aircraft in the size of the SAS needs.

Aerospatiale and the Italian ALENIA, which already cooperated in the ATR, formed in January 1996 with BAe a new company, AERO International REGIONAL (AI(R)). The company would advertise and manage the "product support" for the owner's former products. AI (R) would also be responsible for new aircraft development.

AI (R) manufactured the ATR 72 and ATR 42 turboprop aircraft and the AVRO RJ-family of jets. AI (R) also worked on a new jet project, AI (R) JET, which was planned to include a family of aircraft with about 58-84 seats.

Bombardier Inc, is a group that is involved in many business sectors, financing, snowmobiles, transportation equipment, and aircraft. They bought de Havilland Canada in the early 1990s with the Dash 8 production and had previously acquired Canadair CRJ manufacturing. Bombardier Regional Aircraft Division (BRAD) had in 1997 produced a total of, including orders, 563 Dash 8s and CRJs.

The ATR 42 had, in 1987, been studied as a candidate when SAS Commuter acquired Fokker 50s. At that time there was much discussion about the ATR's wing design, its stall characteristics, and de-icing systems, after an accident in Italy in icing conditions. In that study SAS had also made comments on the propeller deicing system. However it had been modified and improved. In October 1994, American Eagle in the US had an accident involving

SAS Commuter Fokker F50.
Photo Fokker.

Dash-8 300
Photo Widerøe

an ATR 72 caused by severe icing, however, in combination with crew management problems in a holding pattern.

Dash-8 300 was also included in the 1987 Commuter study and I had at that time some conceptual discussions with de Havilland Canada on a type with a larger capacity and higher speed than the typical turboprop aircraft. The idea of a higher speed, propeller-driven aircraft came from the concept studies of the so-called Propfan aircraft.

These studies also came to initiate analyses regarding cabin environment with regard to noise and vibrations. There were concerns in the industry about major problems with higher-loaded propellers. Manufacturers invested therefore much on research and development in the field of acoustics, which was welcomed by the airlines and especially by SAS.

Bombardier chose to use a cabin noise damping system, "Active Noise and Vibration Suppression" (ANVS). With high aspirations for improved cabin environment they named the Bombardier Dash 8 models with ANVS to "Q-Series turboprops," Q200, Q300 and Q400, where Q stands for Quiet.

SAS Commuter operated as a subsidiary in the SAS Group with its own technical and operational organization that assisted Fleet Development with requirements definition and evaluation.

As usual, we specified requirements for both candidates, ATR 72 and Q400, and received proposals.

The application was still mainly feeder services and frequency increase in the larger system at Copenhagen.

In order to effectively assess the cabin environment and comfort, demonstration flights were organized in the spring of 1997 with both manufacturers' products. The Bombardier Q400 was not yet in production so the demonstration was done with a Q300. To provide SAS management with the opportunity to participate, flights were carried out on the same day from Arlanda. Both aircraft were also parked "nose-to-nose" so it was perceived as a real "Fly Off" to win the battle at SAS.

The ANVS-system function was demonstrated by turning off and on the system, which clearly demonstrated that some form of noise reduction in the cabin was necessary.

ATR's old icing accidents were still mentally present in the background and surely influenced some. In connection with a business trip to the US, I visited American Airlines (AA) and American Eagle, which was AA's commuter operator, to question them about their experience with the ATR. According to the chief pilot of American Eagle, then the largest ATR operator, they had no problems with icing or handling of the aircraft model.

An always current issue in connection with the purchase or leasing of new aircraft types is the risk of poor dispatch regularity because of teething

AIR with its ATR 72 at Arlanda after the demonstration flight for the SAS evaluation group and SAS management.
Photo Bengt-Olov Nas.

Christer Ek, SAS Asset Management and Kenneth Marx SAS Commuter on the ATR 72 demonstration flight.
Foto Bengt Olov Nas.

SAS Commuter Q400.
Photo Hans Norman, www.Scanliners.com

problems before enough operational experience has accumulated. ATR had many years of operating experience, while the Q400 was still a project that had not even flown or been certified. Most new types of aircraft go through a break-in period in which problems and risks must be weighed against the benefits of new, more efficient types and a "launching incentive" on the price. Despite warranty provisions, costs can arise both in money and goodwill and can become very large and are usually not covered in the acquisition calculations. Experiences of the specific manufacturer's capabilities and ways to solve these types of problems are also a factor in the assessment. Smaller manufacturers such as Bombardier do not naturally have the same resources as larger manufacturers and the risk could be slightly greater that the problems are not resolved quickly and efficiently.

Both manufacturers worked very hard to meet the SAS and SAS Commuter requirements. The selection eventually went to Bombardier's Q400 which had the following advantages:

- Slightly better overall economy
- Best unit costs
- Larger capacity, 72-76 seats compared with 62-66
- About 30% higher cruising speed which can potentially provide additional productivity and greater flexibility in flight planning
- Some advantage in ground handling such as docking at the gate

When the contract was written, a few other airlines were supposed to get the very first deliveries. Due to delays and changes to the delivery sequences, SAS Commuter was, in 2000, the first to operate the Q400 in service.

It soon became obvious that the aircraft had a large number of quality problems. It often led to long delays or cancellation of flights, which was reflected in the operating statistics. It showed unusually low availability for a very long time. The low reliability did also burden the station staff, who had to take care of dissatisfied customers.

Saab 2000 at SAS

In connection with the development of the Saab 2000 at the beginning of the 1990s Saab tried to promote the project to SAS. Fleet Development followed the project and I participated in the "Saab 2000 Airline Advisory Board." There was also an SAS specification developed.

Basic requirements were that the existing Fokker 50 would be trade-ins since we considered that it was not reasonable to have two types of aircraft in the commuter fleet. A proposal was submitted in the autumn 1993.

SAS analysis assumed that the Saab 2000 would replace the Fokker 50 and F28 on the Swedish part of the route network. An alternative fleet plan therefore contained 40 Saab 2000s. Additionally, we made comparisons between The Saab 2000 and Canadair's new jet of the same size, the CRJ. The conclusion was that it was not economically feasible to implement a replacement of the Fokker 50 with Saab 2000s even if it showed slightly lower operating costs. Detailed analyses were made by both SAS and Saab to clarify what benefits SAS would have with the Saab 2000's higher speed. The traffic patterns with feeder services to Copenhagen meant that the higher speed did not provide any added value. The conclusion was that even if SAS could possibly reduce the number of aircraft it still would not be economically feasible.

To continue the strategy with good access to departures it was decided in 1996 to open a SAS Commuter base at Arlanda, Sweden mainly to be used on the domestic routes and the immediate area around the Baltic Sea. In order not to increase the number of types it was planned to lease six F50. As SAS looked for Fokker 50s on the second-hand market, Saab had picked up the news. So again SAS was courted with a proposal to set up the Arlanda base with Saab 2000, instead of Fokker 50. In terms of capacity both were equivalent aircraft. The main difference between types was the cruise speed. Saab had invested in an airplane with speed comparable to jets. For the planned operation from Arlanda, it was again not certain to provide any benefits because the majority of flights were short.

Given the scale of investment and the economic risks associated with aircraft purchases the grounds for a selection need to be very clear.

We let Saab again try to convince us that there would be scheduling benefits because of the speed. With the usual conservatism in the evaluation, it was not obvious that there were clear benefits. A disadvantage with the Saab 2000 was that it would be a new type, which would give new type costs; SAS Commuter only had Fokker 50s and no operating experience with the Saab 2000. SAS already had many different types of aircraft and had taken a decision in principle to minimize the number of types. Type costs also become proportionally higher for small fleets with few units. In this case it would only involve six aircraft.

Maintenance costs was the area we were most concerned about and that was the most difficult to assess. The technical reliability and thus the availability of the aircraft on the routes are essential for an economically successful operation. We therefore requested that Saab would take responsibility for the technical availability by managing the maintenance of the aircraft. Saab finally accepted to take on this responsibility and the entire maintenance became part of the aircraft lease. SAS leased the aircraft for six years. The rental period was based on there already being ideas about replacing the 50-seaters and growing with larger commuter aircraft.

The model to purchase more of the maintenance

Saab 2000 in SAS Commuter colors
Photo: Saab.

SAS Commuter Saab 2000 SE-LSC at Kalmar Airport in 1997.
Photo John Berggren

activity than to have it "in house," became a strategy we used later at many procurement discussions, referring to the Saab 2000 as a good example.

SAS had in the mid 1990s consolidated and developed its position in the local market, i.e. Scandinavia and the Baltic region. The first year in which SAS seriously faced competition on the so-called capital triangle, Copenhagen-Oslo-Stockholm, was in 1997. SAS increased flights to Finland, which by now was regarded as a part of the home market.

In 1997, the new commuter base in Stockholm, was established. Two Saab 2000 were put into service in the spring of 1997 in order to expand the number of departures and to increase the timetable to a large number of destinations. The number of flights with jets had also been extended to the competitive routes from Stockholm to Malmo, Angelholm, and Sundsvall. A number of smaller destinations in Finland were served with the Saab 2000.

The Saab 2000s proved very flexible when used together with the then jet fleet used in the same markets. Thanks to its relatively high speed, domestic routes could be flown on the same block times. It could therefore replace an F28 or DC-9 without affecting timetables.

The aircraft's range was also good, which meant that it was put on some longer international routes to Archangelsk and Budapest.

SAS Commuter had a lower cost structure than the Airline. In this way, SAS used the production resources to optimize profitability on flights of varying numbers of passengers. One example is that the Stockholm-Archangelsk route became profitable when it could begin to be served by the Saab 2000.

Technical availability was very good and the lease agreement contained an incentive for high utilization, which was also the case. Thanks to the very high availability and flexibility of schedule, the introduction went largely trouble-free. One drawback, which was sometimes experienced at peak times, was that the number of seats (47) was too small in relation to the rest of the fleet.

SAS had generally tried to adjust flight deck systems to achieve operational compatibility across the fleet when there were opertunities. For the Saab 2000, which was a transitional solution of about six years, the standard Saab cockpit was chosen. It was considered to be "state of the art" by Jan Ström, a SAS pilot with extensive experience in flight deck design, and SAS avionic expert Bengt Nilsson. They had also been involved in its development.

The cabin was equipped with 47 leather-covered seats of the same type that Crossair had. Seat pitch was especially large in the first row, which was appreciated by tall people. Seating comfort was very good. Seat width was namely about an inch more than in the Fokker 50, Dash 8, and 737. Boarding and deplaning could be perceived to have some limitations due to the low ceiling height.

The cabin was equipped with a very effective noise reduction system. However, it also had a peculiarity that in some places external noise sources were attenuated to the extent that conversation from a seat row ahead or behind could clearly be overheard. Something that is rare in airplanes!

The contract between Saab Aircraft and SAS Commuter stipulated that Saab would be responsible for:
"Perform line and base maintenance according to SAS Commuter maintenance programs." "To provide specified group support equipment." "To provide spares and handling."

The Saab 2000 maintenance program could be planned such that it did not require any technicians in the morning after a night stop at an "outstation." The flight crew and ramp personnel managed the necessary procedures themselves, which meant that all the mechanics were stationed at Arlanda airport, and only in case of a technical failure at an outstation would a technician was required on site.

Regularity was high during the whole lease period and the setup between Saab and SAS Commuter worked well. Both organizations benefitted from the lessons learned. Aside from aircraft SE-LSF that was badly damaged by a ground incident at the airport in 1999, all aircraft were transferred to Finland and SAS-owned AirBotnia, currently Blue1 in Helsinki, after the contract period.

Saab 2000 cabin.
Photo Saab

Aircraft Projects and Evaluation

During aviation's early buildup, aviation technology developed very quickly with new projects every so often. When SAS was formed after the Second World War, new technologies developed within short time intervals. Much of the reconstruction of postwar civil aviation also demanded innovations and knowledgeable technicians to further develop flight operations, aircraft, and equipment. SAS involvement in many aircraft projects has been presented in previous sections that led to the types SAS bought, but also some that were not selected.

The airline industry was very technology oriented but with deregulation of the various markets and changed competition, more influence from the business and financial sectors also came in the 1980s. Management structures changed and therefore priorities regarding expertise in projects, aircraft valuation, and procurement. SAS maintained an adequate expertise in projects and evaluation until the early 2000s but has since gradually decreased these resources. This also applies to many other airlines, so resources and expertise in the area vary widely between companies.

Alliances between airlines within the evaluation process took place early in an organized form such as within the "Association of European Airlines" (AEA) in the 1970s and 1980s. "Fleet Planner" and evaluators met regularly and exchanged experiences and compiled an evaluation model that manufacturers could use to evaluate their products against others. KSSU did also play a role.

Bilateral contacts were taken with other airlines for aircraft projects and it was natural to help each other in aeronautical matters, despite the commercial competition. Only once, did I encounter a problem.

A meeting had been set up by Finnair when SAS was studying the MD-83, which Finnair already had. At the same time, we studied the possibility of extending the range of the DC-10-30. The meeting, which took place in the normal spirit of friendship, I asked some questions about Finnair's DC-10 operations. There was suddenly a different atmosphere and they cordially but firmly told me that the DC-10 was not to be discussed. The reason was that Jan Carlzon at a press conference in Helsinki said that Finnair would not be able to fly nonstop from Helsinki to Tokyo with the DC-10 because the SAS experts said that SAS could not do it.

The shortest route to Tokyo goes over northern Siberia, but the Soviet Union allowed at that time only a very limited number of flights, so the shortest path without flying over the Soviet Union was straight north over the North Pole and down through the Bering Strait and from there around the Kamchatka Peninsula towards Japan. Helsinki

Finnair's first DC-10-30 delivery.
Photo SFF archive.

airport is significantly closer to the North Pole than Copenhagen and even slightly closer than Stockholm. From Helsinki the flight was on the verge of what a DC-10-30 could manage but the longer distance from Kastrup or Arlanda was outside the aircraft's range with an economically justifiable payload.

Star Alliance cooperation

Air Canada, United Airlines, Lufthansa, SAS, and Thai Airways formed Star Alliance on 14 May 1997. Star Alliance is today, in 2014, the world's largest alliance of airlines whose 27 members control a fleet of 4,570 aircraft.

The partnership is built on essentially six points:

1. Coordinated networks and schedules, which will facilitate passenger connections among the companies.
2. Common profile.
3. Common bonus scheme – as a member in one alliance member's program also earns bonus points from all members of Star Alliance.
4. Access to airport lounges.
5. Joint offers from more than one airline
6. Collaboration on technology and logistics.

Star Alliance entails a deeper cooperation than just "code share" flights, even if it's the part of the cooperation that the customer usually comes in contact with. Quite early a number of areas were

767-300 with the original five Star Alliance companies´ logos plus Varig who became the sixth member in autumn 1997.
Photo Hans Norman
www. Scanliners.com.

Star Alliance celebrated its 10th anniversary in Copenhagen in 2007. Photo Star Alliance.

investigated that could make the operations more efficient and reduce costs through economies. An area of great potential was joint purchasing of office supplies, spare parts, aviation fuel, and aircraft.

Purchase of aircraft with high capital cost was a very interesting area. So a working group Star Alliance "Aircraft Purchasing Working Group" was established with four companies involved from the beginning. It was chaired by Lufthansa the first two years and then SAS took over presidency.

In late 1998, five of the Star Alliance companies put in individual orders for more than 500 aircraft including options. Capital expenditures corresponded to approximately $ 20 billion. If you could coordinate such purchases it should be a great potential to reduce costs. Star Alliance was not legally an organization that could sign the airplane contracts for its members, which required other solutions. If a jointly-owned leasing company had been formed with the right to purchase and lease aircraft to the Star Alliance companies, that would have possibly solved the issue.

Bombardier CRJ900. Photo Bombardier.

Boeing 717-200. Photo: Javier Bravo Muñoz.

One area, which however is a question of cost and also often a problem area, in disposal or in- or out leasing, is specification. Coordinated specifications were therefore an area that we agreed to develop. With new products proposed by the manufacturers, the Star Alliance companies that had an interest in this type of aircraft cooperated and developed a common basic specification. Individual airlines could then add special commercial "features" to the basic specification in order to get their "branding" of the product. Common Requests For Proposal, (RFP) and lease agreements were developed.

The coordinated specifications were discussed with aircraft manufacturers, which were basically positive; they would also benefit from more standardization in their production.

It soon turned out that joint aircraft purchasing was not so simple and that each company had different internal processes to come to a decision and kept their right to determine when orders are submitted and are to be delivered. Cooperation in the Aircraft Purchasing Working Group continued, but turned into what was called the Star Alliance Fleet Coordination Group. This occurred in connection with employing one full time person to coordinate the work of the group. The first person was Tore Landfald, seconded by SAS.

The exchange was valuable and it put additional pressure on manufacturers that was not there before. One example was the dialogue with Air Canada (AC) when SAS evaluated a 767 replacement and AC shared its reasons for choosing the A330-300, which was described in the 767-replacement section.

New Regional Jet

In the late 1990s, new regional jet projects came forward from Fairchild Dornier, Embraer, and Bombardier. Lufthansa early on signed an order for the Fairchild Dornier 728s, but the company went bankrupt before the first prototype flew. There were needs for additional smaller aircraft with 50-90 seats in Star Alliance, so a joint evaluation and procurement project was launched in January 2003 with the airlines that had an interest. Air Canada, Austrian Airlines, Lufthansa, and SAS formed the nucleus. Manufacturers offering appropriate products were Bombardier with the CRJ family, Embraer with the E170-E195, and Boeing 717s. The Boeing 717 was on the high side in terms of size, but the group wanted more competition and requested that Boeing develop the 717 into a family with several sizes.

Specifications were developed for all the candidates, along with a request for proposal, which requested one proposal valid for all involved airlines. The producers were initially very negative, but delivered in the end one common proposal. It was, however, potentially an order for 200 aircraft.

The inquiry also included a new component,

advanced by SAS, namely that manufacturers would also offer and sell a support and maintenance program that basically contained all maintenance. We called it "Total Support Program" (TSP). Some airlines were not so keen on it because they had their traditional large in-house maintenance operations.

There were also divided views on the value of the TSP within SAS, but it was tested when SAS leased the Saab 2000 with very good experience.

The aim was to get better control of maintenance costs and by involving manufacturers more in the process to create incentives for better quality in design, production, and product. In too many new aircraft, there are quality problems and design errors showing up only when in service, causing major disruptions and costs for operators.

The final negotiations were jointly taken to a certain level, but above that level, it was up to the individual companies to finalize.

The result was that only Air Canada ordered new aircraft. Others waited due to their internal decision-making processes being different but also their different need and timing. Air Canada ordered aircraft from both Bombardier and Embraer.

The Star Alliance companies learned from each other by "best practice sharing" but it also taught manufacturers that future fleet issues would be addressed at the Alliance level. The greater leverage airlines had through a well coordinated collaboration became quite clear in this project. Among the manufacturers in some cases better internal coordination was required between the responsible sales departments and it resulted in some reorganization to best meet the Alliance's questions and requirements.

An interesting episode during the evaluation of the RJ candidates occurred in the summer of 2005. Payload Range ability was evaluated also with regard to potential limitations of takeoff performance such as at high temperatures or reduced runway braking effects. I realized that some versions' performance was deficient. One of Boeing's marketing people, who worked with SAS, gave me an idea of a useful way to evaluate the extent of load limitation on a network. He did not however realize how I used the method.

I let the manufacturers themselves do quite detailed analyses of the planned network based on certain conditions regarding the limiting factors. The

results were very interesting and revealing. It turned out that the larger models in both the Embraer and Bombardier families had such great takeoff weight restrictions in more demanding conditions that the Payload Range was so limited that the maximum load on a given route was less than the smaller version could take under the same conditions. It was actually quite logical in view of the unchanged wing area, higher weights and the same engine thrust of some of the larger versions. In other words, the utility of the larger versions was limited and an efficient utilization of the family concept was limited as well. We told the manufacturers that their larger versions could be eliminated from the evaluation.

After a visit to Boeing in Long Beach in July 2005, I was flying on America West's new CRJ900 via Phoenix, Arizona to Hartford in Connecticut. The CRJ900 was one of the versions we had identified with performance issues. The takeoff from Long Beach was midday and the temperature was around 86 degrees F. Long Beach has two runways, one long and one short, a length similar to the runway at Bromma, Stockholm City Airport.

After boardimg the aircraft, which became fully loaded, and some time beyond the normal departure time the captain showed up in the cabin and informed the passengers that the long runway had closed due to an aircraft that had landed on its belly in the middle of the runway and that the shorter runway had to be used. It required, however, that eleven passengers would have to voluntarily leave the plane to reduce the load. After an hour had passed, minus the load of eleven passengers, and before taking off, part of already loaded fuel was "burned" off to reach the reduced takeoff weight required for the short runway. The takeoff went OK but the delay made me miss my connection in Phoenix.

The first thing I did the next day was to contact Bombardier and ask them to reconstruct the takeoff performance that applied in Long Beach and thereby confirm the criticism SAS presented previously . Bombardier could now only confirm that the CRJ900's takeoff performance was limited to the degree what I had experienced practically and had

Embraer 170 in connection with demonstration flight for SAS at Bromma airport. Photo Hans Norman, www.Scanliners.com.

Air Canada Embraer 175. Photo Air Canada.

CRJ 900 wing with winglet. Photo SFF archive.

Boeing's 787 "Dreamliner" is constructed with much more composite materials than previous generations of aircraft. The fuselage is manufactured with carbon fiber composite. The 787 will be manufactured in three different sizes. The 787-8, which is the first version, is just a couple of seat rows larger than the 767-300.
Photo Boeing.

previously calculated.

Bombardier, however, took charge of the problem and modified the CRJ900 wing by increasing wing area and by changing the winglet and the trailing edge of the wing. In this way CRJ900 takeoff performance improved very much and the previous weakness was eliminated. The modification of the wing later became "production standard" for both the CRJ900 and CRJ700.

Star Alliance long-haul study

In connection with the offering of the Airbus A350 project and Boeing's already launched 787, the Star Alliance Fleet Co-ordination Group started evaluating the new long-haul aircraft. Star Alliance specifications were also developed. Some of the airlines were already in the acquisition process at this point in time. The evaluation resulted in an internal report to the Star Alliance Presidents meeting, the "Airline Management Board" (AMB).

The study presented some weaknesses, which were communicated to the manufacturers, but also showed the advantages of the new technologies applied on the 787 and A350; primarily the increased payload-range capability but also improved environmental characteristics in noise and emissions.

The next generation narrow-body

Star Alliance's Fleet Co-ordination Group had early in their cooperation identified a relatively great need for a new aircraft in the 150-200-seat class. In the long run all airlines had certain needs for new equipment. SAS had the MD-80, the oldest individual in the fleet being almost 15 years old, and some had first-generation A320s and 737 Classics (737-300, -400 and -500).

The Group, now with 16 members, decided in the spring 2006 to start a new project for a "Next generation narrow-body." It began with reviewing the companies' needs in detail and developing a common specification. Then a dialogue started mainly with Airbus and Boeing, but also with the engine manufacturers on an entirely new aircraft. Boeing and Airbus had appeared in the media with statements that indicated that there were ongoing internal studies. From the engine manufacturers there were also signals that enough new technology would be available to justify a new aircraft. Especially interesting was if the engine manufacturers now

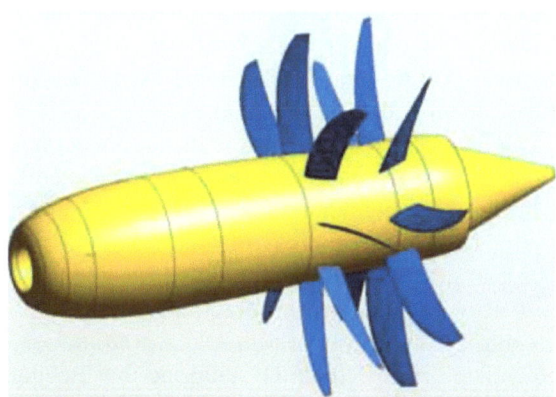

Open Rotor concept.   Picture by Rolls-Royce.

were prepared to invest in more unconventional solutions like the "Propfan" or "open rotor" as it was now called. The dialogue with Boeing and Airbus was mostly a discussion of requirements and specification and not so much about more concrete configurations. It was indicated, however, that a new aircraft could be available at the earliest in seven or eight years, i.e, about 2014, which then (2006) seemed to be a long way off.

For SAS, the issue was retaining MD-80 and switching to a brand new type as it became clear that it would yield greater and more sustainable improvements than to take the step via the then current generation A320 or 737NG. United and Lufthansa had similar issues with the 737 Classics.

In 2010, however, Airbus announced that it would launch a modernized A320 family, the A320neo with new engines, but not with a new airframe. It took until 2011 before Boeing matched Airbus, by launching a 737 version with new engines called 737MAX. It had been speculated that Boeing would have great difficulty squeezing in a new and bigger engine under the 737 wing. With these derivatives of existing models a new aircraft was pushed out into the future and probably at least 10 years from the introduction of derivatives.

Star Alliance fleet planning cooperation was unique in that so many companies were involved from different continents and with different market needs. It did also work well, although more tangible results might have been expected. A confidential source revealed that the One World Alliance (American Airlines, British Airways, Finnair, Iberia, etc.) made a similar attempt, but it did not lead to an active group due to disagreements among the companies.

Superjet International

In 2004 I was invited to participate in the Sukhoi RRJ "Airline Advisory Board" (AAB). It proved to be a very interesting project. Russia's Sukhoi, mainly involved in military aircraft, had plans to develop a civil regional aircraft family with variants from 60 to 90 seats. The Russian aviation industry would be totally reorganized and rebuilt more like an Airbus organization. At the first AAB meeting in Moscow, attendees from the west were, Air France, Brussels Airline, and myself. From Russia, Aeroflot plus a number of other companies.

Unlike previous Russian aircraft, this project was as international as many western aircraft programs. The same subcontractors were responsible for most systems, and in some cases in cooperation with Russian manufacturers. On paper it seemed to be a worthy contender to Embraer and Bombardier. Boeing had an agreement with Sukhoi in an advisory role. The first specification indicated that Boeing tried to have Sukhoi more or less copy the 737 specification.

The Italian aerospace company Alenia Aermacchi bought 25 percent of the Sukhoi Civil Aircraft Company (SCAC) in 2005 and formed a new joint venture company, Superjet International. The company is based in Venice, Italy and is responsible for sales and support of aircraft outside Russia, China, and India, which are managed by SCAC in Moscow. Internationally the aircraft is called Sukhoi SuperJet 100 (SSJ100).

When I informed the Star Alliance Fleet Coordinating Group about the project Lufthansa also joined the AAB. It turned out early that Air France and SAS had similar views and thus a particular bilateral cooperation developed with the Air France evaluation group, which had a high level of expertise and a lot of influence in various projects. Among other things, the western airlines and I influenced the design of the cockpit so it more closely resembles the Airbus concept regarding system integration, the "side stick," and large digital displays.

The aircraft was certified in 2011 in a 95-seat version, the SSJ100, and can sometimes be seen at Kastrup and Stockholm-Arlanda in Aeroflot's color scheme. Interjet in Mexico also flies the SSJ100, but otherwise the sales have been rather modest.

737MAX. Picture Boeing

Airbus A320neo. Picture Airbus

Cooperation within the SAS Group

In parallel with the Star Alliance Regional Jet study, we carried out a corresponding study within the SAS Group, which in 2005 included Spanair, Widerøe, Estonian Air, Air Baltic, Blue 1, and SAS. Commercial proposals from Bombardier, Embraer, Boeing, and Sukhoi were evaluated, but it did not result in any decisions at that time.

Fleet Development performed a consulting role for those companies regarding fleet planning. The companies' organizations were smaller witout dedicated resources for fleet planning. The CEO and CFO typically discussed among themselves and possibly with the technical manager. The planning horizon was often short. Decisions were taken ad hoc e.g. when an aircraft lease had to be extended or aircraft were required to be replaced when a lease expired. We helped companies with evaluations and discussed the longer-term solutions. When capacity needs or surpluses emerged Fleet Development and SAS Asset Management helped by first trying to resolve the situation within the SAS Group with lease-in and lease-out.

Superjet 100 at Moscow Sheremetyevo airport September 2013. Photo Bengt-Olov Nas.

The Q400 operations end in 2007

The introduction of the Q400 was unusually difficult with many technical failures caused by quality problems. As described in the chapter on the acquisition the situation improved very slowly and never reached availability levels on par with other types in the fleet.

In 2007 there were three accidents in the space of barely two months:
- 9 September, SK1209 Copenhagen-Aalborg. During landing the right landing gear collapsed. Passengers and crew evacuated the aircraft. The preliminary report of the Danish Accident Investigation Board pointed to a design of the main landing gear actuator leading to corrosion fatigue.
- 11 September, SK2748 Copenhagen-Palanga. The aircraft's right main landing gear collapsed so that the aircraft was forced off the landing runway and stopped. Passengers and crew evacuated the aircraft without injury. The preliminary report of the Lithuanian Accident Investigation Board pointed to a design of the main landing gear mechanism, leading to corrosion fatigue.
- 27 October, SK2867 Bergen - Copenhagen. During the approach to Copenhagen the right main landing gear could not be extended completely. Passengers and crew evacuated the aircraft without injury. The preliminary investigation from the Danish Accident Investigation Board indicated that an o-ring had come off a component of the hydraulic system. This o-ring had subsequently moved to the main landing gear mechanism and got stuck.

The SAS Board decided on 28 October 2007 to permanently withdraw the entire SAS Group's 27 Q400 fleet from service. The Norwegan subsidiary Widerøe was operating on Swedish domestic routes, Danish domestic routes and international routes,

Counting the number of seats, this represented about 5 percent of the fleet's seat capacity. To take care of the loss in seat capacity, SAS was forced in the short term to compensate with wet leasing from other airlines. Because the Q400 was replaced with larger aircraft in the fleet, e.g. 737s, changes in route structure had to be done, with fewer flights and in some case giving up destinations. The smallest aircraft unit necessary for many domestic thinner routes, increasing frequencies, and the feed to Copenhagen and Stockholm-Arlanda was thus removed from the fleet. The Danish authority responsible for accident investigations, SLV (Statens Luftfarts Vaesende), concluded that there were design flaws on the Q400, so SAS was not blamed because they had not discovered the flaws. The Q400s operated by SAS and Widerøe were upgraded before being sold to other operators.

SAS made a deal with Bombardier and Goodrich, the landing gear manufacturer, for compensation to SAS for the incidents involving the Q400 aircraft in the fall of 2007. As part of the agreement reached in 2008, an order for 27 new aircraft was placed, with an option for another 24. To permanently replace Q400 SAS ordered twelve CRJ900s for SAS Denmark and six Q400NGs for Widerøe in early 2008, who also leased four Q400NGs.

To the right, Q400 main landing gear
Photo HansNorman
www.Scanliners.com.

CRJ900 at Kastrup.
Photo HansNorman
www.Scanliners.com.

The MD-80 replacement

The MD-80 was developed during the second half of the 1970s, and was certified in 1980. It was developed from the DC-9 and was certified as a derivative designated DC-9-80. The type was produced for 20 years until 1999.

In the MD-80 size class Airbus had launched the A320 family and Boeing developed the 737 during this period, both with more modern technology for lower fuel burn, more range and lower noise.

More modern engines accounted for a large part of the improvement. Both the 737 and the A320 offered a family concept in the form of several sizes. The later generations were also much quieter, especially during takeoff. It was therefore natural to evaluate, as new models were launched, the potential benefits adding value so it would be economically justified to replace the MD-80.

The service life for this type of aircraft is technically about 25-30 years, with some variation depending on the utilization with regard to the number of landings (cycles). The economic life can vary for an airline depending on many factors such as the company's internal costs. The fuel price, which increased significantly for many years, has now an increased role in the aircraft's economic life.

Changing airplane types also means major adjustments for an airline with re-training of crews and technicians. For a relatively large fleet to be replaced, it therefore takes several years of phasing in and out with elevated costs during the transition.

The SAS MD-80 fleet reached its maximum size in 1998 with 67 units of the MD-81, MD-82, MD-83, and MD87. In addition, there were 26 DC-9-21 & -41 aircraft and nine leased DC-9-81 in1998, SAS received its first 737-600, which started the final DC-9 replacement program. Since the 737-700 and 737-800 in terms of capacity were closer to the MD-80 these were compared regularly. The same type of comparison was also carried out when the A321 in 1998 was selected and became Big. In this case, however, there was no remaining MD-80 and MD-90 production. At that time calculations showed no direct economic benefit to begin a MD-80 replacement. The difference in fuel costs did not offset the difference in price of new aircraft compared to the depreciated value of the MD-80.

During the period 2005-2007 several airlines discussed with the manufacturers the need of an entirely new aircraft in the 150-200 seat class . There were proposals from airlines and hopes of completely new aircraft types that would be produced by Airbus and Boeing, which possibly could then be a suitable replacement for the MD-80. 737NG and Airbus A320 families did not yield sufficient economic benefits, but if you could skip a generation, the reduction in fuel costs might be twice as large and easier to motivate purchases. It could be shown that even with assumed certain traffic and capacity growth, the total Medium fleet fuel consumption to be less than for the MD-80 fleet over a long period with a brand new aircraft. If the trade was made instead with new 737s or A320s, the total consumption would be higher after a fairly short period because of the assumed and expected growth in the market and the SAS fleet.

The timing of a new aircraft was very uncertain. The most optimistic scenario indicated 2013, but it seemed more likely about 2015-2016. One of the major uncertainties was the engine configuration. Would Open Rotor, i.e. propfan technology develop

MD-82.
Photo Hans Norman,
www.Scanliners.com.

Bombardier's C Series prototype.
Photo Bombardier.

in these timeframes? This technology promised some benefit in terms of fuel consumption, but there was greater uncertainty about noise and certification.

In 2007, a new strategic fleet plan was presented including a major evaluation of SAS's MD-80s, which had an average age of 18.4 years. The utilization of the MD-80 in hours flown and the number of landings was not a problem. It turned out that the fleet utilization was at about 50% of its technical lifetime in terms of number of cycles.

A threat was the environmental requirements that had continuously grown were a risk locally at airports and also the more general in nature concerning CO2 emissions. The most obvious was the MD-80's noise levels during takeoff. During landing, the MD-80 is as quiet as many of the much more modern aircraft due to its engine location.

With the uncertainty around the noise situation at Kastrup airport and what might happen if Kastrup management could not report to the Danish Ministry of Environment that environmental regulations were met, we recognized a potential threat to the MD-80. In December 2010 however, Airbus launched an upgraded version of its A320 family with new engines with about 12-15% lower fuel consumption. The new family was called the A320neo, neo meaning "new engine option." The current A320 is therefore known now as A320ceo, "current engine option." Boeing responded later with the launch of a "New Generation 737MAX" also with the next generation engine technology. This meant that the brand new aircraft were pushed out in time to an even more uncertain future. There were now no longer reasons to wait with the MD-80 replacement.

The candidates were now mainly the Airbus A320neo family and Bombardier's new C-series, since Boeing waited until the second half of 2011 before deciding to offer the 737MAX. SAS had gradually reduced the number of MD-80 to 25 units in 2010. A certain replacement had already been provided with the acquisition of 737-700 and 737-800. The Boeing 737-800 has significantly more seats than the MD-80 and can therefore not only offer more "peak" capacity, but also very cost-effective charter flights. Since the two candidates are not available until 2018 for SAS, leasing of interim capacity to meet capacity requirements was needed.

The choice of the MD-80 replacement fell in 2013 finally on the Airbus A320neo family, with an option to choose the A319neo, A320neo, or A321neo at a time closer to the delivery date. The order is for 30 firm and 12 options. The decision means that the Airbus A321 / 319 fleet that was purchased in 2000 is being expanded with new and more modern aircraft from the A320 family based at Kastrup. For the Arlanda base the 737NG aircraft replaced MD-80 and Gardermoen in Norway was already a pure 737-base, however, in need of replacement of the 737-400 and -500 with the 737NG.

SAS A320neo
Illustration Airbus

New long-haul fleet

In October 2013 SAS signed the final agreement for the purchase of four A330-300 "Enhanced" and eight A350-900s for delivery from 2015 and 2018 respectively. The contract includes options for the purchase of an additional six Airbus A350-900s.

Developments in engine technology and aerodynamics have meant that the new types of aircraft that are now being put into service and those, which will shortly be on the market, provide major savings in fuel consumption and costs. The A330 Enhanced Max TakeOff Weight (MTOW) is increased to 242 ton wich increases the range by 500 nm compared to the current 233 ton MTOW Airbus A330-300 and about 15 percent lower fuel consumption compared to today's Airbus A340-300s. The Airbus A350-900 will have over 30% lower fuel per seat consumption than the Airbus A340-300, and noise is reduced significantly. Compared to competing aircraft of the same size, one of the advantages of the A350 is that the fuselage cross section is wider, providing greater passenger comfort.

SAS plans to increase its efficient A330 fleet from four to eight aircraft by replacing four A340s with four A330-300 Enhanced, when the current A340 leases expire.

Since SAS signed the A330 Enhanced Agreement in late 2013, Airbus further developed the A330 due to pressure from their customers. On 14 July 2014 on Bastille Day, Airbus announced the launch of the A330neo with newer versions of the Rolls-Royce Trent 700 engines. With the engine exchange and some aerodynamic improvements, 14 percent less fuel per seat-mile is promised. SAS was premature with their A330 orders and missed the A330neo enhancements. A330neos will be in service from 2017, which is a couple of years later than SAS 2015 deliveries of the A330 Enhanced in 2015. In September 2014 SAS announced that it couldn't wait for the A330neo.

SAS A350.
Illustration Airbus.

A330-300 Enhanced, LN-RKS delivered 25 September 2015
Photo Hans Norman
www.Scanliners.com

Aviation and the environment

In 1942 US authorities introduced operating and safety regulations for civilian flights with aircraft that were certified by the US FAA. These regulations were adopted in principle by the authorities in other countries.

When ICAO was formed in 1948 the corresponding regulations were drafted as recommendations for international air traffic. These recommendations are described in a number of annexes to the ICAO Convention on International Civil Aviation. The annexes have over the years been updated and evolved along with the development of aviation.

As a result of increasing noise problems around airports when jets were introduced in the 1960s, regulations were demanded. The US FAA published in 1968 its requirement documents, FAR 36 and ICAO issued the same rules, with ICAO Annex 16, in 1969.

SAS's project function was from the beginning committed to work with the new rules by participating in the working groups that were established in various international government and airline organizations such as ICAO, IATA, and in Europe AEA (Association of European Airlines).

Later, it was also time to introduce design requirements for the engines to reduce the amount of harmful emissions. It became absolutely necessary for SAS to have environmental knowledge since environmental issues increasingly influenced the fleet planning. The department for Aircraft Analysis became involved in this work. The training was mostly learning by doing by being active in the various international working groups and through contacts with the authorities and the manufacturing industry.

The regulatory framework for environmental protection, ICAO Annex 16

Annex 16, Volumes I and II, deals with the environmental aspects with respect to aircraft noise and emissions from aircraft engines, two areas hardly contemplated when the Chicago Convention was signed in 1944.

Aircraft noise was a problem already when ICAO was formed. It increased when the first jet aircraft were introduced in the early 1960s and accelerated with the growth of international jet aircraft traffic.

The ICAO General Assembly adopted in 1968 a resolution recognizing the severity of noise around airports, and instructed the ICAO Council to establish international specifications and associated guidance for aircraft noise. The 1971 General Assembly adopted a resolution that recognizes the negative environmental impacts related to aviation, Annex 16, adopted in 1971, deals with various aspects of aircraft noise problems and contains:
- Procedures and description of noise measurement
- Human tolerance to aircraft noise; noise Certification
- Criteria for establishing noise abatement procedures
- Land management and procedures for reduction of noise during ground run of engines.

Following this meeting the Committee on Aircraft Noise (CAN) was established to assist ICAO in developing noise certification requirements for different classes of aircraft.

The first meeting of CAN drafted the first amendment to Annex 16 that includes noise certification of produced and derivative versions of existing subsonic aircraft. During the following CAN meetings certification requirements were developed for future subsonic jet airplanes and propeller-driven aircraft, and for future production versions of existing civil supersonic planes and helicopters.

A resolution adopted by the ICAO General Assembly in 1971 led to measures relating to aircraft engine emissions. "Committee on Aircraft Engine Emissions" (CAEE) was formed with the aim to develop specific "standards" for aircraft engines. These "standards" (requirements), adopted in 1981, set a maximum level of emissions of smoke and some emissions for future large turbojet and turbofan engines. Annex 16 was expanded to include engine emission requirements.

Requirements included limits on emissions of carbon monoxide, unburned hydrocarbons and nitrogen oxides for large turbojet and turbofan engines intended for subsonic aircraft manufactured after 1 January 1986.

In 1983 CAN and CAEE Committees were combined and the "Committee on Aviation Environmental Protection" (CAEP) was formed as a technical committee under the ICAO Council. Since the formation, CAEP has further developed the requirements of Annex 16 for both aircraft noise and aircraft engine emissions.

Aircraft noise Definitions

"Effective Perceived Noise Level," EPNdb, is a measure of the subjective effect of aircraft noise on people with respect to instantaneous perceived noise level and exposure with time. Different measurement points have been defined for maximum noise level: lateral, during landing, and during takeoff and also measurement procedures.

Noise Certificates issued by the issuing State for an aircraft type are based on satisfactory evidence that the aircraft meets the requirements.

Depending on year of certification for the type, aircraft are classified in "Chapters":

Chapter 2 includes subsonic aircraft for which application for type certification of the prototype was accepted before 6 October, 1977.

Chapter 3 regulates aircraft that were accepted from 1977, as well as propeller-driven airplanes over 12,500 lb, for aircraft with less weight, for supersonic airplanes certificated before January 2, 1975 and for helicopters for which the application for certification of the prototype was accepted from January 1, 1980.

The ICAO Council adopted CAEP´s Chapter 4 recommendation in 2001. This new aircraft noise standard tightened the requirements in relation to Chapter 3 by ten EPNdb cumulatively over the three measurement points. Chapter 4 applies from 1 January 2006 for new type certificated airplanes and Chapter 3 aircraft re-certified on request.

The stricter standard was adopted and the ICAO Assembly embraced the concept of "a balanced approach to manage noise issues" that CAEP developed consisting of four elements, reduction at the source of the noise, land use planning, operational procedures, and operational constraints.

The 2013 ICAO General Assembly sharpened additional certification requirements with seven EPNdb cumulatively for new types from 2017, through the introduction of Chapter 14.

With respect to aircraft engine emissions, a change in the organization's work has started. From the beginning the issue was local air quality around airports. Since 1990 the issue has been broadened to include global atmospheric problems such as climate change. ICAO has therefore considered to further develop emission standards to not only cover takeoff and landing phases but all flight phases.

CAEP/8, 2010 adopted a new work program that includes the development of a Carbon Standard (CO_2 standard). Since CO_2 emissions are proportional to fuel consumption it means in principle a regulation of fuel efficiency for commercial aircraft. The ongoing work of this new standard is aimed at CAEP/10 in February 2016 to decide on the design of this standard with a recommendation to the ICAO Council. It is expected that the 2016 General Assembly will eventually endorse the new standard and that it could apply from 2020 on.

The environmental impact has become one of civil aviation's biggest challenges in the new century. Since Annex 16 was adopted, it has evolved to meet new environmental concerns and to incorporate new and more environmentally friendly technologies. ICAO will continue to evaluate Annex 16, consistent with its goal to maintain maximum compatibility with safety and environmental quality as civil aviation develops.

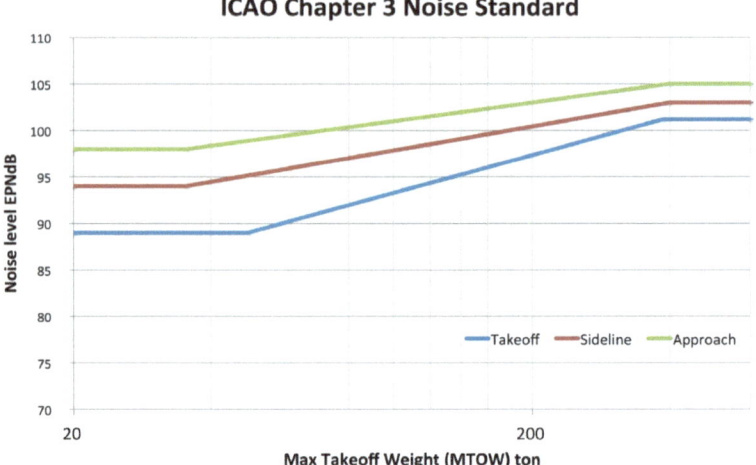

ICAO Chapter 3 aircraft noise standards
Picture Bengt-Olov Nas.

SAS fleet and the environment

DC-9 was the first SAS type that was certified by the ICAO noise standards, Annex 16, Chapter 2. The generation of jet aircraft before the DC-9, such as the Caravelle, DC-8 and 707 were known as non-noise certificated (NNC).

In the late 1970s and early 1980s restrictions were discussed on the use of NNC aircraft. This led to a US-imposed ban in 1980 which was followed by Europe beginning in 1982.

Since SAS still had some remaining DC-8s we investigated the possibility of modifying them to Chapter 2 standards. In situations where airlines have aircraft that cannot be used, there is a market of "fixers," i.e., new ventures or subcontractors who offer modification opportunities that meet the more stringent requirements. The manufacturer of the plane, in this case MDC, does not offer solutions voluntarily. MDC was actually very negative towards SAS's request for assistance in certifying the DC-8 to Chapter 2. The sales organization that would rather sell new aircraft had greater influence on the MDC position than the support organization, which we turned to. To ensure the continued use of the DC-8 we therefore evaluated the market regarding the so-called Hush Kits (noise dampers). Five modification kits were eventually bought.

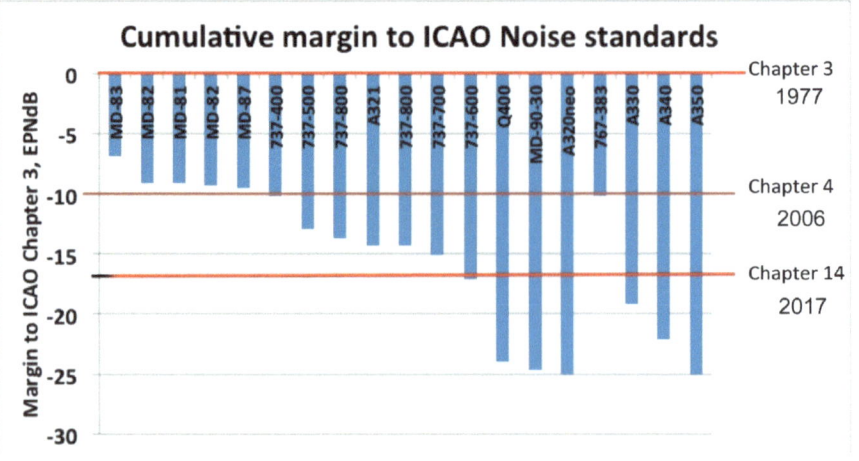

SAS aircraft fleet status of meeting the ICAO certification requirements.
Picture Bengt-Olov Nas.

Another modification that was offered was the engine replacement with the CFM56-2 engines. About 100 DC-8s were modified in total, most of which eventually were converted into cargo planes.

After development of noise-suppressing modifications for the NNC aircraft, kits were also developed for the DC-9 and 737-100 / -200, which enabled certification to Chapter 3. SAS acquired kits for 20 DC-9-41s as the airports in Europe began to introduce various rules detailing when and how Chapter 2 airplanes would be allowed to operate. It was also necessary that the DC-9 was Chapter 3-approved to be sellable, among others, to the US.

Late 1980s and early 1990s, the environmental impact of aviation became a point of discussion in Sweden because of the environmental assessment required for the development of a third runway at Stockholm's Arlanda airport. A lot of newspaper articles circulated, which attributed the majority of the problems to the airlines. SAS felt that the information was inaccurate and misleading. Lars Bergvall, head of the airline, was a proactive person in SAS Management. So in order to educate all employees an information leaflet "The Little Green book" was produced. It was sent to all employees with a letter from Lars Bergvall.

A new position, Head of Environmental Affairs, was established relatively high up in the organization and an environmental policy was established in order to work in a more systematically and transparent way with environmental issues. Jorgen Grauengaard, former head of SAS Commuter was put in charge

When Jan Stenberg in 1994 took over as CEO, Niels-Eirik Nertun was appointed as SAS Environmental Director and the environmental work was even more in focus as a key strategic challenge.

In 1995, SAS presented its first special environment annual aeport. It received an award as Sweden's best environmental report by the accounting consultants' annual ranking of reports. Each year thereafter there were annual environmental reports submitted and presented at the same time as the airline's annual financial report. For several years SAS won awards for the annual environmental report. Eventually social responsibility was added and the environmental report was integrated with the financial as a sustainability report. Just a few European airlines had earlier publicly presented environmental reports, but after SAS all European companies followed. Eventually, also overseas and even US airlines!

The MD-80's noise was certified in 1979 according to the FAA FAR36 Stage 3, which basically corresponded to the ICAO Chapter 3. MD-80 was at that time one of the first in its class to be certified under Chapter 3 and was considered to be in a quiet class by itself. SAS used the MD-80 to a very large extent from Kastrup to European destinations and the rest of Scandinavia. For Kastrup there was an environmental approval, which basically meant that the airport's overall noise emissions would not exceed one-day maximum values nor an annual level, in principle a "noise cap."

During periods when air traffic increased, the total noise exposure grew, thus approaching the noise ceiling. The airport had no rules for each airline but felt a potential threat from SAS's relatively large contribution from the MD-80.

If the airport would "hit the roof" there were, from what we knew, no prepared measures they would take. At many airports in Europe noise charges had been introduced with the hope that they would control the companies' planning towards quieter aircraft. At Kastrup there were no noise charges. The airport's environmental management also did not believe that it would be an effective tool.

In 2004 SAS reorganized the business to separate national companies with their own fleets. SAS Denmark with its base at Kastrup airport received a portion of the MD-80 fleet and the Airbus A321 / 319 fleet. The airport management reacted with an amount of dissatisfaction and said that it looked as if the SAS had "dumped" more MD-80s in

SAS first published environmental policy in 1990. The policy regarding aircraft: We will buy or lease aircraft that meet the most stringent generally applicable international environmental requirements, Aircraft that do not meet the requirements should be replaced as soon as is operationally and economically possible. At the same time, we actively encourage the development of new additional noise reductions, cleaner and more energy friendly aviation types. Photo

1995: SAS's first separate environmental annual report. From 2002 incorporated yearly environmental accounts in the ordinary Annual Report under the concept of a sustainability report. From 2011 on a summary is provided in the Annual Report and a more detailed Sustainability Report is published separately via the internet. Photo Bengt-Olov Nas.

Copenhagen in favor of SAS Sweden at Stockholm-Arlanda being awarded 737NGs plus a smaller number of MD-80s and SAS Norway at Gardermoen receiving only 737s.

An old story about the MD-80's noise data also affected Kastrup management and the way the aircraft type was percived. In the early 1990s, a consultant who Kastrup Airport used to check that the airlines operated according to recommended procedures, made some noise measurements that led him to believe that the MD-80 official certification data was not accurate.

As soon as I got knowledge of this claim I contacted the engine manufacturer, aircraft manufacturer, and certifying authorities to sort out the facts. After a long process with a review of existing data and an additional test flight that MDC arranged, it was found that the certification data was accurate within the required measurement accuracy.

The Swedish Civil Aviation Administration wrote a joint report that the US FAA approved. The consultant was not entirely happy because he thought that surface conditions during the measurement were not consistent with Annex 16, thereby dampening the sound energy more than what was stipulated in the certification requirements!

We engaged in a dialogue with the airport to secure the ability to evaluate and decide on the MD-80's future in good order and with sufficient discretion.

I had for some time discussed the need for noise-reducing modifications with MDC, Boeing, and Pratt & Whitney. Pratt & Whitney made a number of developments of noise suppression modifications to the engine exhaust and inlet parts. MDC was moderately interested and Boeing even less after its takeover of MDC 1997.

I also had contact with Aviation Partners Boeing (APB) in relation to the winglet modifications that were available for the 737NG. I persuaded APB to offer a winglet solution also for the MD-80. It

would contribute to noise reduction notably through improved climb performance.

This SAS Activity created an interest among some European airlines. The problem was more evident in Europe than in the rest of the world. We also managed to interest GECAS, a leasing company that had a big number of MD-80s in its portfolio.

Several entrepreneurs In the market now appeared with an interest to develop a noise-suppression

engine modification. SAS initiated a dialogue with two of those, Comtran and Aviation Fleet Solutions (AFS), and requested tenders to noise dampen the MD-80 fleet. The plan was to keep the MD-80 in the fleet until a completely new aircraft was developed.

The modification consisted of a new "mixer" in the exhaust nozzle of the engine that mixes airflow from the by-pass duct with the air from the core engine. With better mixing the exit velocity is reduced, which results in lower noise. The inlet section was also modified with a small extension and with noise absorbing material to attenuate fan and compressor noise.

Noise Technology and calculations of relatively small changes are not sufficiently secure to base an investment so we demanded to test the modifications prior to making decisions and choices of manufacturers. Both producers lined up with the modification parts and test flights were conducted at Kastrup in 2006. The idea was to use Kastrup's own noise measurement system to see if a noticeable improvement could be recorded. If that were the case

Project meeting on the ability to reduce MD-80 noise. Participants representing APB, Boeing, Pratt & Whitney, GECAS, and a number of airlines, at SAS headquarters Frösundavik October 2003.
Photo Bengt-Olov Nas.

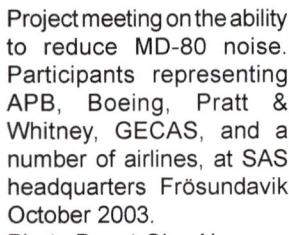

Exhaust nozzle mixer installed on the MD-80 engine.
Photo Bengt-Olov Nas.

To the left: Comtran exhaust mixer demonstrated at Farnborough in 2006. From left Jack Anderson Jet Engineering, who designed the mixer, Bengt Olov Nas SAS and Dougls Jaffe co-owner of Comtran.
Photo Bengt-Olov Nas.

Standard Instrument Departure (SID) Chart. Flight paths that must be followed within certain corridors at some airports are very demanding depending on the onboard navigation equipment and weather conditions.
Picture Patrik Nas.

the airport should accept the result. The relatively coarse measurement system was not designed for this type of test but we needed a noticeable improvement if the modifications would be valuable. The measurement results did not provide the level of improvement that was proposed.

After many years of pressure on manufacturers that actual hardware for modification was developed, it turned out that the result was not good enough, so SAS declined to modify the MD-80s. A few aircraft are reported to have been modified in the United States.

Another noise problem that the MD-80 wrestled with was departure and approach procedures from the noise-sensitive airports. The navigation system was not accurate enough for the sometimes very demanding procedures, which implied to follow a very precise track and in some cases many turns. When a flight path discrepancy occurred it showed on the airport noise monitors and reports were sent to SAS for explanation why flights diverted from prescribed tracks. In some cases fines were levied. In order to improve the operability a GPS system was installed that would assist the autopilot with heading information. However the GPS refresh rate was too slow for the system to work as expected.

In conjunction with the DC-9 replacement study during 1994-1995 and with Jan Stenberg's strong interest in environmental issues, SAS tightened the requirements regarding the current replacement candidates. The fleet should achieve an overall improved environmental impact. Noise was quite easy to manage because SAS basically swapped a 1960 generation aircraft against the "next next" generation, i.e, 1990s generation.

With engine emissions, it was not so easy. The engines had become very effective with lower fuel consumption at higher combustion temperatures and pressures, providing a cleaner burning, but increasing nitrogen oxides (NOx)

Swedish authorities and the Swedish Civil Aviation Authorities (SCAA) in particular, had since the late 1980s tightened the requirements for nitrogen oxides. Within ICAO, SCAA had been pushing for more stringent certification standards. The permission to build a third runway at Arlanda airport included as part of the environmental assessment, a requirement that the airport's total annual NOx values be limited to a certain level, i.e, a NOx bubble at the airport.

To replace the DC-9 with moderate NOx emissions and allow room for expansion of the fleet, required low NOx emissions of the candidates.

The CFM56-7B that was the only option on the Boeing 737-600 was virtually identical regarding basic engine parts with the CFM56-5B, which Airbus were offering on the A320 family. The CFM56-5B was already certified with a low emission combustor called "Dual Annular Combuster" (DAC). Swissair and EQA had the corresponding discussion and demands in the 1990 Joint Assessment.

DAC reduced NOx by about 30 percent, by affecting the combustion in stages, depending on the thrust level.

Boeing had not yet offered the DAC. We demanded however that even the CFM56-7B be certified with the DAC combuster. It was more difficult to convince the US companies Boeing and CFMI's part owner General Electric to agree to this condition than CFMI's European partner SNECMA. There was a clear difference in the perception of environmental adaptation by different cultures.

The other main candidate, the MD-95 with BR715 engines, had no corresponding background. However, there was probably some insight by Rolls-Royce's collaboration with Pratt & Whitney, since in the EQA study of 1990 a combustion solution was actually proposed for the V2500, with similar combustion technology for the MD-90. MDC was already aware of the requirements Rolls-Royce was also willing to develop the BR715 engine with a staged combustor. The Rolls-Royce and Pratt & Whitney solution seemed technically more elegant, but no customers chose this solution.

When the 737-600 was selected the DAC configuration was also selected.

DAC engines already had a few years experience in the Swissair and Austrian Airlines A320 fleets. The DAC configuration had an early problem with

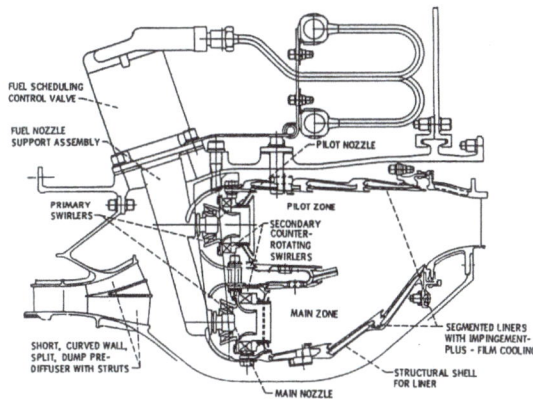

Cut through drawing section of the "Dual Annular Combustor" (DAC) showing the two combustion chamber parts "Pilot" and "Main".
Picture SNECMA.

cracks in a structural member at the exhaust of the A320 engine, but otherwise nothing alarming. When SAS introduced its 737-600s, turbine blade fatigue issues surfaced relatively soon and operational measures were needed to address the problem.

Relatively early on there were also reports from the Frankfurt Airport noise measurement system, which registered unusually high levels at approach; however relatively far out so it was not an annoying problem but, compared with other airplanes of the same size, quite higher levels. It was shown in the Frankfurt measurement data that this was also true of the Swissair A319 with DAC. The reason was that at idle power DAC created a relatively high noise level measured in dB (A), a difference that was not revealed in the certification values EPNdb. The levels were not so high that it was a disturbence on the ground, only different in comparison with measured general values for approach.

SAS also had cabin noise requirements and a guarantee, which was not in compliance due to the DAC selection. When the DAC was chosen, it was estimated that the combustion chamber would cause about 0.5% higher fuel consumption due to less efficient combustion at idle.

The difference between the DAC configuration and the later development of "Singular Annular Combuster" (SAC) on the CFM56-7B has increased the difference to about 1.5%. SAS has therefore found reasons to modify all DAC engines to the later SAC configuration during engine overhauls. DAC engines are quite unique because very few airlines followed the SAS and Swissair engine choice.

SAS had from the 1980s strict requirements in the working environment on the ramp at Scandinavian airports, especially Kastrup. The issue was noise and emissions levels at the workplace. At Kastrup and several Scandinavian airports the use of the APU on the ground is therefore regulated to maximum five minutes before the "Block On" and five minutes after the "Block Off." In connection with the aircraft evaluation and contract negotiations we always imposed demands for improvements in this area, which in general was neglected by all manufacturers. In connection with the 737NG agreement a modification of the air inlet for the APU to reduce noise levels was adopted.

"Aviation Partners Boeing" (APB) developed what is called "Blended Winglets," wing tip devices, first for the Boeing 737NG and later also for the 737 Classic, 757, and 767. The purpose of winglets is to reduce the so-called induced drag arising from the wing tip when the reduced air pressure from the wing upper side is mixed with higher air pressure from underneath, forming a vortex of air flow. APB "winglets" for the 737NG reduce fuel consumption, depending on the 737 model and flight distance, by about 1-4% due to the reduced drag. If the distance is very short, it is of no advantage because winglets do increase the empty weight.

737-800W with winglets. Photo Bengt-Olov Nas.

SAS begun to procure 737-800s back in 2000 as part of the 737-600 order and used these aircraft also on weekend charters, which meant very long flights. A winglet-modification evaluation seemed to show a fairly safe investment. Despite several attractive offers it took until 2009 before the modification was introduced. Since fuel consumption is proportional to the CO_2 production it is not only an economic gain but also an environmental benefit.

SAS Environmental work generated wide interest far outside the company. A university that wanted to study the way we worked with the issues contacted us. This resulted in a doctoral thesis entitled "Motivations for Environmental Commitment in the airline industry" by Jennifer Lynes at the University of Waterloo in Canada. Another university that used SAS environmental commitment as a case study was the University of Sacramento, California, where a thesis for an Masters Business Administration, (MBA) is entitled "Scandinavian Airlines: The Green Engine Decision."

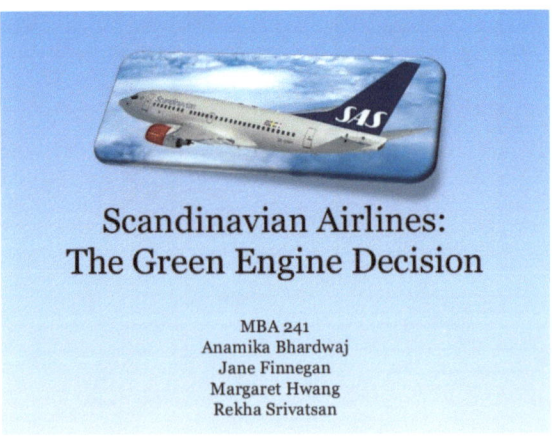

Title page on the MBA 241 paper by the University of Sacramento. Picture via Internet.

Aircraft come back

Ex Braathens' 737-500 LN-BRM in SAS colours. Photo SFF.

When a certain type was chosen by SAS one or more candidates lost the competition. In some cases, however, the "losers" for various reasons at a later stage were used in the SAS system and with SAS colors.

The F50 was selected in 1987 for SAS Commuter and a competing candidate was the Dash 8-300,

Wideroe Dash 8-300. Photo Wideroe..

which later entered the SAS family through Wideroe during the period from 2002 to 2013 when SAS had majority ownership of Wideroe

The 1987 Commuter evaluation also included the ATR 42 and in the subsequent evaluation to upgrade the SAS Commuter fleet with the larger ATR 72 turboprop, was a hot candidate that lost to the Dash 8-400.

The ATR 72 was leased by SAS via Cimber Air in the 1990s and is available from 2013 now in SAS colors for some domestic and shorter feeder services in Scandinavia and neighboring areas. It

ATR-72-500. Photo Hans Norman, www. Scanliners.com.

can be stated that the ATR-72 since the 1987 study and accidents in Italy and the United States during icing conditions, has technically worked impeccably among the many large and small operators.

The options of the 1992 DC-9 replacement study were the Fokker F100 and Avro RJ85 and RJ100. This study resulted in no change to the fleet. In 2006-2007, two Avro RJ70s were leased for flights to London City Airport (LCY). None of the former

Avro RJ70 Photo Hans Norman, www. scanliners.com.

SAS types had the takeoff and landing performance required for LCY.

The 737-500 and 737-300 were studied in 1993 because SAS bought Linjeflyg. The question was whether there was reason to "change course" and go with Boeing or to continue to develop the fleet of MD-80. The study was concluded that SAS should continue the MD-80 track. The purchase of Braathens SAFE in1999 incorporated a number of 737 Classics into the SAS fleet.

The 1994-1995 DC-9-replacement study rejected the MD-95. When Boeing took over MDC in 1997 the MD-95 was incorporated into the Boeing system and renamed 717. Within the SAS Group during the 2000s there were a few 717s in Spanair's fleet. Spanair planned to expand their 717 fleet, as there was a need for smaller aircraft in a part of the system. SAS, as principal owner of Spanair, guaranteed therefore a number long term leases.
In Blue 1, SAS's wholly owned Finnish company since 1998, there was also a small aircraft needed to replace the Avro RJ85. When Spanair went bust these 717 were available for Blue 1. The 717 is thus used now by SAS network planning as one of SAS's available capacities. Since its introduction

Blue1 Boeing 717-200. Photo Hans Norman www. Scanliners.com.

into service in 1999, the 717 has demonstrated a very high technical reliability. Unlike many other new or derivative aircraft, the 717s have performed better than average.

The Saab 2000 is also back in the SAS traffic programs since 2013. The aircraft are flown by Braathens Regional on a lease, and are now painted in today's SAS color scheme.

Reflections Bengt Olov Nas

It is a privilege to personally have been a part of the aeronautical development over more than 30 years. Commercial air travel is barely 100 years old at the moment (2014) and SAS's development described in this book spans about 70 years of the commercial aviation and SAS development.

At SAS a highly capable project department was build up very early by Birger Holmer and was further developed by Ulf Abrahamsson. The management from time to time gave the project department great confidence with the realization that the fleet was an important tool for implementing business strategies. It's probably rare that three individuals have been responsible for, and having an impact on the fleet development for so long.

It has of course meant that a lot of experience has been built up, which also demonstrably contributed to the great respect among manufacturers and other organizations within the industry.

Among airlines this kind of function has varied in size, expertise and influence. When I joined Ulf's Central Engineering in 1982, and was given responsibility for the evaluation of new aircraft and engines, and met with my European colleagues, all companies had almost similar departments. In these circles, there was a lot of camaraderie and a spirit of support. We collaborated as best we could between companies to have a stronger voice to influence manufacturers and the development that the airlines felt was needed.

As the airlines over time have struggled with profitability and cost cutting, many companies have downsized these resources. The trend to lease a larger part of the fleet as an alternative to ownership has also affected how airlines can influence the manufacturing industry.

It is clear from Birger's story that some manufacturers had a strategy to "sell directly to the company's CEO" rather than sell the product to the company. This approach persists still among some manufacturers, and as resources have been reduced for cost reasons, it has become easier to sell products without detailed evaluation. Manufacturers do also risk getting less feedback and specification requirements. The influence that SAS had on the design and specifications have been both positive and sometimes negative. Generally it can be stated that more standardization in the industry is a good thing, but when it did not fit the individual company's needs, individual solutions were created, often with additional cost for both the airline and sometimes the manufacturer. Company unique solutions can also be profitable, like the DC-9-41 was for SAS.

I experienced corporate cultures that clearly differed. There were those that took "the alligator approach" i.e. a big mouth and no ears, (knows best and not listening). There were also those who really tried to understand the customer's needs with the conviction that a "win-win" strategy was the best for the aerospace industry. The latter category was of course the easiest to work with.

Towards the end of the 1990s it became a trend in the industry to establish so-called Asset Management departments to handle the increased proportion of leased aircraft. SAS established its Asset Management inside the finance department. It was the beginning of the fragmentation of Fleet Development, which had been responsible for the evaluation, procurement, leasing in and out, and termination of fleet types. It started with those who worked with leasing and as people retired, Fleet Development was decimated to a few and finally written off completely in 2007 in an organizational change when the Asset Management took over two people and the others retired.

One area that will continue to have an increasing impact on the aviation industry is the environmental issues in commercial aviation. I took over SAS's representation to the IATA Environment Committee in 1986 and soon realized that the requirements for environmental adaptation would in a big way steer the development of the industry.

It is often stated by the industry that total environmental impact from aviation is small, which is correct, but with a traffic growth greater than the relative efficiency improvement, aviation's total environmental impact is growing. The challenge is to further develop aviation while reducing its total environmental impact.

Improvements will be gradual with the launch of new, more efficient aircraft. For the industry to contribute positively to development programs, steps need to be large enough and within certain time frames. It requires that all new and more efficient technologies be developed and implemented.

Now several "engine swap" projects like Boeing 737MAX and Airbus A320neo are launched, which give relatively small steps, resulting in postponement of larger efficiency improvements. We were showing as part of the 2007 strategic plan that the replacement of the MD-80s by an all new aircraft gave the greatest, and most importantly, better long-term improvement. This cannot be achieved if airlines are bound to derivatives of existing models for the foreseeable future.

The trend towards less evaluation resources for estimating what future aircraft can provide makes airline decision-makers less equipped for specifying requirements and they will be more in the hands of the manufacturing industry.

Aircraft Financing

Financing of aircraft purchases is of great importance since large amount of capital are involved. SAS usually arranged this either by using funds generated within its own operations or by partial or total borrowing from banks or other financial organizations.

During the 1970s, a few large companies were established that dealt solely with the so-called leasing of aircraft. They bought the aircraft directly from the manufacturers and rented (leased) the aircraft for longer or shorter periods to airlines. Large leasing companies often had many different types of aircraft in their fleets.

SAS went into this industry at the beginning of the 1990s as a part owner in a startup leasing company, Aviation Holdings PLC, together with Allied Irish Bank and Electra Investment Trust. The company had its headquarters in London and offices in San Francisco, Stanford, and Hong Kong. The operational part of the company consisted of Electra Aviation, which at that time had three years of leasing operations, but needed more capital. In connection with the re-launch, Lars Rantzen was appointed as COO and later CEO.

Electra Aviation had a large number of aircraft the largest part was eleven A300s on lease to Eastern and Continental. In the wake of the Iraq war and the adverse impact of air traffic leasing companies were also severely affected. The biggest company, Guiness Peat Aviation (GPA), went bankrupt, a fate that also affected Electra Aviation. Electra filed in 1993 for protection under the bankruptcy laws of the United States (Chapter 11) via the US subsidiary. The lenders, several major international banks, took over the business and sold the assets and liquidated the company during 1993/1994.

Some of the forms of leases that were available for SAS are described briefly below.

Financial lease

Financial lease means that the airline, instead of self-financing, included a long-term lease agreement with a bank or financial institution that is the owner of the aircraft that the airline intended to use in its operations. The lease payments, which also includes amortization, are paid by the airline during the contractual period and the airline is thereby given the right to use the aircraft in their operations.

The airline has responsibility for the maintenance of the aircraft during the rental period and shall normally allocate funds for major expenses such as major engine overhauls.

The contract period is often long (12-18 years) and normally the airline has a purchase right at an agreed residual value when the lease expires.

In a financial lease agreement, conditions are defined if and to what extent the operator can perform modifications and what condition the asset must meet when returned to the owner. In order to adapt the aircraft's potential for changes in market needs it may require different types of modifications. If they are large and costly maybe the owner is not interested to invest more in the plane, which may mean that improvements the operator would really like to do and benefit from are not made. The operator can therefore be limited in an optimal use of the aircraft if funding limits these possibilities.

Operating lease

Operating lease is usually for a shorter period to handle a capacity need. The aircraft is returned to the owner after the lease period in an agreed operational condition, but without the airline facing any residual value risk.

The operating lease is usually a "dry lease" which means that the airline leases aircraft but has its own crew as opposed to "wet-lease" where even the crew is included in the lease agreement (sometimes even fuel) but the airline has operational responsibility.

Sale-leaseback

The concept means that the airline sells and then leases the aircraft back directly from the buyer. This is a way to finance the acquisition of aircraft if the airline has difficulty in arranging financing. This method is usually also used in conjunction with a planned phase-out of aircraft from the fleet and can effect a sale at a favorable moment and then lease it back for a shorter time to fit in with the delivery of new aircraft.

SAS fleet

After 1980 SAS used several of these lease options. Most of the SAS 767s were financial leasing.

In September 1966, SAS had 58 aircraft in the fleet. 52 were used on its own routes, and six were leased out. SAS owned 100 percent of its fleet.

At the end of 1995 the number of aircraft increased to 178, of which 142 were owned or financially leased. SAS now owned 80 percent of its fleet. This trend towards a smaller proportion of owned aircraft continued and by the end of 2013 SAS (the airline) owned only 25 percent of its fleet.

Finance leases created some problems, especially the agreements in 1980 for the last two Boeing 747s the lease term was 18 years, which complicated the premature phasing out. In addition, included in the contract, the aircraft had to be US-registered, which meant that the crew and mechanics have to have certificates issued by the US FAA

"This is your captain speaking"

Here are some personal comments from pilots who flew the types in the SAS fleet. The stories are, it should be emphasized, each pilot's personal experience of their workplace.

Douglas DC-3, Goran Swensson

The Douglas DC-3 can best be described as an institution. Hardly has any single type of aircraft been tied to so many exciting events and experiences in its existence. Those who belong to the older generation are happy to tell you his/her youthful memories of how as a child they experienced their first flight with the DC-3. Many are also those who worked with and around this beautiful metal bird. The DC-3 has been used both in civil and military service for many decades. It is thus natural that this lady, now over 70 years old, carries a great aviation history.

Today there are two flyable DC-3s in Sweden, a privately-owned yellow one, which is attached to Vallentuna Aviatorforening, and a silver-colored plane operated by the Flying Veterans. So far it has been possible to keep the aircraft airworthy thanks to a highly competent and ambitious maintenance team. In the long term there may be some concern because the technician training today has no notion of systems and engine knowledge associated with precisely the DC-3.

I am full of admiration for all those aviators during the middle of the last century, making flights in tough weather situations with icing and strong winds and even taking off and landing on airfields with questionable quality.

To the pilot flying and controlling the DC-3 it differs in many respects from modern aircraft. The procedure before it is ready to take off takes considerably longer because the systems and engine functions require some preparation. Before each take-off the propeller feather setting is controlled, (propeller blade put in a position to reduce air drag in the event of engine failure). Magnetos are checked to ensure that all spark plugs have enough spark. Each engine has a dual ignition system. The deicing system, consisting of rubber bladders on the leading edges of the wings, tailplane, and fin are checked. Alcohol deicing of the propeller, the front cockpit windows and carburetor are tested. Preheating of air to the carburetor is tested.

From the time the engine has been started, the checklist has another 41 points to be examined and checked. This obviously takes a few extra minutes to complete. If the engines are cold, it may require additional time to warm-up.

To taxi and turn the DC-3 on the ground is done by using the motors by varying the thrust and assisted by the wheel brakes. The tailwheel is not controllable but moving freely. At takeoff and landing and in flight the tailwheel is locked. This gives a course stabilization during takeoff and landing as well as the tailwheel does not "flutter" in flight.

The takeoff is not particularly complicated when trained on the technique. Since airflow over the fin is disturbed by the fuselage as long as the tailwheel has contact with the runway, it is important to relatively quickly lift the tail portion so that the aircraft reaches a horizontal position. You can then obtain an acceptable effect on the rudder. During the first part of the ground roll it's possible to compensate for crosswinds with the engines. Since crosswind has a relatively large impact on the fin and wants to bring the nose into the wind so use a little more power on the windward engine. Wheel brakes should not be used to compensate for course deviation

DC-DC-3, SE-CFP "Daisy" cockpit.
Photo by Ulf Abrahamsson

Captain Goran Swensson
Photo Ulf Abrahamsson.

during takeoff. Climb performance may not be as impressive compared with modern aircraft.

Once in the air the DC-3's flight characteristics are prestigious. Good rudder harmony with effective trim tabs. The fuel tanks are located near the center of gravity which causes the trim position to be affected very little as the amount of fuel decreases during flight.

The landing technique is different from modern aircraft. The most common method is to make a landing where the main wheels first meet the runway and then lowering the tailwheel at an easy pace. Three-point-landings require a lot of training to feel comfortable. The aircraft lacks spoilers (equipment that reduces the lifting force at touchdown) and it is therefore very easy to make an extraordinary leap into the air if you reflexively make one by rotation in connection with the first ground contact. This is an experience that almost all are surprised by during the checkout on the DC-3. Crosswind landing is perhaps what requires the most active operation since no servos are connected to the rudders. Easy crosswinds are no major problem but a strong gusty wind straight into the side puts a little extra spice to the craft.

Being in the environment around the DC-3 allows one to experience a nostalgic stimulation of the senses. It smells of a really genuinely aircraft, a mixture of metals, aviation gasoline, and oil. The aural experience is also special. The engine sound elicits a melody that only the aerospace and engine enthusiasts can interpret.

Convair 340/440, Metropolitan, Roland Karlsson

My first flight with passengers on board the Metropolitan was a little unusual. The Captain and I would fly an evening flight from Sundsvall to Östersund and I flew as a passenger to Sundsvall in a Linjeflyg F28 on a winter evening in early 1978. I was the "Flying Pilot" on the flight to Östersund and when I had lifted the nose wheel from runway 34, we had an engine failure on the right engine. After the comprehensive training, mostly flights on one engine, it felt quite normal to depress the pedal rudder and fly around in a visual left turn and land. But, of course it is unlikely that this happens on one's first flight.

In the Metropolitan one of the first officer's duties was to check that the doors were closed and locked. "Hooks and handles in locked position," I think was the phrase reported to the captain after a walk through the cabin.

Since the Metropolitan has radial engines you must satisfy yourself during engine start that the cylinders are not filled with gasoline or oil through leakage past the pistons, the so-called water hammer effect, which may damage the internal parts of the engine. Therefore you rotate the engine several times with the starter before the ignition and fuel supply are connected. With a cold engine, count an estimated 15 propeller blades and when the engine is hot, six blades, by leaning out the side window, "Fifteen blades, respectively, Six Blades - ignition ON." The side window was then left partly open during the first part of taxiing.

The Metropolitan has a pressurized cabin, a major advantage over previous airliners such as the DC 3. However, it required a bit of caution to activate the pressurization of the cabin. When the engines are started the cabin pressure compressor begins working and if you close the side window too quickly a small pressure shock occurs in the cabin that can be an unpleasant experience. Thus, it was the first officer's task during taxiing to slowly close the side window to protect passengers' eardrums.

We flew mostly night mail during the last years with the Convair in Linjeflyg. Gasoline was cheap in those days and we started often towards airports, even though the weather forecast at the destination was below landing minima. Instead we uplifted more fuel, up to 12-13 hours of flight time, in order to be in holding mode until the weather got better.

In 1969 jet fuel cost 7 cents per liter and gasoline (108/135 octane) cost 13 cents, roughly equivalent to 54 cent in today's money!

We had crew catering onboard the postal flights. But that was placed in the back of the plane, where also the hot jugs of coffee were. Mail sacks were loaded in the cabin, and then the rows of seats folded up against the cabin wall. Often there was so much cargo on board that we were creeping across the load, just under the roof, to reach the longed-for sandwiches and coffee. On the way, one could also view the beautifully glowing engine exhaust pipes in the darkness.

The Metropolitan has ten controls for controlling the motors: two throttles (for each pilot), 2 for fuel mixture, 2 for speed control, 2 for Carburetor, and 2 for controlling the damper in the exhaust pipes for temperature control for the de-icing system for the wings and tail section. After adjustment of one of the controls all others must in principle also be adjusted, so it was a constant job with tuning the engine and to keep them synchronized. When it was really cold outside you have to occasionally reset the propeller speed, so warm oil would come out to the hydraulic changeover in the propeller hub.

Overall, I think the Metropolitan was a good and reliable aircraft that was easy and fun to fly. The autopilot was good enough to keep the course and altitude, but the approach was done manually. The course gyro and ADF indicators had large dials and one could fly with high precision and PAR approaches were fun features at some airports, such as at Bromma.

Sud Aviation Caravelle, Gunnar Fahlgren

Caravelle - well, just the name itself was like a passion, as former aircraft designations contained as a rule, manufacturer names such as Douglas, Boeing or Lockheed with one digit after.

Caravelle became a personality from the outset and was undoubtedly feminine. Not only the name but also her shape and what she could do, attracted men around her.

"When beauty came to the village" ...., well then, according to Nils Ferlin - "they were all so wise." Without a doubt some follies sneaked into the operations by the attendant cavaliers. That, for example, it was decided that she would be flown with the lowest possible speed, "Minimum Final Approach Speed," all the long way from the outer marker to the runway, scared us new and green mates in SAS. We had in all cases, in contrast to the captains, many years of experience in jet operation in the Air Force. But the reality is of course now so constituted, that sometimes degree and position are listened to more than knowledge and experience.

The tragic crash in Ankara, January 1960, was of course caused by adapting this crazy invention, which subsequently was changed. From the outer marker at Ankara airport, it took about six minutes! That the operations of the Caravelle at Bromma went so well was because of her trustworthiness. An engine failure there, just before lift-off, would undoubtedly have led to plane and cars being intermingled on Ulvsunda Road in both lanes. This is despite the allure that men's mathematically theoretical calculations showed the opposite. And they taught us to believe in that!

She also had an enormous negligé of nylon in the form of a brake parachute to be used at each landing. When the Nordic winter hit her, she was so cold in the behind, that the chute froze! When we pulled the trigger handle after landing at Bromma, out came just a frozen packet, which bounced around on a string behind her. Well, the attending cavaliers came in to warm her bottom with hot air. And then she behaved as expected again.

Her powerplant, in the form of two Rolls-Royce Avon engines in the stern, was a revolutionary innovation. Both we the pilots and passengers soon learned to love that variety. For the first time in aviation history it was now so quiet on board, as advertising always said that it was, even on the noisy DC-6s time.

Another major innovation was that she did not have control cables all the way to the rudders. Instead, there was hydraulic transmission of power to the control surfaces. Many conservative pilots were skeptical of this and many expressed doubts. I also want to remember that this was a major obstacle for her to be approved (certified) in the United States. Only when additional cables were installed parallel to hydraulic lines, she became certified there. Maybe a scary accident involving a Swissair Caravelle could have been avoided with these extra cables. She was at that time completely uncontrollable in the air, as the hydraulic lines were severed by a tire explosion, after the landing gear with overheated brakes was retracted into the body.

She was pleasant to fly! She was beautiful to behold! She slipped through the atmosphere with idle engines like a dolphin in the water. She had a glide ratio which could compete with contemporary gliders. Through its clean wing, without slats, she glided in for landing in a soft and comfortable way. She flew where the nose was pointed. Man and the aircraft was a natural entity.

Captain Gunnar Fahlgren. Photo Gunnar Fahlgren.

Her followers with slats and T-tail behaved in a completely different way. And many were the accidents, during the 1960s, which slowly taught the world's pilots to "beware."

She was quiet and comfortable to fly. What do you mean silent? Well, for us who sat in her arms. The neighborhood became more and more irritated when she flew over the houses and she was even forced to night work. You may recall the frequent slogan "Clear as a day to fly at night." That she rumbled, she could not help. She arrived at a time when the buyer thought the noise was force and not, as now, energy waste.

Dear Caravelle! Without a doubt you have written an important and glorious chapter in the history of aviation.

Fokker F28, Roland Karlsson

I flew F28s for more than twenty years at Linjeflyg, eleven of them as captain. It was a very robust and easy to work with airplane. With the help of the "speed brake" in her tail we were not so sensitive to height adjustment during approach and were able to accept high and low in terms of both height and speed. The speed brake had no speed restrictions and no trim change or vibrations, just pull the lever to increase the rate of descent, or reduce speed.

The Rolls-Royce engines were very reliable and easy to handle. However, you have to be timely with the "engine anti-ice" in moist air, otherwise you could get vibrations that were difficult to overcome.

We flew in recent years at Mach 0.65 (Mach

0.7 in exceptional cases) and the maximum flight altitude was FL350 (35,000 feet), which meant that it was often overtaken and had to keep clear of other traffic, especially on charter flights in Europe.

At the maximum altitude the aircraft felt rather "spongy" and if you turned with normal turning speed, it could happen that you got "buffeting," light vibration and a faint rumbling sound i.e. "be careful."

Range with maximum load was not so great and it could be a problem on charter flights and far away alternative airports. I remember some captain had the aircraft towed on to the runway not to burn the amount of fuel for taxi and thus have enough fuel to conduct the flight without stopover for refueling.

The smaller version, F28-1000, was a little "wobbly" once in cruise flight, which could not be tuned out completely, while the slightly larger F28-4000 was better in that regard. The autopilot worked fine but lacked an "auto-throttle," so you had to control speed manually with the engine throttle. One tricky thing with the autopilot was "altitude capture" a feature that was very sensitive. The desired altitude was set with a small crank, after which you pressed "auto" on the panel. If we then happened to touch the little crank the very least, or change the "pitch" of the panel, the auto function disconnected without warning. You had therefore to closely monitor the airplane to really level out at the selected altitude.

The lack of "thrust reverse" was not a problem, wheel braking was perfectly adequate. Touchdown speed was so low that an "engine reverse" on the engines would have lost most of its force when the F28 touched down. However, you had to be on guard for slush on the runway, but it is not unique to F28s.

In the first years we had some issues with the display of the nose gear in the extended position. During the winter it happened that the pin which gave the green light was covered with dirt or ice from the runway and it gave a red light. It happened to me a few times. A special inspection and cleaning of the pin was introduced, which solved the problem. Many pilots found that the noise level in the cockpit was high, and we always used the headset, both for internal and external communications.

MDC DC-9, Ulf Johnfors
We were a few "oldies" as new officers, and with jet-experience from the Air Force, where we flew the swept wing aircraft with high wing loading. Despite this experience, it was a great surprise that one had to fly at so high an "alpha" (angle of attack) and thus high attitude in the lower speed range both at takeoff and during landing.

The swept wing properties also meant that the aircraft was less speed stable in the low speed regime. During various types of manual approaches you were forced to "stay ahead" with the throttles and expect the level of drag you would get during the configuration changes. Douglas had not succeeded in producing a control law for "auto-throttle" that was good enough to be used for instrument approaches. The only possibility was to manually find a stable position and then connect auto-throttle. Then it was as good if not better to fly "manual throttles" even if the autopilot was in ILS mode.

Another characteristic feature of the swept wing is the change in center of lift force position depending on the angle of attack and speed. This meant that the pilot constantly had to trim the aircraft during speed changes. Sometimes you experienced flying the DC-9 with the trim button.

The DC-9 had both slats and trailing edge flaps to increase the lift at low speed. Especially the higher flap positions affected trim during situations that were sometimes difficult to handle. During a manual NDB approach, you must really be on the ball with the trim in order to be stabilized and keep the desired approach profile. There are many DC-9 pilots that got a real "balloon" by extending full flaps.

In summary, one can say, however, that when the aircraft was well trimmed, it was harmonious to fly in both pitch and roll.

The DC-9 was the last generation transport plane with "bells and light bulbs" in the cockpit and servos manually switched on and off. Autopilot and "flight director" were different systems that complemented each other. The autopilot could be linked to a VOR or ILS but mostly used in "heading select" and "vertical speed," since in locked modes the control laws were poor. The same thing happened with "auto-throttle."

As a pilot, you get used to the system you are currently flying. DC-9 was flown mostly in a kind of semi-automatic way with quite a large amount of manual handling.

MDC MD-80, Ulf Johnfors
Auto brakes were a new feature on the MD-80. That feature shortened braking and stopping distances, particularly on slippery and wet runways. In addition, if initiated it triggered the system for an aborted takeoff. It was a safety-enhancing factor, but it created some problems if you flew both the DC-9 and MD-80. On the DC-9 you had to practice stepping on the brake pedals at an engine failure before lift-off in order to stay on ground. Stepping on the brakes with an "auto-brake" coupled system disconnected it. This was one reason why the pilots did not fly the DC-9 and MD-80 simultaneously.

MD-80 originally had a "Performance Management System" (PMS) that helped pilots to optimize the flight in the vertical plane with respect to altitude and speed. This feature was later taken over by the Flight Management System (FMS), which navigated in both the vertical and horizontal plane. FMS could be linked to the Flight Guidance System (FGS) on both planes.

Navigation and precision in flight with FMS increased significantly. Fuel consumption decreased by providing more direct flights, more optimal and precise speed control, and better planning for the descent from cruising altitude.

With an FMS onboard the EFIS could feature a MAP (map display),which is a stylized map of the route and surrounding airspace with navigational information. This presentation provides a very good description and awareness of the aircraft's position.

Finally, I want to emphasize, that the MD-80 cockpit had a pleasant acoustic environment. It was so quiet that we often flew without headsets.

Boeing 747, Sten Hjalmarsson

For the last eight years before my retirement I got on the Boeing 747 and it was the height of happiness. I was impressed by the size; I came from the DC-8 and it was not so small either.

I had flown the Caravelle earlier and liked its flight characteristics a lot, but after a period on the 747 I had probably come to the "ultimate."

Flight characteristics were outstanding as well and it was, if one may so express it, easily flown even though it was large and heavy. You soon became accustomed to the size. On landing the nose was quite high, like a 2-3 story building. Never a problem with landings, always soft and stable, like the Caravelle!

Over the years that I flew 747s I never had any technical or other problems with this aircraft.

Douglas DC-10-30, Thomas Lanz

On a fine spring day in 1978, I stood, as newly appointed officer and the third pilot, in front of my first workplace at SAS, a DC-10-30. For me it was a very large aircraft and the beginning of a new life.

The DC-10 had a real flight deck. For it was half a step up from the cabin floor. Its flight deck was set up for two pilots and a "flight engineer." Besides my "cruise only" pilot certificate, I also had a flight engineer certificate. My task was to keep track of the aircraft's various systems such as fuel, hydraulic, pressure, electrical, and air conditioning systems. All displayed and operated from the flight engineer panel. This was also the main location of all the fuses for the on board electrical system.

The pilot's instruments were of the traditional model. The navigation equipment was in addition to ordinary VOR / DME, ILS, and ADF equipped with inertial navigation and a navigation computer that navigated the aircraft. The navigation database was stored on magnetic tape in two tape recorders. The system worked great once you had entered your route. It took some time for the tapes to drive back and forth to find all the data and it happened occasionally that a tape got stuck. Then you had to restart the process from the beginning and hope that it would succeed.

Later after a period on the DC-9, I came back to the DC 10 as first officer and had the opportunity to fly the aircraft for real. But given that it was a large aircraft it operated fine. It did not feel big. DC-10s had one single mode on the autopilot called "Control Wheel Steering," CWS. In this mode you flew the aircraft with input from the pilot's steering wheel. For my part, I thought it facilitated the manual flight considerably. The DC-10 was also equipped with "autotrottle." It was switched on and off with two levers on the "glareshield" panel. During decent it was disconnected so it would not increase or decrease the engine thrust. With autotrottle off there was no "speed protection" so you had to remember to engage them before the aircraft leveled off at the set height. After a long flight and many altitude changes it could be forgotten, and it happened despite the fact that everyone was aware of the danger.

Boeing 767, Thomas Lanz

After many years on the DC-9, I came to the 767 as a captain. The biggest shift was to have flown the aircraft to operate an aircraft. From old-fashioned instruments to a "glass" cockpit. According to my definition 767 cockpit had no flight deck. The floor was at the same level as the cabin floor. Aside from all the automatics you could fly the 767 manually. Then I think it flew fine and did not feel big.

The Cockpit was a typical two-pilot environment. We usually had with us, however, a relief pilot. It was only on shorter flights to London and Greenland when there were two pilots on board. I arrived quite late into the 767 when the route network shrank during my time. In the beginning we flew however, to many destinations, both in Asia and North America. In the end it was only Washington

767-300 cockpit. Photo Boeing.

Saab 2000 Flight deck. Photo Saab.

DC. It's not a bad place but perhaps a bit monotonous.

On long flights and night flights the sleeping compartment area behind the cockpit was a welcome opportunity for individual rest during the flight so you were much more alert during approach and landing than if you just rested in the cockpit seat.

The aircraft was equipped with a variety of auto functions and other equipment that allowed us to operate under more extreme weather situations than previous aircraft. We operated with CAT3 which was landing in very poor visibility. With my previous experience, I thought it was fascinating to land in CAT3 weather with autoland. To see the runway so late, then make a quick decision to land or go around, just by your pressing a button or not. The autoland worked great. The same controlled landing and roll each time. Navigation wise, there were three (IRS, Inertia Reference System, inertial navigation system) supported by the DME and integrated by a "performance" computer. Easy and intuitive to operate once you had learned the logic. What we can say though was that if you wanted to get a good descent towards the destination you would begin about 15 miles before top of descent. Then it worked great.

A small weakness of the 767, was that it could not climb directly to a sufficient altitude after takeoff in relation to thunder clouds and turbulence. This made it uncomfortable for passengers and cabin crew. Thunderclouds had to be navigated around but the turbulence you had to put up with.

Another thing we had to pay attention to was "standing waves." We often flew close to maximum speed and "auto-throttle" was not sufficiently alert to manage the "downhill" after a wave. Then you had to intervene manually to not exceed the maximum speed. But even the sun has spots.

Compared to the DC-9 the maximum speed with extended slats and flaps was quite low which made the speed and height loss less forgiving.

Another small detail that annoyed us was the placement of the speakers in the cockpit. They were placed at knee height. Who listens with his knees? Despite this, I got on fine with the 767. Easily flown, good destinations, and fine crews.

On the whole, the 767 workplace is a nice place to be and work at.

Saab 2000

The Saab 2000 was a very convenient machine. The working environment in the cockpit was generally good and very well thought out. Modern technology and the latest avionics (1997), made it a bit of a pilot's dream. Technically it worked very well. Saab's organization that maintained the aircraft also had really skilled technicians.

Operationally, it was something of a success. In the first month 100% regularity was achieved, which was quite unique. With speed comparable to jet aircraft, but with fuel consumption about half of a jet's for similar work performed.

Maximum cruising altitude of 31,000 feet, made it possible to avoid most of the bad weather that turboprops otherwise need to fly through.

Despite the advanced "noise cancellation" - the system was felt somewhat noisy in the cockpit combined with vibration. Headsets were used all the time. Flights over 1.5 hours could sense there was something stressful in the cockpit.

Boeing 737 NG, Roland Karlsson

This is a real workhorse, which I flew over two years in SAS. The instrument panel electronic displays are great, large, and with very good colors and resolution. The so-called scan-flow system, rather than point after point with the checklist before the flight was new to me.

It is noticeable, however, that many of the aircraft's systems have been around from the early sixties. Some procedures are perceived as cumbersome and some are left over so certification shall be "backwards compatible" to the extent possible.
For example, the warning system in front of each pilot station feels archaic, various warnings are shown on the left and right side and remaining warnings are displayed only when you press the small panel. There are many "by heart items" on "non-normal" checklists, even if nowadays being reduced to fifty.

It is a crowded cockpit, very crowded, and no places for the coffee cup exist and even less for the now much-needed meal tray. There is also quite a lot of aerodynamic noise in the cockpit. Trim wheels for attitude trim spin wildly at speed change or attitude with the autopilot, or manually. It is important to keep the fingers away.

The 737 NG goes pretty high. FL 410 is the max and then you fly over most of the weather and can surf on the best downwind area. "Auto Brake" is very effective and the braking distance is considerably shorter at reduced friction than with manual braking. The default mode is very well balanced. The longer 737-800 can be a bit tortuous during approach on autopilot, but becomes firmer if you fly manually. Landing with Flaps 40 (full flaps) all variants of the 737 NG are sensitive in the roll plane and the pilot must be careful so as not to over-compensate and get oscillations in the roll plane. With Flaps 30 the aircraft is much more stable; the situation is therefore used whenever possible. Some of the SAS 737s have a so-called head-up display on the left pilot position, which allows one to fly manually by visual symbols projected onto the windscreen.

Airbus A321, Roland Karlsson

The A321 is my favorite. It is noticeable that this airplane is designed and built as a whole, and not a patchwork of different design and eras. Note, however, that the aircraft was developed in the early eighties, which is why some automatic features can be perceived as slow. At the time of the introduction of the A320 concerns were heard about the "electrical" steering system reliability, "non-moving throttles," individual "side sticks" without feedback between the right and left of the pilot, no manual ground spoilers activation etc. Problems with these, in some cases revolutionary innovations, seem to have been relatively small.

However some noticable accidents happened in the early history of the airplane, which was considered to provide support to the criticism. On closer examination, the main cause was probably inadequate training in the aircraft's particular system. Airbus responded to early criticism of the claim that you can fly the aircraft exactly the same way as that of a conventional aircraft. However, the pilot must have some basic knowledge of how key systems work, because the aircraft has comprehensive monitoring and security systems, which in some conditions initially "take over" control of the airplane.

The modern Airbus fleet, the A320 to A380, applies the same general concept for flight operation, which results in very short conversion times for crews and technicians between the types. According to Airbus one needs only about two weeks of training for pilots from e.g. 320 to move up to the 380 Series, which of course appeals to both operators and pilots. The first thing that meets you in the cockpit is a bright and generous space. The lack of control lever in front of the pilots made it possible to place a folding table there, which is a great advantage. Besides that you can put maps, manuals, etc., on the table, you get access to a generous place for the meal tray, not insignificant in today's many and long flights without a break.

"Electronic Centralized Aircraft Monitor" (ECAM), is the aircraft's automatic system for monitoring the technical parameters and it also contains a privileged system of "non-normal checklists." In case of a malfunction, the necessary actions are shown on the screen and on the relevant control a light stays on until the correct action is performed, and then the message disappears from the screen. If several errors occur simultaneously, actions are placed on the screen in order of priority. The screen also displays references to the manuals and any limitations that need to be observed, such as longer runway length, changed speed, higher fuel consumption, etc. Another result of the ECAM feature is that the procedures for abnormal situations only contains about ten "by heart items."

An innovation in this Airbus generation is the "ground speed mini" system. It means that the aircraft is flying at a constant ground speed during approach, instead of a constant airspeed that most other aircraft with the auto throttle does. The pilot enters the current wind at the airport in "Flight Management System", which then makes sure to constantly maintain the speed over the ground. In gusty wind changes, it is known that indicated air speed goes both up and down. An increase in indicated air speed, on encountering a headwind gust, means that the "auto throttle" in a conventional aircraft, reduces the thrust to keep the speed down, and the next moment increases thrust when the gust has ended. With ground speed mini the opposite occurs. Encountering increasing headwinds means thrust is increased to keep the momentum over the ground constant and when the gust stops, reduced thrust, which means better margin because the engines are already "spooled up" if the indicated airspeed tends to become too low.

The aircraft fly "track," i.e. it takes care of itself for any sidewind if you fly manually on a particular course. Furthermore, there is a system of compensation for gusts, "gust compensation," which, however, can be perceived as a bit slow. The risk is that the pilot will manually try to help with the joystick, which can lead to so-called pilot induced oscillation (PIO), as the aircraft and the pilot's rudder commands are added. A weakness in the control system can also be that the left and right joystick work individually, you cannot make

Captain Roland Karlsson in his A321 cockpit. Photo Roland Karlsson.

To the right
A340 cockpit.
Photo Airbus

out the second pilot's stick position and not "help" to correct the situation. The aircraft is designed primarily to be flown with the autopilot.

"Auto Brake" has three modes in which position 1 has a time lag and slowdown is often perceived as too small, but in position 2 slows the aircraft quickly. Many pilots prefer manual braking.

Today, probably the Airbus 320 family in some respects seems a bit old in comparison to the latest example, from Boeing and Embraer, e.g. when it comes to computer screens in the cockpit that are smaller and have a lower resolution than those found in the 737NG. However, one should remember that the A320 was introduced for more than twenty five years ago and it still is both conceptually and technically leading in the aerospace industry.

The Airbus A330 / 340, Tomas Dal

I was attracted directly by the Airbus elegant shapes and the "side stick" controller in the cockpit which did not feel totally wrong for an old Air Force pilot! It was a very pleasant feeling I got the first time on the flight deck, I sank into the pilot's seat and just enjoyed this bright, spacious and luxurious working environment with excellent air conditioning.

I will admit that many of us "old" pilot sorts were skeptical about these modern, almost fully automated systems. Pilots are a little conservative and reluctant to abandon tried and tested methods, which are built on hard earned experience. Eventually, however, I fully appreciate the systems that actually raised the level of flight safety, not least since the two-pilot system also is introduced on the long haul.

Manual flight with a fly-by-wire system gave a pleasant feeling of harmony and rudder control of the aircraft. Completely new was the enormous amount of information that was available.

Two things I quickly learned to appreciate, the details of the nearest adequate aerodrome, including flight time and fuel consumption, as well as during standby mode at the destination, the exact time when you are forced to go to your alternate airport, to meet the requirements on minimum fuel. Technical problems in flight are presented with a list of actions on a screen and as each measure is implemented, the points disappear until the checklist is "completed." If a new more serious problem emerges in the midst of the solution to the first problem, a new action list is shown and the previous checklist will return only when the more serious problem is solved. On older aircraft types it was very difficult when encountering multiple faults, to see the warning that came first and which checklist would be a priority.

SAS has both the twin-engine A330-300 and the four-engine A340-300. After the training we received government authorization to fly both types. The biggest differences are experienced during takeoff and landing. A heavy A340 rises very slowly and it is sometimes difficult to reach the minimum altitudes (e.g. noise consideration) during departure from certain airports. Engine failure on one engine at the takeoff is managed in terms of performance, but if two engines fail immediately, dumping of fuel is required. The A330 has, like all twin-engined aircraft, good climb performance and an engine failure is handled by the remaining engine.

Both types are "gliders" and speed reduction for "slats" and "flaps" must be implemented in time to avoid an involuntary "go around". On the A340 the touchdown is complicated by the center wheels. When the main wheels touchdown, the aircraft has a relatively high angle of attack so to get a soft setting of the center wheels, it is important to "release" the joystick and let the aircraft itself begin sinking. Immediately after the center wheels are on the ground the stick should be moved forward and then "capture" it for a soft touchdown of the nose wheel. Easier said than done!

Captain Tomas Dal on a "walk around" before an A340-flight
Photo Tomas Dal.

"Welcome to SAS," it's your cabin crew's salute to welcome you aboard.

Convair 440 Metropolitan, Reidun Fjærvoll Boëthius
It was used on flights both domestically in Norway and abroad. Many flights to northern Norway and on the "milk routes" such as the Oslo-Bergen-Stavanger-Kristineansand-Aalborg - Copenhagen. Especially on this plane there was a built-in staircase the hostess extended after landing.

There were usually two attendants on board. The service was simple. There were no tables on the blue-gray seats so the tray was placed on a pillow in the passenger's lap. It went well! The food was loaded in metal cabinets, a portable system designed by a Norwegian purser, Arne Olsen. On international routes, we also had the sale of duty free goods. The price list was in 34 different currencies! The Convair often had problems with weight and balance. If it was not completely full we had to move some of the passengers either further forwards or backwards.

Scandia, Reidun Fjærvoll Boëthius
I flew on it only once. There had to be in addition to advertising, the need to inform passengers that "there will be flames from the engines during the flight, and it is quite normal."

Douglas DC-6, Reidun Fjærvoll Boëthius
On the DC-6 there were three of us in the cabin: purser, steward, and a flight attendant. The purser had a white mess jacket during service and the steward had a real chef outfit with a high cap. Everything was so elegant and you really felt like a hostess when you received the guests. The plane had room for 48 passengers, including 16 in first class. The DC-6 had fine patterned curtains in bright colors and red seats, and a "Ladies Lounge" in the back. We had real ovens and refrigerators so the food that was served was of a very high class. There were beds on board the longer routes. I got to experience a trip where we bedded down passengers. The seats in first class were converted to four beds separated by curtains. Four beds were pulled down from the ceiling. It was no easy task!

Sud Aviation Caravelle, Reidun Fjærvoll Boëthius
SAS entered the jet age in 1959. The French-built Caravelle was a stunningly beautiful aircraft. It had first and tourist class for a total of 80 passengers, and there were four of us in the cabin. Many were concerned to fly with Caravelle. At Fornebu you could hear when passengers crossed the tarmac to the plane, "Can you fly with that thing? It has no propellers!" To calm the passengers soft music was played before takeoff and landing. The plane was very comfortable to work in.

It flew so quietly and landed so that it was almost not noticeable. The Caravelle had a parachute at the rear for additional braking. It was often used at Torslanda where it was always windy. It must have been an amazing sight. I've never seen it. I was sitting on board!

Douglas DC-8, Reidun Fjærvoll Boëthius
In 1960, came the DC-8, SAS's first long-haul jet. The cabin was light and delicate and initially with green seats and reading lamps mounted in the back of the seat. Now we got trolleys, an incredible relief. Previously we had brought all the trays through the cabin. It had a galley in both the first and tourist classes. Besides the purser, who was now called "the maitre de cabine," there were two stewards and three flight attendants on board. At the front there was an elegant lounge where passengers in first class gladly took a drink or played bridge. There were flowers on the table in the lounge and a nice sidewall decoration by Otto Nielsen, the Dane who made the SAS calendar years from 1956-1976. The DC-8 was a wonderful machine to fly.

Douglas DC-9, Karin Jans
In the 1970s, it was the DC-9 that was the workhorse in Europe. The Caravelle was on the way out. One of the advantages of the DC-9, as well as the Caravelle, was that we were "self-sufficient" with built-in airstairs in the front and rear. It saved us a lot of time. We would not have to wait for stairs to be moved up to the plane. At that time the passengers walked on the tarmac out to the aircraft and back. The DC-9 galley was well designed with ovens and location for food carts and various standard units, so much could be stored on both sides of the service door and the main door and the cabin. The closet was minimal and there would be room for first class passengers' coats, the large log purse, often a couple of sacks of diplomatic mail and also the collapsible trolley to be loaded with everything we needed in the way of beverages for the food service. Because the service arrangement and the flight time were not always consistent, it was often

stressful at the end when the trolley would be folded up and secured before landing. It also worked as a sales cart. We had awesome sales even on flights like CPH-GOT and CPH- JKG-NRK and it was an incredible amount of Marabou Shipping Boxes (mixed children sweets) and half-pound chocolate boxes sold from the cart. How did we do it? From a work standpoint, the DC-9 may not be the world's best. But was there a best one for short haul in the 1970's? The engines were making some incredible noise and it was not easy to make announcements to those that sat at the back between the engines. But we had nothing to compare with.

Boeing 747. Bengt Landelius and Sverre Nordtvedt

The first two Jumbo aircraft were passenger versions with 32 first class seats and 321 economy class seats, for a total of 353.

They were very popular among cabin crew, with relatively large galleys, plus the toilets and galley were separated which we were not accustomed to. We came from the DC-8 and found that there had been a tremendous development with the automatic coffee maker, food carts, drinks carts, and lots of ovens to heat the food in.

To begin with, there was a first a class lounge on the upper deck, but later this was rebuilt to accommodate 16 tourist class seats. Each galley serviced individual sections.

Number three and four 747s were so-called combi aircraft that could be reconfigured from a completely passenger version to one with 12 or 6 pallets of cargo behind the passenger cabin. A large heavy net was installed in front of the cargo compartment. This reconfiguration was done in Copenhagen within 24 hours.

I remember especially a flight when the cargo consisted of six pigs in a specially designed enclosure. Besides the pigs, there were also two new Ferrari cars carried.

These two 747s had more modern galleys and an elevator to the upper deck galley for loading catering supplies. The upper deck had 32 Economy Class seats.

Sometimes we had horses. It was usually to Los Angeles. Then there would be a wrangler (or horse handler) on board, if the horse would fall or be frightened of turbulence. He would, in extreme cases be able to kill the horse on board. I remember one flight when a passenger travelled with his two horses and a Ferrari! It was also to Los Angeles. Initially there were 15 people who worked in cabin: a purser, five stewards, and nine stewardesses. At that time we flew to New York and later Chicago. When more aircraft were added to the fleet the route network increased to include destinations such as Los Angeles, Bangkok, Singapore, and even across the North Pole to Tokyo via Anchorage.

With the 747, we also made Hajj flights from Algiers and Niger to Jeddah with pilgrims. 550 passengers with a leased former Alitalia aircraft.

DC-10 economy class with 2 + 5 + 2 seats abreast. Photo Karin Jans.

Douglas DC-10, Karin Jans and Kristina Anker

Then came the DC-10, a personal favorite. On the long haul for many years you flew either the combination B747 / DC-10 or DC-8 / DC-10. At the annual bidding most of us looked more at the destinations than at the type of aircraft. There were two groups of us that had completely different requirements. Those who chose the B747 were the ones who wanted to be at home as much as possible (they flew to NYC very much with 24-hour layover). Those who chose the DC-8 / DC-10 wanted to be out on the long layover and see and experience as much as possible. DC-10 destinations were very attractive, USA, South America, and Asia.

DC-8 destinations were certainly not attractive (Africa, Middle East), but there was no time zone difference, and that was where we got to know each other, because we were simply forced to stay together. In some places we could not even go out, especially at night in Lagos and Monrovia.

We came from three different bases, and often you knew some of the crew, but far from all, and sometimes none at all. The compositions of the crew were not the same on two flights in a row. There were pros and cons. But even with a crew where no one knew any of the others everyone knew in advance all the time exactly what to do on board at all times, both from the service / hospitality point

747-200 cabin. Photo SAS

of view and the "In Case of Emergency." We had a fantastic atmosphere on board in the cabin and passengers often asked: "do you always fly together?" Can you get better grades?

A very appreciated bit of DC-10 news was prepackaged drink carts! What a help! On the DC-8 we had the small foldable cart that we knew from the DC-9. On long flights, we had time enough to mount and load, unload, fold up, but it contained so little that we had to run and reload all the time, or signal the steward out in the galley what was needed. Now we were spoiled with a carriage with five boxes above each other on both sides, filled with wine, beer, miniatures, soft drinks, etc.

Another important step forward for us in the cabin of the DC-10 was that overhead bins, where you previously were only allowed to stow clothes, now had doors. Here, there were considerable luggage compartments, which could be closed, and that could accommodate carry-on baggage (of reasonable size). On the DC-8 much time was spent before take off to take down everything that was not allowed on the open shelf and discuss the removal with the passengers.

Those who flew 747s found that the DC-10 was bad. The rumor was that it was very difficult and harder work and that the cabin floor sloped downward toward the tail.

We who flew the DC-8 found "the Ten" was absolutely amazing! So easy to work on and with the two center aisles! We were not so spoiled on the DC-8.

The DC-10 was not optimal in furnishing and the seating configuration in tourist class was to say at least problematic with 2-5-2 abreast. The middle seat was a perpetual source of conflict when we had a full house. Up front was also not entirely successful in the SAS version. At the front was a first class compartment with ten seats and the rest became a small tourist class cabin. The wall between compartments could be opened, so those in the small cabin did not miss the movie, when it would appear. The problem was that a full first class catering took just over three hours with individual table settings, silverware and real plates, and a steward who cut filet of beef on a rolling table dressed in white chef's clothing. But serving tourist class took half the time. Those who really wanted to see the film had to wait a long time, and it irritated passengers in first class when the wall was opened to intrude into their "domain".

At the back of the small cabin's right side, close to the galley, the DC-10 had something completely new: the purser had its own office! From there, he could command movie projectors and sound for the film, plus music. It was still the same movie for the whole plane, but the three projectors could be started independently of each other and the purser would no longer go up with a huge roll of film to projectors in the ceiling like on the DC-8. What progress!

On the DC-10 the cabin crew also received four seats, where we could sit down and eat undisturbed. Seats that were ours and could not be sold! On a ten hour flight, you do need proper food.

Also a lot had happened regarding safety, The old lifeboat on the DC-8 had been replaced by a slide, which could also serve as a lifeboat ("slide raft"), which was blown up automatically if you opened the door with the slide secured to the floor. I often thought aboard the DC-8, in which the 132 lb. heavy bales of lifeboats were up in the ceiling, that if we experience a ditching (landing on water), we will never be able to get them down and drag them to the doors. On the DC-10, it was also the end of breaking one's fingernails while on your knees before departure and trying to get the "slide bar" in place in the small holders on the doorsill. All one needed now was a simple operation with a handle at shoulder height at the side of the door, and the slide was "armed."

When Jan Carlzon arrived, all of SAS got a huge boost, with both planes and crew. Old planes became like new with new interiors, new colors, and new exterior design. We in the cabin suddenly felt that we were also worth something! The whole attitude towards us changed. We were SAS's outward face. It also helped with Calvin Klein's new dark blue uniform. We were again proud to show ourselves in an SAS uniform. And also we got the Business Class, the "revolution" of the 1980s. Although we would serve hot food to many more in Europe and in less time, our galleys and our equipment did work, and soon we had honed our routines, so much so, that we were able to serve over 100 "Business pax" hot food to and from London, a flight time of 1.20 hours!

MDC MD-80/90,
Anna Håkansson Öreberg

In the 2000s the MD-80/90, an old workhorse, was the type you always first got checked out on and I started in 2006. A good machine to work on as a hostess, especially if you had a position in the forward part of the cabin. Partly because of the generous front galley, but partly also the noise level. It was indeed always quiet and comfortable at any time, while the aft cabin boomed from the engines sitting directly on the fuselage at the rear. In the rear cabin there was a minimal galley on the left side where you hardly had room for two people. Ergonomically bad, as you had to stand sideways to reach cabinets, trolleys, or the like in the rear.

When I started working, there were four or five people in the cabin: a purser and three or four hostesses / hosts. In position number two you sat at

MD-80 cabin with removable cabin separator (curtain) between Business Class and Economy Class. Photo Karin Jans.

Karin Jans in the 767 in the rear galley.
Photo Karin Jans.

the back in a crowded little jump seat folded down from the rear emergency exit wall and had primary responsibility for the cabin announcements. It was so noisy, something completely horrible, as soon as you walked halfway down the cabin, sometimes you could not hear what you said in the speaker system.

Because of the noise we received great-looking earmuffs, we were advised to wear during takeoff and landing, but they were used by only a few. On each flight, there was almost always some passengers who would go mad over the noise. The only remedy you could give them, except for a seat reassignment if the flight was not full, was a pair of yellow earplugs that were taken from a big box at the base office. There were always a bunch of small bags in my apron to quickly offer this aural soothing . If they were not furious because of noise, there were people who were horribly afraid of flying and panicked to be able to see and hear the engines just outside their window.

One of the MD's ace up the sleeve was that it had its own stairs. The emergency exit in the tail could also serve as a staircase that was folded up and down with a big lever. In the front entrance door there was also a built in staircase that could unfold. Useful when the "gate" or stairway was not available at certain destinations.

Working on board the MD was a delight, as I realized in retrospect after trying even newer airplane types. The gangway was generous, the front galley was large and they had been listening to cabin-crew wishes for galley furnishings and also what was needed to get to a decent working environment. There were large closets and lots of cabinets. Today, all such amenities have been peeled away in order to be able to fit in an additional row of seats.

The MD was nice to fly when it was windy; it was always as a trusted farmer's plow with the weight in the back. Other long aircraft with the engines on the wings tend to wiggle significantly in the tail in strong wind and storm, something the pilots rarely notice. Sometimes you get down, lying on the floor, holding on to a trolley, call and inform the pilots that back here indeed everything is flying about. We need the "Seat Belt Sign On" Now! Meanwhile they drink coffee and do not notice the slightest turbulence in the front.

The MD was phased out slowly over a few years and disappeared completely in 2012. Many mourned; others were delighted to get rid of misery. It arrived in the 1980s and was as reassuring as a tractor, but it had also become horribly worn inside; it was time to say goodbye.

Boeing 767, Karin Jans

In the late 80's the DC-10 was up for retirement and the replacement became the Boeing 767. It came with only business and economy classes, so it worked in many areas better than the DC-10. Seating configuration of 2-3-2 instead of 2-5-2 was a big plus for both us and the passengers, but it felt small and cramped compared to the DC-10 as it lacked space in the cabin.

The 767 was the first plane that had individual entertainment screens; the idea was brilliant, but there were quite a lot of problems with the system. It was often full-time employment for the purser to make it work. All too often he/she did not succeed. But you could instead rejoice over the industry's swankiest toilets (at least in Business), generous in size and with windows, natural light and views! In the late 1980s someone had concluded that SAS would no longer be blue but gray. The 767 came with the gray. They also tried to introduce the gray on the MD. A few planes were rebuilt, but there was so much protest from customers and crews, that they gave up. It was cloth in the middle and leather on the seats´ sides. That skin smelled abso-

Crews during training on A330-300.
Photo Lars Björling.

lutely horrible. To spice up the extremely boring, gray interior, the seats were fitted with bright red head covers, called by us "Christmas napkins." Handsome it was certainly not! They eventually went back to blue.

We even had the smaller 767-200ER on the longer range flights, e.g. to fly 13 hours nonstop to Singapore. They were the "easiest" long haul flights we had; fewer passengers and an additional purser to monitor the authorities' crew rest regulations. We were not overworked, just tired of having too little to do in the 13 hours. On the way to Singapore when it was dark almost all the time, and most of the passengers slept, so you had to have plenty of books to read. The 767 remained until 2004, but the successor had already been introduced in 2001, the Airbus A330/340.

AIRBUS A330 / 340
Anna Håkansson Öreberg

In 2008 it was time for my next aircraft, the Airbus A330 / 340 aircraft for long flights. At last, one would have to try to be a real flight attendant! Time to learn to live with jet lag, night work, shift work, and get used to large exotic cities around the world. The Twin-engine A330 was used on shorter long-haul routes, e.g to the US East Coast i.e. New York and Washington. The four-engine A340 flew all the longer destinations to Asia and the US West Coast.

The difference in the cabin is that the A340 has a larger business class, a large and a small compartment, located behind the front galley and adjacent to today's Economy Plus section. The A330 has only the Business section in front of the front galley and therefore more Economy seats which in turn means that the A330 will take more passengers, 265, while the A340 only takes 245 passengers.

The machines are wonderful to fly in and are also laid out in a comfortable way for cabin crew with "comfort jump seats," wide aisles, and a quiet, dark crew rest module. The rest module is located on the right side aft and looks like a closet. In this small, but highly appreciated area, four crew get a nap in accordance with regulatory requirements to have the "unwinding rest" between the two great services. You divide into two teams, where one team is on duty while the other go to bed. Without these modules, I would say that you can no longer handle any long flights. Just for the little while to get in seclusion and silence makes it possible to handle night shift work, jetlag, and the usually short layovers of 24 hours without being devastated.

Typically, there are ten attendants including a purser on all routes to Asia, and nine on the US routes. Of these ten, six are "AH" (air hosts), and three are stewards who have primary responsibility for galleys and food service. Even today, wearing the chef jacket and plaid scarf even though there is no longer any meat carving, but it looks handsome. SAS has a business concept on "long-haul" that you can really be proud of and that is precisely on the long flights that you feel you may unfold your service wings completely and can provide a really good service. One simply has the tools and the time in a completely different way than on short-haul. In 2015, all existing long-haul planes underwent a major facelift with new interior, new seats, modern 'on demand' video systems, and in Business Class real "flat bed" seats were installed.

In 2018 five brand new Airbus A350 will be delivered and then we're talking big, new, fresh, and fuel-efficient airplanes that we really look forward to!

A321, front galley.
Photo Karin Jans

Airbus A321, Karin Jans and Anna Håkansson Öreberg

The A321 with seating for 198 passengers gave the European fleet a real boost. Finally a plane within Europe with air and space and a reasonably wide center aisle, so you can get past a cart, and there are large galleys both front and rear. What if we had it when we had so many passengers in business and they would all have hot meals on short flights! The A321 is a beautiful, comfortable and quiet plane, an ergonomic dream in many ways. All the electronics are computer signals with sublime, soft little tinkles for all sorts of matter. Calls from the cockpit, passenger call, fire in the toilet or whatever it may be, one become aware in a calm manner. Screens showing safety demonstration, entertainment with music and film, (wonderful on charter trips), flight information, maps, and what the cameras in front of the nose wheel or under the plane sees (like the A 330/340). When passengers can "see" take-off and landing, so a blessed tranquility falls on the cabin! Many people forget that they are afraid to fly when they actually can see the runway, both during takeoff and landing

Slides can be armed with a small handle at chest height, so no more getting down on all fours to attach girt bars to the floor. On a screen in the front galley the purser can check that all doors are armed before she/he does a Conference Call and thus minimizes the risk of pulling a slide. Previously there were always 5-6 crew in the cabin, but today there is a minimum crew of four in general. It's a long airplane that takes 198 passengers, so with 4 it becomes a challenge to catch up with a full load on the shorter routes. In an emergency, it is definitely an Airbus you want to be on! 8 exits make an evacuation smooth and fast. There are slides on all doors and all can be used as rafts for a ditching in water. That is always a secure feeling.

CRJ 900, Anna Håkansson Öreberg

My third aircraft was the CRJ900, a smaller guy that takes 88 passengers, and two crew in the cabin. The CRJ always operate without purser and instead have a "Senior Cabin Crew" as cabin chief. It flies in Europe and can handle longer distances but on trips over two hours it is demanding for both passengers and crew to be inside the small metal tube. An ultra narrow aisle means you have to swing your hips like a salsa queen to get past the rows of seats where passengers sit more or less wedged in their small seats. Many passengers get a slightly panicked look when they come up the stairs and become aware that all people over five feet ten inches tall must duck to not hit the ceiling. "It's small but fast" are usually our comforting words when greating the passengers. The aft hostess position is in a position in the back between a minimal toilet and an even smaller galley.The four emergency exits are located over the wings and we have to brief passengers thoroughly, as it'll be those who have to open the doors in an emergency.

The front galley is also minimal and is one that I, at five feet seven inches tall, with a pair of heeled shoes on, has to stand like a bow when I make coffee or when I say hello and goodbye to passengers, because it is so small and cramped .

The CRJ is too small for many gate systems so entry and exit is always straight to and from the plane. Blazing sun, pouring rain or storm, nothing can be avoided. With stairs in the down position, you sometimes get both rain and snow inside. Because of the latter, there is actually a small mini broom in one of the closets! It is intended for snow removal, which is not uncommon in the winter. One of the CRJ's strengths lies in "boarding / disembarking" which is both fast and smooth so it will usually get away quickly. It can fly high and fast, which means that often it lands a little ahead of time, which is appreciated by both passengers and crew. It operates generally on shorter routes, much in Germany,so it means many flight legs in a 10-12 hour day,

Best memories with all types, however, are all of those wonderful colleagues we fly and work with. All the laughter, conversations and moments together. Flying with golden oldies you know but also almost every day with someone new that you've never met. Each check-in is composed of a new crew constellation, ever new mixes. The magic of being a team on the small briefing hour before each flight! Even before you have passed through security you have a team spirit, cohesion and good atmosphere that cannot be compared with anything else. In a small space, trapped together during many hours you get to know each other in a very unique way. Old, young, men, female, straight, gay, married, single, all variations are found in crews and are comfortable enough, with few prejudices!

CRJ900 with entrance stair extended. The stair is integrated in the door Photo Hans Norman, www. Scanliners.com.

Chief Excecutive Officer 1946-2016

SAS has in the period 1946-2010 had thirteen Chief Excecutive Officers and currently, Currently Rickard Gustafsson is number fourteen. Several have been involved in SAS aircraft aquisitions and all had important messages to the staff and customers.

SAS CEO	Period	Message	Aircraft purchase
	Per A. Norlin 1946-1948 1951-1954	Take care of the SAS-pin.	DC-4 DC-6 Saab Scandia DC-6B DC-7C
	Per M. Backe 1949-1951	Private and public interests can work together	
	Henning Throne-Holst 1955-1957	Scandinavismen.	Convair CV-440 DC-8-33 Caravelle
	Åke Rusk 1958-1961	We shall get SAS on its feet by being patient	Convair Coronado

SAS CEO	Period	Message	Aircraft purchase
	Curt Nicolin 1961-1962 (nine months)	The company can not be managed like the UN but has to be managed more professionally on business terms	Cancelled Coronado orders and leased two from Swissair..
	1962-1969 Karl Nilsson	SAS must keep up its service and technology advantage	DC-8-55 DC-8-62 DC-8-63 DC-9-40 DC-9-20 DC-9-33 AF 747-200
	Knut Hagrup 1969-1978	Save, save on everything to maintain the technology advantage.	DC-10-30 Airbus A300 747-Combi
	Carl Olov Munkberg 1978-1981	Cooperation and patience gives results.	
	Jan Carlzon 1981-1993	We Fly people not aircraft!	DC-9-81 MD-81 MD-82 MD-83 MD-87 767-200ER 767-300ER LIN incl. F28 & 737-500

SAS CEO	Period	Message	Aircraft purchase
	Jan Reinas 1993-1994 Seven months		
	Jan Stenberg 1994-2001	We can and must do a little better every day.	737-600 737-700 737-800 A 330 A 340 A321 Q 400 Saab 2000
	Jörgen Lindegaard 2001-2006	SAS group shall be a group that is known for: • creating value • punctuality • caring	The Braathens ASA aquisition includes 737-400 and 737-500 Version change A321 to A319 for four firm orders
	Mats Jansson 2006-2010	SAS is a fine company with fantastic people with great potential. We shall together strive to be the obvious choice for our customers.	CRJ900
	Rickard Gustafsson 2010-	We create a more competetive platform. We are more relevant for people who travel much, and we invest in our future.	A320neo A330Enhanced A350

Two old SAS-ladies: Daisy and Tante Ju

Writing about the SAS aircraft without mentioning these "ladies" that still fly feels wrong.

Daisy, a DC-3, was built in 1943 in Long Beach, California, as a military transport aircraft and was probably named Daisy. She was rebuilt after the war and was delivered to the DNL in 1946 and was named Nordfugl. When DNL became a part of SAS she was baptized as Fridtjof Viking, received SAS colors and flew SAS routes in Scandinavia and Europe. Then Lineflyg became owner of the aircraft in 1957, and with the Swedish registration SE-CFP, but was sold in 1960 to the Swedish Air Force and all the great names disappeared. She became Tp 79 with the number 79006 but became a civilian again in 1982 when two enthusiasts bought her and sold her to the newly-formed foundation, Flying Veterans (FV).

It was the start of a new life for Daisy when the foundation signed a contract for use with the Flying Veterans Association.

To the right
Lindegaard signing the agreement with the Flying Veterans (FV) 2005 in the presence of FV-President, Solveig Leijon and Treasurer Mona Cedwall. Photo Ulf Abrahamsson.

Jan Carlzon back in 1986 gave support for FV and Daisy painted in SAS original decor. SAS hostess Reidun Boethius and Hans Blank. Photo Michael Sanz.

Jan Carlzon, was contacted and with the help of Hans Boethius, and SAS signed a support agreement with Flying Veterans.

The contract was renewed every three years almost automatically. When Jan Stenberg was told about Daisy he was initially hesitant to fly with such an old aircraft, but he changed his mind and signed the agreement with FV. Perhaps after having met Lufthansa CEO Juergen Weber. Lufthansa then sponsored a Ju 52, called Tante Ju.

Ulf Abrahamsson became, after leaving SAS, a member of FV's board of directors and a natural contact to SAS.

The next CEO of SAS, Jorgen Lindegaard, did not hesitate to extend the contract and he was very happy to get a small model of Daisy when signing the contract.

Mats Janson gave his opinion by saying, "if it's something SAS must support, it's FV and Daisy"!

SAS Arlanda also gave good support to FV for many years by providing hangar space at the airport. Difficult times for SAS resulted in the support for FV ceasing in 2011.

Daisy is still flying in the SAS color scheme and has now flown about 34,000 hours.

Lufthansa Tante Ju has also a history of SAS. DNL had in 1946 five Ju 52 in its fleet, two of which remained until 1950, and they flew Norwegian domestic routes on floats. The plane wandered around among many owners before Lufthansa bought and renovated it. Tante Ju is still flying and has made several visits to Scandinavia.

To the right Lufthansa Ju 52 "Tante Ju" Photo Lufthansa.

Flying Veterans DC-3 Daisy over lake Malaren. Photo Freddy Stenbom.

Aircraft data

Aircraft type	In SAS fleet	Number into the fleet	Number of seats	Crew Pilots/Cabin crew	Max Take off weight ton	Max payload ton
Shorts Sandringham	1948 - 1951	2	37	5/2	25,4	
JU 52	1948 - 1956	5	15-16	2/1	10,5	1,85
Douglas DC-3	1946-1957	47	21-32	2 / 2	11,43	2,7
Douglas DC-4	1946 - 1956	9	28-60	3/5	33,2	5
Douglas DC-6	1948 - 1960	13	48-63	3/4-5	43,2	6,9
Douglas DC-6B	1952 - 1961	14	53-82	3/3-5	49,0	8,5
Vickers Viking	1948 - 1949	5	21-38	5/2	15,354	
Saab Scandia	1950 - 1958	8	24-32	2/2	16,5	3,5
Convair CV-440	1956 - 1976	20	56	2/2	22,3	5,7
Douglas DC-7C	1956 - 1967	18	44-94	3/3-6	64,9	9,3
Sud-Aviation Caravelle	1959 - 1974	21	81	3/2-3	46,0	7,7
Douglas DC-8-33	1960 - 1971	7	142	3/5	142,9	17,3
Douglas DC-8-55	1965 - 1971	3	145	3/5	147,4	17,7
Douglas DC-8-62	1967 - 1987	10	154	3/5-7	151,9	22,2
Douglas DC-8-63	1960 - 1971	8	200	3/7-9	161,0	26,2
Douglas DC-9-41	1968 - 2002	50	110-122	2/4	51,7	11,7
Douglas DC-9-21	1968 - 2000	10	78-85	2/3-5	44,5	9,3
Douglas DC-9-33AF	1969 - 1988	2	0	2	51,7	16,0
Boeing 747-200B	1971 - 1987	3	352-396	3/9-15	351,5	71,8
Douglas DC-10-30	1974 - 1991	14	286	3/7-10	251,7	40,0
Boeing 747 Combi	1977 - 1987	3	209-230	3/5-7	371,9	371,9
Fokker F28-4000	1973-2001	19	65-75	2/2	33,1	8,4

wing span m	length m	Engine type	Engine power / thrust	Cruising speed km/h	Fuel kg/ASK	Range km
34,4	26,0	4 PWA R-1830	1200 hk	295	0,048	2500
29,3	19,2	3 PWA 550 hk	550 hk	240	0,123	1 900
29,9	19,7	2 PWA R-1830	1200 hk	260	0,040	1 900
35,8	28,9	2 PWA R-2180	2 180 hk	345	0,035	5 450
35,8	30,9	4 PWA R-2800	2 800 hk	450	0,050	5 000
35,8	38,5	4 PWA R-2800	2 800 hk	435	0,034	7 900
27,22	19,66	2 Bristol Herkules	1 675 hk	228	0,035	1850
28	21,3	2 PWA R-2180	1 800 hk	290	0,047	4 600
32,1	24,1	2 PWA R-2800	2 500 hk	410	0,038	6 400
38,9	34,2	4 Weight R3350-TC	3 400 hk	510	0,041	7 200
34,3	32,0	2 RR Avon	5 170 kp	800	0,053	4 600
43,4	45,9	4 PWA JT3D	7 600 kp	870	0,075	6 300
43,4	45,9	4 PWA JT3D	8 200kp	870	0,053	8 800
45,2	48,0	4 PWA JT3D	8 600 kp	870	0,045	9 800
45,2	57,1	4 PWA JT3D	8 600 kp	870	0,044	8 300
28,5	38,3	2 PWA JT8D-11	6 800 kp	815	0,054	2 400
28,5	31,9	2 PWA JT8D-11	6 800 kp	815	0,068	2 300
28,5	36,4	2 PWA JT8D-11	6 800 kp	815		2 400
59,6	70,4	4 PWA JT9D-7	21 300 kp	890	0,033	10 400
50,4	55,4	3 GE-CF6-50C	23 100 kp	880	0,042	9 800
59,6	70,4	2 PWA JT9D-70	24 000 kp	890	0,041	9 800
25,1	29,6	2 RR Spey	4 500 kp	680	0,057	1 800

Aircraft type	In SAS fleet	Number into the	Number of seats	Crew Pilots/ Cabin	Max Take off	Max payload
Airbus A300 B4	1980-1986	4	242-291	3/6-7	148,0	33,0
MDC MD-81	1986 - 2001	19	133	2/3-5	63,5	15,5
MDC MD-82	1986 - 2013	28	150	2/3-5	67,8	16
MDC MD-83	1987 - 2001	2	133	2/3-5	72,5	14,5
MDC MD-87	1988 - 2011	18	110	2/3-5	61,2	15,3
MDC MD-90-30	1996 - 2004	8	141	2/3-5	75,3	18,1
Fokker F-27	1984 - 1990	9	40	2/2	19,7	4,5
Fokker F-50	1989 - 2010	22	46-50	2/2	20,0	5,2
Boeing 767 -300ER	1989 - 2010	16	161-209	3/10	186,88	31,5
Boeing 767-200ER	1990 - 1993	2	155	3/8	175,5	24,1
Boeing 737-500	2003--2012	13	120	2/3-4	60,6	13,5
Boeing 737-400	2003-2012	4	150	2/4-5	68	17,3
Boeing 737-600	1998 -	30	123	2/3-4	59,6	13,2
Boeing 737-700	1999 -	24	141	2/4-5	69,6	15,2
Boeing 737-800	2000 -	21	186	2/5-6	79	19,6
Saab 2000	1997 - 2001	6	46	2/2	22,8	5,9
Airbus A321	2001 -	8	198	2/4-6	89	23
Airbus A320	2013-	12	165	2/4-6	75,5	18
Airbus A319	2006 -	4	141	2/3-5	75,5	16,7
Airbus A340-300	2001 -	7	245	2-3/8-11	275	44
Airbus A330-300	2002 -	4	265	2/8-11	233	43,8
Bombardier Q400	2000 - 2007	24	68	2/2	29	8,7
Bombardier CRJ900	2008 -	12	88	2/2	38	9,6

wing span m	length m	Engine type	Engine power / thrust	Cruising speed	Fuel kg/ASK	Range km
44,8	53,6	2 PWA JT9D-59A	24 000 kp	840	0,041	3 600
32,9	45,1	2 PWA JT8D-217C	9 070 kp	800	0,045	2 650
32,9	45,1	2 PWA JT8D-217C	9 530 kp	800	0,041	3 150
32,9	45,1	2 PWA JT8D-219	9 530 kp	800	0,045	4 900
32,9	45,1	2 PWA JT8D-217C	9 070 kp	800	0,046	4 260
32,9	46,5	2 IAE V2525	13 150 kp	815	0,033	4 200
29	23,5	2 RR Dart	2 300 kp	460	0,058	1 850
29	25,3	2 PWA 127	2 750kp	520	0,029	2 015
47,6	54,9	2 PWA 4060	25 580 kp	860	0,038	10 500
47,6	48,5	2 PWA 4060	25 580 kp	860	0,046	12 100
28,9	31	2 CFM56-3B	9 070 kp	800	0,039	4100/
28,9	36,4	2 CFM56-3B	9 070 kp	800	0,034	3150
34,3	31,2	2 CFM56-7B22	10 900 kp	840	0,038	2400
35,8	3,6	2 CFM56-7B25	10 900 kp	840	0,032	4400
35,8	9,5	2 CFM56-7B27	10 900 kp	840	,029	4200
24,76	27,28	2 Allison AE 2100A	4 152 kp	685	0,045	2200
34,1	44,5	2 IAE V2530	13 600 kp	840	0,029	3 800
34,1	37,6	2 IAE V2524	12 620 kp	840	0,031	3 900
34,1	33,8	2 IAE V2522/24	12 620 kp	840	0,033	5 100
60,3	63,7	4 CFM56-5C4	15 400kp	875	0,039	12 800
60,3	63,7	2 RR Trent 772B	32 660 kp	875	0,033	10 100
28,4	32,8	2 PWA 150	4 570 hk	667	0,035	1800
36,2	23,4	2 GE CF34-8C1	6 250 kp	840	0,039	3 100

Authors

Royal Institute of Technology in 1943, Low current technology, was employed in the defense industry in 1940 and came to SAS's technical office in 1945.

Appointed in late 1950 as head of the entire engineering department, responsible both for the daily operations of existing aircraft and future aircraft projects.

Appointed in 1960 as Vice President and was given the responsibility for the newly formed research department which was responsible for the evaluation of new aircraft projects from technical and operational standpoint.

SAS was now an organization with overall responsibility for the project issues. Birger´s department soon became a qualified contact both with the manufacturing industry, cooperating airlines and the aviation industry's international associations IATA and AEA.

Birger Holmer developed a wide network of contacts with people at the highest levels within the industry that contributed to SAS being deemed a highly qualified customer whose views on new projects manufacturers gladly accepted.
Birger Holmer retired in 1981.

Birger Holmer

Royal Institute of Technology, 1961. Employed at the Aeronautical Laboratory at KTH 1960 to 1965. Joined SAS from 1965 to 1969 within the Department of airplane analysis, then at the Aviation Safety Authority as responsible for Airworthiness Office 1969-1973, including type certification of the Boeing 747, DC-10 and F28. Was the Swedish representative in numerous international aircraft noise committees and for a time was chairman of IATA's "Technical Committee."

Returned to SAS in 1974, first in the operational planning function and then the technical division in various roles. Ulf assumed responsibility for Birger Holmer's project department at his retirement in 1981, and took also over the responsible for fleet planning.

Ulf was appointed as Vice President. The department was called Fleet Development since being given overall responsibility for all changes in the aircraft fleet including responsibility for the contract on purchase and sale of aircraft.

Ulf started after retiring in 1995 consultancy Consulf AB with assignments from both aircraft manufacturers and the airlines.

Ulf Abrahamsson

Royal Institute of Technology, Aerospace 1981. Joined SAS operations department in 1978 as performance engineer. 1982 head of aircraft and engine analysis department of the "Central Engineering," reporting to Ulf Abrahamsson. The Aircraft and Engine Analysis Department evaluated all the possible candidates for the replacement of older aircraft and maintained contacts with the manufacturing industry and research organizations regarding the aerospace technology.

Bengt Olov represented SAS on AEA and IATA's environmental committee, including periods as chairman. Aviation environmental issues developed from the 1990 on into a more strategic important issue for SAS contributions and Bengt-Olov was involved as a technical expert in SAS's internal environmental forums, including great contribution to SAS's environmental annual reports.

Bengt Olov kept his role as head of aircraft and engine analysis within the department Fleet Development as Director Aircraft Evaluation & Environment until his contractual retirement in 2008.

Bengt Olov has since worked through his company NACE AB mostly as a consultant to IATA on ICAO's Committe for Aviation Environmental Protection, CAEP, as an independent expert regarding technological development and elaboration of new environmental rules for the aerospace industry.

Military service 1966-1967 in the Air Force as a navigator.

Bengt Olov Nas

Abbrevation	explanation	Abbrevation	explanation
ABA	Aktiebolaget Aero Transport AB	IATA	International Air Transport Association
AEA	Association of European Airlines	ICAO	International Civil Aviation Organization
AIDS	Air Integrated Data System	IAE	International Aero Engines
ALPA	Air Line Pilot Association	ILFC	International Lease Finance Company, USA
APG	Airline Planning Group	JAA	Joint Aviation Authority, Europe
APU	Auxiliary Power Unit	JAR	Joint Aviation Regulations, Europe
ATR	Avions de Transport Régional, French aircraft manufacturer	KLM	Dutch Airline
		KSSU	KLM, SAS, SWR, UTA
AVIANCA	Airline in Colombia	LIN	Linjeflyg
AVRO	A.V. Roe and Company, English aircraft manufacturer	Mach	Relative to The speed of sound
		Max pass. loadt	The aircraft max load accounted for in number of passengers including baggage
AUA	Austrian Airlines		
BAC	British Aircraft Corporation	MDC	McDonnell Douglas, aircraft manufacturer in USA
BMI	British Midland, Airline in England		
BMW	Bayerische Motoren Werke AG	MPH	Miles Per Hour
BOAC	British Overseas Airways Corporation	MUSD	Millions US dollar
BRAD	Bombardier Regional Aircraft Division	NM	Nautical Miles
CAB	Civil Aviation Board USA	NNC	Non Noise Certificated
CAEP	Committee on Aviation Environmental Protection	OSAS	Overseas SAS
		Pan Am	Pan American Airways
CAN	Committee on Aircraft Noise	PDM	Post Delivery Modification
CFIT	Controlled flight into terrain	PWA	Pratt&Whitney
CFMI	CFM International, French-US engine manufacturer	RR	Rolls-Royce
		Saab	Svenska Aeroplan Aktiebolaget
DAC	Douglas Aircraft Company	SAS	Scandinavian Airlines System
DDL	Det Danske Luftfartsselskap A/S	SABENA	Airline in Belgium
DLH	ICAO code for Lufthansa	Seat-mile cost	Operating cost per seat and mile
DNL	Det Norske Luftfartsselskap A/S	SEK	Swedish Kronor
EASA	European Aviation Safety Agency	SILA	Svensk Intercontinental Lufttrafik A/B
EFIS	Electronic Flight Instrument System	SLV	Statens Luftfartsväsen
EPNdB	Equivalent Perceived Noise Level dB	SNECMA	French engine manufacturer
EROPS	Extended Range Operation	STK	Skandinaviska Tillsyns Kontoret
ESAS	European SAS	SWR	Swissair, Swiss airline
ETOPS	Extended Range Twin engine Operations	TCAS	Traffic alert and Collision Avoidance System
EQA	European Quality Airlines	THAI	Thai International Airline
FAA	Federal Aviation Administration, USA	UDF	UnDucted Fan ^{tdm} General Electrics propfan concept
FAR	Federal Aviation Regulations, USA		
FMS	Flight Management System	UTA	Union de Transports Aériens, French airline
GE	General Electric engine manufacturer, USA	VASP	Brasilian airline
GPWS	Ground Proximity Warning System		

www.ingramcontent.com/pod-product-compliance
Lightning Source LLC
Chambersburg PA
CBHW040903020526
44114CB00037B/40